University of Hertfordshire

College Lane, Hatfield, Herts. AL10 9AB

Learning and Information Services

For renewal of Standard and One Week Loans,
please visit the web site **http://www.voyager.herts.ac.uk**

This item must be returned or the loan renewed by the due date.
The University reserves the right to recall items from loan at any time.
A fine will be charged for the late return of items.

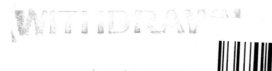

Technology Outsourcing

Related titles available from Law Society Publishing:

Design Law: Protecting and Exploiting Rights
Margaret Briffa and Lee Gage

Drafting Confidentiality Agreements
Mark Anderson

Enterprise Act 2002: The New Law of Mergers, Monopolies and Cartels
Tim Frazer, Susan Hinchliffe and Kyla George

The New Law of Insolvency
Vernon Dennis and Alexander Fox

Titles from Law Society Publishing can be ordered from all good legal book-shops or direct from our distributors, Marston Book Services (tel. 01235 465656 or email law.society@marston.co.uk). For further information or a catalogue call our editorial and marketing office on 020 7320 5878.

TECHNOLOGY OUTSOURCING

A Practitioner's Guide

General Editor:

John Angel

The Law Society

Published in 1998 under the title *Outsourcing Practice Manual* by
Sweet & Maxwell

Published in 2003 by the Law Society
113 Chancery Lane, London WC2A 1PL

Typeset by J&L Composition, Filey, North Yorkshire
Printed by TJ International Ltd, Padstow, Cornwall

Contents

Abbreviations   x
Notes on contributors   xii
Table of cases   xvii
Table of statutes   xx
Table of statutory instruments   xxi
Table of European legislation   xxii

Introduction   1

1. The procurement and bidding process   6

  1.1   Introduction   6
  1.2   Preparation for, and process of, outsourcing   6
  1.3   Customer's procurement process   11
  1.4   Overview of customer's procurement process   14
  1.5   Supplier's bid process   16
  1.6   Due diligence – rationale and examples   17
  1.7   Human resources due diligence – a suggested methodology   33
  1.8   Building the contract around the drivers for outsourcing   43
  1.9   Supplier objectives   44
  1.10 Customer objectives   49
  1.11 Costs arising from contract termination or expiry – a special risk   55
  1.12 Other preliminary legal documents typically used in outsourcing projects   58
       Annex 1A: Specimen confidentiality agreement   62
       Annex 1B: Letter of indemnity/intent in respect of costs incurred by the supplier prior to signature of the outsourcing contract   64

2. The outsourcing contract **66**

2.1 Introduction 66
2.2 Structuring the deal 66
2.3 Structuring the contracts 80
2.4 The transfer of assets agreement 84
2.5 The services agreement 86
2.6 Conclusions 112

3. Information systems outsourcing **113**

3.1 Introduction 113
3.2 Typical information systems outsourcing contract terms 114
3.3 Term 116
3.4 Intellectual property rights 117
3.5 Transfer of third party software and related contracts 119
3.6 The information systems services 123
3.7 Service levels 128
3.8 Service credits 132
3.9 Performance improvement 134
3.10 Charges 135
3.11 Liability 138
3.12 Change management 140
3.13 Data, data protection and privacy 141
3.14 Termination 143
3.15 Exit management 144
3.16 General warranties 148
3.17 Dispute resolution procedures 149

4. Telecommunications outsourcing **152**

4.1 Introduction 152
4.2 Types of telecommunications outsourcing 153
4.3 Sample clauses and commentary I: deal-specific issues 157
4.4 Sample clauses and commentary II: generic telecoms
outsourcing issues 167

5. Website hosting **189**

5.1 Introduction 189
5.2 Selection of suppliers 189
5.3 Terms and conditions of the web hosting agreement 195

5.4	Statement of work	199
5.5	Service levels	200
5.6	Service credits	203
5.7	Conclusion	204

6. Business process outsourcing   **208**

6.1	Introduction	208
6.2	What is business process outsourcing?	208
6.3	Key differences between BPO and IS outsourcing	209
6.4	The BPO market	211
6.5	The range of BPO services	213
6.6	Key contract clauses	217
6.7	BPO developments	224

7. Public sector outsourcing   **230**

7.1	Introduction	230
7.2	Drivers for public sector outsourcing	231
7.3	Public law constraints on outsourcing	234
7.4	The private finance initiative	241
7.5	Commercial and contractual issues in public sector outsourcing	242
7.6	Critical success factors	253

8. Benchmarking   **258**

8.1	Introduction	258
8.2	What is benchmarking?	259
8.3	Why would you benchmark?	262
8.4	The benchmarking process	263
8.5	What is best practice?	264
8.6	Context and where to include benchmarking	264
8.7	What a metrics-based benchmark should cover and deliver	266
8.8	What a commercial benchmark should cover and deliver	266
8.9	Checklist	267
	Annex 8A: Example of a benchmarking approach	269
	Annex 8B: Benchmarking schedule	275

9. Employment issues   **277**

9.1	Introduction	277
9.2	Employment protection in outsourcing	277

9.3	When is a transfer a 'transfer of an undertaking'?	278
9.4	The Directive	278
9.5	TUPE	279
9.6	Outsourcing survey	283
9.7	The amended Directive	285
9.8	Who is protected by TUPE?	286
9.9	What is transferred?	291
9.10	Reorganisations	298
9.11	Consultation	303
9.12	The public sector	307

10. Pension considerations   **310**

10.1	Introduction	310
10.2	Sources of pension provision	311
10.3	Defined benefit and defined contribution schemes	312
10.4	Defined benefit schemes and funding	313
10.5	The regulatory structure of pensions	313
10.6	The legal structure of pension schemes	314
10.7	Pensions and contracts of employment	315
10.8	Pensions and TUPE	316
10.9	The pension aspects of an outsourcing transaction	318
10.10	Transfer calculations	323
10.11	Future service obligations	325
10.12	The public sector	325
	Annex 10A: Due diligence enquiries – asset purchase	329
	Annex 10B: Pensions warranties	330
	Annex 10C: Pro forma pensions schedule	334
	Annex 10D: Annex A to Treasury guidance: *Staff Transfers from Central Government: A Fair Deal for Staff Pensions*	341

11. Tax considerations   **350**

11.1	Introduction – why consider tax?	350
11.2	Definitions	351
11.3	The foreign dimension	352
11.4	Joint ventures	352
11.5	Outsourcing contracts	354
11.6	Agents outside the UK	355
11.7	Withholding taxes on cross-border payments	355
11.8	Transfer of assets	355

11.9 Research and development   356
11.10 Value added tax   356
11.11 Conclusions   362

Index   365

Abbreviations

4Ps	public private partnerships programme
APO	applications process outsourcing
ASP	application service provider *or* provision
ATM	asynchronous transfer mode
BAFO	best and final offer
BPO	business process outsourcing
BSP	business service provision
CAF	Common Assessment Framework (EU)
CCA	Call Centre Association
CCT	compulsory competitive tendering
CCTA	Central Computer and Telecommunications Agency
CEDR	Centre for Dispute Resolution
CIP	continuous improvement programme
CPA	Comprehensive Performance Assessment
CRM	customer relationship management
DASD	data access storage device
DB	defined benefit
DC	defined contribution
DDI	direct dialling inward
DID	direct inward dialling
EDI	electronic data interchange
EFQM	European Foundation for Quality Management
EFQMEM	European Foundation for Quality Management Excellence Model
EPOS	electronic point of sale
ERP	enterprise resource planning
ETO	economic, technical or organisational
F&A	finance and accounting
FRS	Financial Reporting Standard
GAD	Government Actuary's Department
GSM	global system for mobile communications
HR	human resources
ICT	information and communications technology

IDeA	Improvement and Development Agency
IP	intellectual property *or* Internet protocols
IPR	intellectual property rights
IS	information systems
ISDN	integrated services digital network
ISO	information systems outsourcing
ITT	invitation to tender
JV	joint venture
KPI	key performance indicator
LAN	local area network
LGPS	Local Government Pension Scheme
LIFT	Local Improvement Finance Trust (NHS)
MIPS	million instructions per second
MVNO	mobile virtual network operator
NAO	National Audit Office
NCC	National Computing Centre
NIH	'not invented here'
OECD	Organisation for Economic Co-operation and Development
OEIC	open ended investment company
OGC	Office of Government Commerce
OLA	operating level agreement
OPRA	Occupational Pensions Regulatory Authority
PBX	private branch exchange
PCSPS	Principal Civil Service Pension Scheme
PFI	private finance initiative
PPP	public/private partnership
PRIME	Private Sector Resource Initiative for Management of Estate
PRINCE	Projects in a Controlled Environment
PSTN	public switched telephone network
PTT	public telephone and telegraph
R&D	research and development
RFP	request for proposal
S2P	State Second Pension
SERPS	State Earnings-Related Pension Scheme
SIP	Share Incentive Plan
SLA	service level agreement
SPV	special purpose vehicle
SSAP	Statements of Standard Accounting Practices
TOGC	transfer of a going concern
Ts & Cs	terms and conditions
VFM	value for money
VOIP	voice using Internet protocols
VPN	virtual private network
WAN	wide area network
WAP	wireless application protocols

Notes on Contributors

General Editor: John Angel LLB, LLM, MSc, FCIPD is a solicitor who specialised in employment law and was a part-time employment tribunal chairman before leaving solicitor's private practice for a period of 12 years to join the information technology (IT) industry where he was CEO of a software business solutions company. In recent years he has worked with City law firms specialising in IT, communications and e-commerce law and was formerly Head of Online Legal Services at Clifford Chance. John has been a non-executive director of several IT/internet-based companies. He is a Visiting Professorial Fellow at the Institute of Computer & Communications Law, a part of the Centre for Commercial Studies, Queen Mary, University of London. John is consultant editor to *Electronic Business Law*, Butterworths Tolley and joint editor of both *Computer Law (5th edition)* (Oxford University Press, 2003) and *Telecommunications Law* (Oxford University Press, 2001).

Mark Catchpole joined Stephenson Harwood in 2002 to head the pensions and employee benefits practice. He has specialised in pensions and share schemes since qualification in 1989 at Herbert Smith and then Theodore Goddard. As a result, he has seen and considered most of the issues that arise in connection with occupational pension and employee share schemes. As well as client work, Mark is involved in the work of the industry's professional bodies. He is a member of the Association of Pension Lawyers and is on the corporate governance committee of the Share Scheme Lawyers Group. He is also a member of the legislation committee of the Society of Pension Consultants and on the SORP1 working party of the Pension Research Accountants Group. As far as publications are concerned, in addition to journal articles, Mark has recently published a book on stakeholder pensions.

Andrew Foster is Company Secretary and Head of Legal at ITNET plc, a company specialising in IT and business process outsourcing (BPO) in both the public and private sectors. Andrew is a qualified solicitor with 11 years' experience of working as an employed solicitor in the IT industry, having previously worked with the UK subsidiary of AT&T. Before that he worked as a private practice lawyer. Andrew's role involves him directly in advising on all stages of an outsourcing project from concept to preparation, transition and delivery through to the end of contract arrangements. As such he has developed a good working knowledge of those practical points that make for a successful outsourcing project.

Rory Graham is a member of Baker & McKenzie's Global Outsourcing Group and leads the UK outsourcing practice. He has acted on over 100 deals, both in the UK and globally, with a value exceeding $15bn. Rory focuses on transactional work, including outsourcing, for users and providers, as well as other strategic and business critical contracts. He has particular experience of representing both user and service provider clients in the financial services sector. Rory represents the legal profession on the board of the National Outsourcing Association, the trade body for users and suppliers, and prepared their industry standard best practice guidelines for technology outsourcing. He has been advising on outsourcing transactions for 14 years and was recently rated a leading practitioner in an independent survey.

Chris Holder is a partner in the Commercial and Technology Group at Barlow Lyde & Gilbert and specialises in advising customers and suppliers involved in large-scale, complex IT and business process outsourcing transactions. He has advised on a number of data centre, desktop, application development and network IT outsourcings, some of which are among the largest transactions of their kind in the UK and Europe, and also human resources (HR) and finance outsourcings. Chris has worked in a range of business sectors including telecommunications, pharmaceuticals, banking and financial services, insurance, retail, utilities and government. Chris was previously a partner at outsourcing specialists Shaw Pittman and was also an in-house lawyer at IBM. Aside from outsourcing, he has broad experience in all other areas of non-contentious IT work including systems integration, website design, development and hosting and e-commerce.

Sandra Honess is the General Counsel for the BPO service line of PricewaterhouseCoopers. She has specialised in outsourcing and technology related matters both 'in-house' and while a partner in the IT and Telecom Group at Landwell and, previously, in the Media, Computer and Communications Group at Clifford Chance. Sandra has experience of the range of outsourcing transactions (with a current focus on BPO) from both a supplier and customer perspective. Sandra has also spoken on the topic of outsourcing at a range of conferences and seminars.

Lucille Hughes BA (Government), LLB (Syd.Uni.) was admitted as a solicitor and barrister of the Supreme Court of New South Wales in 1995 and also admitted to the Roll of Solicitors of England and Wales in 1999. She is a senior solicitor in Nabarro Nathanson's Public Sector Department (Projects Group) and specialises in public procurement law, public/private partnerships

(PPP)/private finance initiatives (PFI) and public sector outsourcing projects, with a particular focus on information and communications technology (ICT) and e-government outsourcings. Lucille has published articles on public procurement issues and other matters in the *Local Government Chronicle* and *Municipal Journal*.

Mark Lewis BA, LLB, LLM is Chairman of Tite & Lewis and leader of the firm's Technology and Outsourcing Group. Mark was called to the English Bar in 1982 and was, from 1983 to 1989, Assistant Parliamentary Counsel in the Office of the Parliamentary Counsel and subsequently a senior legal adviser to HM Treasury, the Central Computer and Telecommunications Agency and other UK government departments. In that capacity, he was involved in some of the earliest bureau processing, facilities management and outsourcing transactions in Europe. In private practice since 1989, Mark has represented public and private sector organisations in many local and international outsourcing projects, including some of the largest in Europe and Asia Pacific. His experience includes all forms of IT outsourcing, BPO, HR outsourcing, shared services centre and application service provision (ASP) and other forms of web-based outsourcing. Mark has been published in the UK and international press and has spoken at international conferences on the subject of outsourcing and related issues, including in the US, Europe, Hong Kong and mainland China.

Robert Morgan is the Chief Executive and founder of Morgan Chambers plc. Robert worked in the City throughout the 1980s at the time of deregulation and liberalisation of the financial services markets. This led to him establishing a company in 1985 whose sole focus was supporting the outsourcing service provider community. As the outsourcing market grew and became steadily more sophisticated and a much more strategic decision, it was increasingly clear that independent, end-client-centric, practitioner-led advice and support was missing from the market. This led to the founding of Morgan Chambers plc in late 1994, since which time it has grown to be the largest independent sourcing consultancy in Europe. Robert assumed the responsibilities of chief executive in April 1999 and retains responsibility for brand marketing for the group.

John A. Newman MA, FCA, MAAT is a Corporate Tax Partner with Smith & Williamson in London. He qualified as a chartered accountant with Coopers & Lybrand in London. He joined Smith & Williamson in 1994 and specialises in international and UK tax affairs of foreign owned enterprises. These include law firms, investment houses, listed non-UK collective investment funds and hedge funds. He also has particular experience in the UK tax law relating to individuals who are not domiciled in the UK. He has written books and articles. He can be contacted on jan@smith.williamson.co.uk

Dr Malcolm Sargeant BA, PhD is a Reader in Employment Law at Middlesex University Business School. He is author of *Employment Law* (Longmans, 2003), co-author of *Essentials of Employment Law* (CIPD, 2002) and editor of *The Law at Work* (Spiro Press, 2003). He is a member of the Centre for Legal Research at Middlesex University and has written widely on employment law issues, particularly on transfers of undertakings, which was also the subject of his PhD thesis.

Michael Sinclair is a partner in the IT and Telecommunications Group at Simmons & Simmons, specialising in technology contracting and outsourcing. His experience includes advising customers and suppliers in relation to global technology, telecoms and business process outsourcings, international framework agreements for global hardware supply, and software development and supply for turn-key solutions. Michael Sinclair has a PhD in law from Cambridge University and is a contributor to *Telecommunications Law* (Oxford University Press, 2001). He is a guest lecturer in outsourcing at London University's Masters degree course in telecommunications law. He can be contacted at michael.sinclair@simmons-simmons.com

Ricky Vassell is a solicitor specialising in employment law. He is a senior solicitor in the international law firm Simmons & Simmons and his experience includes advising clients on both contentious and non-contentious employment matters. Ricky has built up particular experience in the area of outsourcing transactions and is responsible for the employment team's technology media and telecoms sector. Ricky is also one of a team of solicitors who assist the Simmons & Simmons Employment Law Training Group, an employment law training team that advises clients on the practical application of best practice in the fields of equal opportunities and general employment law. Ricky can be contacted at ricky.vassell@simmons-simmons.com

John Voyez BSc, ATII, AIIT is Head of VAT at Smith & Williamson and has worked on a wide range of VAT issues for over 15 years. John specialises in property transactions and advises property investors, developers and their professional advisers. Other work areas include advice on cross-border transactions, e-commerce and the not-for-profit sector. John is editor of *VAT in Europe* (Tolley, 2002) and contributes to a number of other publications. He is a regular speaker at conferences and chairs the London Branch meetings of the Institute of Indirect Tax. John is also a member of the Chartered Institute of Taxation and the VAT Practitioners Group.

Alison Welterveden LLB (First Class Honours) is a partner in the Technology & Outsourcing Group at Tite & Lewis. She qualified as a solicitor in 1995 with Freshfields. She joined Tite & Lewis in 1998. Alison has specialised in technology and outsourcing since qualification and has considerable experience of all forms of outsourcing, ranging from IT outsourcing to business process outsourcing and ASP. She has also been involved in a number of cross-border shared services centre transactions. More recently, she has represented clients in some of the first digital security outsourcing projects in the UK. She has published a number of articles on various aspects of information technology, outsourcing and e-commerce law. She has spoken at public conferences on the subject of outsourcing in the UK, US and Europe.

Table of cases

Abbey National plc *v.* Customs and Excise Commissioners [2002] BVC 2077 359
Adams *v.* Lancashire CC and BET [1997] CMLR 79; [1998] OPLR 119, CA 317
ADI (UK) Ltd *v.* Willer [2001] IRLR 542 281
Alamo Group (Europe) Ltd *v.* Tucker [2003] IRLR 266 .305
Barber *v.* Guardian Royal Exchange Assurance Society (C-262/88) [1990] ECR
   I-1889, ECJ 316
Beckmann *v.* Dynamco Whichloe Macfarlane Ltd [2000] PLR 269,
   QBD 317–8, 320
Berg and Busschers *v.* Besselsen (C-145/87) [1988] ECR 2559; [1989] IRLR 447,
   ECJ 278
Bernadone *v.* Pall Mall Services Group [2000] IRLR 487, CA 294
Berriman *v.* Delabole Slate Ltd [1985] ICR 546 299
Betts *v.* Brintel Helicopters Ltd [1997] 2 All ER 840; [1997] IRLR 361, CA 280, 281
BIFU *v.* Barclays Bank [1988] 3 CMLR 587; [1987] ICR 495, EAT 304
Bork International A/S *v.* Foreningen af Arbejdsledere i Danmark (C-101/87)
   [1988] ECR 3057 288
Botzen *v.* Rotterdamsche Droogdok Montschappij BV. (C-186/83) [1986] ECR
   519, ECJ 138
British Sugar plc *v.* NEI Power Projects Limited [1998] ITCLR 125, CA 138
BSG Property Services *v.* Tuck [1996] IRLR 134, EAT 299
Burgoine *v.* Waltham Forest London Borough Council [1997] BCC 347, Ch D . . .235
Cable & Wireless plc *v.* IBM United Kingdom Limited [2003] All ER(D) 391 . . .108
Card Protection Plan Ltd *v.* Customs & Excise Commissioners (C-349/96)
   [2001] BVC 158, ECJ 360, 361
Clarks of Hove *v.* Bakers Union [1978] 1 WLR 1207; [1978] IRLR 366, CA 305
Crawford *v.* Swinton Insurance Brokers [1990] IRLR 42, EAT 302
Credit Suisse First Boston (Europe) Ltd *v.* Lister [1999] 1 CMLR 710; [1998] IRLR
   700, CA 293
Credit Suisse First Boston (Europe) Ltd *v.* Padiachy [1998] 2 CMLR 1322; [1998]
   IRLR 504 293
Credit Suisse *v.* Allerdale Borough Council [1997] QB 306, [1996] 4 All ER 129,
   CA 235
Customs & Excise Commissioners *v.* CSC Financial Services (formerly
   Continuum) (C-235/00) [2002] 1 WLR 2200, ECJ .358, 359
Customs & Excise Commissioners *v.* FDR Ltd [2000] STC 672, CA 359
Dines *v.* Initial Health Care Services and Pall Mall Services Group Ltd [1994]
   IRLR 336, EAT 280
DJM International Ltd *v.* Nicholas [1996] IRLR 76, EAT .292
Duncan Web Offset (Maidstone) Ltd *v.* Cooper [1995] IRLR 633, EAT 287
ECM (Vehicle Delivery Service) Ltd *v.* Cox [1998] IRLR 559, EAT 57

ECM (Vehicle Delivery Service) Ltd *v.* Cox [1999] 4 All ER 669, CA 281, 282
Electronic Data Systems Ltd *v.* Customs & Excise Commissioners [2002]
   BVC 2190 359
Foreningen af Arbejdsledere i Danmark *v.* Daddy's Dance Hall A/S
   (C-324/86) [1988] ECR 739, ECJ 289, 292
Frankling *v.* BPS Public Sector Ltd [1999] ICR 347; [1999] OPLR 295, EAT 317
Furniss *v.* Dawson [1984] AC 474 362
Hadley *v.* Baxendale (1854) 9 Ex 541 138
Halifax *v.* Customs and Excise Commissioners [2002] STC 402 362
Hay *v.* George Hanson (Building Contractors) Ltd [1996] IRLR 427 289
Henke *v.* Gemeinde Schierke (C-298/94) [1996] IRLR 701 308
Hotel Services Limited *v.* Hilton International Hotels (UK) Limited [2000]
   1 All ER (EC) 173 138
Hough *v.* Leyland DAF Ltd [1991] IRLR 194, EAT 305
Insitution of Professional Civil Servants *v.* Secretary of State for Defence [1987]
   3 CMLR 35; [1987] IRLR 373, Ch D 304
Katsikas *v.* Konstantidis (C-132/91) [1992] ECR I-6577 289
Kenny *v.* South Manchester College [1993] IRLR 265 280
Lightways (Contractors Ltd) *v.* Associated Holdings Ltd [2000] IRLR 247 281
Litster *v.* Forth Dry Dock & Engineering Ltd [1990] 1 AC 546; [1989] IRLR
   161, HL 288, 292
Magna Housing Association *v.* Turner (EAT/198/98) 57
McLeod and another *v.* (1) Ingram t/a Phoenix Taxis (2) Rainbow Cars Ltd t/a
   Rainbow Taxis (EAT/1344/01) 57
Merckx and Neuhuys *v.* Ford Motor Co Belgium SA (C-171/94) [1996] ECR
   I-1253 295
Michael Peters Ltd *v.* (1) Farnfield and (2) Michael Peters Group plc [1995]
   IRLR 190 287
Mikkelsen (Foreningen Arbejdsledere I Danmark) *v.* Danmols Inventar A/S
   (C-105/84) [1985] ECR 2639 286
Mitie Managed Service Ltd *v.* French [2002] ICR 1395 296
Morris Angel & Son *v.* Hollande [1993] All ER 569; [1993] IRLR 169 293
MSF *v.* Refuge Assurance plc [2002] 2 CMLR 27; [2002] IRLR 324, EAT 306
Oy Liikenne AB *v.* Liskojarvi and Juntenen (C-172/99) [2001] All ER (EC) 544;
   [2001] IRLR 171, ECJ...282
Perry *v.* Intec [1993] OPLR 1 317
Prudential Assurance Co Ltd *v.* Customs & Excise Commissioners [2001] BVC
   2201 359
Rask and Christensen *v.* ISS Kantineservice (C-209/91) [1993] IRLR 133,
   ECJ 279, 282
RCO Support Services Ltd *v.* UNISON & Others [2002] EWCA Civ. 464;
   [2002] IRLR 401, CA 57, 281, 282
Re Coloroll Pension Trustees *v.* Russell [1995] All ER (EC) 23; [1994] ECR
   I-4389 316
Rossiter *v.* Pendragon plc [2002] IRLR 483, CA 295
Royal Bank of Scotland Group plc *v.* Customs & Excise Commissioners [2002]
   BVC 2213 362
Schmidt *v.* Spar-und Leikhasse der Fruheren Amter Bordesholm (C-392/92)
   [1994] ECR I-1311 279
Sita (GB) Ltd *v.* Burton [1998] ICR 17 295
South Durham Health Authority *v.* UNISON [1995] IRLR 407 304
Sparekassernes Datacenter *v.* Skatteministeriet (C-2/95) [1997] All ER (EC),
   ECJ 358, 359

Spijkers *v.* Gebroeders Benedik Abbatoir CV. (C-24/85) [1986] ECR 1119 279
Süzen *v.* Zehnacker Gebaudereinigung GmbH Krankenhausservice (C-13/95)
    [1997] All ER (EC) 289; [1997] IRLR 255, ECJ 57, 280, 281, 284
Temco Service Industries SA *v.* Samir Imzilyen and others (C-51/00) [2002]
    IRLR 214 57
Thompson *v.* SCS Consulting Ltd [2001] IRLR 801 300
Trafford *v.* Sharpe and Fisher (Building Supplies) Ltd [1994] IRLR 325 299
Transport & General Workers Union *v.* McKinnon [2001] ICR 1281; [2001]
    IRLR 597 305
Tsangacos *v.* Amalgamated Chemicals [1997] IRLR 4 293
Tucker (HM Inspector of Taxes) *v.* Granada Motorway Services [1977] 1 WLR
    1411, ChD 354
University of Oxford *v.* Humphreys [2000] IRLR 183, CA 296
Walden Engineering Co. Ltd *v.* Warrener [1993] 3 CMLR 179; [1992] PLR 1 317
Warner *v.* Adnet Ltd [1998] IRLR 394 301
Wheeler *v.* Patel [1987] ICR 631 299
Whent *v.* T. Cartledge [1997] IRLR 153 294
Whitehouse *v.* Charles A Blatchford & Sons Ltd [1999] IRLR 492 300
Wilson *v.* St Helens Borough Council; British Fuels *v.* Baxendale [1999]
    2 AC 52; [1998] IRLR 706 . . . . .288, 300
Wilson *v.* West Cumbria Health Authority [1995] PIQR P38 292
Wren *v.* Eastbourne District Council [1993] ICR 955 280

Table of statutes

Arbitration Act 1996. 150
Companies Act 1985. 219
Companies Act 1989. 219
    Sched. A 219
Computer Misuse Act 1990 148
Contracts (Rights of Third Parties)
    Act 1999. 76
Data Protection Act 1984. 141
Data Protection Act 1998. . . 141–2, 162,
                  196, 197, 223
    Sched. 1. 31
Deregulation and Contracting
    Out Act 1994 . . . . 236, 243
    s.69
        (5)
            (a) 237
            (b) 237
    s.70
        (4). 237
    s.71. 237
    s.73
        (2). 237
Disability Discrimination Act 1995 . 217
Employment Rights Act 1996. 217
Finance Act 2002 356
Financial Services and Markets Act
    2000 163
Income and Corporation Taxes Act 1988
    s.592. 332
    s.601. 332
    Pt XIV, Ch.I 335
    Pt XIV, Ch.IV 333
Local Authority (Goods and
    Services) Act 1970 248
Local Government (Contracts) Act
    1997 237
Local Government Act 1999. 257

Local Government Act 2000
    s.2
        (1). 236
Partnership Act 1890
    s.1
        (1). 351
Pensions Act 1995. 336
    s.60. 339
    s.75. . . . . 331, 339
Pension Schemes Act 1993
    s.144. 331
Race Relations Act 1976. 217
Sex Discrimination Act 1975 217
Social Security Act 1986
    s.84
        (1). 331
Social Security Pensions Act 1975. . . 331
    s.57A 332
Superannuation Act 1972. 342
Telecommunications Act 1984 161
    s.22. 174
    Sched. 2, para.27(4)
    (Telecoms Code) 166
        Clause 22 166
Trade Union and Labour Relations
    (Consolidation) Act 1992
        Part IV 277
        Part IV, Ch. II. 305
Trade Union Reform and Employment
    Rights Act 1993
    s.33
        (4). 289
Unfair Contract Terms Act 1977 . . . 252
    s.3 139
    Sched. 2. 139
VAT Act 1994 357
    Sched. 9 . . . . 358, 359

Table of statutory instruments

Collective Redundancy and Transfers of Undertakings (Protection of
  Employment) (Amendment) Regulations 1999, SI 1999/1925 303
Consumer Protection (Distance Selling) Regulations 2000, SI 2000/2334 162
Local Government Pension Scheme Regulations 1997, SI 1997/1612 327
Local Government Pension Scheme (Amendment, etc.) Regulations 1999,
  SI 1999/3438 . . . . .325, 327
Public Works Contract Regulations 1991, SI 1991/2680 . . . . .238, 240
  reg.3 238
  reg.10 239
  reg.13 239
Public Services Contracts Regulations 1993, SI 1993/3228 . . . . .238, 240
  reg.3 238
  reg.10 239
  reg.13 239
Public Supply Contracts Regulations 1995, SI 1995/201 . . . . .238, 240
  reg.3 238
  reg.10 239
  reg.13 239
Telecommunications (Interconnection)(Number Portability,etc.) Regulations
  1999, SI 1999/3449 160
Transfer of Undertakings (Protection of Employment) Regulations 1981, SI
  1981/1794 (as amended) 10, 30, 34, 35, 37, 39, 42, 44, 55, 56, 57, 78, 111, 147,
                  245, 246, 262, 277–308, 310, 316, 318, 342, 347
  reg.5 . . . . .286, 288, 316
    (1) 291
    (2) 291, 296, 297
     (b) 292, 293
    (5) 295, 297
  reg.6 294
  reg.7 316
  reg.8 . . . . .286, 299
    (1) 301
    (2) 301
  reg.10 303
  reg.11 303
VAT (Special Provisions) Order 1995, SI 1995/1268
  Art.5 362

European Legislation

Acquired Rights Directive (77/187/EEC amended by Directive 98/50/EC; consolidated into Directive 2001/23/EC) 277, 285, 286, 287, 342
   Art.1(1) 295
   Art.1.1(b) 285
   Art.1.1(c) 307
   Art.3 286
   Art.3(1) 288
   Art.3(2) 296
   Art.3(3) 301
   Art.4(1) 299
   Art.4(2) 295
Collective Redundancies Directive (75/129/EEC as amended by Directive 92/56/EEC) 305
Collective Redundancies Directive (98/59/EC) 277, 305
   Art.2(1) 306
Distance Selling Directive (1997/7/EC) 162
EC Sixth Directive on VAT
   Art.13 358
EU Licensing Directive (97/13/EC) 171
Numbering Directive (98/61/EC) 160
Public Supplies Directive (93/36/EEC) 12, 239, 243
Public Works Directive (93/37/EEC) 12, 239, 243
Public Services Directive (92/50/EEC) 12, 239, 243
Telecommunications Data Protection Directive (97/66/EC) 188

Introduction

John Angel: General Editor

THE NEED FOR A SOURCING STRATEGY[1]

Outsourcing has made the transition from being an often panic-driven need to reduce costs to an accepted and fundamental tool for providing a competitive advantage. Many successful companies depend on a comprehensive sourcing strategy to enable them to remain agile enough to cope with changing market conditions and to support their global expansion.

Today, outsourcing is such an accepted and widely used strategic tool that most leading companies have a well defined sourcing strategy and frequently revisit the value of outsourcing specific activities. No managing director who wants to retain his or her position would refuse to consider outsourcing today.

Most organisations seek to develop a comprehensive sourcing strategy driven from the top of the organisation rather than an ad hoc approach for individual activities on a decentralised basis. Many successful companies depend on a comprehensive sourcing strategy to enable them to remain agile enough to cope with changing market conditions and to support their global expansion.

THE SIZE OF THE MARKET

The outsourcing market is maturing and growing rapidly on a global basis. Gartner predicts that the global outsourcing market will be US$1.1 trillion by 2004, and the business process outsourcing (BPO) segment will be $345 billion. Taking a more conservative view, IDC predicts the global IT outsourcing (ITO) market to be over US$200 billion by 2004.

The UK has been the leader in Europe regarding adopting outsourcing as a strategic tool, both in the private sector and in UK government entities. Companies in Europe are adopting sourcing strategies as well, in all of the major economies. The need for a sourcing strategy is not unique to Europe. In North America, the outsourcing market is huge and growing, especially in the BPO arena. Outsourcing is an accepted management tool and relatively unfettered by government regulation in the US.

Another component of the outsourcing market that is maturing is those companies/organisations/firms that assist clients in developing their sourcing strategies, negotiating and drafting the outsourcing contract, managing and implementing sourcing transactions, managing the resulting relationships and measuring supplier performance during the life of the relationship.

BUSINESS DRIVERS

There are environmental factors driving towards outsourcing, including the following:

- It is becoming harder and harder to maintain a competitive advantage today. The more one has to manage and support internally constrained organisations, the less flexible an organisation is in coping with the rapid pace of change prevalent in today's dynamic business landscape.
- With these competitive pressures, many executives find it difficult to attack new markets and implement new capabilities given current resource constraints, reductions in capital budgets and cost pressures.
- Getting the management to support new solutions is difficult. Existing corporate structures may be unable to support the implementation of new solutions.
- As well as the need for different skills there may be a need for a culture change within an organisation to enable effective solution implementation.

From a global economy perspective, it is easy to identify a list of business drivers that would suggest that outsourcing be given serious consideration:

- globalisation;
- deregulation;
- impact of the Internet;
- mergers, acquisitions and divestitures;
- buy v. build to reduce capital requirements;
- create market value from internal processes;
- shared services are not effective enough.

Companies traditionally outsourced purely for financial reasons: to get assets off their books or to get an infusion of cash from the supplier who bought their assets. That sort of strategy is not the dominant driver now. Today companies outsource to:

- obtain speed to market;
- get access to capability/resources and improved service;
- better utilise in-house resources by outsourcing legacy or non-value-added activities;
- convert fixed costs to variable costs;
- implement a change in management philosophy/culture.

Companies are looking for flexibility in their operations in order to take advantage of fast developing market opportunities. Companies are seeking quick and effective ways to enter new markets – from either a geographic or a segment perspective. Companies have to deal with the rapid pace of change that presents many challenges. Another challenge is the increasing pressure of global competition forcing efficiency improvements and expanded capability. Most are not willing or able to make the investments to stay competitive. Cost savings are an important factor but not the driving factor. The new issue is how to get that capability or presence in that market and improvement in service levels without having to redirect investment from core R&D or increasing overall costs.

IS OUTSOURCING ALWAYS APPROPRIATE?

While outsourcing is a readily accepted strategic tool, it is not for everyone. A tool is only as effective as a knowledgeable operator applying it to the appropriate task. There are certain risks involved in any change process, including:

- loss of control by the client;
- lack of performance by the supplier;
- business disruption caused by loss of service or poor transition planning.

Such risks can be mitigated by utilising the appropriate advisers in defining the sourcing strategy and assisting with the conduct of a sourcing transaction process. The more past experience of others and current best practices can be leveraged, the more likely it is that a company will have a successful sourcing strategy.

DEFINING THE SOURCING STRATEGY

In order to develop a sourcing strategy effectively, it must be aligned with the organisation's business objectives. Those that will benefit from the services must play a role in defining the strategy. There also needs to be a business case for the strategy, including the appropriate financial analysis.

Most sourcing strategies require an executive sponsor or champion and a steering committee if they are ever to see the light of day. Resources must be identified to help formulate the strategy from all functional areas involved, user representatives, HR and finance. It must be clearly understood that any strategy adopted will result in a major change process. Therefore, the organisation must define the parameters that are acceptable for change, risk and investment within the organisational culture and business environment.

3

In most organisations defining the sourcing strategy also includes determining how to achieve the results articulated in the strategy and how to monitor progress and measure results once the strategy is implemented.

WHAT TO OUTSOURCE

A selective approach is often recognised as the most successful where specific activities that best-in-class experts can provide are outsourced. In the selective approach there is limited risk and exposure. Selective sourcing transactions are usually less complex and represent smaller transactions that can be executed in a shorter time frame. Multiple selective transactions may be conducted over time until all activities identified in the corporate strategy as candidates for outsourcing have been outsourced. While this is a less demanding approach in terms of management time and can be implemented more quickly, it is also suboptimal in that it breaks down major activities into smaller segments such as IT, accounting, finance or HR and then into discrete elements like desktop, networks and software applications requiring additional interfaces and little opportunity for the supplier to produce significant results over time.

Another approach is to be more strategic and outsource all but a few key functions in an area to a single supplier or a team of suppliers led by one prime supplier. This approach is more complex and requires more resources and time to implement. However, the results are usually greater in that the supplier can focus more on providing innovative/creative solutions since it now manages the whole pie and can generate synergies in functional interdependencies. More resources are freed up for internal use by the client to focus on core activities. This approach is usually taken to support a change in management philosophy or to drive a cultural change within the organisation. It is also a public statement of the leadership's desire to move quickly and leverage the benefits of outsourcing on a large scale.

Organisations looking to maximise the value of sourcing and leverage the value of an internal capability might take a value-based approach. This is where the supplier acquires a valuable business operation from the client in return for reduced rates, and an equity position in the supplier or an internal operation has more value externally and may have a market of its own when teaming with an external supplier.

TECHNOLOGY OUTSOURCING

The outsourcing of IT or communications may be part of a selective, key functions or a leverage of a business operation approach. Technology outsourcing is similar in many ways to outsourcing other things but is also different on at least five counts[2]:

4

1. It is not a homogenous function, but comprises a wide variety of IT functions.
2. IT capabilities continue to evolve at a startling pace – predicting IT needs past a medium-term horizon is wrought with uncertainty.
3. There is no simple basis for gauging the economics of IT activity.
4. Economic efficiency has more to do with IT practices than inherent economies of scale.
5. Large switching costs are associated with IT sourcing decisions.

Therefore the decision to outsource IT is particularly challenging and much research has been undertaken to discover the success and failure factors associated with IT outsourcing.[3] From this research it has been identified that the lawyer's role in drafting an appropriate contract can be a key success factor and the steps involved in this process are the subject matter of this book.

Once the strategic decision has been taken to outsource technological aspects of the organisation's business then the implementation of the strategy is necessary. The first chapter of this book covers the procurement and bidding process and only then is the outsourcing contract (Chapter 2) itself considered from a structural point of view along with the key points that need to be reflected in the document. The particularities of outsourcing information systems (technology), telecommunications outsourcing and website hosting are then covered in some detail in separate chapters (Chapters 3, 4 and 5) with examples of precedent clauses. Because of the importance and interrelationship of business process outsourcing a chapter on this subject is included in the book (Chapter 6). Also the particular requirements of public sector outsourcing are identified in a separate chapter (Chapter 7) together with a technical appreciation of benchmarking used widely in the sector (Chapter 8).

The outsourcing contract is recognised as being largely lawyer made with a minimal legislative framework. The only exceptions to this are in the areas of employment, pensions and tax, which are all considered in their own chapters in the book (Chapters 9, 10 and 11). Together with the other chapters they provide a comprehensive understanding of technology outsourcing to assist the in-house lawyer, external counsel and others advising on, negotiating and concluding the outsourcing contract.

NOTES

1. This introduction has been influenced by the work of John Buscher in 'What is Your Sourcing Strategy?' [2002] 1 *The Outsourcing Project*.
2. 'Experience of Information Technology Outsourcing', a chapter by Leslie Willcocks and Mary Lacity published in the *Outsourcing Practice Manual* (Sweet & Maxwell, 1990).
3. *Ibid.*

CHAPTER 1

The procurement and bidding process

Andrew Foster

1.1 INTRODUCTION

The purpose of this chapter is to offer some practical insight into some of the key phases in the procurement and bidding processes within an outsourcing project. It should therefore be read in conjunction with other chapters of the book, especially Chapter 2 (The outsourcing contract) and Chapter 9 (Employment issues). Sections 1.2–1.5 look at the procurement and bidding process from the perspective of both the customer and the supplier. They illustrate through diagrams and commentary what steps each party might typically take to define and secure their respective business objectives arising from the outsourcing. It also considers the level of preparedness that a customer ought to achieve, and what information it should hold, before commencing the formal part of the procurement process.

Sections 1.6–1.7 develop and supplement some of the text regarding due diligence in Chapter 2 on the outsourcing contract. They postulate a broad definition of due diligence and explore the rationale, benefits, timing and processes involved with this part of the process of outsourcing, and then outline and comment upon some example subject areas for due diligence. The sections then consider in more detail arguably the most critical area of all due diligence activities undertaken by a supplier: that relating to human resources.

In sections 1.9–1.10 some thoughts are offered on how some of the key business objectives of each side can be reflected in the outsourcing contract, to ensure it fully reflects the meeting of minds between the parties and the essence of the outsourcing.

Section 1.12 provides some examples of other preliminary legal documents that may be needed at the early stages of an outsourcing project before the main outsourcing contract is signed.

1.2 PREPARATION FOR, AND PROCESS OF, OUTSOURCING

The rapid growth in outsourcing of all types in recent years[1] is testimony to the substantial return – in both cost reductions and/or service delivery improvement – that can be generated from a successful outsourcing project. However, whatever the immediate reasons/pressures are that lead to a decision to outsource, the outsourcing must be seen as a business investment with clearly defined objectives and one that, like any investment, needs meticulous planning and a preparedness to commit human and financial resources to realise its full potential. Indeed, there is increasing evidence to suggest that customers do not come to outsourcing with a view that it will provide a panacea for their service issues, or that outsourcing will provide an appropriate home for an existing major issue within their organisation. Customers have not tended to consider that major strategic issues across their business are suitable for outsourcing.

The planning process will involve significant management time in defining and agreeing the result that should be obtained from the outsourcing, and the circumstances in which the benefits available from the outsourcing would not justify the time, expense and risks involved. Benefit might also be derived from the involvement of external advisers – typically an independent outsourcing consultant and a specialist outsourcing lawyer – to supplement the business objectives of the outsourcing defined by the customer with a procurement methodology and the tactical experience of negotiating with outsourcing suppliers. This should avoid any imbalance in the negotiating position of customer and supplier. There does seem to be evidence of an increasing level of use of outsourcing consultants by customers in the procurement process. At my company, ITNET, for example, in the majority of bids made to commercial division customers there was an external consultant providing advice to the customer.

It is not unreasonable to think in terms of at least six months as being an appropriate time period in which to carry out all the internal preparations for outsourcing, obtain management approval, gather the information that suppliers will need to put together their proposals/tenders, and then to instruct external advisers and assimilate them into the project team. This preparatory stage prior to the formal commencement of the outsourcing project is critical to its overall success. Business Intelligence has captured the key elements of this stage in an IT outsourcing charter set out below. Any organisation wishing to commence an outsourcing project may wish to satisfy itself that it has, prior to commencement of the project, met the requirements of the Charter.

1.2.1 An IT outsourcing charter[2]

The danger for the customer is that an IT outsourcing charter does not have meaning or financial relevance at an individual employee level and therefore is not properly used. A customer might, therefore, consider promoting ownership of the contents of the Charter among those members of the customer's procurement team who will have an ongoing involvement in the

---

Charter

1. We have an outsourcing strategy that fits with our business and informa- tion management, information systems and IT strategies. The strategy includes and goes beyond the period of any outsourcing contract we have or are planning.
2. Our outsourcing strategy includes plans for how to manage the IT supply and services market and how to choose, relate to, manage and retain leverage with outsourcing suppliers.
3. We are able to make decisions as to what IT services to outsource and what to source in other ways. These decisions make sense on business and technical grounds.
4. We have in place a process and management capacity to select a suitable outsourcing supplier.
5. There is a human resource plan in place to deal with the decision, transition and subsequent phases of outsourcing.
6. We have the management and specialist capacity to negotiate and draw up an outsourcing contract.
7. We have retained in house sufficient management and technical capacity to manage the outsourcing supplier, monitor contract performance and keep strategic business and technical options under review.
8. We have in place detailed measurement systems enabling us to draw up a detailed contractual agreement and to monitor the outsourcing supplier's performance.

---

project post-contract signing, and will be in a position to influence the success of the outsourcing project. This could be achieved by the customer ensuring that such individual's performance evaluation and the variable elements of his/her remuneration is in some way tied to the achievement of the business objectives of the outsourcing, and to achievement of performance measures in service level agreements. If the supplier similarly motivates key members of its service delivery team, there will then be a clear discernible benefit to both parties in their employees taking a solution-orientated approach to communi- cating about issues that arise during the life of the contract, rather than simply debating the issue itself and problems resulting from this.

Within the preparatory stage, the customer needs to generate detailed information about the service to be outsourced, so as to educate suppliers about the challenges they will face in meeting the customer's business/service objectives. This information will typically be provided in either an invitation to tender (ITT) or a request for proposal (RFP) document issued by or for the customer. The more information that suppliers are given at this early point in the process, the more realistic their bids will be and the greater will be the likelihood of a real meeting of minds.

A problem sometimes encountered by customers in outsourcing services is that service levels and performance targets for the service available from within their organisation are either poorly defined or non-existent. Where this is the case, an alternative to the provision of such information is to define in the ITT/RFP a basic list of service level metrics against which the level of service performance can be evaluated. These metrics should be based on business requirements and not just a wish list, as the supplier's charges will be partially dictated by the standard of service required.

Prior to despatch of the ITT/RFP to selected suppliers, the customer project team should take a final critical look at it. Does it provide a level of information sufficient for suppliers to offer a detailed costing for delivering the required service? Is it easily understood? Does it ask sufficient questions of the supplier to enable a full evaluation of each supplier's strengths and weaknesses against the customer's predefined evaluation criteria?

The ITT/RFP should contain the sections below.

Introduction

- Purpose of the request for proposal.
- Background on the customer organisation and the function or process being outsourced.
- Organisational information relating to the project, including information on the customer's project team.
- Statement on the confidentiality of the information contained in the RFP and procedures for maintaining confidentiality.

Rationale and scope for the outsourcing

- Statement of rationale/drivers for outsourcing from a business perspective.
- Statement of mission/vision for the service and its future development.
- Statement of scope and objectives for the outsourcing.

Project schedule

- Deadline for questions on ITT/RFP to be received from suppliers.
- Supplier open day meeting (optional) – for suppliers to have an opportunity to raise questions about matters arising from the ITT/RFP.
- Proposal due date and instructions regarding presentation, number of copies, etc.
- Supplier demonstration day (optional) – for the supplier to explain to its prospective customer how it would deliver the required service.
- Preferred supplier selection – process and timing.
- Anticipated start date for service set-up activities (before delivery of live service).
- Expected service live date.

9

- Contract term.
- Contract termination planning start date.

Business requirements

- Detailed business requirements.
- Resumé of how service delivery will be organised, and detail of escalation procedures for handling issues so that problems are resolved effectively at the right management levels.
- Project management and regular service reporting requirements.
- Criteria against which the overall success of the outsourcing will be measured by the customer at a defined future point.
- Draft terms and conditions of contract.
- Service level agreements or performance metrics.
- Quality and other processes to be followed by the supplier.
- Approach to supplier performance default (may include service credits scheme).
- Request for supplier to provide summary insurance details.

Staff issues

- TUPE statement (i.e. does the customer consider that the TUPE regulations will apply to this transaction?).
- Details of staff/contractors currently delivering the service, including costs/liabilities associated with such staff.

Service environment

- Current environment in which or utilising which the service is provided.
- Planned future changes that the supplier needs to take account of in its proposal.

Proposal requirements

- Contents of the proposal, including references and information regarding any key supplier personnel who would be assigned to delivering the service.
- Proposal format and number of copies required.
- Guidelines on how to present costs (see Note below).
- Risk assessment for the service, and plan for containing these risks.
- Proof of reliability of supplier and availability of relevant in-depth resources to offer continuity of delivery of high quality services.

Note

A supplier's cost profile will often show significant investment in the early years of the contract (in order to develop/improve the service) with a lower level of investment in later years. If this cost profile were fully reflected in its proposed charges to the customer the charges in the early years may be uncomfortably high for the customer (quite possibly higher than the cost of delivering the service prior to outsourcing), and this may make it difficult for the customer to gain management approval to proceed. Therefore, the supplier will sometimes be asked to *smooth* its payment profile to the customer by amortising its contract investment costs evenly over the life of the contract, thus delivering the immediate (year one) service cost reduction, which may be a key driver for the outsourcing project.

1.3   CUSTOMER'S PROCUREMENT PROCESS

This section presents a view as to what the customer's procurement process might look like, from the steps leading to the decision to outsource through to the live delivery of the service. The total process is split for convenience into two discrete sections: from concept to receipt of tender/proposal (Figure 1.1, p. 14) and from receipt of tender/proposal to live service delivery (Figure 1.2, p. 15–16).

Figure 1.2 puts forward two alternative process routes that the customer may follow. The first one is based on a procedure of negotiation of all elements of the contract prior to supplier selection (with due diligence taking place before supplier selection). With this route, the suppliers are initially asked to submit a proposal with charges that may still be subject to certain assumptions. The suppliers then carry out a due diligence exercise on the service and are then asked to submit a best and final offer with these assumptions removed as far as possible, so that a *final* price is arrived at. The other route is based on achieving supplier selection at the earliest possible point, with due diligence and detailed contract negotiation occurring thereafter.

The process route chosen will depend on a variety of factors including time and resource availability, bargaining position with suppliers, previous experience of failed procurements and the quality/completeness of the information gathered by the customer in preparation for due diligence. Suppliers will generally prefer a non-negotiated route for resourcing reasons. It is difficult to say which route is best, as this will be governed by the particular customer, procurement circumstances and also the views of its professional advisers. Sometimes, where the negotiated procedure route involves too heavy a resourcing burden for customer and suppliers, it may be possible to design a hybrid process that involves some limited due diligence and contract negotiation, but only on certain key elements of the contract.

The choice of procedures by public authorities was brought into focus in summer 2000 in relation to the Pimlico School project in London. This was a private finance initiative (PFI) project for the design, build financing and operation of a school, in which the contracting authority chose to use the negotiated procedure. In July 2000, the European Commission (EC) sent a Reasoned Opinion to the Office of Government (OGC) saying that, in its view, the use of the negotiated procedure for this project contravened the EC's procurement rules because the scheme was not sufficiently complicated to merit its use.

The OGC sent a reply to the EC in January 2001, asserting that PFI schemes necessitate the use of the negotiated procedure because such transactions are inherently complex and require that the public authority is able to apply a more flexible approach to the procurement exercise than is required under other forms of procurement (i.e. the restricted and open procedures). The case has been closed by the EC and no further action will be taken. At the same time, the EC appears to have recognised the difficulties that the current lack of precision in the procurement rules is causing. It is expected to adopt a new Directive in summer/autumn 2003 that will consolidate the Public Supplies, Works & Services Directives and on a new competitive dialogue procedure. Member states will need to implement the new Directive in the first half of 2005. It is hoped that the extra focus on procurement processes that the changes will bring should reduce the circumstances when the negotiated procedure is used in inappropriate circumstances.

The customer will need to ensure that, before commencing its procurement process, it has developed a supplier evaluation model by reference to, and in conjunction with, the business case. This model brings together the collective thinking of the customer's project team as to what the key factors are in the selection of the right supplier to deliver the required service. The customer will want to assign weightings to each model and to each individual element within the model. This will enable it to generate a score for each supplier based on the assessments made of the supplier within the models. The customer's evaluation model should probably cover the following three main areas:

- cost model;
- qualitative model;
- financial/viability assessment.

1.3.1   Cost model

The cost model should assess among other things:

- tendered charges;
- incremental charges arising from that supplier's specific approach to transition and delivery of the service;
- estimated indirect benefits accruing from the outsourcing over life of contract (such as from being able to take advantage of volume purchasing arrangements of the supplier, offering lower prices to the customer).

ITNET's research into the IT outsourcing market has revealed that, in the United States, over 50 per cent of outsourcing contracts signed are at a higher price than the internal IT budget for the same service. So while price is, and remains, a sensitive issue in supplier selection, there is now more of a tendency to make an economic value-added assessment of what overall measurable financial and business benefits a relationship with the supplier will provide. This type of assessment obviously requires increasingly sophisticated approaches to designing models for supplier evaluation.

1.3.2 Qualitative model

The qualitative model should assess among other things:

- flexibility in supplier's approach to delivery;
- approach to implementing/costing changes (i.e. will some service changes be made without further charges?);
- cultural fit;
- ability to, or proposals to, innovate;
- perception of customer's users about the supplier (derived from initial contact during the bid process/other knowledge);
- level of understanding of service;
- realism of service development plan;
- comprehensiveness of planning for the transition of the service to the point where it becomes the responsibility of the supplier;
- approach to exit planning on contract expiry/termination;
- references from other customers;
- quality of processes/working practices/physical security (from site visit).

1.3.3 Financial/viability

The financial/viability assessment should cover:

- review of financial position/credit rating;
- management stability;
- group/delivery structure, e.g. is local management empowered to make quick decisions about the service?
- current resourcing pressures on the supplier arising from, e.g. recruitment problems/other contract wins;
- degree of dependence on one business activity/market and resultant risk to long-term stability;
- staff turnover levels – above or below industry standard?

The development and use of these criteria are critical to achieving a fast procurement process and a fully informed purchasing decision by the customer.

1.4   OVERVIEW OF CUSTOMER'S PROCUREMENT PROCESS

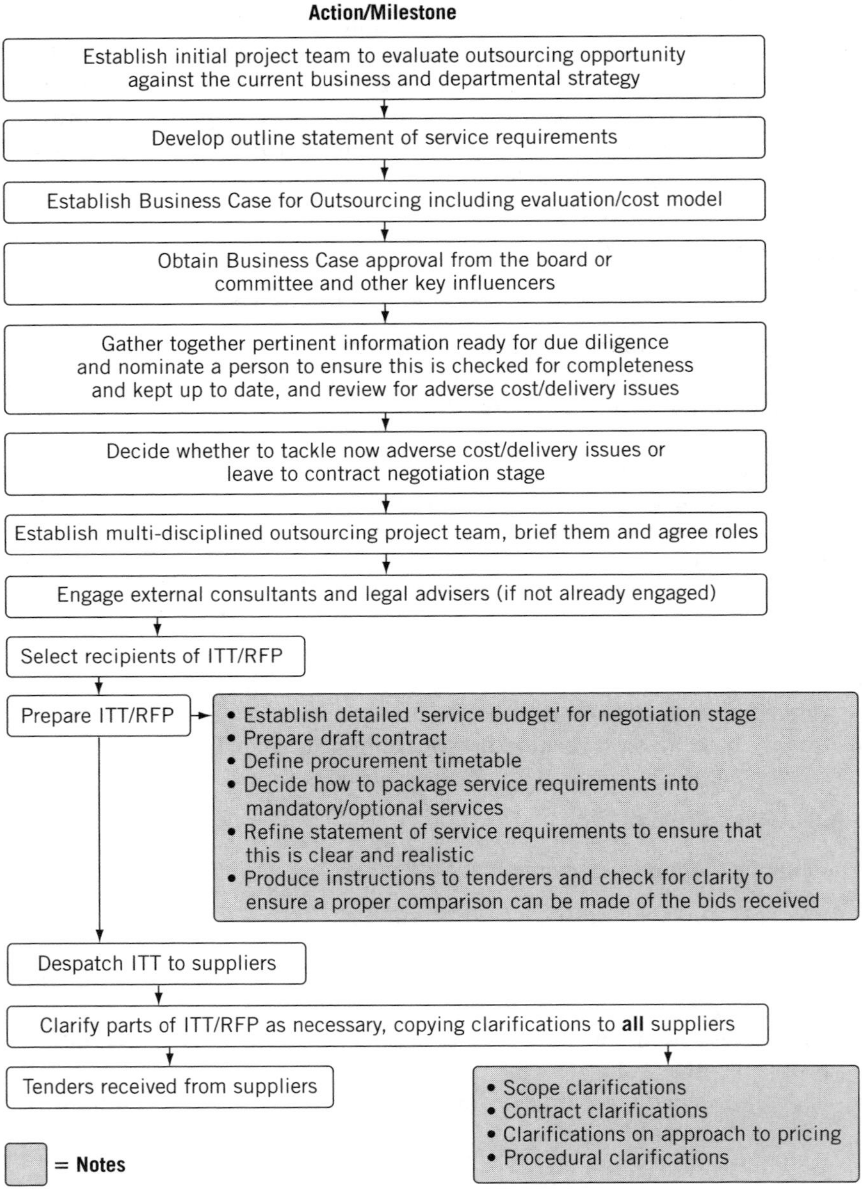

Action/Milestone

Establish initial project team to evaluate outsourcing opportunity against the current business and departmental strategy

Develop outline statement of service requirements

Establish Business Case for Outsourcing including evaluation/cost model

Obtain Business Case approval from the board or committee and other key influencers

Gather together pertinent information ready for due diligence and nominate a person to ensure this is checked for completeness and kept up to date, and review for adverse cost/delivery issues

Decide whether to tackle now adverse cost/delivery issues or leave to contract negotiation stage

Establish multi-disciplined outsourcing project team, brief them and agree roles

Engage external consultants and legal advisers (if not already engaged)

Select recipients of ITT/RFP

Prepare ITT/RFP

- Establish detailed 'service budget' for negotiation stage
- Prepare draft contract
- Define procurement timetable
- Decide how to package service requirements into mandatory/optional services
- Refine statement of service requirements to ensure that this is clear and realistic
- Produce instructions to tenderers and check for clarity to ensure a proper comparison can be made of the bids received

Despatch ITT to suppliers

Clarify parts of ITT/RFP as necessary, copying clarifications to **all** suppliers

Tenders received from suppliers

- Scope clarifications
- Contract clarifications
- Clarifications on approach to pricing
- Procedural clarifications

☐ = Notes

Figure 1.1   From Concept to Receipt of Tender/Proposal

Actions/Milestones

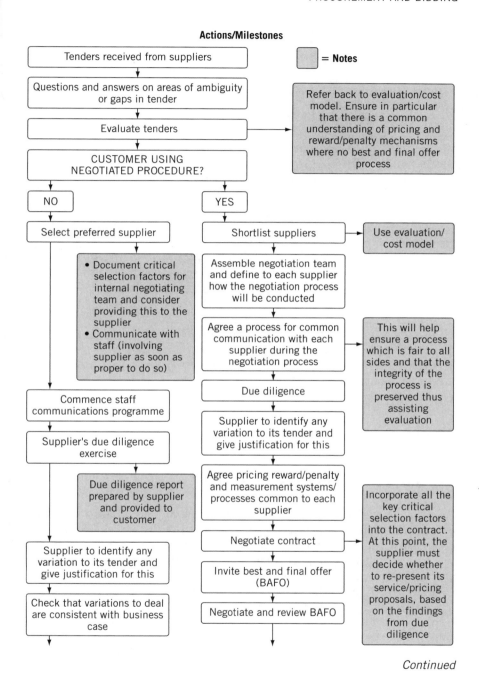

Figure 1.2 From Receipt of Tender to Contract Signing and Service Take-on

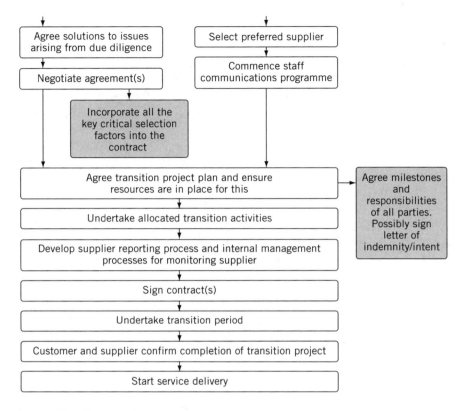

Figure 1.2 Continued

1.5 SUPPLIER'S BID PROCESS

As with the customer's bid process, and taking an end-to-end view of the entire process, this can logically be divided into two distinct phases. The first commences with the identification of a prospective customer and ends with selection as preferred supplier (Figure 1.3, p. 18–19). The second commences with defining and agreeing the take-on process and ends with the internal reviews carried out by the supplier shortly after handover of the responsibility for delivering the service from the supplier's take-on manager (who is responsible for all aspects of planning and executing the transfer of responsibility for delivering the service from the customer or its current supplier to the new supplier) to its service delivery manager (Figure 1.4, p. 20).

The diagrams assume a successful process of bidding and winning the contract by the supplier, and identify the key actions taken and milestones reached at each stage of the process. As can be seen, there is a significant amount of preparation, planning and resource allocation for a bid of a reasonable size. This implied state of preparedness of a professional and well organised outsourcing company is perhaps a further reason why the customer must itself ensure a well planned and properly resourced procurement process (see section 1.4).

On page 21, a suggested checklist for the proposal document to be issued by the supplier is included (Table 1.1). While all proposals need to be drafted so as to respond fully and effectively to the customer's ITT/RFP, the checklist can be used as an outline structure, with items added and deleted as necessary.

1.6 DUE DILIGENCE – RATIONALE AND EXAMPLES

1.6.1 The role of due diligence and when it should be undertaken

Due diligence can take on a number of different guises and be carried out at different points in the outsourcing process. While in its most basic form it can be an information tool used by the supplier to develop a set of warranties and indemnities for the contract, it is normally carried out precontract and used for a more sophisticated set of purposes. These may include:

- The verification of information provided to the supplier during the tender process to enable validation of cost and delivery assumptions that may have been made in the tender, including an assessment of omitted/unavailable information.
- The identification of potential risks to the achievement by the supplier of its business case for the contract, thereby facilitating contingency planning for the service.
- Establishing an early working relationship between customer and supplier at a point prior to the supplier assuming full responsibility for delivery of the service.
- Providing visibility of a wide range of supplier employees/resources to the customer's employees. This assists in team building and confidence building, which helps to ensure a seamless transition of service delivery responsibility to the supplier.
- The output produced assisting those responsible for contract negotiation and drafting to focus on the key business issues.
- Enabling an early assessment to be made by management on each side of the level of cultural compatibility between customer and supplier. This assessment may result in specific recommendations of actions to be taken to promote working together. In an extreme case and bearing in mind the long-term strategic nature of these projects, this may lead to a decision not to proceed and the commencement of a new selection process by the customer, or a withdrawal by the supplier.

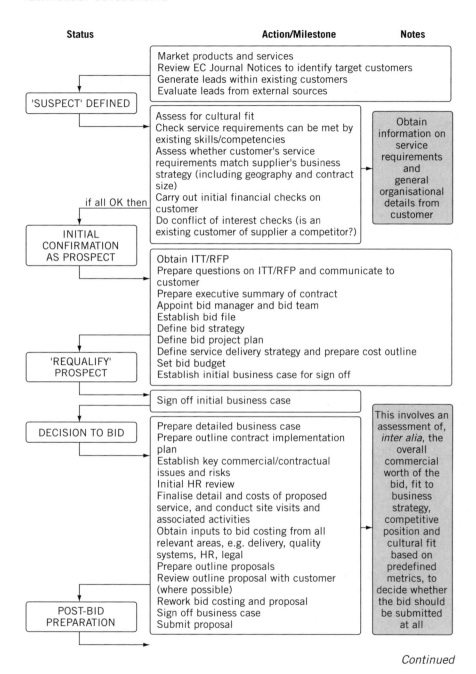

Status	Action/Milestone	Notes
	Market products and services Review EC Journal Notices to identify target customers Generate leads within existing customers Evaluate leads from external sources	
'SUSPECT' DEFINED	Assess for cultural fit Check service requirements can be met by existing skills/competencies Assess whether customer's service requirements match supplier's business strategy (including geography and contract size) Carry out initial financial checks on customer Do conflict of interest checks (is an existing customer of supplier a competitor?)	Obtain information on service requirements and general organisational details from customer
if all OK then INITIAL CONFIRMATION AS PROSPECT	Obtain ITT/RFP Prepare questions on ITT/RFP and communicate to customer Prepare executive summary of contract Appoint bid manager and bid team Establish bid file Define bid strategy Define bid project plan Define service delivery strategy and prepare cost outline Set bid budget Establish initial business case for sign off	
'REQUALIFY' PROSPECT	Sign off initial business case	
DECISION TO BID	Prepare detailed business case Prepare outline contract implementation plan Establish key commercial/contractual issues and risks Initial HR review Finalise detail and costs of proposed service, and conduct site visits and associated activities Obtain inputs to bid costing from all relevant areas, e.g. delivery, quality systems, HR, legal Prepare outline proposals Review outline proposal with customer (where possible) Rework bid costing and proposal Sign off business case Submit proposal	This involves an assessment of, *inter alia*, the overall commercial worth of the bid, fit to business strategy, competitive position and cultural fit based on predefined metrics, to decide whether the bid should be submitted at all
POST-BID PREPARATION		

Continued

Figure 1.3 From 'suspect' to 'preferred supplier' status

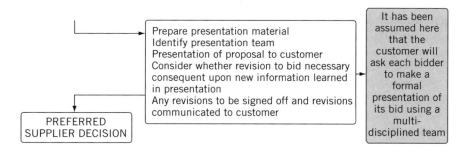

Figure 1.3 Continued

• Where the customer has an incumbent supplier of the services to be outsourced, assessing whether that supplier owns any key intellectual property or physical assets essential for the ongoing delivery of the service and whether this will be made available to the new supplier, and, if so, at what price.

The output from the due diligence exercise should be a detailed due diligence report and this report – or at least those parts that are not commercially confidential – should be provided by the supplier to the customer upon production, and a meeting held to agree actions resulting from the findings.

1.6.2   Can benefit be derived by both customer and supplier?

The answer to this is patently yes. For the supplier, a comprehensive due diligence exercise looking at service issues, cost issues, cultural issues and people issues should generate a high level of understanding of what is being taken on by it. It also underpins delivery of each party's business case by allowing the major adverse findings from the exercise to be identified, discussed and eliminated by agreement between the parties. This may involve adjustments to service requirements or charges, or practical steps to be taken by the parties to remove a particular risk.

For the customer, the exercise reduces the likelihood of additional costs or other surprises arising post contract. It also enables a resetting of expectations within the customer's organisation, if the business objectives on which the service was outsourced were unrealistic by reference to the state of the service, and the barriers to service improvement as identified by the supplier's due diligence.

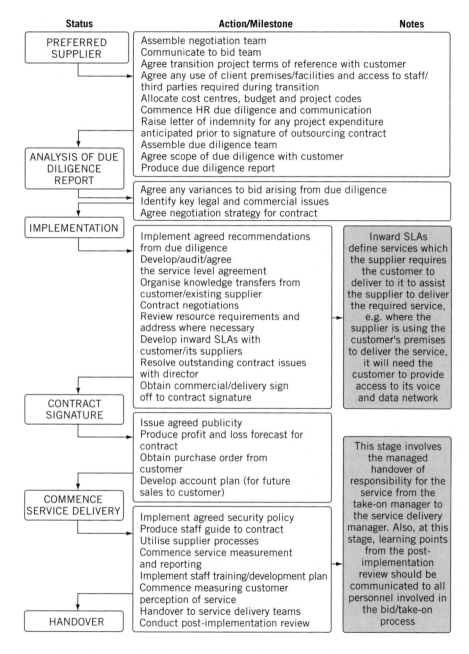

Figure 1.4 From 'preferred supplier' to post-implementation review

Table 1.1 Proposal checklist

No. Main sections of a proposal

---

1. **Cover and title page**
   - Check that the proposal is properly version controlled (to assist updating/reissue).
   - Is customer name and address specified and correct?

2. **Table of contents**
   - Ensure clear indexing of the various sections of the proposal, as outlined below.
   - Use an appropriate point numbering system e.g. 1.0, 1.1 etc., to allow flexibility in making additions or deletions.

3. **Introduction**
   - State the background to the issue of the proposal.
   - Acknowledge assistance from people inside the customer's organisation and name key people.
   - Give brief career details of key members of supplier's bid team.
   - Include appropriate copyright and confidentiality statements.

4. **Management summary**
   - Isolate and summarise from main text of detailed proposal the key service, investment and other commercial features of the proposal, together with the key sales messages.
   - Is the management summary consistent with the detailed proposal?

5. **Customer's current business status and requirements/objectives**
   - Recite pertinent details to show that you have a good grasp/knowledge of the current status of the customer's business, of the business objectives underpinning the outsourcing, and state how these will be met.

6. **Supplier's approach/solution**
   - Outline of the solution.
   - Will the technical solution as described fully meet the customer's stated requirements? If not, define and justify exceptions.
   - Have all technical prerequisites been stated?
   - Are all estimating assumptions clearly defined to assist evaluation by the customer?
   - Are all assumptions on which the technical solution is based defined?
   - Are the project scope and deliverables clear?
   - Are the project responsibilities of each party defined in a way that the customer will recognise? Is it clear where the customer is expected to obtain the co-operation of a third party (e.g. an incumbent supplier) as part of its own project responsibilities?
   - Define how supplier will organise service delivery, and detail of escalation procedures for handling resolution of issues.
   - State how an effective transfer of knowledge about the service can be effected from the customer/incumbent supplier to the supplier, and within what timescales.
   - Outline approach to service performance measurement and regularity of reporting of these statistics to customer.
   - State what quality processes will be followed by supplier and what quality certifications (if any) the supplier holds.
   - Will the supplier require the use of any of the customer's assets or the transfer of third party agreements in delivering the service? If so, what assumptions have been made regarding any payment for this?

Continued

Table 1.1   Continued

No. Main sections of a proposal

---

7. Benefits
  - Summarise the key benefits of the solution, and how it will improve upon the current situation for the customer, in both delivery terms and commercial terms.

8. Pricing
  - Have costs been broken down to an appropriate level of detail?
  - Is the total charge clear?
  - Where relevant, is the approach to charging for expenses clear?
  - Are the payment terms clearly stated?
  - Clearly state the number of days/months for which the pricing is valid. State if prices are subject to change during term of agreement and specify on what basis, e.g. in line with increase in Retail Prices Index or (where cost base is largely salaries) a recognised index of increases in salaries relevant to the staff who will deliver the service.
  - State any expiry date on the proposal.
  - State if any elements of pricing are subject to change and need to be confirmed at time of ordering.

9. Terms and conditions
  - State that all commercial assumptions stated in the proposal will need to be reflected in contract terms.
  - Make it clear on whose terms and conditions the proposal is based.
  - If customer's terms are stipulated, include supplier's response to them.
  - Where neither side has taken a position on what contract terms are to be used then summarise the key points which you would expect to see reflected in the contract.

10. Implementation schedule/transition plan
  - Show time frames and activities from receipt of order and start of the transition project through to successful implementation of all elements of the service.
  - The respective responsibilities of both the supplier and the customer should be clearly spelled out.
  - Spell out any special approaches to risk containment through the transition project.
  - Include draft project plan.

11. Post-sales support and contract review
  - Detail post-sales support services.
  - Define regularity of service review meetings and seniority of supplier staff who will attend.

12. Resourcing and staff issues
  - State, in general terms, how the service will be resourced, e.g. from existing resources of supplier, from new recruits, from staff transferring from the customer or the incumbent supplier under TUPE, or a mixture of these.

Continued

Table 1.1   Continued

No. Main sections of a proposal

12. Continued
- Where TUPE applies:
  - (a) outline the staff transfer and induction process, including when and how the staff (and, where relevant, unions) will be communicated with.
  - (b) summarise the ongoing training which will be provided to staff.
  - (c) outline the credentials of the supplier in successfully handling staff transfers.
  - (d) state the supplier's approach regarding the ongoing terms and conditions of employment of the staff and availability of a company pension scheme.

13. Why buy from the supplier?
- Outline capabilities of supplier, emphasising those services and experiences which are relevant to the project, and any differentiators from competitive suppliers.
- Outline experience of supplier in the delivery of the services required.
- Give 'reference stories' proving experience of delivering these services.
- Summarise historical development of supplier, giving key financial details.

14. Appendices
- This may include terms and conditions, detailed specifications and corporate information on supplier as required by customer, e.g. report and accounts, insurance summary.
- Include CVs, project plans and case studies?

15. Covering letter
- Does it state what customer must do to accept the proposal?

1.6.3   How can the customer help to prepare for due diligence?

When due diligence begins the supplier should already have a large volume of information about the customer and its service requirements from the ITT/RFP, and from answers received to questions raised. However, due diligence will require much of that information to be provided in greater detail to the supplier. To avoid any slippage in the timetable that the customer has set for the outsourcing, this information should have been gathered well before due diligence is due to begin, preferably as part of preparing the ITT/RFP for despatch to the suppliers.

Intellect (formerly the Computing Services and Software Association) provides a helpful checklist of the information that your potential IT suppliers may need (see also paragraph 1.6.8 for some additional subject areas on which information may be required).

1.6.4   Example checklist of information needed by IT outsourcing suppliers[3]

Premises

- Lease and rental details.
- Service contracts.
- Asset values.

Hardware

- Installation dates, model numbers, current maintenance costs and location.
- Present capacity estimates, future requirements and planned upgrades.
- Network diagram with sites, line speeds and hardware installed.
- Any interfaces to external systems and networks.

Software

- All software used, including ownership, licensing and financial arrangements.
- Software support responsibilities for proprietary software together with future implementations planned.
- Definition of who is responsible for application software maintenance, enhancements and new developments, and the number of staff currently supporting this activity.
- New software implementations planned and future strategy.

Third party contracts

- Maintenance agreements.
- Consumables supply agreements.
- Bureau services.

Staff

- Current staff complement costs, including contract staff.
- Policy with regard to transfer or secondment of staff.

Statement of service requirements

- Service availability – online and batch.
- Service priorities.
- User population.
- Output (such as printing) requirements, including distribution.
- Performance targets, monitoring and reporting.

- Helpdesk support.
- Network support.
- Application support.
- Application developments and enhancements.
- Standards and methodologies.
- Data access control and administration.
- Change request administration.
- Backup and security.
- External agency interfaces – contingency services.

It is perhaps also worth considering the question posed by paragraph 1.6.3 in the context of a re-tendering. Many customers find the information gathering necessary on an initial outsourcing a hugely time consuming and gruelling exercise. One can see the potential for this situation to be compounded where, on a re-tender, the customer is reliant on its incumbent supplier to provide key information on such things as the assets used within the service and their ownership, contracts with third party suppliers, staff information and current service statistics. As the outsourcing market matures and contract renewals become greater in number, this becomes more of an issue. One interesting statistic is that, in the IT outsourcing marketplace, there has been an increase in the proportion of renewal contracts being signed. For example, of the total number of contract renewals in the IT outsourcing market in 1999, only 2 per cent of those renewals resulted in a change of supplier. Any customer will want to point to the reason behind this low percentage being satisfaction with the incumbent supplier and with the success of the contract, rather than any practical difficulties that may be associated with changing supplier. Several months before the ITT/RFP is to be sent to prospective tenderers the customer must therefore define to its incumbent supplier the information that is required from the supplier and how this should be presented. Also, on a re-tender, the customer and the supplier should begin to discuss what level of knowledge transfer and general liaison would be needed with any new supplier selected, although the exact details will, to a large extent, be governed by the level of expertise and requirements of a new supplier. The contractual obligation for the incumbent supplier to co-operate in these matters and its ability to charge for some or all of the assistance provided should of course have been defined in the original outsourcing contract.

1.6.5   When should due diligence be undertaken?

When one considers the purpose behind due diligence, it follows that the work must be done at the precontract stage in order for it properly to fulfil its purpose. This is typically done immediately after the selection by the customer of its preferred supplier. This timing may be a reflection of the resource demands that an extensive due diligence exercise places on both customer and supplier.

However, it is becoming increasingly common for a shortlist of two or three suppliers to be asked to do due diligence as a precursor to a re-presentation of their bid (based on the information arising from due diligence), at what is sometimes described as the best and final offer stage. This, it is argued, ensures that both the re-presented bid (best and final offer) and the resultant preferred supplier selection is based on all available information, such that neither side should be able to change its position post selection. However, while the theory behind this approach is sound, it is often difficult for suppliers to commit the level of resource required for the exercise when they have no certainty of their investment in the exercise being repaid by a contract award. It also places a major resourcing burden on the customer, and can significantly delay contract award and the start of the service.

1.6.6   How is it done?

The approach to carrying out due diligence will vary considerably according to the nature and complexity of the service for which the supplier will assume responsibility, the state of the service at the time, and the time and resources available on each side. A suggested process for the supplier of carrying out and reporting upon a due diligence exercise is set out below. This assumes that time and resources permit a relatively detailed process to be carried out.

1.6.7   Suggested due diligence process steps

Preparatory steps

1.   Identify person responsible for managing the due diligence activity.
2.   Identify time needed to carry out exercise and agree with customer.
3.   Identify areas within customer's organisation where due diligence will be done.
4.   Identify individuals who will do, and consider the results from, the work (managerial and technical).
5.   Identify individuals' availability.
6.   Match availability with availability of customer's equivalent staff.
7.   Draw up contacts list – supplier and customer.
8.   Identify what needs to be covered in the due diligence report.
9.   Agree and issue a Terms of Reference for due diligence to the customer. This should include pre-due diligence checklist of information, facilities, access to staff and documentation to be made available, to ensure customer is clear what assistance needs to be provided to the supplier.
10. Distribute all pertinent documentation already possessed to due diligence team.

11. Brief supplier due diligence team on:

- background to contract;
- strategy for delivery of agreed service;
- customer's organisation.

12. Inform the team of what needs to be covered in the due diligence report.

Content

1. The external report (to be available to both customer and supplier) should:

- confirm that the supplier's preferred approach to delivering the service is achievable and can be met within the tendered charges, or required changes to achieve the preferred approach;
- verify the details of the existing service provided by the customer in the ITT, and the numbers of staff assigned to it;
- confirm that the required service performance criteria are measurable and realistic, or suggest alternatives;
- detail existing evidence of level of service performance achieved and user perceptions of the service;
- detail any factual statements made by customer in ITT or any assumptions made by supplier in the proposal that proved incorrect and specify the commercial and delivery implications of those on each party;
- verify service and transaction volumes data provided by the customer;
- identify any recommended actions to be taken prior to transfer of services.

2. The internal report (to be available to supplier only) should:

- confirm internal costing (on which the tendered charges were based), or required amendments with reasons;
- detail actions required to meet the customer's delivery/performance requirements;
- specify any 'show stopper' problems.

Format

1. Timescale and deadlines for completion of the work/production of report.

Carry out due diligence (see also paragraph 1.6.8)

1. On each part of the service, split by function.
2. Generally, with regard to:

- processes and procedures;
- accreditations/quality standards;
- HR: staff details and organisation of the staff;
- third party contracts (including costs and level of dependency on the suppliers);
- assets (condition; how critical to the service; are they owned outright or shared with another part of the customer's organisation?);
- customers' (users') perception of the existing services;
- service dependencies that the supplier will have on the customer (e.g. for provision of fully serviced accommodation);
- accommodation, including any factors that might adversely impact delivery of the services;
- logistics and their impact on the supplier's ability to deliver the service.

Post due diligence

1. Arrange an internal debriefing session.
2. Copy of all due diligence reports to all participants prior to meeting.
3. Jointly discuss and agree preferred approach to issues identified from due diligence.
4. Produce a new version of business case to reflect the findings of the due diligence.
5. Issue a customer due diligence report in the agreed format.
6. As a minimum this should include:

- introduction;
- management summary;
- key areas of variance from information provided by customer or assumptions made by supplier, e.g. pricing, solution, performance, service volumes;
- areas requiring further clarification and assumptions made (including areas unable to be reviewed);
- recommendations;
- appendices of service findings (broken down into functional areas within the service).

7. Issue an internal report of any issues to project sponsor within supplier organisation.
8. Hold a meeting to go through the main points from the report with the customer.

9. Encourage customer to respond formally with responsibility for actions clearly identified.
10. Ensure agreed actions are progressed to agreed timescales.

1.6.8 Some example areas for due diligence

This paragraph outlines a number of other areas on which the supplier is likely to want to focus its due diligence activities.

Current achievement of service levels: the supplier will need to verify the current service performance to confirm any assumptions that it has made with regard to any difference in measured service performance compared with the requested level of service. This assumption will have to be validated by reference to service statistics produced by the customer. These should preferably relate to an extended period of at least one year, to ensure that the supplier's view of service performance is not distorted by seasonal factors affecting service volumes or performance. Examples of this are activity associated with a peak trading period or the end of a financial year. Evaluation over such an extended period also assists in identification of key forward events that need extra resources, e.g. year-end processing connected with accounts preparation. This is of particular importance where payment is wholly or partly linked to service performance, e.g. council tax administration contracts in local government, where part of the supplier's remuneration may be linked to improvements in the percentage of council tax billed that is actually paid by local taxpayers.

Work backlogs/work in progress: the supplier will typically assume that the resources used to deliver the service at the time when it formulates its bid represent a *normal* level of resource, i.e. that which is sufficient economically to deliver the service required by the customer, on the assumption that there is a normal level of work in progress for the type of service. A build-up of a work backlog within the service before the supplier commences service delivery may require immediate resource allocation to clear it, at potentially significant cost. It is therefore key that this is identified and costed.

Assets/consumables to be transferred: these will often have been identified in a list forming part of the ITT/RFP. However, it is not unusual to find that such lists are out of date, incomplete and sometimes suggest exclusive availability of assets that are, in reality, shared with other departments within the customer organisation. Such errors can lead to both cost and service impacts.

Human resources: see section 1.7 for detailed analysis of this subject.

Quality systems/processes employed: as part of the supplier's risk management it should identify what quality systems and processes are actively used in the service. This should provide evidence of a stable process-driven service, which can be relatively easily assimilated into its own processes.

Skills transfer and intellectual property requirements: if the assumption of service responsibility by the supplier will trigger a TUPE transfer of staff (see Chapter 9), the majority of the skills needed to deliver the service into the future should automatically transfer to the supplier by operation of law. However, there is a risk of key personnel being reallocated within the customer's organisation or resigning before such a transfer, and the supplier needs to identify these risks early and prepare a contingency plan. It should also notify the customer of the skills transfer requirements (possibly involving access to third party suppliers or technical documentation) that it needs the customer to arrange for it. There may sometimes be a problem over access to intellectual property on which the service is dependent but which is owned by a third party, sometimes an incumbent service provider. If free of charge access can not be obtained, some replacement resource may have to be obtained, often at significant additional cost.

Health and safety: where the service is being delivered wholly or partially on the customer's site, the supplier needs to be sure that the premises from which the service is delivered, and the existing working arrangements, are compliant with health and safety legislation, and are conducive to achievement of the service performance objectives. The cost of taking corrective actions can in some instances be high, and it might therefore be advisable to pay for an independent health and safety audit, the report from which can be provided to both sides.

Dependencies on customer/its suppliers: the supplier may have identified a continuing dependency on the customer, or via the customer on one of the customer's suppliers, for some key input to the service it is to deliver. The supplier will then want to be sure that such input is working normally and will, for the duration of the contract, be delivered to clear documented service levels. Where these do not exist they will need to be prepared and agreed. One of the outputs from this part of due diligence is a customer responsibilities schedule. This defines all responsibilities of the customer to the supplier, both in the transition period leading to live delivery of the service, and those recurring responsibilities to provide or procure the provision of inputs to the live service by the customer or its suppliers.

Communications/technology: the supplier will want to evaluate how well the communications infrastructure utilised by the service operates and any limitations/restrictions or planned changes to this that could impact on the service, or the cost of delivering the service. This could cover post, phone systems, e-mail systems, network and Internet links, and the absence of contingency plans for any of these.

Accommodation: the supplier needs to check any assumptions it has made about the total cost of occupation of any customer-provided accommodation. It also needs to be sure that the current basis on which the service has access to other facilities, such as storage facilities, is adequate, and meeting rooms, rest rooms, staff restaurants, car parking, toilet and other facilities are adequate and will be maintained. A dilapidations survey will generally be advisable to identify those dilapidations existing at the service start date, which will then be used to identify responsibility for any repair costs to the accommodation at the end of the supplier's period of occupation.

Third party agreements: in addition to software licences referred to in Chapter 2, there may be other third party agreements on which the service is dependent. The supplier needs to review these to establish:

(a) whether it is reasonable and appropriate for these agreements to be assigned or novated to it (i.e. where this causes no adverse cost or service impact on it);

(b) if the agreement is to be transferred, are the arrangements for communicating issues and obtaining support from the third party clear and working well?

Where the third party supplier refuses to give consent to the assignment/ novation or demands terms that are commercially unreasonable, it may be necessary to leave the third party agreements with the customer but agree with the supplier any necessary changes to allow the supplier to make such use of the licences/agreements as is necessary to enable it to deliver the services (e.g. limited use of software; right, on behalf of customer, to place help desk calls, etc.).

In practice, this issue rarely presents an insurmountable problem, but early discussions with third parties are advisable to nip potential issues in the bud.

Security: the supplier must be happy that the physical and information technology security arrangements under which the service operates are robust. There will normally be a particular focus on premises security arrangements (including access for visitors and arrangements for out of hours and weekend working) and network access. Where relevant, there may also need to be clear procedures for identification verification of individuals requesting information by phone or in person in connection with the service.

Data protection: where the service involves the handling or processing of personal data, both customer and supplier should check that their current registrations under the data protection legislation are adequate to permit the activities envisaged, and change their registrations if necessary. Additionally, the service must be designed to incorporate a level of security that will ensure compliance with the data protection principles (Schedule 1 to the Data Protection Act 1998). The parties need to be clear about whether the roles and responsibilities of the supplier could encompass its becoming a data controller rather than simply a data processor. In the former case, the supplier needs to register as such.

One should also consider such points as:

- Will the new service involve disclosures of personal data to a broader group of persons than previously, and if so, do the customer's data protection registration and data subject consents permit this?
- In relation to personal data of staff to be disclosed prior to the start and end date of the contract, has the data subject consented to disclosure of this information to contractors and, if not, can explicit consent be obtained from the relevant employees, or can anonymised information be disclosed instead to sidestep this potential legal difficulty?

Invoicing and payment arrangements: the supplier will wish to establish how it will be paid for its services, and what administrative arrangements it needs to comply with to have its invoices approved for payment. This is of particular concern where the work involves some element of time and materials working, where the amount of resource expended and/or cost incurred needs to be proved to the customer.

1.6.9   Barriers to due diligence[4]

It is not uncommon to find that the due diligence exercise is made more difficult, or even (for some elements) impossible for a variety of reasons.

The biggest barrier to due diligence is often that the customer has not sufficiently prepared information for the service, and has not secured the availability of its staff. There may also be a problem with a particular individual or individuals having a conflict of priorities. This problem should be easily resolved by customer management.

Another more problematic barrier can be the actions of an incumbent supplier. Where the total business relationship between the customer and the incumbent will come to an end on the assumption by the new supplier of responsibility for the service, little commercial leverage is available to get the incumbent to respond to information requests. Sometimes the issue may be one of confidentiality *vis-à-vis* the incumbent and the new supplier, and most such situations can be resolved by a combination of legal and practical protections for the incumbent, agreed by the new supplier. However, the incumbent may have exclusive rights to information or intellectual property that are critical to running the service. If it is not prepared to provide these to the new supplier at a reasonable cost and cannot be compelled to do this under its contract with the customer, there is a problem. Unless the new supplier can find some economical substitute for this resource the very viability of the outsourcing project may be in doubt. Of course, there may be other ways of exerting pressure on the incumbent, particularly if it is a member of a professional body with a relevant code of practice. For example, the CSSA Facilities Management Code of Practice[5] requires that member suppliers of the CSSA should:

- commence contract renewal negotiations in sufficient time to allow the user to seek alternative suppliers;
- provide all reasonable assistance on termination to transfer service provision;
- destroy or return all materials belonging to the user.

A failure by a member of a trade association to comply with its rules could be reported to the association, and any indirect pressure thereby created may be sufficient to get the co-operation required.

Obtaining access to third party suppliers of the customer may also pose a problem. Understanding what they deliver to the customer, and how it inter-relates with what the supplier will deliver, may be of fundamental importance to the supplier. Additionally, where third party supply contracts are to be novated or assigned from the customer to the supplier, it is crucial for there to be proper access to the relevant contracts so that the supplier can identify exactly what it will be assuming responsibility for.

Time may also be a problem. If the customer has had to delay its decision to appoint a preferred supplier such that the project is now running late, it may need to compress the rest of the outsourcing timetable to ensure that the service starts on schedule and delivers in full the benefits that the customer's business case defined. An obvious target for the customer to bring the process back on track is due diligence. However, the supplier is likely to resist attempts to significantly shorten due diligence, and may argue that, in such a situation, more extensive warranties and indemnities will be required by it in the outsourcing contract.

It may be the case that data are not available against which to verify the claims of the customer as to existing service performance. In such a situation, the only real option may be for the customer and supplier to agree an interim set of performance measures pending the finalisation of detailed service measures, after the supplier has been delivering the service for a reasonable period. This approach has obvious risks for the customer.

One thing is certain: if a customer is ever unfortunate enough to be faced with an unco-operative incumbent supplier, it is sure to place the highest emphasis on the exit provisions of the next outsourcing contract that it signs.

1.7   HUMAN RESOURCES DUE DILIGENCE – A SUGGESTED METHODOLOGY

In any outsourcing situation the supplier will have to allocate significant amounts of resource, involving a wide range of staff, to the due diligence process. However, if timescales/resources did not permit the luxury of a full due diligence exercise, it is interesting to speculate on which areas the supplier would focus. It is very likely that very high up the list of priorities would be human resources due diligence, and for good reason. The staff delivering a service are self-evidently the engine behind that service. Their motivation, trust and confidence in the outsourcing project will be key to that engine continuing to operate normally when the supplier assumes service responsibility. However, a typical outsourcing project will also involve an improvement in performance levels, sometimes of a significant nature, and this will only be achieved where the pre-existing level of motivation, trust and confidence has been improved. This can be a major challenge, especially since it involves making that improvement at a time when insecurity, demotivation and low morale may well have taken a grip on significant numbers of the staff. These feelings may have been exacerbated by poor communication from their employer in the weeks and months prior to the supplier being named as preferred supplier.

This section looks at the broad due diligence process needed with, and regarding, the staff before the contract is signed. This precontract activity accounts for substantially the whole of the total effort needed within the HR due diligence programme. The section also looks at the ongoing efforts that need to be made to assimilate the staff into the supplier's organisation. The objective of this must be to ensure, by reskilling and reinforcing their vision of how the service will develop and how they will contribute to that development, that staff are retained and their commitment is secured.

Human resources due diligence is normally carried out at two levels: formal and informal due diligence. The formal process is intended to verify the cost base to the service represented by the staff, now and into the future. It also identifies current and future liabilities (e.g. prospective redundancy liability) that will transfer to the supplier, and facilitates a thorough understanding of the terms and conditions of employment of the staff. Much of the information gathered will be used to put together a TUPE schedule to the outsourcing contract, and a number of warranties will be sought from the customer based around the accuracy and completeness of this information. It is not unusual for the customer's human resources department to feel uncomfortable about confirming the accuracy of the employment information around which their management is being asked to give warranties and indemnities. However, in the light of the obligations arising from data protection law and obligations of confidentiality that the customer has towards its staff, which act as a barrier to effective due diligence, it is hard to see how the supplier could ever obtain a level of comfort and knowledge about the staff, such that it could dispense with such protection. Also, since the proportion of the total cost of delivering the service attributable to staff-related costs is often very significant, then this is an area of business risk that the supplier will wish to have underwritten by the customer.

Informal due diligence involves extensive contact with the staff at all levels, both in groups and in one-to-one sessions. It allows the supplier to evaluate the quality of the staff, areas of weakness that may need management action, and individuals whose abilities are not being fully utilised. It also provides a further opportunity for the supplier to validate information that the customer has provided about itself and the service, with the very people who are best placed to give a full and frank assessment of this.

1.7.1 Formal due diligence – checklist of employment information required by supplier

There follows a checklist of employment information that a supplier will wish to obtain through its formal due diligence.

Primary information

This information will help to formulate the TUPE schedule that will form part of the contract.

1. Staff numbers:
   - number of permanent staff assigned to the undertaking being outsourced and their roles – these staff may have TUPE rights – see Chapter 9;
   - number of contract staff (direct and agency) within scope of service being outsourced and their roles;
   - whether these are permanent roles or temporary roles;
   - if staff are not wholly engaged on work being outsourced, percentage of time allocated to it (to test degree of *assignment* in order to establish whether TUPE will apply to transfer the employment of these staff to the contractor – see Chapter 9);
   - any staff absent through career break/secondment/maternity/long-term absence;
   - staff who may be 'acting up', i.e. fulfilling responsibilities additional to their normal responsibilities, but on a temporary basis.

2. For each member of staff:
   - name;
   - job title;
   - location of work;
   - start date (or start date for continuous service);
   - sex;
   - date of birth;
   - salary (including date of next review);
   - other monetary allowances or benefits;

- grade;
- normal retirement age;
- hours worked (normal or part time);
- notice periods (from the company);
- whether or not in pension scheme (and if different pension schemes, which scheme);
- contract term/rate/notice (contract staff only);
- entitlement to be paid for overtime worked.

3. General:

- redundancy terms, including any special terms for over 50s;
- pension scheme details;
- car/car loan arrangements (consider whether those are easily transferable to the supplier, or need to be replaced);
- whether any of the above information potentially varied by established custom and practice in the customer organisation, e.g. regarding supposedly discretionary bonus schemes or redundancy entitlements.

Other information

This information is required in order for existing terms and conditions of employment to be understood and seamlessly implemented within the supplier's organisation:

- copies of standard employment contracts/offer letters;
- terms and conditions of employment;
- other benefits of employment;
- staff take-up of benefits, e.g. car/health cover/season ticket/loans;
- copies of grading structures;
- copies of job evaluation or performance monitoring schemes;
- copies of staff handbooks.

Costing information

- accrued levels of holiday entitlement;
- overtime costs in last 12 months;
- sickness levels in last 12 months;
- outstanding loans;
- existing training costs for individual.

Industrial relations information

- details of union presence;
- current areas of dispute with unions;

- historical disputes;
- collective and local agreements;
- any established custom and practice in terms of union consultation/involvement in decisions;
- outstanding employment litigation/industrial tribunals/disciplinary or grievance procedures.

Commitments given to individuals

- variations to terms and conditions agreed by current employer;
- training commitments.

Personnel and payroll details

- names and home addresses;
- bank/building society details;
- national insurance numbers.

Contacts in

- payroll department;
- pensions department.

1.7.2   Informal due diligence

As a separate issue to the commercial need for formal due diligence, the supplier must also carry out informal due diligence. This is partly driven by the mandatory consultation requirements under the TUPE regulations (see Chapter 9), and partly by the imperative to establish open and honest channels of communication between the staff and the supplier, brokered by the customer. This should establish trust in this new developing relationship, and mitigate the feelings of anxiety and uncertainty that are likely to affect at least some of the staff. If this relationship of trust can be established, its by-product will be to give the supplier access to information and opinions that may in some cases be both new and of real relevance to the seamless take-on and future development of the service. This may lead to management action being taken to contain newly identified risks, but information that is of direct commercial significance will need to be considered within the contract negotiations. Great care is needed in the management of staff morale and expectations through the procurement process, and the customer and supplier should ensure that they have a comprehensive staff communications strategy, which is fully resourced and to which they are both fully committed. There is set out below a list of areas that may be covered during the informal due diligence process so as to realise the human and business objectives outlined above.

1. *Staff presentation on the big picture*: an early part of the take-on process should be to present the big picture of the outsourcing project to all staff whose employment will transfer to the supplier. This is used as an opportunity properly to make the staff aware of key messages about the supplier's organisation and to announce the identities of the take-on team and their roles. This session is intended to give them a level of understanding of what is going on, and subtly to introduce the plans for developing and improving the service in a positive way.

2. *Staff terms and conditions (Ts & Cs) presentation*: depending on the policy of the supplier, staff may be offered the option of joining it on their existing terms and conditions of employment, or on the supplier's standard terms, although the supplier needs to exercise considerable caution about offering new terms and conditions in view of the case law on this point (see Chapter 9). If such an option is offered, the process of making the choice and the differences between the choices need to be explained to the staff, and this is best done initially in a presentation. Even if only existing terms are being carried across, a short presentation should be given to explain how the staff's employment rights are protected and what the supplier's policies and arrangements are for such things as holiday years, pay awards, pay day, etc.

3. *Staff pensions presentation*: often combined with the Ts & Cs presentation, this is a presentation and question and answer session about the pensions options and arrangements offered by the supplier. The customer's own pensions adviser should also be present to help explain differences between the schemes and whether the employees have the option to stay in the customer's scheme and continue to make contributions into this scheme post transfer (this is increasingly common in the public sector) (see also Chapter 10).

4. *Staff familiarisation with contract/service level agreements and with changes from the existing requirements of them*: this is part of the wider communications programme and clearly something that the staff should understand before they assume responsibility for delivering the contracted service.

5. *Brief staff on supplier/customer security policies*: staff should be briefed on the supplier's security policy, which needs to be understood alongside any policy that the customer might have that is also relevant to service delivery and to the observance of contract conditions.

6. *Supplier HR representative to meet customer HR team*: at this initial meeting there will be Ts & Cs information to obtain or check, and strategies to agree. One important point is that neither party should from then on put out a communiqué to transferring staff without having first agreed it with the other party, so that a consistent message is put out to staff at all times.

7. *Meet trades union representatives*: the supplier's HR representative, possibly accompanied by the service delivery manager if required/available, should meet local union representatives to listen to any concerns, and again describe the HR process that the supplier will be undertaking.

8. *Any special current payroll deductions*: check whether the current employer is making payroll deductions for staff as part of other benefit arrangements, e.g. in a local authority, special arrangements may be made for payment of the individuals' council tax or housing rent. In some public companies, share schemes – such as Sharesave or SIP (the Share Incentive Plan) – are operated with deductions from an individual's salary via the regular payroll payment made to him/her. It may not be desirable or possible for some of these to be continued by the supplier. With share schemes, it may be possible to replace them with the new supplier's scheme, where it has an equivalent scheme to offer to the transferring staff. If it does not, the transferee employer should provide an equivalent benefit to transferring staff who currently enjoy the benefit to avoid any possibility of a breach of contract claim by transferring staff under the TUPE regulations.

9. *Any benefits requiring arrangements to maintain*: are there any benefits that the supplier can continue to provide but only if special arrangements are made, such as access to building, catering facilities, social clubs, subsidised use of local amenities, etc.? The supplier must identify these and use reasonable efforts to secure their continuation. Sometimes the loss of what appear to be benefits of little value can have a disproportionate effect on staff morale.

10. *Staff skills audit*: as early as possible in the process, the supplier needs to ascertain the coverage and depth of skills in the staff transferring their employment to it. This enables the supplier to plan for any necessary recruitment or training to fill gaps or cover areas of weakness.

11. *Rare skills dependency check*: is the supplier vulnerable in certain areas as there are only one or two members of staff who can undertake certain work? What will it do in the event of sickness/holiday/resignation? It may be necessary to draw up contingency plans.

12. *Decide on any permanent recruitment*: will the supplier need more staff or new skills to deliver the service? If so, decide numbers, and start the recruitment process, recognising the lead time in getting suitable staff recruited.

13. *Identify technical training requirements*: from the skills audit, the supplier will identify what training it needs to provide.

14. *Staff perceptions survey*: the perceptions of the transferring staff about the outsourcing are critical. These can be obtained by talking to them, but also by conducting an anonymous survey. The supplier should find out how well the staff think they are being communicated with. The results should be provided to the customer in project meetings to show openness, and actions agreed to address any negative feedback from

39

staff. If the results are particularly negative the customer and the supplier may agree on a major new initiative to encourage staff to stay, e.g. a loyalty bonus, payable to those staff who are still employed by the supplier and working on the service at a defined point after their employment transferred to the supplier.

15. *Circulate pensions literature*: this should be done at an early stage.

16. *Confirm pensions decision timetable*: communicate clearly to staff what the timetable is covering, e.g.:

   - what is the deadline for them deciding whether to join the supplier's scheme(s)?
   - does this differ by scheme?
   - when is their last payment into their current scheme?
   - when can they expect to be able to find out transfer values between schemes to assist their own evaluation of pension options?
   - is there any deadline on transfers of their pension fund into the supplier's scheme?

17. *Produce staff offer letters*: the HR team will produce formal offer letters to all transferring staff. Depending on the policy of the supplier, there may well be two letters to each member of staff, one offering employment upon their existing Ts & Cs and the other offering employment on the supplier's Ts & Cs. The letters will state that the job offer is conditional upon the outsourcing contract being signed.

18. *Individual staff one-to-one sessions*: a key part of the HR process is for every transferring member of staff to have a one-to-one meeting with an HR manager from the supplier's organisation. Key features are:

   - first major part is to hand over the one/two offer letters, explain the acceptance process and answer any questions about personal circumstances. If questions asked cannot be answered, the supplier's manager should take them away and later respond with an answer;
   - second is to talk about the individual to learn more about them. A pro forma will normally have been circulated earlier for them to fill in and this information can be used to guide the discussion about their background, current job, likes and dislikes, aspirations, etc.;
   - although intended as a one-to-one meeting, the member of staff can bring a colleague or union representative if they feel particularly in need of support at the session;
   - scheduling of these meetings, with rooms for them to be held in, is likely to be a large administrative exercise for any large number of staff. Clerical help from the customer to make the arrangements may well be required.

19. *Identify how temporary staff contracts are to be handled*: need to be clear what contract/temporary staff will also be a feature of the service at the

live service date. Be aware that these staff will have been taken on at different times and for different reasons, so expert HR help will probably be necessary to understand their contractual arrangements. In general, it is useful to involve these staff in as much of the communications process as possible to maintain their morale and ensure a shared vision of staff and contractors about the direction in which the service will develop.

20. *Staff Ts & Cs acceptance*: there should be a clear published date by which signed acceptance copies of offer letters are needed back. This is so that staff can be set up on the right payroll and be paid on time.

21. *Outstanding holiday reconciliation*: if staff transfer with their existing holiday entitlements, pro rata calculations are done to get them on to the supplier's holiday year basis, where different. If they accept new Ts & Cs and their entitlement also changes, the pro rata calculation should also take this into consideration. It is also important to understand the position with regard to outstanding holiday entitlement at the contract commencement date. It may well be a commercial negotiating point that the supplier will want to raise with the customer, if staff who are to transfer to the supplier are entitled to significant accrued holiday entitlement (e.g. because the previous employer has asked staff to do additional paid work rather than take holiday).

22. *Understand expenses profile*: understand the historical pattern of personal expenses claims and amounts for budget and forecasting purposes and to check on why expenses have been incurred. This should be done early in the take-on process, in case it uncovers something that needs discussion with the client.

23. *Set up new payroll arrangements*

24. *Staff aspirations audit*: to build on the data collected at one-to-one sessions, it may also be worth collecting more formal/detailed data on personal aspirations, especially about flexibility/wish to work as a manager or consultant, at the original site or others, for their original customer or for others, etc. These data must be passed to, and clearly understood by, the supplier's service delivery manager and HR department.

25. *Transfer personnel records*: ensure that the customer's HR department transfers historical personnel records at the contract commencement date. These files are clearly necessary for the supplier to maintain a full record of the employment history of the staff.

26. *Health and safety representatives/briefing*: one or more persons should be nominated as health and safety representatives. They need to be given training/awareness sessions and have responsibility for a proactive role in accident prevention, etc. in their areas.

27. *Devise staff induction programme*: a comprehensive induction programme should be implemented for transferring staff, and staff recruited into vacant positions, which should be communicated to the staff.

28. *Briefing on supplier's organisation*: a presentation should be given (building on the big picture presentation) that covers:

- the supplier's organisation;
- its main groups of customers;
- its product sets;
- its business strategy and outsourcing track record (including record on winning contract renewals);
- its strengths and market differentiators;
- its financial position;
- its approach to training and career development;
- its culture and emphasis on particular behaviours, etc.;
- its outline implementation plan for this contract. This must have a clear link to the staff induction programme.

29. *Development centre for managers*: as soon as possible the supplier should arrange a development centre workshop, to evaluate the capabilities of staff in management roles, and of staff who have been identified as prospective managers/team leaders. The HR department should arrange this. Staff should receive feedback as soon as possible and counselling about changes in role, if the session shows their management abilities to be lacking, or underutilised.

30. *Set staff initial objectives*: make sure that, promptly after contract start, staff are set personal objectives for the remainder of the current year. These first objectives should have a particular emphasis on personal development that is necessary to the supplier's achievement of SLA/contract measures. Where the supplier has promised the customer to improve service performance by the introduction of new technology or working practices, the speedy implementation and understanding of these by the staff is of critical importance.

31. *Establish staff bonus plans*: identify what the annual bonus scheme will be for transferring staff and make sure each individual fully understands any linkage that the supplier is making between remuneration and individual performance.

It is hoped that this section provides an indication of the level of detail involved in a properly managed HR due diligence/take-on exercise, and how much planning is involved. It is important not to underestimate how long the whole process can take. In view of this, and the mandatory consultation requirements under TUPE, those in the customer organisation responsible for the planning of the total outsourcing project should build the timetable around the amount of time to be set aside for those matters. While the law gives no definitive guidance on how long a period should be allowed, it is unlikely that a thorough and effective HR exercise dealing with the relevant issues outlined in this section could be completed in less than a month from the point where the customer selects its preferred supplier and allows it to commence the consultation and communication process.

1.8 BUILDING THE CONTRACT AROUND THE DRIVERS FOR OUTSOURCING

Outsourcing projects require complex contracts in which the lawyers have fully reflected the business objectives of each party to the contract, both initially and into the future. The contract should also give consideration to the dependencies that the parties have on third parties, to ensure that the contract will work successfully. In the larger outsourcing contracts, there can be a very intricate web of interdependent relationships on which the proper operation of the contract depends. Reflecting in the contract how these interact with the rights and obligations of the customer and supplier under the contract is a key challenge for the lawyers. Additionally, it may well be that the supplier has a major dependency on the customer for some key input to the service. Careful thought needs to be given to expressing what the contractual position of the parties will be if there is a failure by the customer to deliver this input that has an adverse impact on the supplier. This is perhaps best illustrated by an example.

One of the highest growth areas in the outsourcing market is business process outsourcing. This involves the supplier assuming responsibility for a major administrative function of the customer. In the local government marketplace, one area where work is outsourced is revenues collection (billing and collection of payments). It is not unusual for contracts to be let on the basis of the customer providing to the supplier a full information technology service supporting the delivery of the supplier's revenues service. This may well involve provision of all the hardware, software and network/telephony services that the new service needs in order to function. While it is sometimes the case that this service is provided for the full length of the contract, it is more usual for it to be provided for a transitional period prior to the supplier implementing replacement hardware and software, which it will operate and support itself. In either case, the supplier has a critical dependency on the customer for this IT service. Indeed, in practice, the service would, in all likelihood, grind to a halt, or at least be incapable of achieving acceptable levels of revenue collection, within a very short period if the IT service were not available. How should the lawyers deal with this contractually? Is it sufficient simply to define the customer's obligation in terms of a contract output that must be delivered to the supplier, and then rely on the common law to determine what remedies will apply?

In a simple purchasing situation, without the complex interdependencies inherent in outsourcing, this may be an acceptable approach. But since outsourcing is, in its purest form, founded on the principle of the parties acting together in concert over an extended period, and recognising the need to act in a way that promotes business and financial benefits to both sides, then simply relying on the common law may not produce an acceptable result. What is needed then, is for the parties to think beyond the possible failure of the customer to deliver the IT service required of it. They also need to define how such an issue would be escalated for resolution by management of each party, and how the commercial position of the supplier would be protected from any adverse cost impact or from its inability to meet service perform- ance levels because of the failure of the IT service.

It is normal, and preferable, to include as part of the ITT/RFP a draft contract setting out the key commercial and legal principles against which the supplier is required to put forward its proposal for delivering the service. If the customer is asked to make its position clear on the draft contract as well as the rest of the ITT/RFP, the customer should then obtain the fullest pos- sible picture of the totality of what the supplier is proposing. This makes the task of evaluating the tenders of competing suppliers on a proper objective basis that much easier. However, many draft contracts included with ITTs/RFPs suggest a lack of communication between the draughtsman and the project manager/sponsor for the outsourcing. The contract sometimes fails to reflect the true nature of the requirement, and does not attempt to reflect even the most basic likely commercial requirements of the supplier. Equally, there can be an overemphasis on 'input' requirements (relating to such things as staffing requirements, and the location from which the service is delivered), and insufficient attention given to reflecting in the contract the business objectives of each party identified through the tender process, and the outputs required to be delivered by the service.

The following sections 1.9 and 1.10 identify some possible business objec- tives of each of the supplier and the customer and how these might be met in a way that satisfies that party's business objective, and that does not impact on the position of the other party in a negative way.

1.9 SUPPLIER OBJECTIVES

1.9.1 Access to new/additional skills

It can be a great benefit to a supplier to have transferred to it under the TUPE regulations a group of staff who may have skills that are new to the supplier organisation or (more likely) that supplement skills already existing among the supplier's staff. The new skills may enable the supplier, using this valuable new resource, to bid for other contracts requiring similar skill sets, and the transfer of such staff by operation of law may also offer a considerable saving in recruitment costs that might otherwise have been incurred. And where, as is sometimes the case, the transferring staff had become demotivated when employed by the customer (perhaps because of poor management, or rumours of the function being outsourced), these new career development opportunities may persuade the staff to stay when they would otherwise (had outsourcing not occurred) have left the customer.

In such circumstances, and when the staff deliver a service that is changing fast through the introduction of new technology and is defined in the contract solely by reference to service outputs, one has to ask how reasonable it would be for a supplier to be faced with very detailed restrictions on how it could use these staff within its organisation, particularly in relation to delivering services to other customers.

On the other hand, there is a risk of losing the service knowledge of the transferring staff if, immediately after transfer, they were totally free to work on other contracts for the supplier. A professional outsourcing company would recognise this concern.

A possible compromise position might therefore be for the contract to restrict a proportion of the transferring staff for an agreed period of time (perhaps six months) from working on other contracts for the supplier, unless otherwise agreed between the parties. This gives the customer a period of guaranteed staff stability, and gives the supplier time to assess the ability of the transferring staff before reassigning or reskilling them for other duties. This should enable the full realisation of the abilities of the staff, for their benefit and the benefit of the supplier. Although this may seem like a short period, it may very well provide more staff stability than if the customer had not outsourced the service (to the obvious benefit of the customer). The customer is in any event protected by the ongoing obligation to meet the service output requirements defined in the contract (which the supplier will generally only be able to do by using a reasonable complement of appropriately skilled staff).

1.9.2 Ability to change hardware platform

Another common requirement of the supplier is to retain the maximum flexibility regarding the assets it uses to deliver the service. This allows optimal efficiency of use of assets across a large number of contracts, and the ability to acquire even more cost-effective assets if technological advancement makes this possible in the future. Conversely, it is not unusual for a customer to stipulate that it should have a high degree of control over the assets that will be used by the supplier in service delivery, both initially and into the future.

At a time when, particularly in the area of information technology, new products can offer tangible improvements in performance and in their lifetime cost of ownership (e.g. through lower ongoing maintenance costs), this apparent philosophical conflict between customer and supplier is deserving of some careful analysis. If the supplier is able to have a high degree of

45

flexibility over how it delivers the service, this may provide major/commercial benefits to the customer, which may be:

- a price that reduces progressively over the length of the contract; or
- a price that is set at an unusually low level at the start of the contract (when the customer may perhaps be under particularly severe budgetary pressure), but that returns to a higher level thereafter.

And if the service involves the use of assets that are subject to rapid technological change, then there may be little point in trying to exert control over which assets are used by the supplier in the delivery of the service. This is because at the end of the contract in, say, five years time, the asset base used at the start of the contract may well have become largely obsolete.

However, where the contract term is only short and the customer has provided to the supplier equipment that it expects to re-utilise (either itself or through a replacement contractor) at the end of the contract term, then it may be reasonable to impose some limitations on the supplier's ability to use alternative equipment. It should be recognised, however, that this could increase the price.

1.9.3 Ability to retain ownership of intellectual property rights developed in connection with delivery of the service

The issue of intellectual property rights (IPR) ownership is often one of the more emotive of the commercial issues under discussion between the customer and the supplier. The customer will frequently take the view that it has some stake in intellectual property derived from the delivery of the service, as it will feel that it must in some way have paid for this. The supplier will be strongly motivated to retain ownership in such property for use in its ongoing business. The difficulty for the lawyers in trying to navigate between these positions is that it is generally difficult to establish with any clarity, from the pricing document produced by the supplier and the discussions on pricing that follow this, whether the customer is in any way contributing to the cost of development of the intellectual property and, if so, to what extent.

It is therefore sometimes more helpful to analyse the overall business objectives of the parties that brought them to the meeting of minds that is to be reflected within the outsourcing contract. If this approach is used, then it may well be the case that the customer had not placed any emphasis in the negotiations on achieving intellectual property ownership, but did have a requirement to avoid 'contract lock-in'. If this is the real concern, then a fair and commercially balanced approach to intellectual property ownership may be the following:

1. The customer or its third party supplier (as appropriate) will own any enhancements or modifications made by the supplier to pre-existing

intellectual property owned by the customer, or (in relation to items supplied by third parties) used by the customer.

2. The customer will own any intellectual property that is developed by the supplier and wholly funded by the customer.

3. Unless (1) or (2) above applies, the supplier will own any intellectual property that it develops or enhances in the course of delivering the service.

4. To avoid contract lock-in, the customer will have non-exclusive rights to use the intellectual property created by the supplier in the delivery of the service (at the point of expiry or termination of the contract) for such a period as is necessary to preserve the integrity and continuity of the service for the customer. What this means in practice will vary greatly from situation to situation. For a service where there are many alternative suppliers, contract lock-in may be an unlikely scenario, in that each supplier has a different but similarly effective method for delivering the service, which would not need to utilise the previous supplier's intellectual property. Where this is not the case, the customer will typically want a perpetual free of charge right for itself and future contractors to use the intellectual property. The supplier is likely to resist this where the intellectual property is a leading edge tool that gives the supplier a competitive edge over its competitors, especially where the greater part of that tool was in use before the contract between the customer and supplier was signed. In this situation, a compromise position (while the new supplier develops/implements some alternative tool) may be a right to use during a short transitional period of, say, three months.

5. Where the customer has real concerns about the supplier using intellectual property derived from the service with another customer of the supplier that is a competitor of the customer, there may be a discussion about the supplier being restricted from using the intellectual property with that competing customer for an agreed period. There may of course be related issues of confidentiality arising in this scenario, but whether it is reasonable for the supplier's use of its intellectual property to be restricted in this way must depend on the commercial terms agreed between the parties, and the real competitive threat posed by this.

The customer may argue that some sort of revenue or profit sharing on future sales may be required on intellectual property of significant value, where the customer has clearly made a significant contribution to the cost of development. However, given the obvious difficulty involved with the customer monitoring this issue, and providing a workable procedure in the contract for assessing what amounts are due to the customer, it should only be pursued where there is a real likelihood of a reasonable level of future sales, and when it is commercially fair for the customer to have a stake in these. The commercial worth of the intellectual property will determine the size of the opportunity for exploiting its worth and the type of joint venture structure – which may be a simple contractual structure or might involve the creation of a joint venture company in which customer and supplier each have equity – appropriate to the situation.

1.9.4 Protect contract investment

An increasingly common feature of outsourcing is the investment of significant amounts of capital by an outsourcing supplier in a service, to improve the quality and lower the cost base of the service in future periods. There is a strong accounting logic for this. If the customer were to make the investment then it may, in some cases, need to recognise this investment in the accounts of the internal cost centre and/or in its balance sheet in the financial year in which the investment is made. Notwithstanding the potential longer-term savings that may be generated by the investment, the immediate accounting impact may be a substantial capital cost that cannot be justified unless counterbalanced by an immediate cost saving of equivalent value (which will rarely be achievable).

However, if the supplier makes the investment, its accounting policies may permit it to spread the total investment cost over the full life of the contract, thus reducing or eliminating the negative accounting impact that would have resulted from accounting for the investment in the year it is made; where this is not possible a special purpose vehicle may be set up to make the investment and contract with the customer, and if set up correctly, this will be off balance sheet for the supplier. This can make a real difference to the customer's business case for outsourcing and where, as in the public sector, resources for new investment are particularly difficult to obtain, it can facilitate capital investment where, without outsourcing, this investment would have proved beyond the customer's means. However, such a situation can create challenges for the lawyers in considering how to deal with the financial position of customer and supplier in a situation where the contract is terminated by the customer for breach, perhaps shortly after the investment programme of the supplier has been completed. Where the investment cost has been amortised over the life of the contract, the supplier will not have recovered its investment through charges made to the customer at this point in the contract, but the customer may well have received the full benefit of the investment made (assuming that the contract is terminated for reasons other than reasons connected with this investment). This creates a potential for imbalance between the legal position of the parties and the new accounting position of the supplier arising from the termination of the contract. The supplier will be required to account for any unrecovered investment costs in the financial year in which the contract is terminated and this can cause a significant adverse impact on it, perhaps beyond that which is justified by its failures that led to contract termination. The question for the lawyers is whether the application of the common law rules relating to the assessment of damages will achieve a result that is just and fair to both parties, and that is sophisticated enough to have regard to the accounting impact on each party of the unplanned termination of the contract. If there is any doubt about this it may be advisable to provide in the contract for any specific steps that the parties should take in the light of the termination of the contract in particular circumstances, e.g. the customer paying for the remainder of the investment, perhaps over the period over which the contract would have run had it not been terminated.

1.10   CUSTOMER OBJECTIVES

1.10.1   Exercise control over the cost of change

One of the major sources of dissatisfaction of customers of outsourcing service providers relates to the amounts charged for implementing changes requested by the customer to its original requirements. Equally the customer may be disappointed that reductions in its service requirements do not necessarily attract a proportionate reduction in charges. When the customer is producing its business case for outsourcing it is advisable to provide in this for an assumed level of change to the day one service requirement. It will also be important to the customer to have a good level of understanding of how changes will be costed and to have agreed mechanisms by which the net commercial impact of change can be kept to a minimum. The customer should seek to obtain a commitment from the supplier that, where it is possible for the supplier to spread the cost of a major change across a number of its customers, then it must do this. An example of this would be the cost of upgrading computer systems to make them capable of processing transactions in Euros. There are set out below a number of possible mechanisms that might help the customer realise these objectives.

1.   A comprehensive change control procedure under which the process of requesting, quoting for and deciding upon changes will operate is essential. This will help to bring some order to the implementation of changes. Also, where a reasonable time frame is given to the supplier to quote for and make resources available for implementing the change, this will undoubtedly help in reducing the circumstances where premium rates are charged, because of short lead-times given to the supplier for making the change. Further discussion on changes can be found in paragraphs 2.5.5 and 2.5.6.
2.   It may be possible to define in the contract rates that will be charged for certain types of change or, in some cases, to pre-agree a fixed cost for a change that might already be anticipated and well defined. Where possible, the parties should try to agree the service metrics that determine the

49

price for the service and how any change in those metrics would alter the price. This may be especially appropriate to services such as computer desktop support (where the pricing may reflect the number of desktop PCs supported in any one charging period) or payroll services (where the charge may be made on a per-payslip basis). In some cases, where the price depends heavily on how many transactions are carried out within the service – e.g. phone calls made or answered, post opened and actioned, personal visits made to a counter service – it should be possible to agree price adjustments for any rise or fall in those volumes. For both parties, such an approach will provide greater certainty around the commercial implications arising from changes in the service or in the number of transactions dealt with, and will avoid matters becoming subject to the slowness and bureaucracy sometimes characterised by change control procedures.

3. Some suppliers may, depending on the overall commercial terms of the contract, be prepared to consider some form of open book accounting for the cost of changes. This will require the supplier to produce detailed evidence of actual cost incurred to accompany its invoice (to avoid excess profits being made by suppliers), and it may further involve the supplier agreeing to carry out all changes for a pre-agreed level of margin/profit over the proven cost incurred by the supplier in making the change.

4. In the larger outsourcing contracts, the level and regularity of change can be quite significant and the administrative overheads associated with agreeing commercial terms for a change, raising invoices and processing payments can be a real issue for both customer and supplier. It can therefore be attractive to both sides to agree that, until an agreed aggregate level of charges that could otherwise have been made for the changes has been exceeded in an agreed assessment period (e.g. a financial year), the supplier will not invoice the customer. This agreed amount of *free* changes already embodied in the recurring charge to the customer is sometimes referred to as a buffer zone. Once the agreed amount is exceeded, the supplier will be entitled to invoice the customer on the agreed basis for the cost of all changes in excess of that amount in that financial year. If this kind of mechanism is used, it may be appropriate to distinguish between routine, evolutionary changes (for which the buffer zone potentially serves a useful purpose for both supplier and customer), and unforeseen changes (e.g. major legislative changes) or foreseen but financially unquantifiable changes (such as European Monetary Union). In the case of the latter two categories of change, it is arguably fair for the full cost of the change to be met by the customer.

1.10.2 Ability to vary the level of resources used in the service to meet the changing needs of the business

One of the reasons for outsourcing may be that suppliers are able to offer some flexibility regarding the allocation of their resources to delivering a service to the customer. This can mean that peaks and troughs in the customer's business can be accommodated by the supplier within a charging profile that takes these into account.

A good example of this is charging for computer mainframe processing capacity. The customer's capacity requirements over the course of a financial year may vary significantly. This is particularly true of retailers who have significant seasonal trading peaks, and local authorities who have significant amounts of year-end processing to do immediately after the end of their financial year on 31 March each year.

This has led to a demand from customers for suppliers who can adjust upwards or downwards the amount of capacity available and charged to the customer and the level of associated resources available to the customer, on a reasonable agreed period of notice from the customer. This avoids the customer having to pay a constant price when its requirements do not always justify this. While the supplier will clearly also have a cost base that is not totally flexible, it may be that, through its greater purchasing power, it has arrangements with the suppliers of mainframe capacity that allow it to reduce its requirements and also reduce (though not necessarily in the same proportions) the amount paid to that supplier. Alternatively, it may be that a dip in the customer's processing requirements may coincide with an increase in the requirements of another of the supplier's customers, such that the supplier is actually purchasing a relatively constant level of processing resource from its supplier of capacity.

However, it is important for the customer to be realistic about what level of flexibility can be achieved; the contractual arrangements of the supplier with its suppliers, and the time it will take for human resources to be reallocated from one customer to another or back again, means that a notice period of three to six months may be required to increase or decrease its resource requirements of the supplier. The supplier is also likely to stipulate a base level of resource that has to be purchased at all times, in order to retain a level of revenue and profit that is acceptable to the supplier. A further possible variation to this type of scheme (which may be especially appropriate where the supplier has limited scope to meet the level of flexibility required by the customer) might be a revenue replacement scheme. Where the customer has a range of service requirements, a number of which can be met by the same supplier, it may be acceptable to the supplier for a reduction in service requirements in one area to be offset by a corresponding increase in requirements in another area. The supplier will of course expect the profitability and risk profile of the replacement work to be similar to that of the replaced work, and will need a period of notice to implement the requirement, especially where the replacement service will be delivered by different personnel of the supplier.

1.10.3 Linkage of charging provisions to delivery of commercial benefits to the customer

Sometimes, a service is outsourced because it is in need of new ideas and, in particular, new investment after a period in which the customer has been either unwilling or unable to make the significant investment that the service needs.

This scenario presents an opportunity to both customer and supplier. The supplier should be able to make quick and tangible improvements in the service and may, over a period of time (by improved processes and the use of new technology), drive down the cost of delivering the service and perhaps be able to offer a reduction in the charges to the customer. The customer might well be able to achieve a double benefit with the users of the service getting a higher quality service, and the finance director seeing a long-term service cost reduction. However, it has to be recognised that there may in some cases be choices for the customer to make between service improvements and charge reductions, where it has stipulated major improvements in both.

Nevertheless, there is the potential for a win-win scenario for the two parties, with a clear motivation for both sides to make the outsourcing a success. Yet, in a fixed-price contract, the supplier's motivation may only extend so far as achieving the revenue and profit position derived from the fixed price.

In order to realise the full potential of the new alliance between customer and supplier, the parties might, in appropriate cases, consider a risk–reward mechanism where the supplier agrees to receive part of its remuneration based on its contract performance. This might relate to reducing the charge to the customer, where the customer is prepared to allow changes to be made to the service to generate cost savings and then to agree to a sharing of the savings made. However, it might also relate to the supplier being incentivised to increase the income from the customer by means of a more effective delivery of the service. An example from local government is the outsourcing of the collection of council tax and national non-domestic rates, where an improvement in the percentage of such monies collected by the supplier could similarly trigger a sharing of the benefits to the customer of the increased income, cash flow and of the additional interest derived from the income. If the mechanism for sharing these benefits is sufficiently generous to motivate the supplier to invest further amounts in service improvement, then this brings the possibility of performance being improved to an extent where the business case of each of the supplier and the customer have been exceeded. The approach of linking charging at least partially to the delivery of measurable business benefits for the customers is sometimes described as gainsharing.

However, while such a risk–reward mechanism can undoubtedly be attractive to both customer and supplier, the customer should consider the following points, and their potential impact on the supplier's ability to adopt this approach to charging.

1. The supplier's business case might already have built into it a level of risk associated with progressively reducing both the resources allocated to, and the charge for, the service, while maintaining or improving service performance. If that level of risk is already significant, its willingness to accept further risk – by linking part of its remuneration to performance improvement – may be necessarily limited.

2. The supplier will need to link *reward* payments purely to the supplier's *own performance*. This is a particularly difficult issue where the supplier has service dependencies on both the customer and/or suppliers of the customer. Their failures may prevent the supplier generating rewards at the levels it would have achieved had it not been for such failures. The contract should provide for the supplier notifying the customer of such failures promptly when they occur, and for the parties agreeing upon the level of impact of the failure on the ability of the supplier to generate the level of revenue it had anticipated. The contract should also deal with how this will be reflected in the ongoing assessment of reward payments in order that the supplier is not unfairly penalised for matters outside its control.

3. The supplier may also be concerned about the impact of external factors on its perceived performance. Using the same example of council tax collection, the percentage collection rate achieved could be affected by demographic change within the local authority area, a downturn in the national economy, the closure of a significant employer in the area or other factors that are outside of the control of the contractor. A force majeure clause might offer negative protection to the supplier, i.e. that it would not be liable to compensate the customer for poor performance attributable to such matters. However, it is unlikely that a typical clause would deal with the positive protection needed by the supplier, i.e. that the external factors are isolated and removed from the assessment of whether the supplier's contractual performance has in fact improved, thus triggering a reward payment to the supplier. The complexity of such an assessment is not to be underestimated. It may be that, where agreement cannot be reached as to how to deal with the impact of these external factors on contract performance, some form of benchmarking of the service against comparable customer situations may assist the parties to reach agreement.

In appropriate cases, the supplier may also be prepared to agree to some form of credit mechanism to compensate the customer for performance that is worse than the customer itself achieved.

1.10.4   Retaining control of the service

The customer will sometimes be concerned about a loss of control over a key internal service as a result of it being outsourced. While the concern may centre around the possibility of contract lock-in (see paragraph 1.9.3), it may also relate to the ongoing ability of the customer to monitor the effective and secure delivery of the service. These legitimate concerns can be met in a variety of ways:

1.   The basic need to monitor the supplier's service performance should be met by detailed agreement between customer and supplier in relation to what service level reports should be produced and provided to the customer, and with what frequency. Effective monitoring also requires feedback, both positive and negative, from the customer, following receipt of these reports, and the parties should therefore also agree the details of an appropriate forum in which these views can be given and received, and from which appropriate actions will be taken by each side to address reported issues. In addition, audit access may be required to verify the reliability of the reports.

2.   A specific concern of a customer may relate to service security. This could be because of legislative or regulatory rules with which the customer must ensure compliance, or it may be because of the specific quality/security requirements that are mandated within the customer's organisation. The supplier is unlikely to have any difficulty with providing reasonable evidence of the systems it uses to ensure the security and integrity of the service, although it will need to know how to cost into its charges the associated resource requirements on it. It will also need to be satisfied that the security checks carried out by or for the customer will be carried out under proper conditions of confidentiality, and without using external organisations that may pose a competitive threat to the supplier. The *modus operandi* for the security check may be a report from the supplier's quality assessors or a site visit by the customer's representatives or a report by some agreed external body. Issues of cost, time and reliability will determine the correct approach in any particular contract.

3.   A customer may be required by legislation to reserve the right of audit of certain aspects of the supplier's contractual performance. For example, a local government customer will wish to ensure the right of access and audit for the District Auditor in connection with the discharge of his statutory duties. Extensive audit rights for customers can however represent major potential resourcing issues for the supplier where used. The customer should therefore be prepared to agree an audit clause that is proportionate to its legitimate and necessary audit requirements, and that respects the commercial confidentiality of the supplier's business case (including the supplier's detailed calculations of the cost of delivering the service) and related documentation. This is particularly true

where the customer has the benefit of detailed service reporting provisions in the contract (see point 1 above).

1.11 COSTS ARISING FROM CONTRACT TERMINATION OR EXPIRY – A SPECIAL RISK

An emerging area for debate between customers and suppliers is which of them bears the risk of prospective redundancy costs at the end of a contract where there is no transfer of an undertaking, and therefore no transfer of the supplier's staff assigned to the undertaking. This is an issue of real commercial significance as customers become more prepared to change supplier, and since the sums involved can be quite significant.

When a supplier bids for an outsourcing contract, it should take into account all costs connected with the take-on of the contract, and also those costs arising from expiry or termination. It will probably assume that it is able to cease paying sums (e.g. licence fees, lease rentals, maintenance costs) to third party suppliers for goods and services connected with the contract at the point when, at the end of the contract, it ceases to receive revenue from the customer to cover this expenditure. But this still leaves one major area of cost to the supplier where the costs cannot be turned off quite so easily – the costs related to the ongoing employment or termination of employment of the staff who have hitherto delivered the service to the customer.

At the end of the outsourcing contract, there are three possible scenarios in relation to these assigned staff:

1. The staff transfer their employment automatically from the outgoing supplier to the incoming supplier under TUPE, and this has the effect of removing from the outgoing supplier all future costs of employment connected with such staff. Although in theory pre-transfer employment liabilities also transfer from the outgoing supplier to the incoming supplier, the outgoing supplier is likely to be asked to indemnify the incoming supplier against such costs.
2. The staff do not transfer their employment from the outgoing supplier but are redeployed by the outgoing supplier elsewhere in its business.
3. The staff do not transfer their employment from the outgoing supplier, and since no suitable redeployment opportunities are available, their posts are redundant at the point of contract termination/expiry. The outgoing supplier will of course be liable for the redundancy costs unless they are recoverable from the customer under the terms of the outsourcing contract.

Generally, either point 1 or 2 will apply. The difficulty arises where one of the parties does not want one of these scenarios to occur but is also unable or unwilling to allow the alternative scenario to be implemented.

This situation will normally occur where the customer takes the view that it is not in its commercial interests for there to be a TUPE transfer. The incoming supplier may have proposed a different way of delivering the service at a lower charge on the assumption that not all, or none of, the staff transfer their employment under TUPE. In such a situation, the TUPE regulations can be a blunt instrument for facilitating the transfer of staff from an outgoing to an incoming supplier. While there may be an arguable legal case for TUPE applying to transfer *all* the staff from the outgoing to the incoming supplier, if the incoming supplier does not want this to happen, the outgoing supplier has little commercial or legal leverage to bring to bear. This is because the remedy available is one that needs to be sought and obtained by the staff affected, by requesting the court/tribunal to make a declaration that their employment has indeed transferred. While the outgoing supplier could seek to persuade the staff, either directly or through any union representing the staff, to bring such a claim, it is hard to imagine that an individual is likely to do this, particularly since the incoming supplier has shown a clear disinclination to employ that person. Moreover, the individual is likely to wish to focus his/her time on finding alternative employment rather than making headlines in the local press. Additionally, the responsible outgoing supplier may feel it is not acceptable for it to request an employee to find his/her own solution to the need for ongoing employment.

For these reasons, the outgoing supplier will probably then concentrate its efforts on redeployment of the staff affected, but this will not always be available, particularly where the make-up of its work is geographically and technically disparate.

When redeployment is not available for an employee, then when the contract terminates, his/her post is redundant and the outgoing supplier will be responsible for the redundancy payment due to the employee.

In view of the above analysis, the commercial problem that may arise will typically impact on the outgoing supplier. That will be so unless it is able to persuade its customer to take some or all of this end of contract potential redundancy cost by negotiating indemnity or contribution provisions into the original contract.

The outgoing supplier should therefore take one of the following approaches when submitting its original proposal/tender to the customer:

1. Ask the customer to indemnify it from redundancy costs arising from the TUPE regulations not applying to transfer staff from the outgoing to the incoming supplier at the end of the contract.
2. Analyse the skills that it will use to deliver the service and the degree of probability that they can be redeployed at the end of the contract (given a reasonable period of notice) on to other work of the outgoing supplier, and decide not to seek an indemnity for prospective redundancy costs.

3. Seek a compromise solution with the customer to this issue, somewhere between points 1 and 2 above.

One should recognise that the above represents a very difficult piece of legal and commercial analysis, particularly since one has to do a certain amount of crystal ball gazing to reach an assessment of what services will be delivered (and how) by an incoming supplier at the end of the contract (and therefore whether TUPE is likely to apply to transfer the employment of the staff of the outgoing supplier to the incoming supplier) and (if not) what redeployment opportunities are likely to be available. But, difficult though it is, it is important to analyse this issue, as redundancy costs can make a significant dent in the outgoing supplier's profit in the final year of the contract if they are to be met fully by the outgoing supplier.

This is the position based on the European Court's decision in *Süzen* v. *Zehnacker Gebaudereinigung* [1997] IRLR 255, which appears to allow a contractor to submit a non-TUPE bid (i.e. not offering to take on the assigned staff) where no assets or employees are required by it to meet the ongoing service requirement. In such a situation, a TUPE transfer would only arise if the new contractor actually wanted to take on a major part of the workforce. This left the law in a parlous state and capable of manipulation by customers and suppliers alike, to meet their commercial ends.

A number of cases in the UK have suggested an attempt by the judiciary to distinguish the *Süzen* decision and thereby prevent employers avoiding the application of TUPE simply by submitting non-TUPE bids. (see *ECM (Vehicle Delivery Service) Ltd* v. *Cox* [1999] IRLR 559 and *Magna Housing Association Ltd* v. *Turner* (EAT/198/98)). However, the case of *RCO Support Services Ltd* v. *UNISON & others* [2002] EWCA Civ 464 upholds the *Süzen* decision in so far as it decided that a TUPE transfer may be held to have occurred even though the incoming contractor may not wish to take on the staff assigned to the undertaking.

The recent case of *McLeod and another* v. *(1) Ingram t/a Phoenix Taxis (2) Rainbow Cars Ltd t/a Rainbow Taxis* (EAT/1344/01) and the decision of the European Court on 24 January 2002 in *Temco Service Industries SA* v. *Samir Imzilyen and others* (C-51/00) [2002] IRLR 214 confirm that the courts will be prepared to find that TUPE applies even where there is no transfer of any tangible or intangible assets and where the transferee employer has refused to take on any of the staff previously assigned to the undertaking.

We are left with an uncertain legal landscape into the future and plenty of scope for commercial conflict between the players involved in end of contract negotiations. Indeed, research carried out by the law firm Pinsent in 2003 indicates continuing concern about this uncertainty: some 77 per cent of respondents to the survey had experienced difficulty in applying the law on TUPE, whilst over 85 per cent always felt the need to take legal advice on whether TUPE applied to their transaction. The government announced in summer 2002 its intention to legislate to ensure that TUPE will apply to local government contracting out unless there are exceptional circumstances. Revised TUPE legislation is expected to be placed before parliament in autumn 2003. For further discussion of this complex area see Chapter 9.

1.12 OTHER PRELIMINARY LEGAL DOCUMENTS TYPICALLY USED IN OUTSOURCING PROJECTS

This section considers some of the other legal documents that may be required by customer and supplier before the main outsourcing contract is signed, in order to protect their respective legal positions and allow the outsourcing project to commence. The legal documents discussed here are confidentiality agreements and letters of indemnity, which, from the perspective of an outsourcing company, tend to be the most frequently used documents.

1.12.1 Confidentiality agreements

It is not unusual for a customer to request the supplier to sign a confidentiality agreement before releasing to it the ITT/RFP. This is unsurprising as a comprehensive ITT/RFP is likely to contain sensitive information, typically including detailed financial information and details of business and service strategy. At this stage, the agreement proposed will often be one way, protecting only information disclosed by the customer to the supplier.

The supplier, for its part, is also likely to need protection from disclosure of its confidential information at some stage in the procurement process. This will not generally be before it submits its proposal but, before submission, it may well take the view that some of its contents (particularly in relation to service delivery methodology, use of new technology or pricing approach) may be sufficiently leading edge or sensitive as to need protection. Since the customer, by this time, is likely to have engaged consultants and lawyers, it may be necessary for each to sign the supplier's confidentiality agreement, to offer a proper level of protection to the supplier.

For both customer and supplier in a bidding process, there is an important judgement to be made about the timing and detail of disclosures of confidential information. While the signature of a confidentiality agreement offers a measure of protection, the evidential difficulties of proving the source of disclosures of confidential information are not to be underestimated. The disclosing party therefore should seriously consider adopting a drip-feed approach to disclosures, providing information that is at an appropriate level of detail for the stage reached in the procurement process, and providing it only when necessary to allow the other party to evaluate properly what it is saying. Consideration should also be given to reserving some of the information to a selected group of people in the other party's organisation, rather than making it generally available to their entire project team. Provisions regarding how the information is to be held securely and regarding its destruction or return (at the option of the disclosing party) are important features of this document.

An example one-way confidentiality agreement is included as Annex 1A to this chapter.

1.12.2   Letter of indemnity/letter of intent

This document is of increasing importance to both customer and supplier where the customer has selected its preferred supplier and wishes transition activity to commence before the main outsourcing contract has been agreed (or sometimes even drafted).

The requirement

Having been made the preferred supplier, the supplier should assess if there is a need to raise a letter of indemnity. Such a need arises if the supplier will need to utilise internal resources or incur any third party costs prior to the main outsourcing contract being signed, and should already have been identified when the proposal was submitted. Indeed, the potential for the requirement should have been noted in the text of the supplier's proposal as follows:

> Once nominated as Preferred Supplier, [ ] will commence its investment in the transition of the service. [ ] will inform the customer of the extent of this investment and the planned timetable of its execution. [ ] will require the customer to indemnify [ ] for such investment costs in the event that the proposed outsourcing contract does not (for whatever reason) proceed to signature by [date].

The logic for this request is that, prior to being made preferred supplier, the supplier will already have incurred significant costs in carrying out the sales campaign, putting forward a proposal, and resourcing a due diligence exercise. Once a customer has decided to make the supplier its preferred supplier, it can be argued that the supplier should be protected from incurring any further costs without a clear contractual right to recover those costs. The recovery of these costs would of course preferably be provided for in a signed outsourcing contract. But it is unusual for the parties, at preferred supplier stage, to have agreed detailed contract terms and assembled and agreed all the schedules, sufficient to allow the contract to be signed. Therefore, a letter of indemnity is often proposed, which acts as a contractually binding cost indemnity, giving the supplier order cover for certain agreed preparatory work in the period prior to the signing of the outsourcing contract. The document may be expanded to act also as a letter of intent from the customer to the supplier, defining the key elements of the outsourcing contract that it has decided to award to the supplier. The example letter of indemnity in Annex 1B to this chapter is drafted on the basis that this aspect is dealt with only briefly, since the main purpose of the letter is quickly to obtain a cost indemnity. However, the supplier may feel that it needs for its own reasons (e.g. to make an announcement of the new contract award) to go into this aspect in much more detail.

Key contents of the letter of indemnity

The letter in Annex 1B to this chapter covers the following main points:

1. That the customer has decided to enter into an outsourcing contract with the supplier upon the terms defined in outline in the letter.
2. That the customer is prepared to indemnify the supplier for costs that it incurs if the outsourcing contract does not get signed, up to an agreed maximum amount.
3. The type of costs that will be incurred, being:

    (a) goods purchased;
    (b) services purchased;
    (c) staff time;
    (d) other reasonable costs and expenses.

4. In the event that the outsourcing contract is signed, the indemnity then becomes redundant and does not apply.
5. The customer will pay the supplier's costs incurred pursuant to the indemnity if the contract is not signed within an agreed period (three months). The supplier will issue a fully itemised invoice, which should be paid within [30] days of date of invoice.
6. Appendix 1 to the letter summarises what services are to be provided under the outsourcing contract.
7. Appendix 2 to the letter summarises what work will be carried out prior to the contract being signed, and provides summary costs associated with this work.

    Some examples of costs that may need to be covered are:

    (a) staff costs of managing the take-on of the service;
    (b) staff costs of acquiring knowledge about the service;
    (c) staff travel expenses;
    (d) installation of network between customer and the supplier;
    (e) project work to prepare for the transfer of part of the service;
    (f) recruitment and related costs connected with providing staff additional to those being transferred from the customer to deliver the service;

(g) purchase of new equipment;

(h) extension of software licences to permit use of software by the supplier.

The cost of doing all the work summarised in Appendix 2 to the letter needs to be calculated and the total amount is included in paragraph 5 of the letter.

It should be noted that if the full outsourcing contract was to proceed, the costs for the preliminary work would be recovered from the customer together with a margin (profit and overhead) through the charges made under the contract. It is therefore reasonable to consider that the value of the costs specified in paragraph 5 should include a margin.

NOTES

1. The UK IT outsourcing market (comprising information outsourcing, application management, processing services, application outsourcing and ASP) was worth £5.8 billion in 2000, £6.9 billion in 2001 and £7.54 billion in 2002 (Source: Ovum Holway).

2. *New Strategies in IT Outsourcing* (Business Intelligence). Tel: 020 8879 3355. Business Intelligence is an independent, research-based publishing, conference and exhibition company, which predicts and tracks important management trends.

3. *An Introduction to IT Outsourcing*, Computing Services and Software Association Briefing Note (1995).

4. *Ibid.*

5. *Computing Services and Software Association Code of Practice* (1995).

ANNEX 1A

Specimen confidentiality agreement

THIS AGREEMENT is made the   day of   200X by and between [   ] of [Address] (hereinafter 'Company') and [   ] of [Address] (hereinafter 'Recipient').

WHEREAS the Company has already disclosed or will disclose to the Recipient certain of its proprietary information which may include, *inter alia*, operations, processes, product plans, customer details, trade secrets, business plans, service development plans, formulae, software programs, know-how, test results, design rights, drawings, models, photographs, sketches and specifications and which are considered proprietary by the Company ('Confidential Information') and

WHEREAS the Company agrees to disclose to the Recipient the Confidential Information for the sole purpose of [*to be completed as appropriate*] ('the Purpose')

and both parties require the Confidential Information to be protected on the terms and conditions following:

NOW THEREFORE, the parties agree as follows:

1. In consideration of the disclosure of the Confidential Information pursuant to the Purpose the Recipient agrees that for a period of five (5) years from the date of this Agreement, it shall take all reasonable steps to prevent disclosure of such Confidential Information it receives from the Company to any third parties except as expressly agreed in writing by the Company.
2. The Recipient shall be entitled to disclose such Confidential Information to those of the Recipient's employees who have an absolute need to know such information in connection with the Purpose, provided that:

   (a) any such Confidential Information is clearly marked Confidential or Proprietary, or designated as Confidential or Proprietary by appropriate statements, markings or notices; and
   (b) use of such Confidential Information is restricted to the Purpose; and
   (c) the Recipient shall advise its employees of the obligations contained in this Agreement and shall ensure that they observe such obligations.
3. The Recipient shall use at least the same degree of care to avoid disclosure of the Confidential Information as it employs with respect to its own confidential/proprietary information.
4. The Company agrees that the Recipient shall have no obligation hereunder with respect to any such Confidential Information which:

   (a) is already known to the Recipient; or
   (b) is or becomes publicly known through no wrongful act of the Recipient; or
   (c) is received from a third party without similar restriction and without breach of this Agreement; or

(d) is independently developed by the Recipient without breach of this Agreement; or

(e) is disclosed where necessary to do so by law or request of a governmental agency so long as the Recipient shall first give the Company notice of such request.

5. All tangible forms of the Confidential Information such as written documentation, delivered pursuant to this Agreement shall be and remain the property of the Company.

6. Nothing contained in this Agreement shall be construed as granting or conferring any rights by licence or otherwise, expressly, impliedly, or otherwise in relation to the Confidential Information.

7. The Company does not guarantee the accuracy or completeness of the Confidential Information supplied and the Recipient accordingly shall not hold the Company responsible for losses, claims or liability incurred by the Recipient using the Confidential Information.

8. The Company may request in writing at any time that any Confidential Information disclosed by it and any copies be returned with a written statement that it has not knowingly retained in its possession or under its control, either directly or indirectly, any Confidential Information or copies and the Recipient shall comply with such request within seven (7) days of receipt of such request.

9. The Recipient shall not and shall not assist any other person to make any announcement or disclosure of any possible transaction which may arise from the Purpose without the prior written consent of the Company.

10. This Agreement expresses the entire agreement and understanding of the parties with respect to the Recipient's obligations hereunder and supersedes all prior agreements and understandings.

11. This Agreement shall be subject in all respects to the laws of England and the parties agree to submit to the exclusive jurisdiction of the High Court, London, in the event of any dispute.

IN WITNESS WHEREOF the parties hereto have caused this Agreement to be executed by their respective duly authorised representatives.

Signed for and on behalf of the Company   Signed for and on behalf of the Recipient

Signed: _____   Signed: _____

Title: _____   Title: _____

Name: _____   Name: _____

Date: _____   Date: _____

ANNEX 1B

Letter of indemnity/intent in respect of costs incurred by the supplier prior to signature of the outsourcing contract

THIS AGREEMENT is made on   between

[   ] of [   ] ('the Customer') and

[   ] of [Address] ('the Supplier').

1. The Customer has indicated its intention to award to the Supplier a contract for the supply of the goods and/or services summarised in Appendix 1 to this Agreement ('the Contract'). Pending the negotiation and signature of the Contract, the Supplier intends to carry out certain preliminary work relating to the Contract, such preliminary work being summarised in Appendix 2 ('the Preliminary Work').

2. The Customer acknowledges that in carrying out the Preliminary Work, the Supplier shall incur staff and other resource costs and is prepared to indemnify the Supplier against such costs should the Contract not proceed to signature.

3. Subject to paragraph 4 below, in consideration of the Supplier carrying out the Preliminary Work the Customer hereby indemnifies the Supplier against:

   (a) all costs incurred by the Supplier in purchasing any goods (including without prejudice to the generality of the foregoing any computer hardware and computer software) intended to be used by the Supplier in carrying out the Preliminary Work; and

   (b) all costs incurred by the Supplier in purchasing any services (including without prejudice to the generality of the foregoing the services of any independent contractors, subcontractors and the purchase of any computer software) intended to be used by the Supplier in carrying out the Preliminary Work; and

   (c) the time taken by the Supplier's own staff to carry out the Preliminary Work; and

   (d) all other reasonable costs and expenses incurred by the Supplier in carrying out the Preliminary Work.

4. In the event that the Customer and the Supplier agree the terms of and sign the Contract, within [3] months of the date hereof which provides for the recovery of the amounts specified in paragraph 3 above, the Supplier shall not be entitled to operate the indemnity set out in paragraph 3 above.

5. The indemnity shall be operated by the Supplier submitting at any time after such 3 month period a fully itemised invoice to the Customer setting out the items listed in (a) to (d) inclusive of paragraph 3 above and the Customer shall settle such invoice within 30 days of the date thereof PROVIDED THAT the

maximum aggregate sum which may be invoiced to the Customer under this letter of indemnity shall be £[   ] + VAT.

6. The Customer will pay value added tax where applicable on the items invoiced under paragraph 5 above at the rate specified by law from time to time.

7. This Agreement shall be governed by and construed in accordance with the laws of England and the Customer and the Supplier hereby irrevocably submit to the exclusive jurisdiction of the English courts.

SIGNED by a duly authorised
signatory for and on behalf of
the Customer:

SIGNED by a duly authorised
signatory for and on behalf of
the Supplier:

_____

_____

CHAPTER 2

The outsourcing contract

Rory Graham

2.1 INTRODUCTION

One of the games lawyers play in negotiation meetings relating to outsourcing is to bet on how long it will be until one party describes the outsourcing as a 'partnership'. Nothing could be further from the truth: the parties' interests overlap, but they are not congruent; and neither party will put its existence on the line for the other. However, it is equally foolish to see an outsourcing merely as an arm's length commercial transaction, or – worse – as a kind of corporate disposal with a services contract tacked on.

The best approach is to see the outsourcing as the creation of a long-term, flexible relationship, but one that exists within a framework of rules that support its success while addressing failures practically. The contract, therefore, has a sophisticated role not only as the passive record of the parties' agreement but also as the guidebook for the evolving transaction. This chapter considers the structure of the contractual documents and the key points that need to be reflected in them. Prior to this, it considers the structure of the deal itself.

The assumption in this chapter is that the parties are contemplating the initial outsourcing: that is the transfer of an in-house technology department from the user to the provider. However, in preparing the contracts to support that transaction the parties should also be mindful of what should happen on re-tendering and exit, where the services may be transferred to a new service provider or taken back in house. This requirement will be addressed throughout the discussion of the initial contracts.

2.2 STRUCTURING THE DEAL

The shape of the deal should determine the contractual structure, rather than the other way round. However, it is tempting to see the contracts as the checklist for the deal without first considering the drivers for the structure of the arrangements.

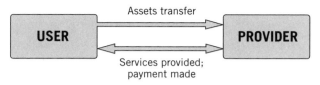

Figure 2.1   Simple outsourcing

The simplest structure assumes that there will be a monolithic user out-sourcing a technology function to a monolithic service provider. This could be dealt with in just one contract, but for convenience the one-off provisions relating to the transfer of assets and people are usually split out into a separate agreement (see Figure 2.1).

However:

- the user is often a group of companies with the contracting party either a parent or a procurement company, buying services on behalf of the group. The group itself may be spread over a number of countries;
- the user may be taking the services in order to supply elements of them on to its customers – for example, if it is buying in call centre services. The scope of interested parties on the user side of the equation therefore may well extend beyond its corporate family;
- the provider may itself be contracting to provide the services using members of its group and also subcontractors outside that group;
- the parties may want to explore other structures, such as the creation of a joint venture.

2.2.1   User group structures

Where the user is the parent company contracting on behalf of its subsidiaries

At first glance, this structure should not cause any problems for the provider: it still has one legal agreement with the parent, and what happens behind the scenes should not matter. However, this simple view is often complicated by other factors:

- The provider may want the user to enforce compliance with certain terms of the outsourcing agreement against the user's subsidiaries. An obvious example would be in respect of use of intellectual property or confidential information, which was sub-licensed or made available to the subsidiaries, where the provider would have no contractual right against a subsidiary (although it might have other causes of action). The parent user may be reluctant to agree to procure compliance by its subsidiaries or to be placed in breach of the services agreement by the actions of a subsidiary.

- The provider may be offering a discount or other benefits on the assumption that the user will ensure that its subsidiaries are either obliged or encouraged to use the provider's services rather than seeking an alternative source of supply. In practice, there may be competition law/anti-trust problems in some jurisdictions or a reluctance or inability on the part of the user to compel its subsidiaries to take the services.
- The subsidiaries may not in fact be majority owned or otherwise controlled by the user, which exacerbates the above issues.
- The user may not be a parent company but instead (as is common) a dedicated procurement company acting on behalf of its group. The user may therefore only have a common parent with other group companies, rather than being at the apex of a pyramid, and therefore have even less influence over the group.
- Whether the user is a parent or a procurement company, the provider may not be confident that the user has the ability to back its financial obligations to pay the charges, especially if the user is in effect simply onward supplying the services and recharging the fees. This can of course be addressed by means of guarantee or letter of credit, albeit not without some resistance.

A number of these issues of course affect the user's position too, in terms of trying to take advantage of a group-wide deal while not necessarily being able to impose the discipline required to make it work. In addition, the user and its group have the following issues to address:

- As the group members have no direct contract with the provider, there can be problems with the user recovering damages that are suffered by a group member as the user has not actually suffered the loss. There are technical legal ways round this, by creating a trust or agency arrangement or by back-to-back agreements between the user and the group members, but these can be cumbersome and politically unpalatable. See paragraph 2.2.3 on third party rights.
- The user, of course, is not just a legal conduit for managing the provision of services on to its group, it is also a conduit for billing and payment. This may be an advantage, in terms of managing group spend (especially measured against a global discount from the provider) but it can also be an administrative burden both for the provider, in terms of the billing information it has to provide in order to allow recharging, and for the user, as regards the effort involved.
- Outsourcing is not just about creating a contract – even hard-bitten lawyers acknowledge that there is a long-term commercial relationship that is intended to go beyond the arm's length contracts. A critical part of this relationship is based round communication and liaison, particularly as regards:

- managing day-to-day changes in the services;
- achieving transformational outsourcing where the aim is to develop value beyond the simple transfer of services and to achieve innovation and mutual business benefit;
- dealing with the (all too common) need to react to market forces where, for example, there is a fundamental business change for the user and it has to refocus or divest businesses;
- avoiding and resolving disputes.

Each of these is made more difficult if the real users of the services are concealed behind the apparent user.

Where there are other stakeholders

As noted in the introduction, services are not always acquired just for internal use by the user or its group. Increasingly, outsourced services either underpin the user's own services to its clients or actually form part of them. An example of the first situation would be where the provider operates an e-commerce or m-commerce portal for the user. Although it is the user that is selling its goods or services, it is dependent on the provider to be able to do so. The second situation is exemplified by the reselling of mobile telephony services by a mobile virtual network operator (MVNO), such as Virgin in the UK and US and OneTel. Here the user is entirely dependent for a core part of its offering on the third party provider.

In these circumstances, the user has a number of additional concerns:

- The level of dependency on a purely contractual relationship is high, as is the ability of the provider to affect the profitability – and viability – of the user. This means a careful negotiation by the parties of the allocation of risk and reward, and the contentious issue of whether the provider should accept some liability for business losses, such as lost profit.
- Major customers, aware of this dependency, may seek some transparency as regards the back-to-back agreement with the provider, i.e. the outsourcing services agreement. They may also insist on having some rights in respect of these contracts (see paragraph 2.2.3 on third party rights later in this chapter). The user, therefore, has to be aware, when negotiating for services that will be onward-provided to large sophisticated customers, that these concerns may need to be anticipated and negotiated into the outsourcing services agreement from the outset.

2.2.2 The virtual user

Taking this forward to another degree, the user in fact may be at the centre of a web of outsourcing contracts – the trend has been for users that begin with, say, IT outsourcing, to move into business process outsourcing or other areas too.

At its extreme is the virtual company, which is totally reliant on outsourcing and has little by way of infrastructure itself (see Figure 2.2).

A similar model applies in the pharmaceuticals industry, where research and development; running clinical trials, and manufacturing and distributing the products can all be outsourced, with the user retaining only the brand and other intellectual property and strategic control. While giving the user maximum flexibility, these models also pose management and legal issues:

- Negotiating and then managing parallel but interdependent agreements takes both time and a high degree of project management, which a start-up venture may not be able to devote to the process.
- Where the providers have to exchange information or co-operate in some other way, it is important to minimise the possibility of finger-pointing should something go wrong. One way of addressing this is to have common operational procedures, which are annexed to the service schedules of the relevant providers' outsourcing services agreements. This avoids having to disclose each provider's commercial terms to the others, but does mean that, at the operational level, the providers have a common understanding of service boundaries.

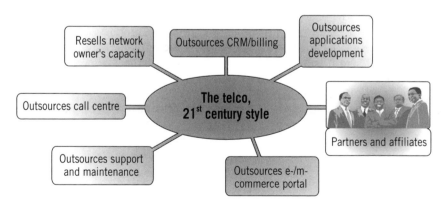

Figure 2.2   A virtual company

2.2.3 Multiple provider structures

Of course it is not only on the user side of the equation that the concept of one legal entity being involved is unlikely to be the case in practice. If the services either involve a number of elements or have to be provided in more than one country, almost inevitably the provider will have to subcontract either within its group or to an unrelated third party, or enter into some other joint arrangement.

There are three basic structures that can be used, each of which has benefits and drawbacks:

- joint priming;
- provider consortia;
- prime and subcontracts.

Joint priming

Figure 2.3 shows joint priming.

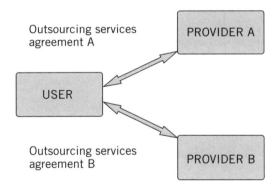

Figure 2.3 Joint priming

Ignoring for these purposes the issue of having potentially two sets of asset transfers, the issues with this structure are outlined in Table 2.1.

Some of the negatives can be addressed by adopting the joint operational procedures manual concept mentioned above, so at least the interfacing between the providers is agreed between them. The providers may also wish to enter into a more formal agreement between themselves to govern their relationship; the user may want to make this a tripartite agreement. However, this still suffers to some extent from the fact that there are multiple relationships involved.

This model becomes increasingly unwieldy as the number of providers involved increases.

Table 2.1   Issues with joint priming

User's perspective	Each provider's perspective
Positives: maximum control and flexibility, with both providers being directly answerable to the user; the user has the ability to change one without affecting the other	*Positives*: strong direct relationship with the user; possibility of taking over the other provider's share in the longer term
Negatives: two sets of negotiations to manage; two relationships to manage; danger of 'finger-pointing' between providers if something goes wrong	*Negatives*: having to cohabit with a potential competitor that may attempt to muscle in on its relationship and/or blame it for any service failures

Provider consortia

Taking the concept of the provider A-provider B agreement one stage further is the creation of a joint venture (see Figure 2.4).

The joint venture company may either be an ad hoc 'Newco' created specifically for the deal, or a consortium arrangement for other business ventures. Again, this structure has advantages and disadvantages (see Table 2.2).

Prime and subcontracts

The main alternative to seeing the two (or more) providers as being essentially in parallel is the structure shown in Figure 2.5.

Again, this is a simplification: there could of course be many subcontractors. It is also possible that there may be a transfer of assets and staff not only

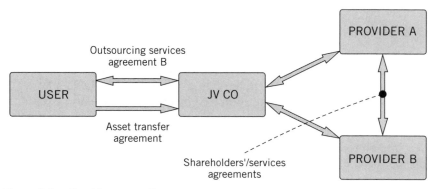

Figure 2.4   Provider consortia

Table 2.2 Issues with provider consortia

User's perspective	Each provider's perspective
Positives: single point of contract and contact; clear line of responsibility and liability	*Positives*: can present a unified service offering to a user or the market; can allocate responsibility and liability with other providers via the shareholders' agreement; can use to limit legal exposure by contracting through a limited liability Newco; can limit commercial exposure by not putting its brand to the service
Negatives: the Newco may have little substance so there may be concerns about it meeting its obligations; there is no direct contract with the actual providers of the services and no lever if there are service issues as between them	*Negatives*: lack of communication directly with the user hence less ability to cross-sell; all the pros and cons of joint ventures (see below)

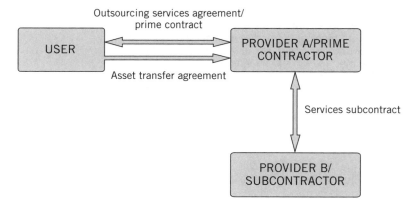

Figure 2.5 Non-parallel providers

to the prime contractor but also to one or more subcontractors. However, at its most straightforward, as above, there are issues as outlined in Table 2.3.

Obviously, as with the other structures, the relative balance of these pros and cons for each party will depend on the nature of the services and the parties' relative bargaining power. This structure has the huge benefit of being simple to set up and to understand.

Table 2.3 Issues with prime and subcontracts

For user	For prime contractor	For subcontractor
Positives: as with the provider JV, there is a single point of contact for management and legal responsibility	*Positives*: control of the services and the interface with the user; freedom to choose and change subcontractors	*Positives*: can regard it as a simple service relationship; divorced from the business impact of its service failures so can resist sharing liability for this
Negatives: all eggs are in one basket – if the prime contractor fails to provide the services properly or goes out of business, the user may have difficulty in replicating the structure and end up losing the benefit of all the subcontracted services; the user may want to have some say in the appointment of key subcontractors but the prime contractor will resist this; there may be a lack of transparency about the passing through of the subcontractors' charges; the user may want the subcontractors to be involved in liaison, for example over changes to the services but again the prime contractor may resist this	*Negatives*: real risk of being squeezed by the user and major subcontractors (especially if they collude) – over pricing and the passing on of liability, for example; the user is likely to demand some degree of transparency and also some say in the changing of subcontractors so the freedom may be more apparent than real; may not be able to charge for the value of the management of the subcontractors. The prime contractor will, of course, be liable for the activities of the subcontractor, including any service failures, but may be able to ameliorate this if the user has insisted on the choice of subcontractor	*Negatives*: lack of relationship with the user and chance to cross-sell or develop the services; at risk of being replaced by the prime contractor; lack of visibility of the main outsourcing services agreement

2.2.3 Third party rights

It will be clear from the above discussion that structuring a multi-party outsourcing is a balancing act of risk, convenience and manageability. Where there is – as is frequently the case – a group or similar structure on both the user and the provider side, a number of the problems are exacerbated.

Under the law of England and Wales, there were until recently three main structures that could be adopted:

1. The trust/agency structure: under this, there would still just be a single outsourcing services agreement as in Figure 2.1. However, the user would purport to be entering into the agreement on behalf of its group, either acting as agent for the group members (hence claiming to create a contractual nexus between the provider and each sub-user) or as trustee of their rights. Both of these options were commonly regarded as being of debatable merit both legally and practically. On the provider side of the equation, the user could insist in the outsourcing services agreement that the provider insert certain terms in its subcontracts, but this was still largely dependent on being able to compel the provider to enforce these terms. These terms would generally cover specific rights of access or audit (especially where the user was a regulated entity) and rights to step in to the relationship with the subcontractor, such as when the provider was failing to provide the services or was insolvent and the user wished to ensure the continuity of service provision.

2. The back-to-back structure: to add greater legal certainty to the above, albeit at the expense of simplicity, the user could enter into services agreements with the group members such that it was obliged to provide the same services on to those companies. Thus any service failure by the provider under the outsourcing services agreement would entail a similar failure by the user under these subsidiary agreements and the subsidiaries could claim their losses from the user and the user in turn could claim against the provider. This got round the problem highlighted at the beginning that the real losses arising from a service failure often are not suffered by the user but by members of its group, the true end users. However, the system is cumbersome for the user to set up and manage and can be politically unpalatable within a group structure. There can also be adverse accounting consequences of setting up potential inter-group liability in this way.

3. The umbrella structure: in this model, the two top companies enter into a master services agreement, which establishes the basic terms (legal and commercial) that will apply to the provision of services from one group to the other. However, at (say) country level, the user's subsidiary in that country will enter into a direct agreement with the provider's domestic subsidiary. This agreement will be called off under the terms of the master or umbrella agreement and its terms will largely reflect those agreed at the top level, with any necessary variations. The aim is therefore to minimise the level of renegotiation each time a local agreement is entered into, but without imposing a straightjacket. The master agreement could govern the way in which, for example, group discounts were to apply, and take a holistic approach to the allocation of risk and liability

between the groups. Used properly, this model can provide a good balance between the legal uncertainty of the first option and the unwieldy nature of the second.

Nevertheless, none of the above is perfect and even the third can lead to a proliferation of contracts – as well as the risk that the user's subsidiaries will not stick to the pre-agreed script set out in the master agreement. However, a recent change in the law in England and Wales has added a new option, which has been adopted in many subsequent group outsourcings, including where English law is applied to multi-jurisdictional agreements.

The problem that each of the above structures sought to address was the fundamental principle of English contract law (known as the doctrine of privity of contract) that only the parties to a contract could enforce its terms or take any benefit under it. Hence, even when an outsourcing agreement was intended to benefit the user's group, only the user could enforce it or recover in respect of breaches, even if the loss were actually suffered by another group member. Similarly, if the user wanted to have rights against the provider's subsidiaries or subcontractors – such as audit rights or step-in rights – it had to rely on the provider to enforce these, rather than having legal rights directly against them. This could be unsatisfactory where the provider was unwilling or unable to enforce the terms of its subcontracts, or was (as mentioned above) insolvent.

The Contracts (Rights of Third Parties) Act 1999 came into force in 2000 and to a large extent removed the notion of privity of contract. Instead, it provided that third parties on whom a contract conferred benefits could in fact enforce these benefits. The principal provisions of the Act and their application to outsourcing are summarised in Table 2.4.

Table 2.4 Discussion of Contracts (Rights of Third Parties) Act 1999

Provision	Comment
The effect of the Act can be excluded in the contract	The provider will of course not wish to see any party other than the user itself being able to take legal action against it, so will seek to exclude the Act. The Act will therefore generally only be applied as a result of negotiation and on a carefully circumscribed basis
The Act confers rights on two classes of third parties – those on whom the contract expressly confers a benefit or 'purports' to confer a benefit	Generally, it is in neither party's interest to confer rights on third parties without some degree of control: best practice is therefore to identify the beneficiaries of the rights conferred under the Act

Table 2.4 Continued

Provision	Comment
The third party beneficiaries need not be named specifically but can be a class of persons	The provider, in particular, will want the range of beneficiaries to be as narrow as possible. The user will often seek to have the following three classes of beneficiaries included as persons having rights to enforce the outsourcing services agreement:
	• members of its group of companies – the provider will usually accept this, subject to the protections as to procedure and liability, described below
	• customers who rely on the services (as referred to in section 2.2 above under 'Structuring the deal') – the provider will be very reluctant to accept this as it implies that it accepts liability for business losses arising out of the onward supply of its services. The issue of business losses is covered in more detail below in paragraph 2.5.7
	• successor service providers who may take over the arrangement from the provider and who may need to rely on statements made by the exiting provider as to, for example, transferring employees (see paragraph 2.5.11), but who will not have a direct contractual relationship with the provider
The Act gives limited protection to the party against whom the contract is being enforced, for example by providing that it can rely on the limitation of liability clauses as against the third party beneficiary	The provider will want to specify carefully how claims by third party beneficiaries are to be handled (for example by compelling the user to act as a central liaison point) and by adding provisions to make it clear that it will not suffer increased aggregate liability as a result of the increased range of parties that can bring actions against it in relation to breaches of contract
	Where the user has insisted that the Act is applied to subcontracts, so as to give it direct rights of action against subcontractors, the provider will usually seek to prohibit the user from exercising these rights unless the provider has itself failed to do so or is insolvent

2.2.4   Joint ventures and consortia

The final main alternative structure is where the user and the provider themselves enter into a joint venture. In this case, the parties initially contribute as follows:

- the user:

    - transfers into the joint venture company (JV Co) the assets constituting its existing department; its employees also transfer into the JV Co by virtue of TUPE (see Chapter 9);
    - enters into the services agreement with the JV Co, so providing a commercial basis for its existence as a business;

- the provider:

    - may also contribute assets or finance;
    - enters into a back-to-back services agreement with the JV Co to provide management and other services.

The parties are issued with shares in the JV Co and also agree how the financing of the operation is to be achieved – whether by way of further subscription or debt financing or otherwise. The arrangement is set up as in Figure 2.6.

This way of operating an outsourcing may seem to fly in the face of the usual intent of the user – to cease to own or care about how the services are provided but only to purchase the services it needs. What, therefore, are the reasons why the parties may choose this method of arranging the outsourcing and what are the drawbacks? The principal pros and cons about creating a joint venture for this purpose are set out in Table 2.5.

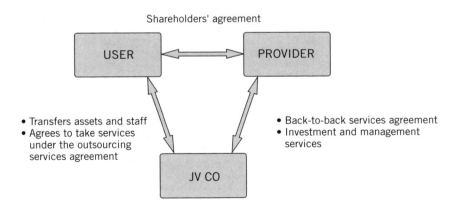

Figure 2.6   JV Co financing

Table 2.5   Pros and cons of joint ventures and consortia

Pros	Cons
Tax: where the user is VAT exempt (such as many financial institutions) it may be able to avoid paying VAT on the charges for the services if the shareholding of the JV Co is arranged such that the JV Co is part of the user's VAT group. [This is covered in more detail in Chapter 11]	*Economies of scale*: it will be more difficult for the provider to leverage its other assets and, for example, to cancel transferred third party contracts where it has existing arrangements with the third parties. This will have a limiting effect on its ability to realise savings or to draw on its other resources such as backup facilities
Finance: if external finance is needed (e.g. to fund the initial acquisition of the assets or for future investment), the funder may insist that the assets and revenue stream are ring-fenced in a separate company over which it can take security	*People*: the user's staff may be reluctant to transfer to a JV Co rather than to the provider itself, seeing a lack of job prospects and flexibility in a ring-fenced operation
Politics or regulation: some government or other public bodies may find it politically or legally impossible to dispose absolutely of their assets or people and a JV may be the only alternative	*Management*: it may be more difficult to allocate responsibility for failure and to enforce legal rights against a company that is partly owned by the user rather than at the other end of an arm's length contract
Sharing reward: one reason for the outsourcing may be that the parties expect that spare capacity may be used to sell services to other potential customers of the provider or otherwise expect to realise benefits – these are easier to identify and allocate if the outsourcing is run as a distinct business. This may also be true in terms of tracking future investment and efficiency savings	*Assessing investment*: in allocating the share of any reward to be realised by a party, it can be difficult to assess the investment which that party has in fact put in – allocation of administrative costs and overheads is notoriously contentious
Exit: if the assets and staff that are being used to provide the services are ring-fenced in this way, it is easier for the user to take them away from one provider and transfer them to a replacement or take them back in house, by using options over the provider's shares. Conversely, the provider may have an option to buy out the user's shares after a period of time or on the happening of certain events, such as the growth of third party business as referred to above	*Risk and liability*: care needs to be taken in applying service credits or other remedies: deducting these from the profit share that would otherwise be paid to user would amount to a somewhat Pyrrhic victory

Apart from these issues, which are specifically related to outsourcing, there are the general points that apply to any joint venture arrangement, chief among which are:

- How are the shares to be divided? Is either party to have a controlling interest, or the ability to block certain votes? What other rights are to attach to the shares, such as the ability to appoint and remove directors; pre-emption rights on transfer of ownership; preferential rights on distribution of assets; or rights to dividends?
- What obligations will either party have to contribute future funds and on what basis – can one party dilute the shareholding of the other?
- Related to this, how is the board of directors to be constituted and operated? Is either party to have a majority of voting rights or a casting vote? How much day-to-day involvement and commitment will the directors need to undertake? Are certain matters to be reserved to the shareholders or require a unanimous vote – what if there is deadlock?
- How can the JV Co be dissolved or either party dispose of its shares?

As noted above in relation to provider JVs, the parties will need to enter into a shareholders' agreement as well as the obvious services agreement, to address the above issues.

2.3   STRUCTURING THE CONTRACTS

The documents encapsulating an outsourcing do, of course, reflect the structure of the deal. At their simplest, though, there are two principal contracts:

- the transfer of assets agreement;
- the outsourcing services agreement.

The distinction between them is as much a matter of convenience as law, as there is no compelling reason why the transfer of the existing department to the provider should not be included in the same document as deals with the ongoing provision of the services. However, convenience suggests that a split is made between contract terms dealing with a one-off transfer and those with ongoing application – so that the services agreement is not cluttered with clauses that have no continuing relevance. Similarly, any claims that might arise in relation to transferred assets can be dealt with in relation to the transfer of assets agreement without necessarily impacting on the services agreement.

2.3.1   The transfer of assets agreement

The best practice therefore is to set out in the transfer of assets agreement only those provisions that establish the outsourcing rather than having an application to the parties' long-term relationship. A useful discipline can be to analyse the existing technology department in two different ways:

- As the sum of its parts, i.e. the assets that constitute it. These will typically include physical assets such as hardware and cabling; real assets such as data centres or network management centres; intangible assets such as intellectual property rights and the benefit of third party contracts and licences; and, of course, human assets – the people who operate the department. The transfer of assets agreement deals with these.
- As the sum of its activities, i.e. the services that it provides to the user of which it forms part. These activities may, initially, be dependent on the transferring assets but will typically decouple from them over time as the services and the method of providing them evolve. These are therefore better dealt with in the services agreement, which underpins the long-term relationship between user and provider.

This distinction is further highlighted by the fact that an outsourcing is often done by way of a 'big bang', such that the contracts are signed, the assets transfer and the services commence at the same time. The transfer of assets agreement therefore only exists to effect the instant transfer of the assets and then has no continuing role and can fall away. There are some important qualifications to this that affect the structure of the contracts and the distinction between them – which make it important not to fall into the trap of treating an outsourcing as a simple corporate transaction (see Table 2.6).

The process of the parties' due diligence is examined in Chapter 1, but part of that should be to identify those assets that will be transferred to the provider as opposed to those that will be retained by the user and simply made available to the provider. The best practice is for only those in the first category to be dealt with in the transfer of assets agreement.

The agreement therefore consists largely of lists, of assets and people, and operative provisions that relate to these lists and to their transfer to the provider.

The content of the transfer of assets agreement is examined in section 2.4 below.

2.3.2 The services agreement

It follows that the services agreement deals with the long-term relationship between the parties. In doing so, it has to achieve the following:

- define the services that are to be provided and the standards they are to meet;
- describe how the services are to be implemented, if there is any transition or migration of the services from the premises or platform of the user to that of the provider;
- provide for any dependencies on the user (for example, the retained contracts as referred to above);

Table 2.6   Qualifications affecting the structure of contracts

Factor	Qualification/impact
The parties to a pure corporate disposal by way of sale of assets generally have the intention to effect a one-off deal, which centres round the value of the assets and the business that those assets generate. There is usually little ongoing dealing between the parties so the value of the assets is critical. Thus, in addition to the due diligence process that the purchaser undertakes to 'kick the tyres' of the business it is buying, the purchaser will insist on detailed warranties (i.e. statements of fact) from the vendor as to the condition of the assets – and, more importantly, the business they support. The aim of these warranties is, in their draft state, to elicit information to enable the parties to set the correct value on the business, as part of their negotiation. Post contract, they give the purchaser continuing rights against the vendor should the warranties prove to be incorrect: in effect they allow the parties to adjust the contract price.	In an outsourcing, the focus is not on the value of the assets and there is no business being transferred: the activities (i.e. services) described above are usually there to *support* the user's business, rather than to comprise it. Although this may be less the case with a virtual user, it is not the assets themselves that are the main part of the deal but the ongoing services and the capability of the assets to support their provision. Thus it is in both parties' interests for there to be a thorough understanding of the assets, because a marginal adjustment to their purchase price post live date is much less important than ensuring that the services continue to be provided – the parties' ongoing relationship is what matters. The transfer of assets agreement in an outsourcing transaction therefore tends to have far fewer warranties than in a corporate transaction – the purchaser (i.e. the provider) will concentrate less on the intrinsic value of the assets than on their effect on its ability to provide the services. In addition, while a purchaser of a business will need to bear the future investment costs in replacing assets, in an outsourcing both the up-front and continuing costs will generally be amortised by the provider over the life of the outsourcing and be reflected in its charges to the user. Of course, the valuation of the assets in an outsourcing must be justifiable – both for tax reasons (especially VAT – see Chapter 11) and if there is to be external financing, as noted above.
Corporate asset disposals tend to involve a period between the date of signature of the transfer of assets agreement and the actual date of completion when ownership passes. During this period, the parties are generally resolving outstanding issues or seeking the	As noted above, an outsourcing tends to be a 'big bang' with no gap between signing of contract and live date (the equivalent of completion in a corporate deal) – live date marks the real beginning of the parties' relationship. The migration of the services and other transitional provisions are usually seen as being part of the services themselves and therefore addressed in the services agreement (see below).

Table 2.6 Continued

Factor	Qualification/impact
Fulfilment of conditions on which the sale depends. The contract therefore will deal with the conduct of the business – and therefore the treatment of the assets and the allocation of risk in relation to them – during the period from signature until completion. Completion therefore marks the end of the parties' relationship.	
It follows that there tends to be little by way of ongoing dependencies between the parties – where, for example, the purchaser needs to have continuing access to premises or services, this tends to be for a short and well defined period and incidental to the deal.	In an outsourcing, the ongoing relationship is of course vital, and there may be indefinite dependencies on the user. Most commonly, these relate to retained contracts (see below) and to IPR that belongs to the user and is licensed to the provider. Because these generally impact directly on service provision, these are best addressed in the services agreement.

- set out a framework for changing the services over time;
- deal with failures to provide the services to the service standards;
- allocate risk and reward;
- establish a basis for communication, liaison and the escalation and resolution of disputes;
- determine the ownership of intellectual property created as part of the services;
- permit the user to verify that it is getting value for money;
- allow the user to re-tender the services and to exit the contract smoothly.

Structurally, the services agreement consists of the terms and conditions and a series of schedules that contain the technical, commercial and operational details. This not only makes navigation around the document relatively straightforward, but also aids the negotiation process by allowing the streaming of consideration of the various aspects of the document. The danger of this, however, is that the services schedule (in particular) is seen as being a separate agreement, a mistake often encouraged by its typical designation as the service level agreement (SLA). The SLA must be seen as an integral part of the legal documentation: a further analysis of the approach to be taken to this document and the services agreement in total is set out below, but the structure is best summarised as in Figure 2.7.

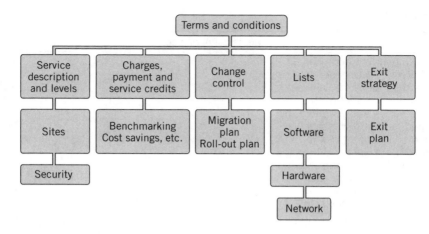

Figure 2.7   Services agreement structure

2.4   THE TRANSFER OF ASSETS AGREEMENT

As noted above, the assets need to be split into various categories, depending on the method by which they are to be transferred or otherwise made available to the provider.

2.4.1   Real property

This could include dedicated data centres, switch rooms and network management centres, as well as the premises and sites of the user. These can be dealt with in two principal ways:

- The provider can be given exclusive occupation of the area, either by way of assignment of freehold (unlikely) or by the granting or assigning of a lease. This is generally referred to in the transfer of assets agreement but dealt with in a separate agreement. There may also be other activities to be carried out, such as excluding a tenancy from the provisions of legislation giving protected rights.
- The provider can be given rights of access short of a tenancy, by way of licence or simple permission, on terms that generally include an obligation to comply with security and safety obligations. These rights and terms are usually set out in the services agreement.

2.4.2   Tangible assets

These could include the kit used by the in-house department, routers and other communications equipment. The kit may be dealt with:

- under the transfer of assets agreement if it is to be transferred to the provider. If it is owned outright by the user, it will be sold to the provider; if it is subject to a finance lease, this lease will be assigned to the provider – subject to the receipt of the consent of the finance provider;
- under the services agreement if ownership (or the finance lease) is to be retained by the user and the asset is simply to be made available to the provider. Again, consent may be required from the finance lessor if possession is to be ceded to the provider.

2.4.3 Intellectual property owned by the user

Principally, this will be software created by the user's in-house department but may include documentation, methodologies and brands. This may be:

- assigned to the provider, in which case the assignment can be dealt with under the transfer of assets agreements (assignments of the principal intellectual property rights generally must be in writing);
- licensed to the provider, which will be dealt with under the services agreement.

2.4.4 Intellectual property licensed to the user

Again, this may be dealt with in two different ways:

1. The licences may be assigned or novated to the provider. In the former case, the consent of the licensor will invariably be required and this will be dealt with as part of the due diligence and negotiation process (see Chapter 1). In the latter case, the agreement will of course be tripartite and the licensor will be a party.
2. The intellectual property (IP) may be sub-licensed to the provider, which will again usually require the consent of the licensor. The user will retain the licence if it uses the IP in the rest of its business or if it considers that exit would be easier if principal licences are kept in the name of the user.

2.4.5 Other contracts with third parties

These could include contracts for the maintenance of software or hardware. These are most likely to be assigned to the provider under the transfer of assets agreement.

The transfer of assets agreement effects the assignment of the assets that are to be transferred to the provider and also addresses the following issues:

- the terms governing the transfer of the employees of the user to the provider, including provisions relating to pensions – these are covered in detail in Chapters 9 and 10;

- the allocation of prepayments under the transferred contracts;
- the giving of warranties in respect of the transferred assets (as referred to above).

2.5 THE SERVICES AGREEMENT

2.5.1 Defining the services

The operative provisions of the services agreement relating to the services themselves are often the shortest and simplest in the agreement: the provider is obliged to provide the services to the service levels and agrees that failure to do so will lead to certain remedies, such as service credits. The substance of what the services and service levels are, and the remedies for failure to meet them, are invariably not set out in the main body of the agreement but in the schedules. The services and the standards to which they are to be provided are, as noted above, set out in a document commonly referred to as the service level agreement (SLA). This must be seen as an intrinsic part of the contract, while also being a practical day-to-day document to be used by non-lawyers.

The specifics of what should be set out in relation to particular technology services are described in Chapters 3 to 6, but the following general principles apply:

- A recurring theme of this chapter is that the period immediately after the transfer of assets and staff is the most vulnerable time for both parties. The user has least commercial leverage and the least practical ability to terminate the arrangement and take the services back or transfer them elsewhere. On the other hand, the provider is also on a learning curve about the capabilities of what it has taken on. The issue of how the services are implemented is addressed below, as is the application of service remedies. However, the setting of the service levels at this point is also very important. It is all too tempting for the parties to put off agreeing the service levels and either to specify that they will be agreed post live date or that there will be a period of verification and adjustment after live date. The baseline for the service levels is therefore stated to be that achieved by the user's in-house department immediately prior to live date, which may or may not be adequately documented. It is highly risky for the user to allow the services to commence without concrete, documented and measurable service levels. It is a legal truism that the courts will not enforce an 'agreement to agree' and it is naïve for the user to believe that the parties will really agree challenging service levels – still less proper service remedies – post contract. If there really is no alternative, the contract must set out the basis for agreeing service levels, the timescales for doing so and how any disagreements over this are to be resolved.

- The services should be described as simply and clearly as possible, and in the active voice, e.g. 'The Provider shall deliver the X . . .' rather than 'X shall be delivered'. The rule of thumb is that the SLA should set out the 'W' questions: *who* is to do *what*, *when* and *where*, and to *what* standard. The key is to break down the services into steps, concentrating particularly on where there is some interface between the activities of the provider and the user or third parties. These service boundaries make it easier to allocate responsibility. See the example below:

> The user is a bank and is outsourcing the printing and despatch of bank statements. The provider will print and send out the statements. The end result should be that each customer receives the correct statement containing the correct information about his or her financial position, together with any marketing inserts the bank wants to send.
>
> However, the provider cannot contractually accept responsibility for this end-to-end service: it can only process and print the information it receives from the user. If that data file is late or corrupted, the provider cannot guarantee that the statements are correct or that they are inserted in the correct envelopes or that they are dealt with in the contractual timescale. Therefore, the contract has to deal with the point at which the provider takes responsibility – and what it should do if the data file is not received at the right time. At the other end of the process, the provider may simply be bagging up the envelopes for collection by the Post Office – its collection and timely delivery is out of the provider's hands.

- The consequence of setting out the services in terms of the 'W' questions, is to raise the issue about the extent to which the service levels should also address the 'H' question: *how* the services are to be provided. There are cultural, technical and legal issues involved in the balancing act as to how far to do this:

  - Culturally, the service levels are often initially drawn up by the user's existing technology managers whose skill lies in delivering services, rather than managing their delivery. These people have never had to make this distinction before and will tend therefore to reflect their concepts of how the services should be provided in their drafting of SLAs. The danger inherent in this approach is that it fossilises one approach and inhibits innovation: it may also give the provider pretexts for avoiding responsibility for service failures: 'We were doing it the way you told us to . . .'.
  - Legally, a lack of clarity about the deliverables and the service boundaries can make it difficult to allocate responsibilities – this is explored further below. In addition, the *how* aspect of the services cannot in reality be frozen in time and will change almost immediately. In theory

then, any change to these provisions will be a contract variation requiring a formal process and documentation, which would be ridiculous for a simple change in, say, the identity of an individual to be called in an emergency or his or her mobile phone number. Further, there may be legitimate reasons for specifying how a deliverable should be achieved. For example, the *what* aspect of data security could include a substantive obligation to ensure that corrupted data can be restored within a certain time frame. However, beyond that, does the user really need to specify the details of how backups are taken, stored, retrieved and verified – in fact, would it not be better to impose an obligation on the provider to use best practice on this (which evolves with time) rather than to specify what the practice should be? There is no right or wrong answer to the question: much depends on the context. For example, a financial institution may have regulatory obligations as to how its sensitive data are dealt with and may be obliged to spell these out in detail to the provider.

– Technically, the *how* and the *what* may be intrinsically linked. For example, in dealing with the communications services to be provided to a critical part of the user's organisation – its head office or data centre – it would be usual to provide that a telecoms provider should install more than one cable into the building, for resilience. However, having two cables entering the building through the same ducting still leaves a single point of failure – for example the proverbial digger slicing through both cables at once. In practice, it may be perfectly legitimate to specify not just that there must be two communications links, but also that they are diversely routed into the building – even that they must be sourced from alternative telecoms providers so that there is no single point of failure at the nearest network node.

• It will be clear from the above that there are no hard and fast rules about where to draw the line about how much detail should go in the contractual service description and service levels. However, the following points should be borne in mind:

– Experience shows that the longer and more complex the documents, the less chance that they will be useful and the more chance that the people who actually have to deliver the services will simply ignore them and come up with their own ways of doing things. It is often the case, when an outsourcing goes wrong and the parties look at the contract, that they discover that what might have appeared to be a clear contractual breach has been muddied by the actions of their representatives on the ground.

– The service level schedules, in particular, must be practical and usable documents, so clarity and precision is as important as brevity.

- A very useful approach can be to split out any necessary details of how the services are to be operated into a separate document, such as an operational procedures manual. This document is not physically part of the contract, but is incorporated by reference, for example the SLA could say 'The Provider shall carry out data backups in accordance with the provisions of the Operations Manual' and the details of this would be in the manual. It therefore has contractual effect, but being separate it is easier to refer to and to update (albeit of course that it must be subject to strict version control, particularly if it is kept in soft copy). An added advantage to this approach is mentioned in paragraph 2.2.3 on multiple service providers, above: the operational procedures can be common to several providers and help to scope their respective responsibilities, without them all having to sign the same substantive contract or see each other's commercial terms.

- Early outsourcing contracts took a very technical approach to defining service levels, measuring output (i.e. compliance with technical specifications) rather than outcome (i.e. has the user's business received the service it needs). Obviously it is much easier to measure hard technical compliance (although see the points below on defining terms) than the more nebulous concept of outcome. However, the dangers with the former approach are:

  - that the user becomes swamped with data that does not give the entire picture about the quality of the service and has difficulty in mapping these data on to the more empirical complaints made by its internal customers;
  - the behaviour of the provider becomes focused on meeting service levels rather than providing a service that meets the user's broader expectations.

- The best approach therefore is still to have some technical measures, or key performance indicators, but to superimpose measures that relate more to the business deliverable. A crude example of this could be in relation to an outsourced call centre. Calls may be answered within the contractual measurement time of (say) three rings, but the callers may then be utterly frustrated by being forced to progress through nested automated menus or by not being put through to someone who can help them or who gives a bad impression. Some of these issues are technical, some may be cultural or a matter of training. Once the problem of negative customer feedback is identified, some of the technical measures may be useful in diagnosing the cause of problem and rectifying it.

- The specifics of defining the technical aspects of services are dealt with in Chapters 3 to 6, but generally the SLA has to be clear about what is to be measured, where it is to be measured, when it is to be measured, who is to measure it and how and when it is to be made available: these are often linked. See the example below for an illustration of the points.

The SLA states that a system is to be available for 99.96% of the time. This begs a number of questions:

- What does 'available' mean in this context and how can it be tested? Does it mean merely that user interface is present on a screen or is there a qualitative measure about the usability of that interface?
- Is the test applied at the provider's data centre or at some part of the user's system? As an obvious point, the fact that a computer system may be running perfectly at the data centre is irrelevant if it cannot be used in real time because the communications links to the user are down. This also reflects the importance of specifying the service boundaries properly: who is responsible for the comms link? Is the provider responsible only up to the user's router or across its LAN too?
- Percentages and averages are dangerous! Is the 99.96% percentage measured at one particular place or across the system as a whole? Depending on how this applies, the service level could be met even if, say, one location has no service at all – is this the intention? Does some other service level deal with that level of granularity? Similarly, 99.96% measured over a day obviously gives a lower number of permitted downtime minutes than a measurement over a week, a month or a rolling three-month or annual period. Are some minutes more important than others: an hour's downtime at financial year-end may be a disaster yet a minor inconvenience at another time. Finally, does the percentage include or exclude permitted downtime, for example for system maintenance. How is this scheduled?
- Who will measure the data? Usually, only the provider will have the technical means to measure network performance, so will the user rely on this? Is there a means of auditing or verifying the data?
- Is the user to receive periodic reports or real time information? What is the format of the data – this may be important if it is being used as the basis for reporting to or charging third party customers.

- It is increasingly common, in the light of the outcome approach mentioned above, for the parties to agree in the contract that user satisfaction with the services will be monitored on a regular basis and this can provider useful information. However, the parties need to take care about what questions are asked, of whom they are asked and how the results are used. The most pragmatic approach may be to feed this information into a contract review process, as outlined below.

2.5.2　Implementing the services

Often there is simply a switch-over of services, with the same people performing the same functions in the same way with the same equipment immediately after the transfer as before. However, there may be a transition or migration of services, for example a relocation of staff and equipment to a new data centre or the replacement of legacy systems with the provider's own systems. The services agreement needs to set out the basis on which this is to be accomplished, as follows:

- The parties should agree – in advance – a project plan setting out not only the start and end points for the migration or transfer, but also key intermediate steps, the dates by which they are to be achieved and the resources to be devoted. The project plan, which will usually include some form of Gantt chart, should also include provisions for how minor variations should be agreed.
- The agreement should deal with how compliance with the project plan is to be measured, which should be as objective as possible and, again, agreed prior to live date.
- The consequences of failure to meet the committed dates should also be set out. In a software development agreement, for example, one of the remedies the user would have is to terminate the agreement: this is likely to be impracticable in the context of an outsourcing, so the user will need a range of other remedies. The user needs to bear in mind that this is the stage, immediately after the transfer of its staff, where its commercial leverage and alternative options are least, and that the aim will usually be to salvage the situation rather than to provoke the end of the relationship. The most obvious remedies are financial, such as liquidated (i.e. pre-agreed) damages. In setting these, the user will need to bear in mind the following:
  - The liquidated damages must avoid being penal – to be enforceable, liquidated damages must be a genuine pre-estimate of the user's losses. These losses may relate to, for example, continuing software licence fees or property rental occasioned by the failure of the provider to relocate the services by the planned date.
  - The liquidated damages are usually intended to ensure that the provider is focused on meeting the targets and remedying problems, rather than being a means for the user to recover damages. The user needs to take this behavioural aspect into account in setting the levels: too low or too high a level of damages may have the opposite effect and lead to the provider losing interest in remedying the problem.

Similar provisions and considerations should apply to the roll-out of new services, or the provision of services to new sites.

2.5.3   Establishing dependencies and qualifications

The provider will want to qualify its obligations to provide the services (which, as noted above, are usually expressed in stark, binary terms) to bring in concepts of fault or other excuses for non-performance. However, if any apparent service failure is immediately followed by a debate between the parties about causation, it will be impossible for mechanistic remedies such as service credits to operate effectively and the parties' relationship will be damaged. There is a tension between the user's legitimate desire to impose clear obligations on the provider and to have meaningful remedies and the provider's equally legitimate need to avoid liability for failures that are not its fault. The parties' aim must be to have as narrow as possible a grey area around fault and responsibility, and this leads to a number of points:

- The services themselves must be expressed within clear boundaries so that it is clear what the extent of the provider's obligations are and equally clear where there are interfaces with the user and third parties. This is vital: none of the other points will compensate for inadequately defined and scoped services.
- Similarly, the services schedule should not contain qualifications, get-outs or questions of fault – these should be addressed in the main contractual terms. One of the biggest dangers of seeing the negotiation of an SLA as being separate from the terms and conditions is that there will be a conflict between the qualifications in the terms and conditions and those that creep into the SLA. This is not the same as setting proper boundaries or parameters (for example that system response times depend on the volume of data), as these themselves can be set out objectively.
- Where the provider is dependent on the user, this should be stated. This generally has two elements:
  - First, the migration of the services is very likely to involve activities by the user, such as allowing access to premises, staff and information. Any delay or failure to do this may prevent the provider meeting the project plan referred to above and the provider will want to be excused from the consequences of such failures, such as paying liquidated damages. As noted above, the user's position can be very weak at this stage so it should take the approach of having such dependencies clearly and exhaustively listed and putting the burden of proof on the provider to show that its failure to meet a date was caused by a failure by the user to provide a dependency.
  - During the ongoing provision of the services, the dependencies are more likely to relate to the continuing availability of the retained contracts referred to above; the services agreement should set this out and also a procedure for replacing or varying them as the services evolve. There are two sides to this kind of dependency. The provider will want

to be excused from service failures if the retained contract is not provided and to be indemnified if the user has failed to obtain the relevant third party's consent; the user will want to be indemnified if actions of the provider in respect of the subject matter of the contracts put the user in breach of the underlying contracts.

- A crucial issue is the application of the force majeure clause. The concept is familiar: a party is excused from liability from a failure because it can show that the failure was caused by an event beyond its reasonable control. In addition to the usual considerations of whether there should be a list of such events, what should go in that list and whether it should be exhaustive, there are additional issues with these provisions in relation to outsourcing services:

  - The interplay with obligations in relation to business continuity and disaster recovery; it is precisely in the circumstances of a force majeure event that such obligations should kick in.
  - The obligations of the provider to take precautions to avoid the onset of a force majeure event and to mitigate its effects.
  - Whether, and to what extent, the user should pay for services it is not receiving during a force majeure event affecting the provider. The theory of force majeure is of course that it would excuse the provider from its failure rather than giving it a right to continue to receive the charges. This may not be commercially acceptable as the user may instead want to contribute to the provider's expenses of restoring the services.
  - Is there a point at which either party should have the right to terminate the services agreement owing to a continuing force majeure?

2.5.4 Exclusivity and 'preferred supplier' and 'most favoured nation' clauses

Generally, there is no reason why the user should agree that the provider should be its exclusive provider of services – there would have to be some compelling commercial reason to do so. In addition, the parties would need to consider the application of competition law to the arrangement.

More common are two related provisions:

- *Preferred supplier clauses*: these range from largely meaningless clauses inserted for commercial comfort, to obligations on the user to notify the provider of new tenders and to give the provider a right to tender for the services. The chances are, of course, that the provider would be asked to tender in any event. The clause may go on to allow the provider to make a best and final offer (BAFO), although not usually to require the user to accept this offer. The parameters of such clauses need to be drawn carefully and they may well be difficult to police or enforce.

- *Most favoured nation/customer clauses*: these clauses generally provide that if the provider offers better terms to another customer, the user will also be offered these terms. Such clauses should be treated with great scepticism, owing to the difficulty of comparing like with like and finding out whether there has been a breach (the arrangements the provider makes with its other customers being confidential).

2.5.5 Changing the services

Paragraph 2.5.2 on implementing the services addresses the initial migration and transition of the services and touches on other pre-agreed changes, such a programme to roll out the services to new locations. However, the contract also has to deal with a range of other potential changes, each of which has different points of difficulty. These are discussed below, but the following general points should be noted:

- A fundamental (but common) error in drafting an outsourcing services agreement is to adopt the 'kitchen sink' approach of trying to pre-empt every conceivable change and prescribe how it is to be dealt with. This is another way to lead to the creation of a large and unwieldy document, as well as being a futile exercise. The contract can only take this approach to known changes (such as call-off services, variations to volumes or moves and changes, all described below); otherwise it must set out a framework to enable changes to be managed.
- This framework approach has four steps:

  - *Identifying the need for change*: can either the user or the provider propose a change? Is there an ongoing obligation on the provider to be proactive in this respect, and, if so, how? This is described in more detail below and in paragraph 2.5.9.
  - *Categorising the change*: does the change fall into one of the more straightforward changes mentioned above (such as a call-off service) or is it a complex change such as new service or a fundamental change that requires more detailed scrutiny and agreement? What is the basis for this categorisation – by likely cost or business impact or some other criteria? In fact, are there more than these two categories of straightforward and complex and therefore more than two sets of procedures to be followed?
  - *Defining the change*: where there is a complex change, the contract will, of course, not contain details of what it is, how and when it is to be implemented and what the knock-on effect on the rest of the services and the charges will be. The contract therefore needs to set out a process for these points to be agreed before work commences.
  - *Implementing the change*: the change, once agreed, must be implemented and this may be against a project plan containing with

milestones and remedies, as discussed in relation to implementing the services (paragraph 2.5.2).

2.5.6 Types of change

Call-off services

These are services that the parties pre-agree may be introduced at a later date at the option of the user, the description of which (i.e. the SLA, service remedies, etc.) and the charges for which have been agreed in advance. Provided that this has been done with sufficient clarity, the contract simply needs to set out the process by which the user can require that these services be implemented. One complication may be whether this is a requirement that the user can compel the provider to take on or whether the provider can refuse and, if so, on what basis.

Moves and changes

This is a generic description for services including the relocation of kit or the introduction of the services at an alternative location. There is obviously some potential for overlap with the previous and next kind of change; these definitions are not terms of art so their application needs to reflect the realities of the particular contract. Generally, these services fall into the straightforward category, as again the services and the implications for the charges are agreed in advance and the contract simply needs to set out how these changes are to be authorised and signed off. Invariably, a particular provider will have its own best practice for this and there is usually little point in rewriting this. The contract therefore normally simply refers to the standard forms and procedures that the provider employs (assuming these are clear and reasonable). Again, the only issue may be whether the provider is obliged to carry out such instructions. As the user is unlikely to be able to go elsewhere for such changes, the provider usually will be obliged to comply with these change requests.

The provision of additional or reduced resources

This could encompass the provision of more person-days of development time or consultancy; an increase or reduction in the number of transactions the system will handle; a change in bandwidth in communications links and a range of similar changes. Usually, these are also counted as straightforward changes and dealt with in a pre-agreed form. Often, the charges for these services are set out on a volume basis so that it is a simple task to calculate the changes to charges consequent on an increase or decrease in the volume of services. The unit price per transaction, for example, may reduce as the volumes increase and vice versa. Generally, the provider will seek to build parameters round these changes so that there is a minimum commitment from the user and a cap on increases within a certain time, to allow it to manage its resources and reflect its business assumptions in pricing the deal. The user may be required to give either indicative or binding forecasts of its requirements and needs to consider with care whether it can do this and what would happen if the parameters were breached in either direction. It would want to avoid an ongoing commitment to pay for services it no longer needed or uncertainty about whether it could increase volumes indefinitely if it increased its business or (say) acquired another company and wanted to pool resources.

New services and fundamental changes to the existing services

New services are self-explanatory. Fundamental changes to the existing services could include moving applications to a new platform or some other major change in the manner they are provided. In either case, there is likely to be an element of risk for one or both parties. In these circumstances, the contract needs to set out a framework to define the project, agree the scope and the method of implementation and the costs involved, together with any dependencies on the user or external resources. The user will be aware of the risk that the provider may have been competitive for the initial deal in the expectation that it will be given all future work. There is nothing wrong with this, unless it means that the user is either compelled to follow this path or is not able to compare the provider's offering with what others could provide. Exclusivity and preferred supplier clauses are dealt with above, but there can be other less obvious barriers to choice. Where the provider uses proprietary methods or has control over, say, a system or network, there may be technical or intellectual property issues, and the contract should make it clear that the provider must co-operate with alternative providers and allow access (on reasonable terms to protect its own interests) to necessary systems, interfaces and people.

The process of agreeing complex changes should therefore follow defined stages:

- Where the necessity for such a change is identified, the originating party should specify as clearly as possible the change to be made.
- The provider, in either event, should then produce a full specification and project plan, spelling out what has to be done and when it will be done, together with the dependencies mentioned above.
- The provider should also produce a fully costed quotation for the work, backed up with explanations of how the costings have been derived, any assumptions affecting their certainty and the implications for the ongoing charges. This will also cover any external financing or finance required from the user.

- At this stage, the user may wish to go to the market and compare the provider's approach with alternative service providers. To do this effectively, it may wish to share with those potential providers the specification and other documents submitted by the provider. The provider will have two principal problems with this. First, it will take the view that it has performed a consultancy service essentially for free, which its competitors can take advantage of without putting in the same effort. This can be addressed by, for example, allowing the provider to charge for this work if it is not awarded the provision of substantive change. Second, the proposal from the provider will draw on its own proprietary knowledge and contain commercially sensitive material. The user should be prepared to agree to reasonable restrictions on the passing on of this information to others, particularly the pricing information.
- If the provider is awarded the change, the process should (as noted above) be dealt with in a similar way to the original implementation of the services.
- If a third party alternative is selected, the provider should be obliged to co-operate as mentioned above.
- Where the change involves the creation of intellectual property, the parties should agree where ownership is to lie and (which is often more important) which party is to have the right to exploit it and on what basis.

There are two other aspects of change that need to be considered, as they can cut across all of the others:

- mandatory changes;
- major business changes.

Mandatory changes

These apply where the user is obliged to change the service as a result of a change in the law or its regulatory environment and must have these implemented by the provider. The issues divide into two:

- *Compulsion*: can the user specify in the contract that the provider must implement the change? In the event of an urgent change, can it also override the processes above? This depends to a degree on the parties' relative positions, but the provider will generally accept such provisions as long as they do truly reflect mandatory changes and as long as it has some protection where implementation may affect its ability to provide the existing services or have a knock-on effect on the rest of its operation. The issue then becomes one of payment.
- *Risk and cost*: the provider may take the view that any such change must be treated as being a change request from the user, entitling the provider to be paid for it. However, the user may counter with an argument that, if

the change were one that the provider would have to implement in any event, the proper way for the provider to deal with this is in increased charges for all its clients in the future. This would be the case, for example, where the provider's costs increased because of a general change in the law relating to the working week or paid holidays. A common approach is to draw a distinction between such changes in the law that apply to all businesses and those that only affect the user or a class of persons including the user (for example a change in the financial services regime). In those circumstances, the provider may have a better commercial argument for passing the cost burden of implementing the change directly on to the user.

Major business changes

Economic circumstances can sometimes undermine the business assumptions on which the parties entered into the arrangement. As noted in respect of joint ventures above, the parties could have formed the JV Co on the assumption that it would attract external business, which does not in fact arise – the shareholders' agreement should address what should happen in this event.

In any outsourcing, though, the user may find that its plans and forecasts as to requirements for services are radically altered, such as in an economic downturn or where it acquires or disposes of a business. The first two events are dealt with above in relation to volume commitments, but it is the effect of a business divestment that needs additional consideration.

Where the user intends to sell a subsidiary or division to a third party, it may be unable to do so (or do so at an acceptable price) without the continuing provision of services on which the business of that entity depends. The provider may therefore be required to split the services into those to be provided to the divested entity and those to continue under the existing arrangements, and consequently into two contracts. If this is a possibility, the contract should set out a process for this and how the services and the charges should be allocated. The provider will want to specify that it can refuse to do this if the new entity or its purchaser is not financially sound or if any increase in its overheads caused by running two relationships is not covered.

2.5.7　Allocating risk and reward

Where the services are not provided to the service levels, the provider will be in breach of contract and the user will have the right to legal remedies. If the user can show that the breach led to a recoverable loss, it will be entitled to sue the provider; more serious breaches may give it the right to terminate the contract.

Of course, these are purely theoretical remedies unless the user really intends to terminate, for it is unlikely to want to sue its sitting provider, given the effect it would have on the relationship between the parties. As noted above, an outsourcing cannot be seen simply as an arm's length contract, because of the effort it takes to enter into one, the long-term interdependency of the parties – and the implications of termination (see paragraph 2.5.11). The practice therefore has been to find other ways of addressing service failures, short of court action or termination. The commonest methods are summarised below.

2.5.8   Remedies

Liquidated damages

This is a general term for damages that the parties agree in advance will apply in certain circumstances: the 'liquidated' description refers to the fact that the amount of money to be paid is pre-agreed, either as an absolute amount or by way of an agreed method of calculation. To be enforceable under English law, liquidated damages must be a 'genuine pre-estimate of loss'; any attempt to specify damages that are greater than this will be 'penal' and unenforceable. This is a matter of fact rather than labels – although it explains why lawyers avoid the term 'service penalties'. The main use of liquidated damages, as such, is for failures to hit deadlines, for example the implementation milestones. Failure to provide the services to the service levels is more commonly addressed by way of service credits.

Service credits

These have become an almost universal way of addressing service failures. The concept is simple: failure to meet a service level will trigger the payment of a certain amount of money. The amount is usually linked to the seriousness of the failure, so if the relevant service level is (say) 98 per cent, £X may be payable for each one per cent below this the provider actually achieves. This has the enormous advantage of being simple and mechanistic; there is no scope for debate and therefore little adverse impact on the parties' relationship.

However, simplicity also has its disadvantages:

* The service credits tend to be set at a low amount (typically the provider will start negotiations at five per cent of the monthly charges) so will not necessarily compensate the user for the impact of service failures or prove much of an incentive for the provider to improve. In fact, it may be cheaper for the provider to pay service credits than to fix the underlying reasons for failing to hit the service levels. The net result of this may be that service credits actually become a way for the provider to limit its liability for all practical purposes, knowing that the user is unlikely to sue for

more unless it terminates. The provider may go further and seek to state in the contract that service credits are the user's only financial remedy. The user therefore needs to see service credits not only in the context of its other remedies, as set out below, but also in its review of the limits of liability.

- To deal with the problem of the low level of service credits, the contract may provide that repeated failures will increase the financial amounts – if in month one there is a payment of £X for each one per cent of failure, the same failure in month two may lead to a payment of £2X and so on.
- The provider will want to avoid double counting, so that one event does not trigger two different service failures and therefore two sets of credits.
- There is a (somewhat arid) legal debate about whether service credits are liquidated damages, as described above, or an adjustment to the charges to reflect the service actually received. The latter interpretation is not the preferred one. The user does not want an implication that the provider can choose to underperform and simply adjust its charges and the provider wants the service credits to be counted against its limit of liability. The contract should clearly specify whether amounts paid in either liquidated damages or service credits over the contract period affect the provider's total liability cap should the user bring a subsequent damages claim.

Other remedies

If service credits are useful but limited, the user is left with a problem: what other remedies does it have short of termination? Earlier outsourcing services agreements left open this gap between service credits and the 'nuclear' option of termination. Better practice is to identify other ways of either recovering money or focusing the mind of the provider on meeting the service levels. These will depend on the context of each contract, but examples include:

- requiring the provider to re-perform services free of charge;
- obtaining benefits in kind, such as free consultancy;
- identifying particular wasted costs and charging them to the provider.

Escalation and allocation of risk and reward

See the comments made on escalation and dispute resolution in paragraph 2.5.9.

The remedies set out above presuppose that the user does not wish to seek remedies in court proceedings. However, the allocation of risk between the parties of course goes beyond this and has to address what will happen if matters do end up in court, on termination or otherwise.

As stated above, the user will be entitled to recover its losses. This will be according to the usual principles of recovery: the user will need to show a breach by the provider and that its losses flowed from that breach; it will need to prove the amount of the losses and that they are recoverable types of loss. It will also have to act reasonably in mitigating its losses, in other words not exacerbate or aggravate its losses by inaction. In the context of an outsourcing, it is hardly conceivable that the user would fail to do all possible to secure alternative services to protect its business.

The above analysis will be examined shortly, but it is also important to note the exception where the user has the benefit of an indemnity. In essence, an indemnity allows the beneficiary to demand payment without having to prove loss or mitigate its losses in the same way. It is therefore a very powerful remedy for the beneficiary and not conceded lightly. Some users seek a general indemnity for all breaches of contract, but this is considered to be unreasonable. A better approach is to focus indemnities on specific issues, such as claims by third parties in relation to intellectual property infringements. In these indemnities, the giver will seek control over the subject matter, for example requiring the beneficiary not to agree a settlement with the third party without the giver's agreement and by seeking a right to change any infringing software so that it no longer infringes.

In the broader context of liability, there are two parameters that need to played against each other: the types of loss that can be recovered and the cap on liability. Of course, these apply to both parties but in practice it is the provider's limitations and exclusions of liability that will be heavily negotiated. The user could take the view that the provider should have unlimited liability, but this is both unreasonable and naïve: why would the user wish to contract with a provider that is prepared to gamble its entire business on one deal? In any event, no prudent provider will ever agree to unlimited liability – a prime example of why an outsourcing is not a partnership. A much more useful debate is over the two parameters mentioned above.

Taking types of loss first, the basic principle of English law is that the innocent party (the user in this context) can recover the losses flowing naturally from the breach, and those that were in the contemplation of the parties at the time the contract is entered into. The first type of loss is usually referred to as *direct*; the latter *consequential*. However, these labels are intrinsically unhelpful and confusing – as well as being controversial, providers have an almost pathological dislike of consequential loss, without necessarily being clear what the term actually means. The focus of the provider's discomfort will be business losses, such as the user's loss of profit. The provider will take the view that it is not underwriting the user's business and that it should not accept these losses.

There is no right or wrong answer as to where the line should be drawn on liability, it is as much a matter of commercial negotiation as law. English courts have established that loss of profits certainly can be recoverable – providers in the past had assumed that this was not the case. However, this is still subject to whether such losses do fit into the tests above. Clearly where the services are bespoke and underwrite a key part of the user's business it is much more likely that loss of profit will flow from a breach than in the case of commodity services. In any event, providers as a matter of course would exclude loss of profit, whether direct or otherwise. The wording of such clauses requires extreme care. Providers have been caught out by imprecision over the exclusion of such losses. It is a basic principle of law that such a clause will be interpreted strictly against the party seeking to rely on it. In addition, there may be supervening rules of law imposing a test of reasonableness on such clauses. As a final general point, some types of liability cannot be excluded under English law, such as liability for death or personal injury or for fraud.

The specific issue in limitation clauses in outsourcing contracts is where to draw the line as to the extent of the provider's liability. Although opinion differs, best practice would be for the parties to agree specifically what losses are included in and excluded from those that the user can claim (of course the user will still need to prove breach and loss, as noted above). Clearly this must depend on the nature of the services – whether they are commodity services or are specialist or business critical; the parties' respective bargaining positions and the interplay with the parties' ability to insure. Some examples of the types of loss, some or all of which may be relevant, are shown in Table 2.7.

Of course, there is also a positive side to allocation of risk and reward, which is where the provider adds value to the user's business. In paragraph 2.2.4 on joint ventures, the option of running the outsourcing as an independent business and sharing the benefits of this was considered. Apart from this, there are other ways of sharing benefits between the parties:

- *Service debits*: the concept is deceptively simple – just as for each percentage point *below* target the provider pays a sum to the user, for each point the provider hits *above* the target it should get a bonus payment. However, the logic is flawed: service credits are damages for failing to hit the contractually agreed service levels; there is no commensurate obligation to exceed the service levels so there should be no entitlement to additional payment. Indeed, it could be argued that the user actually wants 100 per cent service levels, but simply agrees to a lower percentage to be realistic. Equally, it could be said that the provider will always agree to a service level percentage with a margin of error so should be expected to exceed it in practice. The point behind these arguments is that the contracted service level is what the user has stated is its business requirement: over-performance may be entirely redundant and bring it no benefit at all.
- It follows that service debits are a crude way of incentivising the provider. A variation on the theme where over-performance in one month is allowed to be carried forward to cancel out under-performance in the next one (thus reducing the provider's exposure to service credits rather than actually entitling it to bonuses) is more palatable but may allow the provider to get away with poor performance by overcompensating while not actually providing any benefit to the user.

Table 2.7 Types of loss

Types of loss	Comment
Cost of replacing the service	The least controversial type of loss: this covers the cost of the user self-providing missing services and, on termination, the costs of transferring to another service provider (including any incremental increase in charges) or taking the services back in house. Consultancy and legal costs would also usually be included
Wasted costs caused by delayed implementation of services at sites or inability to relocate services on time	If the user is unable to decommission existing equipment or vacate premises, it may have to pay extra licence fees or accommodation charges
Wasted promotional costs, e.g. for brochures or media campaigns	This could apply for example where the implementation of a call centre for a new direct sale insurance product is delayed
Liability incurred to other members of the group or to customers dependent on the services	This would cover the kind of back-to-back arrangement mentioned in respect of user group structures as well as service credits and the like incurred by the user to its own customers where it onward provides the services
Failure to achieve anticipated savings	It may be that the reason for the outsourcing was to achieve costs savings and efficiency, and that these are not realised
Loss of revenue and profit	This would be money the user would have earned from its customers on contracts dependent on the services
Cost of money	This would apply, for example, on the outsourcing of billing and collection services where late billing led to the user receiving money due from its customers later than it should and incurred financing costs

- The key therefore is measuring business benefit to the user of overperformance by the provider and rewarding the provider appropriately for this. Clearly, it may be difficult to do this unless there is a clear and measurable link between what the provider does and the impact on the user's business. An example of this could be the running of a call centre that allows the user's customers to take out insurance over the phone. If the provider can increase the number of calls it handles, this will lead to a measurable increase in business for the user and the parties can decide how to share this.

- Business benefit may involve not increasing revenue for the user but rather cutting costs. If the provider is able to maintain service standards while reducing its overheads, the parties may agree that the user will share in part of this by way of a reduction in its charges.

2.5.9 Communication and disputes

As with any long-term contract, the outsourcing services agreement should set out the means by which the parties will communicate. These communications will range from the formal service of notices on each other to day-to-day liaison and decision making. One critical issue to address is who is to have authority to bind the parties and how decisions are to be recorded. A common cause of disputes is where the parties believe that something has been agreed but the relevant meeting was not minuted or conversation confirmed in writing.

An overriding issue is that touched on above in relation to the cultural issues surrounding defining service levels. The skills required to manage an outsourcing service are not the same as those required to actually deliver those services. Users commonly underestimate the investment they will need to put into managing the outsourcing contract. Worse, some users assume that all responsibility now rests with the provider. The user must retain strategic control over the services and the underlying technological architecture, so that it can be sure that the services fit its business needs and that it has the skills to change providers if need be.

Communications between the parties can be analysed as falling into the classes described below.

Day-to-day conversations

At an operational level, there will be constant communication between the parties, in conversations, e-mails, faxes and letters. As noted above, the parties must be able to distinguish between low level communications and those that may bind or commit either of them – for example where a member of the user's staff agrees to allow some uncontracted downtime, which affects the availability figures of the system. The contract cannot legislate for all of this and the parties must educate their own staff as to the disciplines to follow.

Representatives

The parties will generally appoint various representatives, such as account managers, with particular roles and responsibilities. The contract should identify these roles and responsibilities and how changes to the holders of these roles will take place. The user may insist on terms to ensure a reasonable degree of continuity of the provider's key staff and some say in the appointment of replacements; the provider will resist too much control by the user of the disposition of its staff.

Regular meetings

It is good practice to have regular meetings with a set agenda to review progress of projects and the provision of services and any issues that may have arisen. These are generally monthly although they may be more frequent during a critical roll-out, for example. The contract should specify the procedure for holding meetings, who should attend and how the decisions are to be recorded. Any unresolved issues may be escalated (see below).

Review and forecasting meetings

Most contracts provide for at least annual review meetings to look at the bigger picture of the services and the parties' relationship. This may involve looking at the performance of the services as a whole, including a user satisfaction survey, and may also involve the consideration of a benchmarking report (see paragraph 2.5.10). Looking forward, it may also be an opportunity for the parties to anticipate any major developments in the year ahead in terms of business levels or new services.

Technology improvements

A common complaint from users is that in outsourcing to an expert provider, they expected to receive the benefits of improvements in technology but that these have not been forthcoming. Realistically, unless the provider can see some benefit to itself (for example by being able to sell new services) it is unlikely to be as proactive in this respect as the user may have assumed. There are several ways of overcoming this. The user may specify that the parties will have a quarterly meeting (say) at which technology changes and new services will be discussed and may insist that the provider submits a report in advance of that meeting. It may also wish to be included in any user forum that the provider runs for its major customers to notify them of upcoming plans and pilot schemes, so that the user has a chance to participate in these. As noted above, the parties should agree an overall technology architecture or strategy to ensure that the provider does not, for example, take the user down a proprietary technology route that would prevent it from changing suppliers.

Audit rights

The user will want (and may be required by its regulator) to have rights to audit compliance with the agreement. The contract should set out these rights, including rights of access to information, premises and staff of the provider (and its subcontractors). The audit may be limited to checking financial information or compliance with security or data protection requirements, or may go further and allow full access to the books and data of the provider. The provider will wish to limit this access as far as possible, not least to protect its proprietary information and the data of its other customers.

Dispute escalation

The parties will want to avoid ending up in court if they can avoid it, as this usually will be a precursor to the breakdown of the outsourcing. The contract should not seek to block the user's right to go to court if it chooses, but generally it will contain two sets of alternative routes:

- *Internal escalation*: through increasingly senior levels of management. Sometimes the fact that managing directors or CEOs are about to be troubled by a relatively minor dispute can be sufficient spur to their subordinates to resolve the issue. However this is organised, the contract should spell out the process, clearly identifying the respective management layers to be involved and the timescales for escalation, so that neither party can stall it.
- *External help*: for purely factual disputes, for example over valuations, the parties may appoint an independent expert to rule on the matter. This can be a useful way of preventing a dispute from going any further. The contract should specify which disputes can be referred in this way and the procedure and timescale for doing so, as well as how the expert is to be appointed and paid for. If the parties cannot agree on an expert, it is common for the matter to be referred to the president for the time being of the relevant professional body for that person to select an expert. Failing agreement by an expert, the main alternatives to court action are the various forms of alternative dispute resolution, such as mediation via a recognised mediation body or arbitration. Mediation may be quicker and cheaper than arbitration or court proceedings, and can be completely confidential, although it does not guarantee a binding resolution to the problem. Arbitration may be as lengthy and costly as litigation, but may be useful in international cases and does give more flexibility and confidentiality.

2.5.10 Value for money

Even if the services remained constant for the duration of the outsourcing services agreement, it is unlikely that the parties will agree to a long-term, fixed-price deal. Instead, they will want to reflect the increases or decreases in the provider's overheads as well as market pressures. The principal methods of doing this are summarised below.

Indexation

The principle is simple: linking the charges to an external independent index. There are some drafting issues to be addressed (such as the fact that most indices are actually expressed as absolutes, not percentages, percentage *change* over the relevant period being the required figure). In addition, the parties must select the relevant index. The most common indices used are those relating to retail prices. However, the RPI (in the UK) may bear no relation to the provider's underlying costs. The provider may therefore wish to specify a labour index for specialist technology staff or a specialist index for some raw material (such as paper for a printing contract) or even a range of indices for different parts of its costs, or a composite index.

Negative indexation

Some of the provider's costs (such as bandwidth charges) may decrease over time, so a positive index may not be appropriate. Alternatively, the user may apply a negative index as a way of making the provider more efficient and as a crude way of sharing the efficiency savings.

Benchmarking

The details of benchmarking are dealt with in Chapter 8. Again, the principle is simple: to compare the services being provided, or some element of them, with what is available in the market. This usually involves trying to compare like with like, to see if the provider's charges are in keeping with what alternative providers would charge for similar services in similar circumstances. Irrespective of how feasible (and expensive) it may be to carry out a comparative analysis, the contract must specify the following:

- How benchmarking is to be instigated – for example, can either party start the process or just the user, and in either event, how frequently it is to be carried out?
- Assuming that an independent benchmarking expert is to be used, the process for appointing the expert. Usually, the parties will pre-agree who this will be or have an approved list. It should be noted that each benchmarking company uses different methodologies and processes, so it is important to draft a clause that the chosen expert can actually follow. It can be helpful to clear the clause with the intended expert before the contract is signed: it would be awkward if the clause, when relied on, was unworkable in practice.
- The process for briefing the benchmarking expert, the criteria to be assessed and the timescales for receiving the expert's report.
- Crucially, what is to be done to implement the report. This is unlikely to specify a precise change to the charges that the parties can simply adopt.

Instead, the report is likely to state that the charges are in a particular percentile of the market and the parties will then need to agree any changes – that is, there will be a measure of negotiation. As noted earlier, an agreement to agree is generally unenforceable so the contract will need to set out how the parties are to agree any changes and what is to happen if there is a deadlock (see e.g. *Cable & Wireless plc* v. *IBM United Kingdom Limited* [2003] All ER(D) 391).

2.5.11   Re-tendering and exit

Outsourcing services agreements almost inevitably contain provisions that are to apply on termination, but neglect to think backwards from the point of termination to the decision the user (as it usually is) has to take about whether to terminate. If the user is unable to assess whether there are any realistic alternatives to the provider, it may be forced either to renew the existing contract or to put up with substandard services. Although disentangling an outsourcing is a complex process, the user must at least have the option to do so, even if only to use it as a threat to force a renegotiation. Similarly, if the user cannot realistically go to the market with a proposition to alternative service providers, it will not receive any interest, let alone bids. Service providers do not like to be used as stalking horses against a sitting incumbent without a realistic prospect of winning the business – the cost and effort of making a bid are prohibitive.

All this means that long before the user presses the button to terminate the services agreement, it must be able to find out if there are alternatives in the market and the likely cost of moving so it can decide whether to proceed. This means that the user will need to re-tender the services, either informally (to avoid the provider finding out at this stage) or publicly. The user must be able to give alternative service providers all the same information about the existing operation and services as applied on the initial outsourcing, at least where the new provider is to be expected to inherit the assets and services (the provisions of the contract permitting this are dealt with below).

The keys to this are timing and information. If a typical outsourcing takes a year to negotiate, there is little point in the user starting the re-tendering process a month before the existing contract is to end. There are two points that arise from this:

- The user should avoid entering into a fixed-term contract – it is far better to have the flexibility of a rolling notice period at the end of the minimum term rather than risk hitting a deadline date before the user is ready. In these circumstances, the user would be totally dependent on the existing provider agreeing to extend the contract – and have no bargaining position as to the charges.

- If the contract does provide for a notice period at the end of its term or on early termination, the user cannot assume that this can be used for agreeing the alternative contract – once the termination notice has been served, the user is under severe time pressure as the services will simply cease at the expiration of the notice. The user should therefore have agreed the alternative contract, in an ideal world, before the termination notice is served.

Assuming therefore that the user does begin the re-tendering process early enough, it will need to provide full information to the potential new service provider about the assets, services and staff that may transfer. This information is of course now in the hands of the provider, so the services agreement should give the user the right to receive this information. The user will not want to flag up to the provider what it is considering, so the contract should specify that this information should be provided on a regular basis rather than on request.

Beyond this, the services agreement must inevitably terminate: it is simply a question of when this happens and the circumstances applying at the time. The issue of termination at the end of an agreed term is dealt with above. In addition, as with most contracts, an outsourcing agreement will have two principal triggers for termination: material breach and the financial difficulties of the other party. However, these require some thought:

- The usual trigger for termination for breach is that the breach must be material and either irremediable or not remedied within a specified period (usually 30 days or so). In order to avoid disputes, the user should consider setting out a non-exhaustive list of breaches that are agreed to be material. One way of doing this is to link the clause to the service levels and provide that a certain level of failure or aggregate amount of service credits will amount to a material breach.
- There have been well publicised examples of service providers going into liquidation in the US or suffering similar problems. A termination clause that only allows for termination (or the exercise of step-in rights) when the provider is already out of business will be too late in the context of service provision and it should also include events that may indicate forthcoming problems, such as a major disposal or refinancing or a reduction in credit rating.

Other termination events that the user may wish to consider providing for include those listed below.

Convenience

On a long-term deal, the user may want the ability to break the agreement prior to the end of the agreed term. Generally, the provider's own revenue profile will lead to it refusing to allow such a termination within the first year or so of the start of the agreement. Any termination thereafter, before the end of the agreed term, will lead to the payment by the user of a termination charge. This should of course be less than the charges would have been for the remainder of the term (or there is no point in terminating) but the provider will seek to recover its unamortised costs and lost profits, either as a pre-agreed sum or (more likely) by way of a calculation carried out at the time. The user needs to understand the provider's cost model to work out the extent to which the charges or calculation are justified.

Change of control

If the provider is taken over by another company, the user may wish to terminate – or at least to threaten to do so, in order to receive some reassurance. The provider will (rightly) not see this as being a breach of contract at all and resist its inclusion. A compromise may be to allow termination if the provider is taken over by a competitor of the user.

Loss of licence or other approval

If the user requires that the provider has a certain accreditation or licence or approval (for example, a telecoms licence or financial services accreditation) and this is lost and not replaced, the user may again want to have a right to terminate.

Other events

There may be events that are particular to the contract or the parties to it that should be included.

The termination clause should allow the user as much flexibility as possible. It may allow for partial termination, for example termination of a severable part of the services or their provision to a particular location. The user should take care to set out the services and the charges in such a way as to allow this to be done easily. The provider will want to balance such rights against its overall business case for the services – it may be uneconomic to allow partial termination.

Similarly, the user should not be obliged to terminate the contract forthwith, as contracts usually provide. An outsourcing cannot of course simply be switched off, for all the reasons set out above about the problems of re-tendering. The user should be able to specify the length of the notice period (although the provider will want to put some outside limit on this). The timescale for notice should then dovetail into the exit provisions.

The exit provisions should cover the specific rights the user will require on termination:

- the continued provision of the services during the notice period and for any run-off period;
- the right to approach key members of the provider's staff (even if TUPE does not apply to them) and to offer them jobs, with either the user or a new provider;
- restrictions on the provider's ability to manipulate the undertaking that may come across to the new provider or the user, for example by deploying out its best staff and deploying in less talented individuals or changing their terms of employment;
- TUPE-related information and indemnities;
- to require the migration of data and systems and the provision of information about them;
- to require the assignment or novation of key contracts;
- an option to purchase equipment on an agreed basis;
- to require ongoing licences of the provider's IPR (extending to use by the successor provider);
- to require the delivery of documentation, such as up-to-date operational procedures and system configuration information;
- to have access to premises to retrieve equipment and data (usually as a last resort);
- to have general co-operation and assistance, for example attendance by provider personnel at meetings with the next service provider.

These rights will apply no matter what the cause of termination is, but the provider will rightly seek to limit them where it is not in breach and where there could be a knock-on effect on the rest of its business. Where the provider is in breach, the user will expect to have these rights free of charge (other than the provision of the services); otherwise the parties will agree in the contract how exit costs are to be allocated. The user should take care to understand the provider's cost basis – not least if the provider has already amortised these costs and included them in the charges.

As with service changes, the contract cannot spell out the details of how exit is to be managed; nor can this be left to be agreed at the time. The contract should therefore oblige the provider to produce a draft exit plan for consideration and agreement within a reasonable time and process for agreeing it. The plan should be kept under review and tested from time to time. Since 11 September 2001 and recent new financial services regimes being introduced in the aftermath of Enron, users (and particularly financial services companies) are very concerned to deal with business continuity provisions (see e.g. *What Contingency Planning Should You Demand as Part of Outsourcing Contracts?* by Nick Simms of Cornwood Consulting at www.cornwood.co.uk/articles.htm). Exit, of course, is a key risk event for a business and must fit in with the user's business continuity requirements.

In none of this have the rights of the provider to terminate been mentioned. In practice, these will be limited to circumstances of continued non-payment (late payment can be addressed by charging interest) and the financial difficulties of the user.

2.6 CONCLUSIONS

Properly considered and drafted agreements are an essential prerequisite to a successful outsourcing relationship. Key issues are:

- avoiding the kitchen sink approach to drafting: contracts that amount to hundreds of pages and attempt to pre-empt all eventualities end up being self-defeating and unusable in practice;
- facing up to unpalatable issues and addressing them square on in the contract; these include how disputes are to be dealt with and risks allocated;
- supporting the relationship by building a flexible framework rather than a contractual straightjacket.

CHAPTER 3

Information systems outsourcing

Mark Lewis and Alison Welterveden

3.1 INTRODUCTION

Information systems (IS) functions that are now outsourced typically include one or more of the following:

- data centre;
- voice and data networks;
- communications;
- applications development;
- applications support and maintenance;
- desktop;
- project management;
- contract and vendor management;
- help desk and call centre;
- technology-related training; and
- disaster recovery/business continuity.

The above list is not exhaustive, but it does contain the most frequently outsourced IS functions. It gives us a chance to emphasise that, however an IS function may be characterised in a request for proposal (RFP) or elsewhere, the detailed scope of the function to be outsourced *must* be specified, and as early as possible in the transaction.

For example, the description of an outsourcing as a desktop deal can, and often does, mean a number of different things to different organisations. Recently announced desktop deals have each covered one or more of the following functions: networking services; PC supply under call-off arrangements; remote and on-site helpdesk functions; technology refreshment of the desktop environment; asset management; on-site hardware and peripheral maintenance; and procurement and supply services. That a shorthand description of one kind of IS outsourcing transaction can embrace such a wide variety of IS functions makes it all the more essential to specify the scope of services for the transaction, irrespective of the shorthand description given to it.

While the objectives of the parties to any outsourcing contract, especially those of the customer and supplier, should be aligned, their commercial and legal interests are ultimately different. Contracts can be customer friendly or supplier friendly to varying degrees. The better, more enduring, contracts are likely to hold a reasonable balance between these interests. But for simplicity, our precedent material is drafted with a customer bias, although we do try to maintain a reasonable commercial balance where possible. Those wishing to use our precedents for the benefit of suppliers should adapt them accordingly.

3.2 TYPICAL INFORMATION SYSTEMS OUTSOURCING CONTRACT TERMS

Before moving on, it may be useful to provide a list of the usual clause and schedule headings in a typical IS outsourcing contract. This will not only show just how many provisions of an IS outsourcing contract are common to other kinds of outsourcing, but will also put in context the areas we have selected as specific to IS outsourcing.

3.2.1 Clauses

1. Definitions and interpretation
2. Provision of the services
3. Term
4. Extension of term
5. Transitional arrangements
6. Miscellaneous software
7. Customer assets managed by supplier
8. Customer proprietary software
9. Novated agreements
10. Agreements retained by customer
11. Supplier software and third party applications
12. Standards, service levels and service credits
13. Service charges and invoicing
14. Taxes
15. Regulatory issues
16. Subcontractors
17. Relationship with customer's retained technology functions
18. Liability
19. Parent company/performance guarantee
20. Contract change management procedures
21. Relationship and project meetings
22. Data protection and privacy
23. Security requirements
24. Disaster recovery services

25. Insurance
26. Exit management
27. Customer's facilities regulations
28. Customer's contract manager
29. Supplier's personnel
30. Customer's transferred employees
31. Transferred employees' benefits and taxes
32. Intellectual property rights
33. Customer data
34. Confidentiality
35. Publicity and trade marks
36. Intellectual property rights indemnity
37. Termination
38. Break option
39. General warranties
40. Exclusion of warranties
41. Additional services
42. Audit access
43. Transfer and assignment
44. Communications
45. Severability
46. Force majeure
47. Waiver
48. Dispute resolution procedure
49. Law and jurisdiction
50. Entire agreement
51. Costs and expenses
52. Further assurances
53. Third party rights

3.2.2 Schedules

1. Third party applications software
2. Third party systems software
3. Customer proprietary software
4. Supplier software
5. Customer assets managed by supplier
6. Third party equipment
7. Network services supplier equipment
8. Novated agreements
9. Agreements retained by customer
10. The services
11. Technology projects to be taken over by supplier
12. Service levels and measurement

13. Service reporting
14. Service credits
15. Continuous improvement/technology refresh
16. Leases, licences and contracts
17. Disaster recovery/business continuity services
18. Transition and integration
19. Contract change control procedures
20. Charging method and rates
21. Policies, standards and procedures
22. Security
23. Parent company/performance guarantees
24. Employees in key positions
25. Affected customer employees
26. Employment arrangements for customer employees and secondees
27. Non-disclosure agreement
28. Exit management
29. Principal subcontractors
30. Definitions

3.3 TERM

Underlying the decision about the length of term are a number of factors, most of them strategic. A key factor is whether the customer and supplier will realise their respective financial returns and other benefits from the IS outsourcing over the proposed term. A view widely held by both customers and suppliers is that, because IS outsourcing contracts are difficult to enter into and exit and costs need to be amortised, such contracts must necessarily be long term. Accordingly, there are still a good number of 10-year outsourcing deals signed. But there are also a number of countervailing factors that have led to an increase in shorter-term contracts.

1. The customer's business and business drivers change over time. Long-term contracts can often be inflexible, and using change control as a way of effecting the necessary changes to the contract can be very costly.
2. Customers realise that it may not be in their best interests to enter into outsourcing contracts that will run beyond the life expectancy of the customer's technology. New technologies will become available during the term of the outsourcing contract. Planning for and negotiating with the supplier effective IS refreshment duties is not always easy.
3. Customer experience, supported by widely held industry views, is that, in the first two to three years of its life, a well negotiated IS outsourcing contract should deliver value for money when benchmarked against com-

parable transactions. But beyond that, given the factor referred to in (2) above and other trends, the three-year-plus outsourcing contract is less likely to continue to deliver value for money. There are, of course, other contractual mechanisms that can be used to address this issue, chiefly benchmarking. As with technology refreshment provisions, benchmarking – especially where it could result in contractually enforceable obligations to reduce the price of the outsourcing – is a contentious point for many suppliers. So it is not always easy to negotiate contractually enforceable benchmarking provisions into an outsourcing contract.

4. Some industry analysts have identified a 'two-year itch' in the life cycle of technology outsourcing deals. This is when a number of customers start to become dissatisfied with their deals and press for changes to their contracts.

5. It is recognised as a fact of life that there is a tendency for suppliers to lose interest in long-term outsourcing deals in the second half of, or towards the end of, the term.

There are, of course, other factors that come into play. But the combined effect of those listed above and other relevant factors is that many outsourcing advisers tend now to recommend three- to five-year terms for IS outsourcing.

So, while the standard provisions for the term of an outsourcing contract are, as a matter of contract language, short and straightforward, there are a number of important strategic decisions that underlie them.

3.4   INTELLECTUAL PROPERTY RIGHTS

While intellectual property rights (IPR) are, to a greater or lesser degree, important in all outsourcing deals, they are absolutely critical in IS outsourcing. All of those systems and the information and data they process are, with very few exceptions, protected by IPR – most commonly copyright – frequently belonging to third parties.

Without any doubt, the most common – and potentially the most difficult – IPR issue in IS outsourcing arises from the customer's use of third party software.

The customer has licences to use third party computer programs, whether operating system, applications or utilities (and including databases) that need to be transferred to, or at the very least used by, the outsourcing supplier. Unless the customer has been far-sighted enough to have agreed with third party software licensors specific rights for the customer to transfer that software to the outsourcing supplier, or allow the supplier to use that software as a sub-licensee, the customer cannot transfer, or sub-license the use of, the software. To do so without the licensor's consent would amount to an infringement of the licensor's IPR.

Most software licences now contain, as a minimum, standard terms that:

- prohibit the transfer of the software, either in object or source code, and the associated user documentation to anyone outside the licensee's organisation. (This term is usually wide enough to catch use by third parties (e.g. external consultants or software engineers) even for the customer's own internal business purposes);
- specifically restrict the use of the software to the customer's internal business purposes;
- expressly prohibit the customer's use of the software to provide data processing or outsourced services to third parties;
- impose confidentiality obligations on the customer so as to prevent the customer disclosing the software or associated documentation to third parties.

So unless the customer has the licensor's consent to transfer the licensor's software to an outsourcing supplier or to allow the supplier to use that software, the customer will also be in breach – and almost certainly material breach – of the third party licence terms by doing so.

The software licensor's legal remedies for breach of its IPR *and* licence terms will include:

- the right, at the discretion of the courts, to obtain a court order preventing the transfer of the software or use by the outsourcing supplier, against both the customer/licensee and the outsourcing supplier;
- damages for infringement of its IPR, mainly copyright, both from the outsourcing customer/licensee and from the outsourcing supplier;
- damages for breaches of the terms of its software licences from the outsourcing customer/licensee;
- the right as against the customer/licensee to terminate the software licences concerned and related contracts (e.g. for software support) for material breach.

This is one of the most critical legal issues – if not *the* most critical legal issue – in IS outsourcing, because the inability to transfer third party software and databases containing vital customer data could effectively kill the outsourcing deal.

If approached by the customer or supplier, third party software licensors are almost always willing to give their consent, modify the terms of their licences, or grant new licences, to enable the customer to transfer the software to the outsourcing supplier or all the supplier's staff to use the software. But the consent comes at a cost – sometimes a considerable cost. This is one of potential hidden costs of IS outsourcing.

For all the above reasons, it is vital that both customer and supplier undertake a complete and accurate audit (i.e. due diligence) of the networks, systems, applications and other technology assets that are to transfer to the outsourcing supplier or be used by it to provide the outsourced services. We say more about due diligence below.

In case there is any doubt that this is a real – as opposed to a theoretical legal – issue, all involved in IS outsourcing should bear in mind that, over the years, disputes have arisen in just this kind of case, and that these disputes have resulted in very costly litigation, mainly in the US, but also in the UK.

The most effective way of identifying third party IPR issues is, accordingly, to initiate a full due diligence exercise as early as possible in the outsourcing project.

There are, of course, other important IPR issues that arise. These include the way in which customer-owned IPR in its technology assets (e.g. the customer's proprietary software) are dealt with, and the need for the customer to have licences to use third party IPR after termination of the outsourcing contract. We shall deal with these briefly in sections 3.14 and 3.15 on termination and exit management.

3.5   TRANSFER OF THIRD PARTY SOFTWARE AND RELATED CONTRACTS

From a legal perspective, the fullest and most effective form of transfer is novation. Note that, technically, the legal effect of novation is *not* the continuation of the arrangement as is, simply replacing the customer with the supplier. It is the termination of an existing legal arrangement between customer and third party and the start of a *new* arrangement – albeit on the same terms – between the supplier and the third party. So the question as to who, as between the customer and supplier, remains responsible for historic liabilities and other outstanding issues in relation to the novated contracts is an important one. And the customer and supplier must agree it beforehand.

In this section, we consider the legal mechanics of transferring to the supplier potentially the most problematic of the technology assets and arrangements, namely third party software and related contracts.

The basic contract clause starts:

> The Supplier acknowledges that, in respect of the Third Party Software,[1] the Supplier has obtained, with effect from the Commencement Date, all the consents, licences and permissions necessary to operate the Third Party Software and that the Supplier shall continue to have, for the duration of this Agreement and for such time after the expiry or termination of this Agreement as is necessary for the proper performance of its obligations under this Agreement, all the consents, licences and permissions necessary to operate the Third Party Software.

Where such consents, licences and permissions *can* be obtained before commencement of the outsourced service, the customer and supplier should, of course, do so. This kind of provision is similar to warranties that often appear under general or specific warranty clauses in the contract. Clearly, if the general warranties cover these specific cases adequately, there should be no need for the supplier to offer the second of the two acknowledgements contained in the preceding clause.

> The Supplier shall, in respect of the Third Party Software and such consents, licences and permissions, fulfil all of the obligations and liabilities (which, for the avoidance of doubt, includes payment obligations) which arise on and after the Commencement Date[2] in respect of the Third Party Software and otherwise in respect of the consents, licences and permissions referred to in clause [preceding subsection].

Assuming that the relevant licences have been transferred by novation to the supplier, the supplier will in the ordinary course assume the payment obligations under those licences. But there may also be additional payments required by the third party software vendors. The parties need to agree how to allocate such payments between supplier and customer. And, as between the customer and supplier, the continuing payment obligations of the supplier and such allocation need to be reflected in the contract. In the preceding clause, the supplier assumes the payment obligations, both under the transferred licences and in connection with the transfers themselves, i.e. the costs of obtaining the consents, licences and permission referred to:

> The Customer warrants that, in respect of the Third Party Software, it has fulfilled all of the obligations and liabilities that arose before the Commencement Date.

As the supplier will usually take over the obligations and liabilities in relation to third party software after the commencement date, the customer will usually warrant that it has fulfilled all of those obligations and liabilities up to that date.

> The Supplier shall indemnify the Customer and keep the Customer indemnified against all claims, demands, actions, costs, expenses (including, but not limited to, reasonable legal costs and disbursements on a full indemnity basis), loss and damages arising from or incurred in connection with the Third Party Software in respect of the period starting on, and continuing after, the Commencement Date.

As the supplier will in all respects be in control of the third party software after the commencement date, the customer will want to have the assurance that, if there are any problems that arise after that date, the supplier will be legally responsible for them. It is usual for the customer to seek an indemnity of the kind set out above. Often, the supplier will seek a counter-indemnity from the customer in relation to the fulfilment of the customer's obligations in relation to the third party software up to the commencement date.

The Customer shall use all reasonable endeavours to provide such assistance as may reasonably be required by the Supplier to enable the Supplier to obtain such consents, licences and permissions as the Supplier may require in respect of the Third Party Software, so that the Supplier may use that Third Party Software in the manner contemplated by this Agreement without infringing the rights (including, but not limited to, the intellectual property rights) of any third party.

As the customer will have the primary relationship with third party software vendors and support service suppliers and will be a party to the agreements that will need to be transferred to the outsourcing supplier, it would be reasonable to expect the customer to help to effect that transfer and the completion of the necessary documentation. Here, the customer agrees to use reasonable, rather than best, endeavours to assist in the process. The customer's obligations are further qualified by the need for the supplier's requests for help to be reasonable.

The question that is most frequently asked is: what happens if the parties are unable, before the commencement date of the outsourcing, to get the third party software vendor's consent to the transfer of that vendor's software or a novation of the software licence or other contact?

There are a number of options, including the following.

1. The customer and supplier can agree to defer the commencement date of the outsourcing.
2. The customer and supplier can agree not to transfer the software licences concerned.
3. If neither options (1) nor (2) are feasible, the customer and supplier can agree effectively to defer the transfer of the affected licences. This would mean, in some cases, those of the customer's staff who usually operate the third party vendor's software remaining on the customer's payroll after the commencement of the outsourcing contract, until that vendor's consent to the transfer or the novation is obtained. The staff would continue to operate the third party software as they had always done. The customer would continue to be a party to the licence concerned, until that time. Sometimes, the parties agree that the supplier will be responsible for such staff, and hence for the provision of the full outsourced technology service, even before the third party software is transferred. This would depend on the supplier effectively supervising the staff concerned, but without taking control of the operation of the third party software. These are difficult arrangements to put in place and to work under. At all times the customer and supplier must ensure that the customer complies fully with the terms of the third party software licence concerned and that the supplier does nothing to infringe the third party's rights or put the customer in jeopardy under the terms of the licence. Also, from an operational viewpoint, anything less than a complete transfer of the customer's technology assets and arrangements to the outsourcing supplier is likely to be problematic.

4. As regards third party arrangements other than software licences, e.g. third party support contracts, the customer and supplier might have been unable to obtain that third party's consent to the transfer of the arrangements. If it is open to them to do so, they could agree that the customer will remain a party to the third party contract, but that the supplier will manage that contract for the customer until such time as the third party consents to the transfer. These arrangements, too, can be difficult, as many third party contracts will contain standard provisions preventing or restricting the customer's ability to assign, transfer or otherwise dispose of its rights under that contract. Also, there are often confidentiality obligations imposed on the parties to such arrangements. These could also pose difficulties for the management option described here.

The Customer and Supplier shall use all reasonable endeavours to obtain such consents, novations, licences and permissions as would enable the Supplier to take over the Affected Agreements [those contracts in relation to which the parties have been unable to obtain third party consent to their transfer, whether by novation, or by the supplier managing or operating those arrangements for the customer] as soon as practicable after the commencement date. Until such time as:

the Supplier can lawfully take over, and the Customer can lawfully agree to have the Supplier take over, the operations under the Affected Agreements; or

such Affected Agreements have become Novated Agreements [the term covering those arrangements in relation to which the parties have obtained third party consent to novation for the purposes of the outsourcing]

the Affected Agreements shall continue in accordance with their terms as at the Commencement Date. If the Customer and Supplier are unable to obtain such consents, novations, licences and permissions, they shall negotiate in good faith alternative arrangements in respect of the Affected Agreements and the Third Party Software that reflect as closely as possible the objectives of this Agreement, and these shall be documented in accordance with the Change Control Procedure [the procedure regulated by the change control clause and schedule(s)].

It would, at this point, be open to the parties to agree other options, as described above, and to reflect those in the outsourcing contract. In the event of the parties being unable to obtain third party consent, this clause provides for negotiation of the necessary changes to the contract through the change control mechanism.

Frequently, the IS supplier will have its own corporate relationship with the third party software vendor and will offer to use that relationship to obtain whatever consents, licences and permission might be needed to effect the transfer of that software to the supplier. The extent to which this offer might displace the customer's obligations will vary from deal to deal. But the following clause will be useful in such cases, if the customer accepts that it (as opposed to the supplier) will approach third party vendors for such consents, licences or permission.

The Supplier shall provide all assistance as may be reasonably required by the Customer to enable the Customer to obtain such consents, novations, licences and permissions so that the Supplier may use the Third Party Software in the manner contemplated by this Agreement without infringing the rights (including, but not limited to, the intellectual property rights) of any third party.

3.6 THE INFORMATION SYSTEMS SERVICES

Typically, the provision in the main body of the IS outsourcing contract that obliges the supplier to deliver the outsourced services is short. The real detail of the technology service requirement is always contained in one or more technical schedules annexed to the contract.

For reasons that have been stated in Chapter 2 (The outsourcing contract), it is essential to capture all of the services to be provided by the supplier under the outsourcing arrangements. For example, having identified the main functions to be outsourced, say, data centre operations, the customer should ask at least the following questions.

1. What other, ancillary, services am I going to need from the supplier?
2. Who will be providing the disaster recovery/business continuity service?
3. Who will be providing the service that links my data centre to my desktop and other technology environments?
4. How do I expect the supplier to interact with my in-house technology function and other third party service providers?
5. What additional services or duties should the main outsourcing supplier have, recognising my need that it should work effectively with my in-house and external technology suppliers?
6. Are there any other services that I am likely to need in the future that I would like to see covered by the provisions of this outsourcing deal and, if so, on what terms?

The answers to these and other questions should result in the outsourcing contract listing, in addition to the core IS to be outsourced, a number of other related or ancillary services and obligations. From the customer's perspective, there could be a problem if the outsourcing contract does not include all of these services and obligations within its scope. Either the supplier might refuse – quite reasonably – to provide them, or the parties will have to use the contractual change control mechanism to bring some or all of these related or ancillary services within the scope. And the latter will almost always come at a cost.

A number of IS outsourcing contracts list additional services. These might include a list of specified services, or general categories or service that the supplier will undertake on the terms of the contract, if requested by the customer to do so. The advantages for both parties of listing additional services is that they can plan in advance to have them provided or to provide them, and (from the customer's viewpoint) that the charges or basis of charge for such services are known (because they are specified in the contract) and can be budgeted for accordingly.

Having identified and specified the services to be outsourced and certain other threshold issues (we say more about these below), the customer needs to establish which entities in its corporate structure will receive the outsourced services. It may be that there is one company in the customer group, e.g. the holding company or main operating company, that will take the services. Alternatively, there may be a number of group companies, some wholly-owned subsidiaries, some in which the customer has a minority interest and others that are even more loosely affiliated to the customer. It is essential that, as early as possible in the transaction, the customer identifies these entities and discloses its plans to the supplier. The plans may change, both before and after signature of the contract. But the supplier needs to be able to grasp the scope of distribution of the outsourced services.

A related issue is where the IS services are to be provided. In a multinational corporation, some sites will be situated in locations in which outsourcing could be difficult or costly or both, e.g. because of value added or other service taxes, the complexity of local labour and employment rules and regulatory restrictions, such as those applying to outsourcing in the financial services sector.

Similarly, where corporate group management is decentralised, it may be difficult for the group entity driving the technology outsourcing to require or even persuade local subsidiaries to take the outsourced service. There are commercial and legal implications in such cases: there is a trend for companies to put in place relationship or framework contracts with outsourcing vendors. Typically, these contracts will provide for a centralised outsourced service to be provided to the holding company or principal operating vehicle, with provision to roll out the outsourced services to other group companies as and when they decide, or are persuaded, to take the services. Ideally, the relationship or framework agreement should contain a commercial and legal infrastructure that will enable group companies to adhere to the arrangements and the supplier to roll out the services, without having to negotiate a completely new contract, new charges or different bases of charge each time.

> The Customer shall, subject to and in accordance with this Agreement, perform its obligations with respect to the Services as expressly provided in this Agreement.

This clause recognises certain dependencies: performance by the supplier will, to varying degrees, depend upon the customer meeting its obligations. Accordingly, some suppliers insist on the customer undertaking to perform its obligations in relation to the outsourced services. However, it is important from the customer's viewpoint that its obligations are clearly and specifically set out in the contract – hence the wording 'as expressly provided in this Agreement'.

Without prejudice to clause [first subsection], the Supplier shall, during the Transition Period,[3] supply the Services in accordance with this Agreement, including but not limited to schedule [detailed arrangements for transition of services and integration of systems and customer data].

Not all IS outsourcing contracts differentiate between the services to be provided during a start-up, or transitional, phase and those fully developed services to be provided afterwards. But it is often worth making it clear in the contract that the transitional services might be very different – in scope, duration, level of service and possibly even in the charges – from the services to be provided after that phase. It is clear from this drafting that, while the transitional services may be different in the ways mentioned, they are otherwise subject to all the other provisions of the contract.

More generally, defining the scope of the services to be outsourced is the most fundamental step in the outsourcing process. As mentioned earlier in this chapter, the scope of the services to be outsourced will vary from deal to deal. In each case, the determining factor is whether the customer is proposing to outsource its data centre, networks, call centre and/or the other functions referred to above.

As specification of the IS services varies so much from outsourcing to outsourcing, it is not feasible to produce a range of specifications here. But we *are* including below extracts from various IS service specifications schedules to illustrate the approach and level of detail that is required.

3.6.1 Operations management

The Supplier shall perform all necessary operations management functions relating to planning, scheduling, organising, monitoring and controlling day-to-day operations in accordance with the Customer's Procedures Manual.

Note the reference to the customer's procedures manual – an operating manual produced, in this case, by the customer's IS department that serves as an essential reference point – both operationally and contractually – for defining the scope and content of the supplier's obligations in performing the specified IS services.

Note also that these service specifications are written in technical, but reasonably plain and understandable, English. It is common in technology contracts for the technical schedules to contain incomprehensible language – if it can be called language at all. Without seeing the rest of the contract(s) from which these specifications have been extracted, and without knowing the context in which they feature in the transaction, it is hard to make any sense of them here. But they are still, for the reasons given, intelligible. Accordingly, in the event of any dispute about their meaning, putting these specifications in context, there should be an excellent chance that the customer or supplier (or both) will be able to refer to what they had intended and agreed. This is one of the most important points about the drafting of technical schedules in IS outsourcing contracts: they must make sense to those coming to the transaction without having been closely involved in it. One of the reasons, of course, is that, almost invariably, the staff who negotiated and documented the contract on both buy and supply sides are no longer around when the contract has to be taken out, dusted down and interpreted.

3.6.2 Production control

The Supplier shall perform the following production control functions in accordance with the Customer's Procedures Manual:

maintain [ ] databases as required to reflect changes to the production environment;

investigate [ ] related incidents, develop and recommend refinements and revisions to the [ ] database and implement such refinements and revisions in accordance with the Customer's instructions from time to time;

maintain production library control; and

perform system maintenance functions as required, including, but not limited to, [ ] file allocation, creation/expansion and user file secure and deletion requests for the [ ] system.

Technical Support

Installation and configuration

The Supplier shall install, maintain, upgrade and troubleshoot (including, but not limited to, performance monitoring, tuning and problem investigation, diagnosis and rectification) all components of the Customer's Technology Infrastructure in accordance with the Customer's Procedures Manual.

The Supplier shall maintain the configuration of the software components of the Customer's Technology Infrastructure (including, but not limited to, in respect of environments, tables, parameter lists and macros associated with the operating systems, online and database sub-systems and those in-scope network components detailed in paragraph [ ] below).

Problem response services

The Supplier shall provide on-call support and problem response services for the Customer's Technology Infrastructure and shall be available 24 hours a day, 365/6 days a year to do so.

Production database support

In respect of production databases comprised in the Customer's Technology Infrastructure, the Supplier shall:

perform database administration and maintain data dictionaries;

monitor performance and tune for efficiency and performance;

perform free-space file validation for the [ ] systems;

investigate, diagnose and rectify problems, liasing with vendor technical support services as required; and

design and implement effective database backup and housekeeping procedures, having regard to input from the Customer's applications development teams.

Daily Operations

The Supplier shall, in accordance with the Customer's Procedures Manual (including, but not limited to, production schedules and work instructions contained in that manual), operate the Customer's applications (including, but not limited to, online and batch processing).

Online systems and batch processing

Such online and batch processing shall, include, but not be limited to:

the initiation and shut down of online applications in accordance with the Customer's Procedures Manual;

the execution of daily/weekly/monthly batch jobs in accordance with the Customer's Procedures Manual and the fulfilment of ad hoc run requests which shall be carried out in accordance with the service request procedure referred to in paragraph [   ] below;

the monitoring of online and batch job processing performance and results, and the troubleshooting, recovery from abnormal terminations of programs and re-running of batch jobs as necessary;

in accordance with the problem management procedures referred to in paragraph [   ] below, responses to and resolution of problems in accordance with Schedule [   ]; and

the execution and monitoring of all print jobs (including error handling, restarts, and re-runs). For the avoidance of doubt, the Supplier shall not, pursuant to this Agreement, be responsible for such of the physical aspects of such print jobs as are performed in accordance with the Customer's existing outsourcing arrangement for remote printing with [specified third party service provider] . . .

Note the exclusion of certain functions (here, certain aspects of the printing function). This is a good example of making it clear in some detail in the technical schedules what the supplier's obligations will and will not include.

the receipt, loading, creation and despatch of tapes in accordance with the Customer's Procedures Manual and the execution of any other ad hoc instructions from the Customer; and

the taking of data and program backups as required by the Customer's Procedures Manual.

The Supplier shall not be responsible for applications support of the Customer's Applications. However, the Supplier shall on request assist the Customer in resolving problems that arise in relation to the Customer's Applications, including, but not limited to, providing advice and guidance, restarting those Applications and other related applications, implementing fixes, running utilities and acting on Customer's reasonable instructions from appropriately authorised staff of the Customer.

It is clear from this exclusion that applications support is being provided by another supplier, either the customer's in-house technology department or a third party outsourcing supplier. Nevertheless, this specification recognises that the supplier will still be called on to resolve certain problems arising in relation to the applications. The purpose of imposing this service obligation on the supplier is to ensure that problems arising from the use of the customer's applications do not fall between two stools – here the IS department or third party applications support outsourcing supplier and the outsourcing supplier each saying: 'but it's not *my* responsibility'. This is also a good example of the customer recognising a dependency and taking steps to resolve any likely difficulty.

3.7   SERVICE LEVELS

Service levels are at the heart of the IS outsourcing contract, as they define the quality of the service to be provided by the supplier. 'Quality' is, of course, too wide a term. Specifically, the customer will want to be assured:

- that the services will be available when the customer needs them (i.e. with limited downtime or outage);
- that the services will be responsive and speedy;
- that they will be effective in supporting the customer's business operations;
- above all, that they will deliver the cost savings and other benefits promised by the supplier, as reflected in the technology outsourcing contract.

So there is a lot riding on the service levels. It is, therefore, essential that they are properly drawn up, effective as contractual obligations and that they will result in appropriate remedies when they are not maintained. Unfortunately, because service levels vary so much, there is little guidance to be had from any generally available published works as to how they should be constructed.

Unless the customer's IS department has produced internal service levels before the proposed outsourcing, the customer will need to start as early as possible in the life of the outsourcing to develop service levels with the supplier's support.

This is often a time consuming and difficult process, as few customers – even large companies – have the necessary in-house resource to undertake this task. Suppliers generally offer to help, but customers must appreciate that suppliers have their own concerns, interests and resource issues. So, with the best will in the world, the customer cannot, and should not, rely on the supplier's technical delivery or operations teams to write the customer's service levels. The solution for most customers is to engage IT consultants who have experience of identifying and constructing the right service levels for the proposed transaction.

But it is still essential for the customer to engage the supplier's technical delivery and operations teams in developing the service levels, because they need to understand what obligations the customer is proposing that the supplier takes on and plan accordingly. And the supplier's technical delivery and operations staff should be expected to participate in workshops and other meetings to discuss the customer's requirements and their feasibility.

It has become customary in the IS outsourcing industry to refer to the service level agreement (SLA). This goes back to the time when it was standard practice to sign an outsourcing contract and, separately, an associated SLA. The trend more recently has been to incorporate the service levels in the main outsourcing contract. This is not only good commercial and operational practice, but also good legal practice. The reason is simply that incorporating the service levels in the contract should ensure that the provisions themselves and the terms used in the service level schedules and in the main body of the contract are consistent. This should avoid any actual or potential inconsistency in interpretation and, accordingly, doubt about the meaning of the contract.

Service levels come in many different shapes and sizes, depending on the kind of IS outsourcing transaction concerned. Before looking at the narrower legal provisions governing service levels, it is worthwhile setting out what service levels are, by extracting from a typical outsourcing transaction some relatively simple service levels. The following extracts cover service availability, online response times, call/problem resolution and operational support services (the latter including disaster recovery):

SERVICE LEVELS AND SERVICE LEVEL MEASUREMENT

Service Availability

The actual level of service provided by the Supplier shall be measured by comparing the Actual Service Hours[4] during a calendar month with the Planned Service Hours for that month. For the purposes of this Schedule, the ratio Actual Service Hours to Planned Service Hours shall be called the 'Service Availability' and shall be defined as follows:

$$\text{Service Availability} = \frac{\text{Actual Service Hours}}{\text{Planned Service Hours}} \times 100\%$$

An Online Service is available if full access to the Service can be obtained from a computer terminal or workstation connected to the router interface (LAN to WAN).

The Supplier shall measure Service Availability. Data regarding downtime shall be collected automatically by the Supplier and reported to the Customer in accordance with Schedule [service reporting].

The Service Hours shall be as specified in paragraph [ ] of this Schedule for each of the Services.

Online response times

The Supplier shall monitor the Response Time for Online Services.

The Supplier shall not be excused from liability where it has failed to achieve the Response Time Service Level, because of batch overruns caused by its act, omission or default.

The language is quite simple and readily intelligible, when read with the defined terms referred to in the above paragraph.

Note also that it is sometimes appropriate even in the technical schedules to insert legal provisions – here the reference to the supplier not being excused liability in the case mentioned. This is acceptable, as long as both customer and supplier are comfortable that they have kept track of such provisions and are aware of their respective rights and obligations. This is acceptable, as long as both customer and supplier are comfortable that they have kept track of such provisions and are aware of their respective rights and obligations.

Reverting now to the call/problem resolution and operational support service levels:

> Call and problem resolution
>
> The Supplier shall resolve all problems reported by means of the Call Procedure in accordance with the priorities and resolution times outlined in Tables 3.1 and 3.2:

Turning now to the legal provisions in the main body of a typical technology outsourcing contract, the service levels clause would look something like this:

> The Supplier shall perform the Services in accordance with, or in excess of, the Service Levels as set out in Schedule [   ].

The service levels are, as illustrated above, specified in one or more schedules to the contract. Together, they should be defined as the 'Service Levels'.

> The Customer and Supplier agree that, in respect of any Service Levels applicable to the Priority Services[5] not fixed in Schedule [the service level schedule] at the Commencement Date, the Customer and Supplier shall use all reasonable endeavours to agree within three (3) months of that date service levels in respect of the Services for which service levels have not been agreed. The Customer and Supplier acknowledge that the concept of appropriate service levels applicable to all the Services is fundamental to this Agreement and each shall negotiate in good faith such service levels accordingly, which shall then become Service Levels for the purposes of this Agreement.

Table 3.1 Priorities and resolution times for problems

Priority	Business impact	Example	Resolution service level (during service hours)
Critical	Critical	Impacts on business performance	1 hour*
High	Potentially critical	Threatens to impact on business performance	4 Service Hours
Medium	Eventual	Causes disruption to efficient working	8 Service Hours
Low	Low	No business impact (e.g. change request)	5 Working Days

* Calls logged during Service Hours will be resolved within the Resolution Service Level even if resolution continues outside the Service Hours.

Table 3.2 Operational support services

Service element	Measure(s)	Service level	Critical service level
Online Services Service Availability	Online Services Service Availability production Systems from the Transfer Date	99.6%	95%
	(To include switches, but excluding Unscheduled Downtime caused by software errors which could not reasonably have been foreseen and for which no known fix or workaround then existed)	98%	94.5%
Backup and restore	Backup media to on-site	≤ 30 minutes	None
	Rate of bulk restore	Not less than average of 60 Gigabytes per hour	None
	Rate of ad hoc restore	Not less than average of 15 Gigabytes per hour	None
Disaster Recovery	Successful cutover to Disaster Recovery Site from the Primary Site	Not more than 1 hour	None
	Successful cutover back from Disaster Recovery Site to Primary Site restoring to all Users Service Availability of the System at then applicable Service Levels	Not more than 6 hours	None

It is not always possible to specify all service levels before the outsourcing contract is signed, so there needs to be a contractual procedure for the parties to agree appropriate service levels after signature. This is not, of course, ideal, as most service levels are, if not fundamental to the IS outsourcing contract, then at least central to it. But, for the reasons given at the start of this section, it is often inevitable. The question then is: but what if the parties still cannot agree important service levels even after the contract has been signed?

In the event that the Customer and Supplier cannot agree the service levels to apply to any such Priority Service, the issue shall be referred to the dispute resolution procedure in accordance with clause [escalation procedures and dispute resolution]. In the event, then, that the issue remains unresolved after the time periods provided for in that clause, the Customer shall be entitled, without liability or any charge or cost due to the Supplier, to terminate this Agreement in respect of those Priority Services for which service levels have not been agreed and if such termination right is exercised:

> the Customer and Supplier shall agree any resulting changes to this Agreement through the Change Request Procedure; and
> the Charges shall be varied in accordance with Schedule [procedure for changing charges].

In the event that Customer and Supplier are unable to agree any such changes or variations, the issue shall be referred to the dispute resolution procedure in accordance with clause [escalation procedures and dispute resolution]. In the event, then, that the issue remains unresolved after the time periods provided for in that clause, the Customer shall be entitled, without liability or any charge or cost due to the Supplier, to terminate this Agreement and, without affecting any right or remedy of the Customer in that regard, the Supplier shall within [ ] of the date of such termination repay to the Customer all moneys it has received from the Customer under this Agreement.

There are other variations on this theme and, of course, other ways of dealing with this issue. But the principles are that, if the parties really cannot agree important service levels after the contract has been signed and, having exhausted the contractual procedures for resolving such issues, they are still unable to resolve their differences, either or both should be able, either to terminate the contract in so far as the disputed services are concerned, or to terminate the contract in its entirety. Whether or not compensation for such termination should attach will depend on the transaction.

Breach of service levels, or failure to maintain them, is usually dealt with by means of service credits, referred to in section 3.8.

3.8 SERVICE CREDITS

Service levels, as we have seen, are at the heart of the contract. Service credits go hand in hand with the service levels – effectively providing the teeth behind the performance levels set. They are a stated monetary amount, payable by the supplier on a failure to achieve a service level to which service credits apply. They therefore provide an automatic financial remedy, potentially avoiding the need to pursue lengthy and costly legal claims for damages. The extent to which in practice service credits provide a true level of compensation obviating the need for other claims will be a matter for negotiation.

Careful consideration needs to be given to the level at which credits are set. This is for both practical and legal reasons. From a practical perspective, different services will clearly have a different level of importance to the customer (for example, a failure to answer calls on a helpdesk will probably have less impact on the customer's business than a serious network outage on a network maintained and operated by the supplier) and therefore different types of service will merit different credits. There are legal considerations too. Under English law penalties are not enforceable. Service credits should therefore be a genuine pre-estimate of the likely loss and damage that will be suffered in the event of the service failure to which those credits relate. Customers would be well advised to keep records of their calculations from the time of negotiations in case of later disputes as to the validity of the amount specified.

Service credits are usually set off against the service charges payable by the customer although in some circumstances the supplier pays credits direct to the customer.

Perhaps not surprisingly, not long after service credit regimes became the accepted norm in outsourcing transactions the supplier community began to promote the concept of service debits. As their name would suggest, service debits are a payment or reward where service levels are exceeded. For many, the idea that a supplier should be compensated for performing in excess of a level required and while the customer is still paying for that service is counterintuitive. The respective bargaining power of the parties will ultimately drive whether this concept is adopted into the contract. In any event, it will be extremely rare to find a service debit regime incorporated into a contract which requires the customer to make a payment direct to the supplier for over-performance.

If service debits are adopted, then the most frequent, and generally most acceptable, way of incorporating them is by way of a service credit/debit bank. This requires an account (real or notional) to be established. Service credits are paid into the account on their occurrence. The supplier is then given the opportunity to reduce the amount of credits payable by performing in excess of the service levels. On any over-performance, service debits will be paid into the account, having the effect of reducing the balance of credits. The account should be settled on a regular basis with an appropriate payment to the customer. This payment can be made direct to the customer or set off against the charges, as discussed above.

Where the Supplier fails to achieve the applicable Service Levels, without prejudice to the Customer's other rights and remedies (including, but not limited to, the right to claim damages and terminate this Agreement):

Service Credits shall be credited [in accordance with Schedule [ ] [service credit schedule]] [to the Service Credit Account and that Service Credit Account shall be settled periodically in accordance with Schedule [ ] [service credit schedule]; the Supplier shall arrange all such additional resources as are necessary to perform the Services in accordance with the Service Levels as early as practicable

> thereafter and at no additional charge to the Customer; and where applicable, the Supplier shall promptly re-perform any Service which has not met its applicable Service Levels or which has not been performed correctly by the Supplier, at no additional charge to the Customer.

Service credits are an important remedy. But those drafting the outsourcing contract should not concentrate on them to the exclusion of everything else. Even though the customer may be compensated financially for underperformance through the service credit regime, ultimately termination rights may be required. Termination rights are discussed in more detail in section 3.14. In addition, more practical remedies as referred to in the precedent text above, such as obligations on the supplier to remedy the failure, should be incorporated.

In considering the use of service credits, one of the key questions is whether service credits should be the sole and exclusive financial remedy of the customer in the event of a service failure. IS outsource suppliers will naturally favour such an approach, as it enables them to predict with a fairly high degree of certainty their potential risk exposure. This will only be acceptable where the service credits have been set at a level that does attempt to compensate the customer for the likely loss, rather than at any lower or nominal level. And in any event customers should be aware that the impact of a service failure can never be assessed with complete accuracy at the outset of the contract. Any decision to depart from the right to claim further damages should only be taken with care.

> Clause [ ] [liability] shall not apply in relation to the Supplier's liability (if any) actually accrued during the Term for amounts in respect of Service Credits, which shall, accordingly, be in addition to the amounts of the Supplier's liability referred to in clause [ ] [liability].

The contract should clearly state how service credits are to be treated under the liability provisions. The supplier's liability for service credits can fall within any overall liability cap on loss and damage, be subject to a specific liability cap applicable to the service credits alone, or can be unlimited.

3.9 PERFORMANCE IMPROVEMENT

The typically long life span of an IS outsourcing contract combined with the fast pace at which the technology market moves in today's climate are the prime motivators behind the concept of performance improvement. Contractual provisions are an important mechanism by which the customer can be assured that they will continue to receive a cost-effective and high quality service for the duration of the outsourcing relationship.

A combination of market reviews carried out by both the supplier and external benchmarking consultants will work best to achieve this.

Contracts will often require the supplier to carry out a yearly review of the market to ascertain whether there are any ways in which the services could be improved or the cost of the services reduced, for example by utilising new technology. Usually, it would be in the supplier's best interests to carry out such a review in any event as any ways in which the cost of providing the service can be reduced (and the profit margins increased) would clearly benefit the supplier. However, the technology market is a competitive one and suppliers are unlikely to look to using the products of their competitors, despite any potential cost benefit, unless they are contractually compelled to do so.

Benchmarking provisions are an important protection for the customer, allowing the customer (or an external third party consultant appointed by it) to conduct their own review of the services.

Under the benchmarking exercise, the services are reviewed to see if services of an equivalent nature can be obtained more cheaply or at increased service levels from elsewhere. The basis of the review should be fair. This means that the services provided to the customer should only be compared against services of a similar scope, size and quality. See Chapter 8 for a more detailed discussion of benchmarking procedures.

It is important to note that these performance reviews should form part of the customer's overall review of the service. They should sit alongside, and not replace, detailed reporting requirements in the contract.

3.10 CHARGES

Although any IS outsourcing contract will invariably require changes to be made even to supposedly fixed charges, any changes should be kept to a minimum and carried out in accordance with stated contract procedures (e.g. as a result of applying an inflationary index on a yearly basis or as a result of changes made to the contract through the change control mechanism).

The nature of IS outsourcing contracts means that the level of usage of a service can be difficult to predict. Suppliers will therefore often seek some element of variability (e.g. when the level of use by the customer exceeds an agreed baseline amount or general charging on a time and materials or unit cost basis). Variable charges may also be more appropriate where the customer is able to call on a pool of resources as and when required under the contract. Care should be taken to define some limits around variable priced contracts to prevent costs escalating out of control, e.g. by imposing an estimated costs ceiling, which the supplier is required to monitor, and for any costs in excess of that to be notified to the customer and agreed in advance before they are actually incurred.

Charges can be paid in arrears or in advance. From the customer's perspective, payment monthly in arrears is likely to be the preferred model. It

135

gets a little more complex if the charges are variable, requiring a review at the end of the payment period to which the charges relate to assess whether an adjusting payment is needed or must be reflected on the next invoice.

Any express provisions entitling the supplier to suspend services after a failure to pay should be strongly resisted, not least because of the considerable impact on the customer's business of any cessation in the service provision. If any such clause is incorporated, prior warning must be given by the supplier before services are suspended and a further notification period incorporated in case the failure to pay arises from any administration error.

The nature of IS outsourcing contracts means that often a number of different types of service may be provided or services may be provided for the benefit of a number of companies within the customer group. It may, therefore, be important for the customer to receive an invoice that contains an adequate breakdown of the services provided, whether by reference to each of the types of service provided or by showing the services provided to each member of the customer group. This type of information can be invaluable for any later internal recharging of costs within the customer organisation.

In some more innovative contracts we have seen a move away from traditional charging structures in order to compete effectively in the existing UK market. For example, the company EDS has introduced benefits-based contracts under which the payment it is entitled to is linked to the benefits received by the customer rather than the simple provision of services. The benefits received by the customer can be measured according to that customer's operational performance (e.g. in relation to manufacturing cycle times or purchasing efficiency).

Customers should ensure that any contract based on more innovative charging principles, such as a benefits-based contract, is well drafted to clearly define the circumstances in which the supplier becomes entitled to payment.

> The Customer and the Supplier shall review the Charges on 1 January of each calendar year in light of the [Retail Prices Index as published by the UK Office for National Statistics (ONS)]. As a result of this yearly review the Charges payable shall be increased or decreased automatically to reflect the percentage rate of increase or decrease of the [Retail Prices Index]. Such variations shall take effect from 1 January of that calendar year.

As outsourcing contracts can last for some years, the supplier will look for the ability to increase the charges that apply over the duration of the contract. For this reason, the charges are often linked to indexation with increases (or, even, decreases) being made to the charges on an annual basis to reflect the change in the inflationary index over the previous year. The inflationary index that is to be used is often bitterly disputed.

The Retail Prices Index as published by the ONS is frequently applied. However, this index reflects the general rate of inflation in the economy and is based on the price of goods. It does not take into account the rather special circumstances of the technology industry and the spiralling labour costs within that market. A supplier may therefore look to other indices specific to the IT industry. Market research company, Computer Economics and the National Computing Centre (NCC) both carry out annual surveys of salaries in the IT industry. Customers need to be aware of the dramatic impact on charges that the application of such an index may have.

In respect of any Change:

all external costs incurred by the Supplier (if any) in respect of any Changes shall be passed to the Customer at the Supplier's cost price plus [5]% to cover sourcing and administration costs; and

the Supplier shall provide to the Customer a breakdown of the price of the Change into the following charge elements (as applicable):

i)   once-off site and facilities;
ii) once-off hardware (to cover capital and/or lease costs);
iii) once-off hardware maintenance;
iv) once-off software (licence, support and maintenance);
vi) once-off external services;
vii) once-off labour;
viii) once-off other expenses; and
ix) ongoing service charges.

Changes to the scope of the services and contract will inevitably be required as the customer's needs change over time, so contract provisions should state how the charges will be calculated for any such change. The supplier should provide detailed breakdowns for any new service, achieving maximum costs transparency.

The above formula works on a cost-plus basis with the supplier being able to recover the cost of the new element of the services, together with an additional (profit) element to cover administration costs, etc. Such a formula may not always be appropriate. For example, if there is an added risk to the supplier in delivering that change to the contract (e.g. a performance risk where the change makes it more difficult for the supplier to achieve the then prevailing service levels) then it may be appropriate for a further costs premium to be charged to the customer.

As the outsourcing market becomes increasingly competitive, customers are seeking assurances that the level of charges will remain competitive over the life of the contract, especially as regards other customers of the supplier. Such provisions are often referred to as 'most favoured nation' clauses.

Provisions can be incorporated providing for an annual review by the supplier of the charges against amounts charged to the other customers of the supplier. One of the difficulties from such reviews is the very specific nature of technology services, which are often tailored to a customer's specific circumstances. The prices charged in practice to a particular customer will also reflect the volume of services that is being placed with that supplier under any specific contract. For this reason, suppliers may be anxious to prevent comparisons against services that are not a true match for the services being provided to the customer. The review should therefore only be against services of an equivalent size, nature and scope. In any event, these clauses can be difficult to enforce as confidentiality obligations in the supplier's other customer contracts will prevent the disclosure of detailed price information.

3.11   LIABILITY

Suppliers will generally seek to exclude their liability for indirect, or consequential, loss. Such loss encompasses loss beyond the damage to the value of the property itself, such as loss of profits and loss of revenue. It is becoming increasingly common to try to extend the bounds of the types of loss and damage that the supplier is liable for, so that effectively certain categories of loss and damage that might otherwise be viewed as consequential loss are brought within the scope of the direct loss provisions.

This is particularly the case given the nature of the relationship under the technology outsourcing contract where the supplier is likely to have a detailed knowledge of the customer's business and an understanding of the likely impact of any contract breach.

> Neither the Customer nor the Supplier shall be liable to each other for:
>
> > any indirect or consequential costs, claims, expenses, loss and damage of any kind, even if they are informed of the possibility of such costs, claims, expenses, loss and damage;
> >
> > loss of revenues, profits, interest, anticipated savings or goodwill;
> >
> > loss of or damage to the other's records or data; and
> >
> > third party claims against the other for losses or damages.

Suppliers who wish to exclude their liability for consequential loss will need to draft appropriate provisions with care. Recent case law has thrown doubts over the effectiveness of the, until recently, standard formulations of exclusions for indirect and consequential damages. In particular, the Court of Appeal judgment in *British Sugar* v. *NEI Power Projects Limited* [1998] 87 BLR 42 suggested that the meaning of the word 'consequential' was loss that flows from special circumstances (and therefore within the second limb of the *Hadley* v. *Baxendale* (1854) 9 Ex. 341 damages test). This contradicted the view of many that certain types of consequential loss can constitute direct loss and therefore fall within the first limb of *Hadley* v. *Baxendale*. In the later case of *Hotel Services Limited* v. *Hilton International Hotels (UK)* [2001] CILL 1686 the Court of Appeal held that loss of profits were, on the facts, a direct and natural consequence and prevented the defendant from relying on a clause excluding liability for indirect and consequential loss accordingly.

In light of these conflicting cases, those drafting exclusion clauses are advised to specify in some detail exactly what types of loss and damage are covered by the clause.

The contract will also include a number of provisions regarding the supplier's liability in specific circumstances, e.g. in the event of an infringement of a third party's intellectual property rights, or failure to achieve the service levels. The contract must deal with how these specific liabilities are linked to the general caps on the supplier's liability for breaches.

Whether the supplier's liability under the various indemnity provisions will be capped by the general liability cap is often a contentious issue and will ultimately depend on the bargaining position of the parties. Customers should be aware that the infringement of a third party's intellectual property rights as a result of the provision or use of the outsourced services could have serious costs implications. As a result, customers would be well advised to ensure that the supplier's liability for this type of loss and damage is unlimited.

> In the event that any of the Customer's Data are corrupted or lost as a result of any act or omission by the Supplier, the Customer shall:
>
> be entitled to require the Supplier at the Supplier's own expense to restore or procure the restoration of the Data to the last transaction processed; or
>
> where the Supplier has failed to restore or procure the restoration of the Customer's Data, the Customer may itself restore or procure the restoration of its Data to the last transaction processed and shall be entitled to be repaid by the Supplier any reasonable expenses so incurred.

IS outsourcing contracts will invariably involve data being processed by the supplier's system or on the customer's or a third party's systems or networks. Any loss of that data can cause serious business interruption and liability exposure. Loss of data is a consequential loss and, as such, something for which suppliers will seek to exclude liability. However, to leave the customer with no remedy is unacceptable, particularly as the supplier is running the IS operations and should, therefore, be accepting some responsibility.

Contracts should, therefore, include specific remedies (in the absence of any more general acceptance by the supplier of liability for consequential loss) in the event of a loss of data where that loss is due to the default of the supplier. The precedent text above incorporates a fairly standard remedy in this regard.

Finally, where the parties contract on the basis of one party's standard terms of business, the exclusions and limitations of liability for loss and damage in respect of any contract breach under section 3 of the Unfair Contract Terms Act 1977 (UCTA) must be reasonable. What is reasonable will be assessed in light of a number of factors as set out in Schedule 2 to UCTA. While the courts are generally reluctant to intervene, there have been some recent decisions regarding IT contracts where clauses have been struck out, especially where one of those parties was perceived as being in a weaker negotiating position.

3.12   CHANGE MANAGEMENT

The outsourcing contract will not remain static. Change may be introduced through amendment to the scope of the existing services, to reflect new services to be provided and to bring in new forms of technology. This will be particularly the case given the speed at which the technology market moves as new products and services are devised and given the increasing reliance on technology to fulfil the day-to-day operations of the modern-day business.

Although a certain amount of flexibility can, and should, be built into the standard contract enabling the customer to make minor changes to the services, anything more significant will need to go through a formal procedure.

Some suppliers have acquired a somewhat negative reputation for using the change control procedure as a way to drive up the price of the contract. As stated above, the customer must take some responsibility for ensuring that the initial statement of its service requirements is comprehensive. A services schedule that clearly defines the scope of the service will avoid the need for items that should have been thought of at the outset to be added to the contract subsequently.

Contract change procedures should require a detailed assessment by the supplier of the impact of the change. This will enable the customer to make an informed decision as to whether, and the basis on which, to proceed with any change. Naturally the introduction of a new service will have a price attached but given the interaction between many technology systems, there may well be an impact on other systems and networks. Other provisions that may be affected include the charges, service description and service levels.

The time and internal costs in preparing detailed change proposals can become burdensome, so suppliers often view such procedures with caution (especially if contract negotiations or other early dealings have revealed the customer to be a demanding one). What should be remembered though, is that if the contract scope is extended, then the supplier will ultimately benefit from increased charges.

Either party should be able to propose changes to the contract scope. The procedures for reviewing the change proposal and providing a detailed assessment of the impact of the change on the remainder of the contract are relatively standard. Although mutual agreement is always at the core of any change proposal procedures, provisions that are drafted for the benefit of the customer will leave the ultimate decision as to whether or not to accept or reject the proposal for the change with the customer.

3.13 DATA, DATA PROTECTION AND PRIVACY

The Supplier acknowledges that the Customer's Data and all Intellectual Property Rights that may subsist in the Customer's Data are the property of, and shall belong to, the Customer. The Supplier shall not delete or remove any copyright notices contained within or relating to the Customer's Data.

The Supplier agrees not to assert or exercise, or attempt to assert or exercise, any right or lien against the Customer with respect to the Customer's Data. In consideration of the payment by the Customer to the Supplier of £1.00 (receipt of which the Supplier hereby acknowledges), the Supplier hereby assigns to the Customer all right, title and interest, including, but not limited to, copyright and all other Intellectual Property Rights, in and to all data falling within the definition of 'the Customer's Data'.

The Supplier shall take reasonable precautions to preserve the security and integrity of the Customer's Data and to prevent any corruption or loss of the Customer's Data. Without prejudice to the foregoing, the Supplier shall maintain safeguards that are no less rigorous than those maintained by the Supplier for its own information of a similar nature.

As part of the services provided pursuant to the technology outsourcing contract, the supplier is likely to handle a considerable volume of data. This may be either where the supplier processes or generates data using systems that are utilised by the supplier as part of the services or where the supplier itself directly generates data in the course of performing the services.

Given the value and fundamental importance of the data to the customer's business (without them, the business simply cannot function) it will be important to ensure that the rights to such data are owned by the customer and that the supplier does not attempt to exercise any lien over those data.

Where as a result of the provision of services, the supplier generates data, then the supplier, as the creator of the data, will prima facie own the intellectual property rights that arise in respect of them. In such circumstances an assignment of the intellectual property rights will be required to ensure that the customer has the unfettered right to use its own data as required.

If data processed or generated as a result of the technology outsourcing contract includes data relating to individuals (i.e. personal data) data protection law will apply. In the UK, the Data Protection Act 1998 is the key piece of legislation.

The 1998 Act introduces the concept of the data processor, replacing the earlier concept of computer service bureaux that was contained in the predecessor to the 1998 Act, the Data Protection Act 1984. A data processor is someone who carries out the processing of personal data on behalf of a data controller. The data controller is an entity that (either alone or jointly or in common with other persons) determines the purposes for which, and the manner in which, any personal data are processed. At the outset, the parties will need to determine whether they are data controllers or data processors. In a standard technology outsourcing contract the customer will usually take the role of the data controller. As the supplier carries out the processing of the data in accordance with the customer's instructions (as defined by the contract) the supplier usually will be a data processor.

> The Supplier shall ensure that any person under the authority of the Supplier shall collect, store, use and disclose the Personal Data only upon, and in accordance with, the written instructions of the Customer.

> The Supplier confirms that, to the best of its knowledge and belief, the security requirements, as set out in Schedule [ ], are such as constitute appropriate technical and organisational measures to protect the Personal Data against accidental or unlawful destruction or accidental loss, alteration, unauthorised disclosure or access, and against all other unlawful forms of processing and that such measures shall, having regard to the state of the art and the cost of their implementation, ensure a level of security appropriate to the risks represented by the processing and nature of the Personal Data.

At the heart of the UK data protection legislation are eight data protection principles. The precedent reflects the seventh principle, which states that 'appropriate technical and organisational measures shall be taken against unauthorised or unlawful processing of personal data and against accidental loss or destruction of, or damage to, personal data'. Under the Act, the customer must choose a data processor (i.e. supplier) with sufficient guarantees in respect of the measures it takes. This is unlikely to be an issue when dealing with a reputable technology provider and can be dealt with by incorporating express requirements regarding security measures (both logical and physical security). The suggested wording above shifts some of the burden of assessing whether the security measures are appropriate to the supplier. The customer must take reasonable steps to ensure compliance with these security measures, for example by reviewing security issues as part of a regular audit process.

The Act states that the processing must be carried out under a written contract – which will invariably be satisfied with a complex outsourcing relationship. Importantly, the processor, i.e. the supplier, must only act on the instructions of the data controller, i.e. the customer.

The eighth principle under the Data Protection Act 1998 may also be relevant. This states that data cannot be transferred to a country outside the European Economic Area unless that third country offers an adequate level of protection. This is of particular importance with the recent move to the use of outsource providers based in countries such as India, Malaysia and South Africa to take advantage of the lower cost base in those areas. Cross-border transfer of personal data is a complex issue. The appropriate solution will depend on issues such as the third county involved, the roles of the customer and supplier in relation to the data and accordingly will merit detailed consideration in each particular case.

3.14   TERMINATION

As well as general termination rights (e.g. termination for material breach or in the event of insolvency), termination rights will also need to be considered specifically in relation to the service levels under an IS outsourcing contract. Contracts commonly specify the level at which the customer considers the service to be of an unacceptable standard, triggering a termination remedy.

> Without prejudice to any other rights or remedies that the Customer may have pursuant to this Agreement or at law, the Supplier shall be deemed to be in material breach of this Agreement and that such breach is not capable of remedy pursuant to clause [ ] and the Customer may terminate this Agreement by notice with immediate effect if any Service Level falls below the Minimum Service Level.

Without any such express right, the customer would be left to argue that the particular breach of the service level constituted a material breach, resulting in a termination right under the general material breach provisions. This risks lengthy disputes between the parties as to whether that service level breach was or was not material.

> Without prejudice to any other rights or remedies that the Customer may have pursuant to this Agreement or at law, the Supplier shall be deemed to be in material breach of this Agreement and that such breach is not capable of remedy pursuant to clause [ ] and the Customer may terminate this Agreement by notice with immediate effect if a Service Credit has been paid by the Supplier to the Customer, in respect of a failure to meet the same Service Level, in any [three (3)] calendar months in any [six (6)] consecutive calendar month period.

In addition to this type of minimum service level at which termination rights are triggered, the customer should also consider the impact of long-term, more minor service failures. Although service credits may be payable, a customer will not want to keep on receiving service credits indefinitely for a substandard service. Limits should therefore be placed around the period for which such service credits are to be payable before the right to terminate arises.

The above precedent wording links termination to service credits being paid in excess of a specified period where the service credits relate to a failure to achieve the same service level. The termination right could be extended to apply irrespective of whether service credits relate to one, or a number of, service levels.

IS outsourcing contracts will often involve a mix of a number of different services. Rights to partial termination may therefore be appropriate, and highly desirable, enabling the customer to retain a degree of flexibility as to how its business develops in the future. The contract can also incorporate the right to terminate only part of a particular service.

The practicalities as to whether part of the services can be terminated will depend on the extent to which the services are bundled together and whether they can be easily separated. Rights to partial termination are usually highly contentious. They may be more palatable where there has been a contract breach (e.g. failure to meet an applicable service level requirement) than a general right to terminate for convenience.

The extent to which any termination charge will be payable on partial termination will be a matter for negotiation between the parties. Many suppliers will seek to impose an excessively high termination charge to discourage the exercise of the right by the customer. Again, the motivation for termination will be important here. Where partial termination rights are exercised for breach it will be more difficult for the supplier to justify the imposition of a charge. Where the termination is for convenience, it may be more appropriate for the customer to bear some of the charges (e.g. relating to any third party charges under licences or other contracts that the supplier is required to cancel as a result).

As in any industry, there will be some services that are more profitable to the supplier than others. A key concern for the supplier is therefore that a right to terminate for convenience might result in the supplier being locked into a contract that no longer remains profitable. It may therefore be desirable to define a certain minimum set of services that will always be provided or alternatively to allow the supplier the ability to terminate once the annual value of the contract falls below a certain threshold.

In view of the longevity of outsourcing contracts, customers may wish to have the ability to walk away from the contract after a number of months or years. Break options can be built into a contract to allow for this. Such provisions are strongly resisted by suppliers and, if they are included, are likely to bear a high cost for the customer in the termination payments that the customer is compelled to pay.

3.15   EXIT MANAGEMENT

To contemplate the end of the relationship before it has begun can seem at best like being overly detailed and at worst, a damning indictment of the future partnership between customer and supplier. As a result, contractual provisions relating to exit arrangements are frequently drafted at a very high level with the only obligation undertaken by either party being that detailed agreement will be reached at the time.

Customers must, however, understand that a failure to specify detailed provisions exposes them to a serious risk that at the end of the contract relationship their business will come to a grinding halt and that they will lack the right to use crucial items of hardware or software. In addition, the customer will be in a far better position to negotiate favourable exit provisions prior to entering into the contract when the supplier is anxious to win the business rather than at the time of termination when the relationship has broken down and any goodwill between the parties may be limited or non-existent.

At the very heart of the exit provisions should be an obligation on the supplier to ensure that there is a smooth transition of the services, either back in house to the customer or to a third party service provider, with minimum disruption to the business. Terms relating to assets used and commitments to ongoing service provision during the exit period should be included and are examined in turn below.

> The Supplier shall, on an ongoing basis, maintain and keep up to date the Inventory Record.

> The Supplier shall provide to the Customer such updated Inventory Record in hard and electronic form at least every twelve (12) months, commencing on the anniversary of the date of this Agreement and within five (5) days of the occurrence of an Exit Event.

Exit events (as referred to in the precedent text above) should include the expiry of the agreement or any termination in accordance with the termination provisions or otherwise.

While the choice of technology used to provide the services will often be a matter for the supplier's discretion, the customer should not forget the importance of understanding precisely what the technology infrastructure comprises. An obligation on the supplier to maintain an inventory for the duration of the contract of the items used to provide the services will be helpful in this regard. This inventory should include details of any software (both application and infrastructure software), hardware, data, documentation, manuals and details of any licences, leases or other arrangements relating to the services provided.

> In connection with an Exit Event, other than the termination or expiry of the Run-Off Agreement, if the Customer provides to the Supplier a notice valid in accordance with clause [ ] that it requires the Supplier to continue to provide any or all of the Services for a period after the date of the Exit Event, then the Supplier shall provide to the Customer the Services specified in that notice in accordance with this clause [ ] (and that continuation of the Services shall be known as the 'Run-Off Service').

> In connection with the Run-Off Service:

> if the Exit Event is expiry of the Term or the taking effect of the Break Option, the notice shall be valid if it is served by the Customer at least 60 Working Days prior to the relevant Exit Event; and

> in all other circumstances, a valid notice shall be deemed to be served upon the Exit Event unless the Customer notifies the Supplier otherwise on or before the Exit Event.

> Initially, and subject to clause [ ], the Supplier shall provide the Run-Off Service for a period of three (3) months. The Customer shall, by giving the Supplier at least twenty (20) Working Days' notice, be entitled, at its absolute discretion, to

extend by three months the period (including any period extended pursuant to this Paragraph) for which the Supplier shall provide the Run-Off Service.

The Customer may extend, under clause [ ] above, the period during which the Supplier is to provide the Run-Off Service as many times as the Customer requires, provided that the period during which the Supplier is to provide the Run-Off Service shall not exceed twelve (12) months in aggregate.

In respect of the Run-Off Service, the Customer and the Supplier shall be deemed to have entered into a new agreement (the 'Run-Off Agreement').

The Run-Off Agreement shall be on the same terms and conditions (including in respect of charging) as were subsisting immediately prior to the Exit Event.

In determining the period for which any run-off services are to be required the customer should take into account the complexity of the services and the anticipated time required to locate and implement a replacement contract with a further provider. A good rule of thumb will be the length of time it has taken to set up the original outsourcing contract, from the early stages of defining the customer's requirements and selection of suppliers through to the go-live date under the contract. An equivalent period of time is likely to be required to transfer services to another third party or back in house.

The above provisions give the customer a certain amount of flexibility, allowing the purchase of chunks of services in three-month blocks. The above provisions also state that the existing terms of the contract are to apply to that run-off service. For example, the customer will be required to pay the supplier in accordance with the existing charging arrangements and the supplier will remain committed to providing the services in accordance with the stated service level requirements.

Provisions should then be included regarding the different types of assets that have been used to provide the services. The supplier should return copies of the customer's proprietary software, including copies of any modifications that have been made. Licences should be granted to use any of the supplier's proprietary software. Depending on the nature of this proprietary software, the licence may only be granted for a limited period. Some licences may be granted for use beyond the expiry of the exit period, although inevitably in these circumstances the customer will be required to pay a commercial rate (or close to it) for the grant of that licence. It will be important to ensure the licence provisions allow use by the customer or by a replacement third party contractor.

Licences relating to third party software should be novated to the customer.

Copies of data should also be provided to the customer, together with copies of any leases, licences or other contracts relating to third party items used to provide the services. This will then enable the customer to assess whether those agreements should be assigned to it or whether it wishes to purchase replacement items.

If premises of the supplier are used to provide the services, which the customer requires further access to on termination (such as a data centre), it may be possible to obtain a lease to use part (or all) of those premises from the supplier. Where the premises are leased to the supplier from a third party, this will usually be done by granting a sub-lease to the customer for the appropriate areas of the premises. The provisions of the head lease should be examined carefully. Consent from the lessor may well be required to any sub-lease and the head lease may stipulate terms that must be incorporated into a sub-lease.

A traditional debate will always centre on the extent to which the supplier should be required to transfer to the customer assets, such as hardware and other equipment, used to provide the services. Items that the supplier has used exclusively for the customer should be transferred to the customer. Items that are not used exclusively for the benefit of the customer and that are, for example, used to provide services to a number of customers pose more of a problem. In these circumstances, it may be possible for the customer to rent the use of part of that item from the supplier.

The Transfer of Undertakings (Protection of Employment) Regulations 1981, SI 1981/1794 (TUPE) might apply at the expiry of the outsourcing contract to transfer the staff of the supplier who have been substantially employed in providing the services to the customer (or the replacement contractor) – see Chapter 9 in this regard. Even if TUPE does not apply, the customer may want the right to employ employees of the supplier who have been key in providing the services.

> As soon as the Customer notifies the Supplier that an Exit Event has occurred, or will or is likely to occur, the Supplier shall put in place a plan specifying how its obligations under this Schedule [ ] will be fulfilled. The Customer shall provide input and advice in connection with such plan and the Supplier shall take full account of all such input and advice.

> Compliance with such plan will enable the Customer itself or its replacement third party contractor to provide services of a similar nature and scope as the Services, and to a level of provision at least as good as the Service Levels immediately after the Exit Event.

> Compliance with such plan will ensure that none of the Customer's data are, at any time, lost, corrupted or otherwise damaged or unavailable and that the volume of data processing outstanding at the Exit Event will be minimised.

> Compliance with such plan will ensure that Service disruption and/or Service Level degradation experienced by the Customer during any period leading up to, and immediately after, the Exit Event will be minimised and that the Supplier will inform the Customer of any interim arrangements necessary during such periods.

> The implementation of such plan shall ensure that the transfer of service provision to the Customer or the replacement third party contractor shall occur in the shortest practical time frame.

The above provisions provide for the supplier to draw up a detailed exit plan, the aim of which should be to achieve the seamless transition of the services to the customer. The customer should have the right to contribute to this plan. It should explain in detail how all of the exit obligations are to be carried out, e.g. the granting of licences, novation of third party licences, transfer of equipment, etc.

The extent to which the supplier is permitted to charge in respect of performing the obligations under the exit provisions is likely to be the subject of some negotiation. There may also be considerable costs associated with obtaining any necessary third party consents to the transfer of contracts and assets to the customer. Given that the supplier continues to receive the basic payment for providing the services, the customer will argue that any additional costs incurred through providing exit services should be borne by the supplier and built into their original cost plan.

The supplier is, however, likely to seek payment on a time and materials basis for any assistance provided. This will particularly be the case if, for example, the customer has exercised a right of partial termination of the services for convenience or where the supplier is terminating for a material breach of the customer. It may therefore be appropriate to define some circumstances in which the supplier is entitled to payment and some circumstances where it is not.

3.16 GENERAL WARRANTIES

General warranties should be incorporated into the contract to cover the performance of the supplier, including warranties regarding the performance by the supplier of its obligations in accordance with all applicable laws, that only skilled and experienced personnel will be utilised in the service provision and the supplier's obligations will be performed in accordance with good industry practice. Such general warranties will be incorporated into any outsourcing contract.

The nature of a technology outsourcing contract requires specific warranties to be incorporated in relation to the systems used to deliver the services and in relation to any items, such as hardware and software, that are delivered to the customer as part of the provision of the services.

Where software is to be provided by the supplier, it may be advisable to obtain contractual assurance that the software will not contain any virus, lock or other device that will enable the supplier to prevent its continued operation. For example, if the customer fails to make payment the software is then disabled. Under English law, such locks and time bombs will be illegal (under the terms of the Computer Misuse Act 1990) unless the supplier has notified the customer in advance of its intention to use such coding in the software and their effect.

3.17 DISPUTE RESOLUTION PROCEDURES

Inevitably, disputes will arise during the life of the contract. Dispute resolution procedures are often provided for in some detail in the outsourcing contract. With all these procedures it is important to bear in mind that it may not always be appropriate to follow them and provisions should be specified acknowledging those circumstances. These include where one party simply refuses to participate in the process, where one party has committed a material breach of the contract or where a party suspects that its intellectual property rights are, or are about to be, infringed or believes that its confidential information is, or is about to be, disclosed other than in accordance with the terms of the contract (in which case immediate action, such as obtaining an injunction, will be required to protect the rights of that party).

The first formalised mechanism of dispute resolution usually involves an escalation procedure between various representatives of the parties. For example, the contract managers may first attempt to resolve any disputes and, if they are unable to do so, the matter is then referred to the respective finance directors of the parties and ultimately, to chief executive or managing director level. The intention behind these escalation procedures is to encourage resolution of more minor matters at a low level within the organisations. It will not look good for either party if a dispute about a particular charge under an invoice, or the quality of a particular set of reports delivered by the supplier is referred to the chief executives/managing directors for resolution.

The result of the internal escalation process means that it delays the point at which either party can seek adjudication outside the contract, by referring the matter to the courts or an alternative form of dispute resolution (such as mediation or the use of an expert).

It will not always be to the best advantage of the customer to be compelled to follow an internal escalation process, which may take some months to follow, before being free to pursue legal action in the courts – particularly as it will usually be an alleged default of the supplier to which the dispute relates. As the obligations of the customer under the contract are invariably limited (with payment being the most key requirement) the potential for the dispute to relate to the customer's performance is restricted. The threat of court action, with its attendant negative publicity and high costs, can often encourage an early settlement by the supplier. That said, however, most customers are willing to take the view that they should look to resolve disputes by working together with the supplier rather than automatically taking court action and for this reason, escalation mechanisms are commonplace in most technology outsourcing contracts.

In the event that the parties cannot resolve the dispute through the internal escalation procedure, then typically the parties would refer the matter to the courts. It is well known that the costs of such court action can be extremely high and that court action is very time consuming. A further problem is that disputes can often be of a highly technical nature, so judges may lack the detailed knowledge and expertise to be able to fully understand the issues in question.

For these reasons, the parties may therefore look to building into the contract alternative forms of dispute resolution. This also reflects the need to look at appropriate forms of alternative dispute resolution as a result of the Woolf reforms to the UK litigation process. Litigants will be asked whether they considered or actually participated in other dispute resolution mechanisms before resorting to the courts. For those who have not, there are significant costs implications.

Such other forms of dispute resolution process may involve the referral of disputes of a technical nature to a third party expert and other disputes to mediation.

Where an expert is to be used then the contract may leave it for the parties to determine the identity of the expert to be used. Any failures to agree may require an independent third party to intervene to appoint a suitable expert. The parties will need to provide the expert with all relevant information. Time periods should also be specified for the expert to consider the representations of the parties and to provide a judgment. The expert will usually be asked to determine at the time of giving judgment who should bear the costs of the proceedings, taking into account the conduct of the parties and the outcome of the proceedings.

In relation to the use of mediation to resolve other disputes, again the contract should specify a body that, in the event of a failure by the parties to agree on the identity of a mediator, will be required to appoint one. The Centre for Effective Dispute Resolution (CEDR) is often used in this context.

The use of any such form of alternative dispute resolution process should be based on the mutual consent of the parties.

Finally, arbitration can also be used. Arbitration is a form of binding dispute resolution. An arbitrator is appointed and proceedings are conducted in confidence. The Arbitration Act 1996 details the way in which arbitration proceedings will be conducted by the arbitrator. Decisions cannot be appealed, unless it can be shown that the arbitrator acted in bad faith or unless it can be established that the arbitrator's decision was wrong in law. Arbitration is most likely to be appropriate where the parties to the technology outsourcing contract come from a number of jurisdictions and arbitration can therefore provide a more neutral forum for dispute resolution.

NOTES

1. This term should be defined, as it needs to call up a list of the relevant third party software, usually contained in a schedule or annex to a schedule.

2. The customer and supplier will also need to agree who, as between them, will be responsible for payments and liabilities that arose *before* the commencement date. Usually, the customer will assume that responsibility.
3. This term would usually be specifically defined in virtually all technology outsourcing contracts.
4. There are a number of defined terms in this extract from a service level schedule. Definitions will, of course, vary from transaction to transaction. We have capitalised the terms that are usually defined in service levels of this kind – though even these will vary from deal to deal.
5. It is quite common for the customer and supplier to agree a phased introduction for the services, often starting with those services that are essential to the customer's business.

CHAPTER 4

Telecommunications outsourcing

Michael Sinclair[1]

4.1 INTRODUCTION

The telecoms outsourcing industry, like the telecoms market as a whole, is currently in a state of flux owing to a shortage of large outsourcing deals and of customers willing to make the financial and strategic decisions necessary in order to outsource telecoms infrastructure.

There has been a slow take up of new telecoms technologies (for example, third generation mobile technologies) owing to concerns about the cost and resilience of the technology and because of a widely held view among large users of telecoms services that it is not necessary (and may not even be desirable) to be at the forefront of developments in this field. What matters, the market would have it, is not what a network can potentially do but what it will consistently do. It is better to take on a tried and tested technology rather than one that has yet to prove its worth, so the argument goes.

Difficult market conditions mean it is not just users of telecoms services that need to make decisions about relative competitiveness. Market saturation has meant that telecoms suppliers are themselves under pressure to achieve a competitive edge (and to achieve cost savings) by replacing outmoded systems.

Increasing globalisation of business has meant that customers are seeking global telecoms solutions from their telecoms suppliers. The need to provide global reach has put immense pressure on many telecoms suppliers, forcing them to roll out global subcontracting, billing, reporting and customer relationship management (CRM) systems at immense cost, and pushing them to the brink of (or beyond) their now global service level arrangements.

The result of all this has been a lack of investment and stakeholder confidence in telecoms suppliers, pressure from customers for more competitively priced telecoms services and some rather spectacular collapses.

In these volatile conditions, it is essential that customers entering into telecoms outsourcings effectively manage legal and operational risk in their outsourcing agreements. Greater attention will need to be paid to the areas of high risk: financial stability of the supplier and its subcontractors, implementation, compliance with service levels, rights of termination, step-in rights and exit management. Many of these principles have been covered elsewhere in this book and they apply equally to telecoms outsourcings (they are not repeated in this chapter).

The focus of this chapter, therefore, is on those additional considerations and principles that ought to apply to telecoms outsourcings in particular, as distinct from any other type of technology outsourcing. Accordingly, issues surrounding the transfer of telecoms infrastructure (hardware, software, licences, premises, people, etc.) to the supplier are not dealt with in this chapter as they are in substance the same as those that arise in any other type of technology outsourcing.[2]

This chapter first outlines the various types of outsourcing that can be broadly grouped as telecoms outsourcings. It then provides sample clauses and commentary in relation to various issues specific to telecoms outsourcings. The sample clauses and commentary fall into two groups: those that are deal-specific to particular types of telecoms outsourcings; and those that are relevant to all types of telecoms outsourcings (and that are therefore generic).

Not much has been written on the legal issues surrounding telecoms outsourcings.[3] This chapter is, however, a product of its time and its focus is inevitably about risk management (for example, disaster recovery and risk of insolvency) during a difficult stage in the global economic cycle. At other times a slightly different emphasis may be more appropriate.

The sample clauses and commentary do not define definitively or exhaustively all issues that need to be dealt with in a telecoms outsourcing. They are provided to provoke consideration of the issues, and must not be considered to be an adequate substitute for deal-specific legal advice and drafting. Any detailed analysis of the regulatory framework within which telecoms outsourcing suppliers operate is beyond the scope of this chapter.[4] References in the rest of this chapter to 'supplier' are references to the telecoms service provider to which the telecoms infrastructure and service have been outsourced, and references to the 'customer' are references to the customer which, having transferred its telecoms infrastructure to the supplier, is now receiving the service back from the supplier.

4.2 TYPES OF TELECOMMUNICATIONS OUTSOURCING

4.2.1 Voice

The outsourcing of standard voice telephony infrastructure is a common type of telecoms outsourcing. If an end-to-end service is required (see below for a discussion of end-to-end as opposed to intermediate services) it will involve the transfer of handsets, cabling, switches (including private branch exchanges or PBXs), leased lines and other telecoms infrastructure to the supplier. The supplier will then manage and maintain the infrastructure and use it (or refreshed technology) to supply the voice service using the public switched telephone network (PSTN) according to service levels.

4.2.2 VOIP

VOIP refers to packet data transmission of voice using Internet protocols (IP). Transmission is most commonly over the Internet, although IP can equally be used as part of a dedicated leased line infrastructure. Although VOIP services have been available commercially for a number of years, the uptake has been relatively slow to date because of concerns about quality, resilience and integrity of carriage across the Internet. A VOIP outsourcing is most likely to be considered where the customer is migrating to a data IP network and wishes to include voice within the data carried.

4.2.3 Data networks

Asynchronous transfer mode (ATM) and frame relay are the most common types of data networks used by global organisations at present, although as already mentioned there is movement towards the use of IP and the Internet as acceptable alternatives.[5] The network to be outsourced may be a local area network (LAN), a wide area network (WAN), a combination of both LANs and a WAN, or a virtual private network (VPN).

LANs consist of a localised network of computers (within a building, for example) linked by a central server. WANs, on the other hand, consist of telecommunications links connecting the LANs, and the associated software, switches and routers controlling the flow of data between them. A VPN is a software-created dedicated communications network designed to act as if it were dedicated to the particular customer (even though at any one time circuits used by a VPN may carry the traffic of more than one customer). A VPN is private in the sense that it is intended to guarantee the provision of bandwidth capacity required by the customer at any time, allowing the customer to burst above its usual capacity requirements and have the network meet such requirements. It is a virtual network in the sense that the software driving it does not depend on a dedicated route for the data.

LANs, WANs and VPNs can be used for both data and voice in an IP solution.

4.2.4 Mobile telephony

A mobile telephony outsourcing in many respects looks just like a mobile telecommunications services agreement, except that existing handsets and user contracts in relation to those handsets may need to be transferred to the supplier.

Mobile telephony outsourcings may become more prevalent with the advent of third generation mobile telephony, bringing with it the ability of mobile telephony to provide increased bandwidth capacity (allowing faster and greater access to the Internet in conjunction with wireless application protocols (WAP)).

4.2.5 Mobile data – WAP applications

Mobile data and WAP are not really the subject of separate outsourcings in their own right, but are often included within the functionality provided in an outsourced mobile telephony solution.

WAP is the radio frequency spectrum equivalent to protocols (IP) used for the Internet. WAP does not increase the bandwidth or data carrying capacity of a mobile network but allows the network to carry information otherwise carried through wires in accessing the Internet.

4.2.6 Audio and video conferencing

With recent global events giving rising to a reduction in world travel, suppliers of audio and video conferencing services have seen an increase in the demand for their services from large business customers. Many large organisations see the advantages of cost savings and of an enhanced service by outsourcing their audio and video conferencing requirements. This will usually involve the transfer of the existing in-house equipment to the supplier, followed by the replacement of such equipment over time. There will often be a migration plan to migrate the service to IP and the supplier will usually provide a managed service under which calls may be booked and connected electronically or through human agency.

4.2.7 Call centres

Although not strictly telecoms outsourcings as such, call centre outsourcings often involve numerous telecoms-related issues. A detailed commentary in relation to call centres appears in paragraph 4.3.3.

4.2.8 Maintenance

In an end-to-end telecoms outsourcing, the provision of maintenance to the customer's network will be part of the service. The supplier will be required to fix network downtime and call failures within time frames specified in the service level agreement. However, the customer might wish to maintain ownership and operation of, say, its data network, but outsource maintenance of that network to the supplier. Here service levels will relate to fix times.

4.2.9 E-business-related infrastructure

With almost universal use and reliance by business on the Internet as an accepted means for conducting business, Internet and e-business-related infrastructures are being outsourced. These very often involve telecoms infrastructures. Some examples are set out below.

Dedicated trading and information exchanges

Dedicated trading and information exchanges can take various forms over the Internet. A common example is where a supplier provides a customer and its suppliers with access to a dedicated server containing information posted there by the customer and its suppliers. In this way the customer and its suppliers can exchange information on a secure basis over the Internet without the need to use more complicated electronic data interchange (EDI) arrangements, which had, until the advent of the Internet, been the general way of exchanging supply chain information electronically in a secure fashion. Their establishment sometimes needs to be cleared from a competition law perspective.

The information exchange is 'dedicated' in the sense that passwords are given out by the customer to its suppliers and no one else may (in the absence of hacking) access information held on the server without such passwords. The customer may also seek additional security comfort by requiring the supplier to provide the data in encrypted form when they are released from the server.

IP tunnelling

IP tunnelling uses encryption technology for the creation of what are, in effect, dedicated lines of communication maintained through telecommunications networks into and across the Internet and out into the telecommunications network on the other side between nodes of a WAN. The most common example is a business wishing to exchange information internally to other offices across the globe through the use of the Internet. IP tunnelling can be used both for voice and data, and the technology both overlaps and relies upon encryption software.

Encryption

Because technology in the telecoms and Internet arenas is converging, telecoms service providers providing data traffic carriage across telecommunications lines into the Internet are often being asked to provide a one-stop shop through secure encryption of the data transferred. This can also apply to voice transmissions.

Application service provider applications

Application service provider (ASP) applications are commonly referred to as renting software or bureau use of software over the Internet. Put simply, it means that a customer does not itself need to be licensed to use software in order to have its data processed by that software, but instead pays a subscription fee to a supplier who provides or rents access to the software over the Internet. The use of ASP applications generally involves large bandwidth capacity, and it is for this reason that telecommunications service providers are particularly interested in this kind of technology.

4.2.10 Cabling and related infrastructure

The customer may wish the supplier to take over and maintain all cabling and similar infrastructure. This will usually be part of a managed service.

4.2.11 Co-location/hosting

At the edges of the outsourcing spectrum are co-location/hosting arrangements under which an incumbent operator hosts or permits a competitor to site its own equipment at, say, the incumbent's local exchange so that the competitor can send and receive traffic directly from the local loop.

4.3 SAMPLE CLAUSES AND COMMENTARY I: DEAL-SPECIFIC ISSUES

4.3.1 Managed services – voice and/or data

The service provided by the supplier may be intermediate or end to end. If intermediate, the supplier will connect to existing telephony infrastructure supplied and maintained by the customer. The customer might wish to outsource everything from the exit terminal of its PBX to the supplier. This would mean that the customer would retain responsibility and ownership of the PBX, cabling and related physical infrastructure, including handsets, within its buildings. This kind of outsourcing (less than a full end-to-end service) will require the parties to define precisely where their respective obligations begin and end. This issue is dealt with in more detail in paragraph 4.3.5.

In an end-to-end service, however, the supplier will take on full operational responsibility for meeting all the customer's telephony needs. This kind of outsourcing will require the supplier to have a detailed knowledge of the customer's business requirements (which ought then to be reflected in the service level agreement).

Adjustments to estate

In an outsourcing under which handsets or other high volume hardware estate is being transferred to the supplier, it will often be the case that the customer will not know exactly how many items are in the total estate to be transferred.

This could have two consequences if the number of items to transfer is wrongly calculated. It may affect the transfer price the supplier would have been willing to pay for the estate. It may also affect the ongoing pricing for the service that the supplier would have been willing to commit to (the supplier may well have committed to a level of pricing on the mistaken belief that there were more handsets, and therefore more users, than is in fact the case).

The agreement should therefore provide for an adjustment to the transfer price (both up and down) if the actual number of items to be transferred is different from the number calculated at the signing date. Similarly, a supplier that bases its pricing on an assumed number of handsets should provide in the outsourcing agreement that it may adjust the pricing to reflect any decrease in the number it will take on.

Virtual extensions and hotdesking

Another difficulty in relation to pricing can arise by virtue of the fact that pricing may be linked to the number of handsets for which PBXs are configured (on the assumption that such number represents the number of users). Such number is usually calculated remotely by electronically interrogating all PBXs. However, this approach can lead to overcharging because hotdesking and the presence of virtual extensions registered on the PBX may give rise to an inflated number of theoretical users.

Hotdesking and virtual extensions refer to flexible call routing (often required by businesses whose personnel operate from a variety of locations or from out of the office from time to time).

In the most simple PBX configuration, a virtual extension requires a notional extension number that is allocated to a specific user. This is sometimes referred to as an analogue or digital 0 extension number. This does not include the supply of a handset, but may include PBX features and facilities, calls within the same site, on-net calls and PSTN access to the supplier's network. The analogue or digital 0 extension number can be used alone, or in conjunction with voicemail or hotdesking services.

Hotdesking, on the other hand, includes the supply of the analogue or digital 0 extension number, but, unlike a virtual extension, to work hotdesking requires the allocation of a DDI (direct dialling inward; or DID: direct inward dialling) number. Hotdesking therefore consists of the analogue or digital 0 number with an accompanying DDI number.

The outsourcing agreement should include provisions that entitle the customer to challenge the number of handsets/users calculated by the supplier (by remote interrogation) by insisting on a jointly conducted physical audit of PBXs and sites from time to time (at a cost to be borne by the supplier if its calculation proves to be more than, say, 3 per cent overstated), and to insist on retrospective price adjustments (including refunds) if the actual number of users proves to be less.

4.3.2 Voice

Telephone numbers

Usually the supplier will attempt to provide in the outsourcing agreement that the customer shall have no rights in relation to telephone numbers issued to it:

> Subject to the provisions of any applicable law, regulation or licence condition, telephone numbers allocated to the Customer, and all rights in those numbers, belong to the Supplier and the Customer shall not sell or transfer any telephone number to a third party. The Customer shall have no trade name right in any telephone number that the Supplier allocates to it nor any trade name right that may develop in any telephone number allocated to it, and the Customer shall make no attempt to apply for registration of such telephone numbers as a trade or service mark (whether on their own or in conjunction with some other words or trading style or device).

> The Supplier may change any telephone number allocated to the Customer after giving the Customer reasonable notice.

> After cancellation of any Services, the Supplier shall not issue any telephone number that has been allocated to the Customer to a third party for a period of [ ] months after the date of cancellation.

The purpose of such provisions is to prevent the customer from asserting that it has developed intellectual property rights in association with the telephone numbers, which could prevent the supplier from reallocating the numbers to another customer at a later time.

However, being forced to change telephone numbers is an expensive business (the cost of advertising number changes and replacement of all stationery, etc.). Accordingly the customer might wish to place limits on the supplier's ability to change numbers:

> The Supplier shall not allocate any telephone numbers to a third party already reserved for use by the Customer.

> The Supplier shall not be entitled to withdraw or change any telephone number or code or group of numbers or codes designated for the Customer once such numbers or codes have been allocated to the Customer except in order to comply with any provision of a licence or any numbering scheme or if such change is required by law or by a regulatory authority, and in such circumstances the Supplier shall give the Customer the maximum period of notice practicable and reasonable in the circumstances before withdrawing or changing such telephone numbers or codes.

Number portability

In the UK and within the European Union the provisions of the Numbering Directive (98/61/EC) (implemented in the UK as the Telecommunications (Interconnection) (Number Portability, etc.) Regulations 1999, SI 1999/3449) require that service providers provide number portability in relation to fixed telecommunications services (but not for mobile telephony).

The position in relation to mobile telephony is the subject of a new Directive (Directive on Universal Service and Users' Rights relating to Electronic Communications Networks and Services (COM (2000) 392)). The Directive requires number portability to be provided by mobile operators. It would not initially extend the requirement of number portability to apply between mobile and fixed operators, but such change could be proposed under a review procedure. Implementation in the United Kingdom is likely to be under regulations to be made under the Communications Bill.

As the supplier is not subject to particularly onerous regulatory obligations in relation to portability, it may be advisable to provide specifically for what the supplier is expected to do in relation to porting telephone numbers:

> The Supplier shall, in accordance with the migration plan, at its own cost take all reasonable steps to enable the Customer to port the then current telephone numbers supplied through existing suppliers so that the Customer can continue to use them as part of the outsourced services.

> On termination or expiry of the Agreement, the Supplier shall at its own cost take all reasonable steps to enable the Customer to port the then current telephone numbers allocated to it so that it can continue to use them with a successor supplier.

> The Supplier shall comply with the provisions of the Numbering Directive and all relevant domestic implementations of it.

4.3.3 Call centres

A customer considering establishing an outsourced call centre will need to consider the appropriate location for it from a tax perspective (particularly in relation to liability for VAT).

Establishing an effective call centre outsourcing agreement involves detailed mapping of call resolution from the time the call is received to call closure. This may involve a process map, which may or may not, depending upon the complexity of the issues raised by the call, involve referral into the customer itself for resolution. In any event, the process map will need properly to prescribe the interaction between the supplier and the customer in relation to call resolution (and the boundaries of their respective responsibilities).

The outsourcing agreement must make clear what kind of call the supplier is required to address. A supplier may, for example, dispute that there is any necessity to address a call until it is logged in its call management system. It is increasingly the case that 'call' has come to mean a request for service, whether by telephone, e-mail or otherwise.

A suggested definition for the kind of call that must be resolved by the supplier is:

'Call' means a request from a user (whether written, oral, by e-mail or otherwise) that has been registered on the Supplier's call management system with a unique call log number. 'Call' does not include a follow-up request from the same user made as a result of the first request not being resolved in accordance with the call resolution protocols.

If the outsourced service is being paid for by reference to the number of calls, the definition of call must be precise. For example, a customer would wish to avoid having to pay for the processing of a call that relates to inadequate advice given the first time or where the call is made twice (as a result of the first call being dropped by the call centre's call routing system).

Sometimes a customer might wish the supplier to interface with the customer's own systems (or even to use those systems). An example might be where the supplier processes customer orders and must transfer the ordering data into the customer's supply chain management system. It is important in such circumstances that the supplier is required to achieve compatibility between the systems so that there are no problems with interfacing. This is particularly significant if the customer itself is required at some point in the resolution of a call to provide input, as here it would wish to track the resolution of the call in conjunction with the supplier. A sample clause dealing with compatibility is set out in paragraph 4.4.10.

The outsourcing agreement will need to specify what language/dialects it requires the call centre to use in dealing with calls. This will be important where the customer's services need to retain a sense of local identity.

The starting point in managing legal risk in relation to a call centre is to consider the industry sector in which it operates, as industry-specific laws and regulations may apply to the activities of the call centre in that industry sector.

The way (or methods) in which the call centre conducts business may also be subject to law or regulation (particularly if this involves selling goods or services or financial products).

Where selling or contracting is involved as part of a call centre's activities, the outsourcing agreement must prescribe in precise terms the scope of authority of the call centre representative to bind the customer in contract in relation to the callers. Normally the service level agreement will require call centre representatives within a call centre to follow scripts signed off by the customer in advance.

A call centre's operations will need to comply with the provisions of the applicable class licence under the Telecommunications Act 1984.[6] The licence will include conditions about automatic calls (for example, prerecorded messages) – here the call centre will need to maintain a register of people who have consented to be contacted.

Under the proposed Directive concerning the Processing of Personal Data and the Protection of Privacy in the Electronic Communications Sector (COM (2000) 385)[7] there will be various restrictions on cold calling and unsolicited e-mail and faxes that will apply to call centres.[8] In essence, such direct marketing activities would be prohibited except for customers who have given prior consent. The latest draft includes provision for member states to exercise discretion as to whether opt in or opt out e-spam regimes are permitted.

These new provisions will need to be complied with along with the more general provisions of the Data Protection Act 1998 in relation to the collection and processing of personal data made by the call centre.

The *ICSTIS Code of Practice* (promulgated by the Independent Committee for the Supervision of Standards for Information Services, set up under OFTEL) regulates the premium rate telecommunications industry and applies to call centres used to organise competitions or sales promotions and call centres that provide chat lines or advice services.

The *ICSTIS Code of Practice* establishes standards for the content of premium rate telephone services and applies to call centres accessed by customers in the UK (whether or not the services are provided from within the UK or abroad and whether the service provider is situated in the UK or not).

Services charged at more than £1 per minute, virtual chat services charged at £1 per minute and live conversation services generally require the prior permission of ICSTIS before they can be operated.

The outsourcing agreement should therefore provide that the supplier should comply with the code and directions given by ICSTIS (and generally co-operate with ICSTIS) in the provision of call centre services.

In December 2000 the Call Centre Association (CCA) published a *CCA Code of Practice* dealing with standards of best practice in relation to the operation of call centres. The *CCA Code of Practice* deals with training and development, performance targets, employee consultation and dispute resolution, recruitment, data protection awareness, service standards and complaint handling.

The *CCA Code of Practice* requires that members of the CCA must undertake to subscribe to, and comply with, particular industry customer contact codes of practice and all relevant legislation. It has been endorsed by the Department of Trade and Industry as a model for call centre management.

The supplier may of course not be a member of the CCA. But it is worth considering whether the outsourcing agreement should require the supplier to comply with the *CCA Code of Practice* as a matter of good industry practice.

The Consumer Protection (Distance Selling) Regulations 2000, SI 2000/2334 (in force from 31 October 2000) implemented the Distance Selling Directive (1997/7/EC) (applying to member states of the European Union). The regulations apply to the sale of goods and services remotely, including through call centres (depending on the nature of the goods or services sold).

In general terms, the regulations impose obligations on the call centre representative to provide a consumer contacting a call centre with various information about the supply of the goods or services and the commercial terms relating to them (including delivery and payment details).

If the consumer proceeds with the purchase, similar information must be supplied in writing no later than the time of delivery or supply and such information must include details about the right to withdraw from the sale after delivery or supply. The regulations give a seven-day cooling-off period entitling the consumer to cancel the purchase.

Where a call centre is involved in the sale of goods or services covered by the regulations, it will be necessary for the outsourcing agreement to require the supplier to comply with its provisions. This can best be achieved by requiring the supplier to ensure that its call centre representatives within the call centre follow an agreed script and process in effecting sales and in providing follow-up information.

The Financial Services and Markets Act 2000 (and regulations promulgated under it) includes provisions dealing with the sale of financial products and services sold remotely. Call centres operating in this industry sector must comply with its requirements. As with the other legislative provisions described above, the supplier should be required to comply with its provisions in the context of scripting and prescribing procedures to be followed by call centre representatives.

As with other forms of advertising, advertising relating to services provided by call centres is subject to the usual forms of scrutiny by relevant authorities in the United Kingdom. For example, the Advertising Standards Authority scrutinises advertisements in print media, while the Independent Television Commission and the Radio Authority scrutinise advertising on television and radio respectively. Particular attention must be paid to their codes of practice in relation to premium rate services offered by call centres. The *ICSTIS Code of Practice* incorporates a code of advertising practice applicable to the services offered by call centres.[9]

4.3.4 ASP

In ASP agreements customers often focus on the amount of guaranteed processing time and capacity they have once they have accessed the supplier's application. However, such guarantees are of little comfort if the customer is not able to connect with the supplier's systems at all. Therefore, the customer should also consider whether it should be asking for dedicated capacity through the supplier's pipe connecting the supplier to the Internet or telephone network. If the supplier has not dedicated enough bandwidth to the customer along this conduit, the customer could well find that it cannot achieve connectivity or that processing times are slow, owing to demand from the supplier's other customers. Generally suppliers are willing to agree to dedicated capacity along the pipe for a cost, and to agree service levels relating to such access, but will attempt to make such arrangements back-to-back with any arrangement they have with their own network or connectivity provider.

4.3.5   Data networks and IP

Traditional data network

Voice is excluded from a traditional data network model. Voice and data services are provided on two separate networks (resulting in increased cabling and infrastructure costs). Each user has a telephone and a networked PC, so two ports are required at each desk.

For telephony (voice), there is a PBX at each customer site connected to handsets. Wide area voice connections are likely to use an integrated services digital network (ISDN) over the PSTN.

As regards data, the LAN connecting PCs, printers, etc. within a single customer site will not include softphones (IP telephones). The data WAN connecting various customer sites might consist of frame relay permanent virtual circuits. There will usually be no private or virtual private network.

Convergence solution

In contrast, a convergence data and voice solution converts voice into data packets (so that it can be treated just like any other data). Such a solution might involve a number of building blocks in one integrated network (each of these is discussed below): an IP virtual private network (a WAN), voice over IP, and an IP LAN (including an IP telephony capability).

In a typical convergence solution an IP LAN is established within each customer site. Softphones (IP handsets) are used at each desk. These may be run by software on users' PCs.

All customer sites are interconnected by the virtual private network (WAN) using IP and some form of multi-protocol label switching. This sets up secure pathways between customer sites in the IP virtual private network, based on labels attached to data packets at the point where they enter the network. The purpose of labelling such data is to keep traffic on the customer's IP virtual private network separate from other customers' traffic.

Each customer site on the IP virtual private network can send data packets directly to any other customer site on the IP virtual private network without having to go through a central hub. Predefined pathways connecting every customer site to every other customer site are therefore not required. Multi-protocol label switching therefore avoids the problems of ubiquitous 'hub and spoke' network design.

Voice in the WAN is carried in IP format. Voice packets are labelled as such before they leave the customer's sites, and are given priority over other data to maintain the quality of the call. The system may prioritise transmission of delay-sensitive traffic (such as voice and video) and business-critical traffic over non-urgent traffic.

In most convergence data network solutions suitable bandwidth segments will be allocated to each class of data. If the traffic exceeds the bandwidth allocated to it then packets may well be dropped. Whether they are dropped or not in many solutions may depend on the class of data. Voice packets would generally be dropped rather than delayed (delay obviously unacceptably affects call quality). Other data classes might be permitted to burst temporarily into greater bandwidth or be held back for later transmission.

The new convergence solution presents suppliers, who historically provided within country services only (and not on a pan-European or global basis), with major technical, legal and commercial challenges. This is at a time when, ironically, significant regulatory changes currently occurring are intended to make things easier for suppliers hoping to provide such services on a transborder basis.[10]

First, it may be quite difficult to prescribe the appropriate amount of bandwidth at the first attempt for each class of data. This will usually be because statistics are not available for the precise volumes of traffic generated by the customer in each class.

The service levels to which the supplier contracts to adhere will usually only apply if the relevant class of data traffic remains within its allocated bandwidth. If the bandwidth allocation is wildly underestimated at the first attempt it means that the customer will regularly be falling outside the protection of guaranteed service levels.

Usually requesting the allocation of more bandwidth will have cost implications, with the supplier at this point being able to charge indiscriminately on the basis of the customer being a captive audience. Therefore, it is important to agree the price or pricing mechanism for allocating additional bandwidth to each data class before signing of the outsourcing agreement.

The outsourcing agreement should also recognise the reality of the situation that, at least during the initial stages of the life of the outsourcing, bandwidth adjustments will be required and that the customer needs some minimum key service level comfort at this stage (even if some service levels do not apply by virtue of traffic exceeding bandwidth allocation). The outsourcing agreement should make clear the degree to which (if at all) a change in allocated bandwidth entitles the supplier to revise or modify applicable service levels. The outsourcing agreement could provide for a forecasting mechanism for the requirements of bandwidth (e.g. a rolling six-monthly forecast), which would allow the supplier to anticipate future requirements (and therefore limit the extra cost in providing extra bandwidth).

Second, the supplier will wish very clearly to circumscribe the boundaries of the network for which it has responsibility. For example, where the service is less than end-to-end, the outsourcing agreement might provide:

The 'Service Termination Point' is the physical connector at the Customer facing local area network port on each router. The Supplier provides the Services to the Service Termination Point. The Supplier has no responsibility in respect of any equipment on the site beyond the Service Termination Point.

The supplier might also be using local exchange carriers to carry voice or data across the local loop in countries where it is not the local loop provider. Here the supplier will attempt to exclude liability for this part of the network. This is dealt with in detail in paragraph 4.4.4.

Third, customers wanting pan-European or global data network solutions want pricing models that reflect the economies of scale that global solutions providers can offer. For suppliers more used to local supply arrangements, however, this presents a major commercial challenge – they are being asked to abandon simple pricing models based on allocated bandwidth and dedicated circuits in favour of sophisticated models that address volume of traffic and discounts based on total revenue spend under the global arrangement. These pricing models are discussed in paragraph 4.4.12.

It is important that the customer should have the right to continue to use the relevant IP addresses on termination of the service. Other provisions, such as data security requirements, global reporting, changes in the technology platform, network compatibility, future proofing and providing for new functionality, network security audits, access to the supplier's diagnostic systems, liability for data corruption and network hacking, allocating liability for breaches of data protection laws, providing for disaster recovery and catastrophic network failures, and restrictions on the use of data networks, are all particularly relevant to data network outsourcings. These are dealt with in section 4.4 below.[11]

4.3.6 Cabling

The Telecommunications Act 1984, Sched.2, para.27(4) (the *Telecoms Code*) provides that, as between the owner of land and the telecoms service provider, the service provider owns the cabling installed on, under or attached to, land or any building. This overcomes the outcome that would result from the law of fixtures. Under the *Telecoms Code* a telecoms service provider is required to remove cabling when it ceases to provide the service and there is no prospect of the cabling being used by it (clause 22 of the *Telecoms Code*). Therefore, if at the end of an outsourcing, a customer wishes to retain cabling, etc. installed by the supplier (this will be important where the customer wishes to take the service back in house, and to achieve a smooth transition to a new service provider), the outsourcing agreement should provide that the supplier shall not have the right to remove any cabling installed by it and that it shall permit the customer or a successor supplier to use it to provide the services.

4.3.7   Mobile

The protection of location data (information regarding the location or movements of users of mobile devices) should be addressed in the outsourcing agreement. The customer should consider whether the service ought to be limited to the GSM (global system for mobile communications) platform in order to maintain quality of the service.

4.3.8   Audio and video conferencing

The customer should consider whether the supplier ought to be prohibited from using satellite in the delivery of the service (which can cause unacceptable delays in content delivery). A commercial decision will need to be reached about who bears the cost of any equipment upgrades.

4.4   SAMPLE CLAUSES AND COMMENTARY II: GENERIC TELECOMS OUTSOURCING ISSUES

4.4.1   The service level agreement

The SLA should, in the service description, include separate descriptions for the carriage part of the service, the managed component (i.e. for end-to-end outsourcings it should prescribe the obligations in relation to the hardware and equipment estate) and all other services to be provided. Outlined below are some of the telecoms-specific issues that should be dealt with in a telecoms outsourcing agreement.

Network availability

The customer is likely to want the network to be available for use 24 hours a day, seven days a week. However, recognising that there may need to be a very limited latitude for downtime, many customers for outsourced telecoms solutions are prepared to agree that the service level for network availability shall be something less than 100 per cent. Normally it is something like 98.5 or 99.5 per cent availability. This will, of course, differ according to the nature of the customer's business.

Platform fix

The SLA should also provide for fix times for errors or faults in the technology platform – for example, for fixing a defective switch or router. These are generally specified in terms of hours for critical faults, and hours or possibly even days for non-critical faults.

Logical and physical moves

Logical moves are software-implemented moves relating to the configuration and ability of a switch to recognise a call as a numerical extension number and route it to the appropriate physical extension. A physical move, on the other hand, relates to the physical relocation of handsets connected to the PBX.

If the outsourcing includes handset and extension infrastructure, the SLA should permit the customer to request a certain number of logical and physical moves for free, allowing the customer to relocate offices and personnel as part of its business operations.

Beyond certain limits the customer will be charged. Because the customer will have requirements to have logical and physical moves implemented quickly, service levels for their implementation should be specified in the SLA. These should be expressed as a number of hours or days from the date and time of request, regardless of whether or not the customer is having to pay for the move.

Hotdesking and virtual extensions

The SLA should provide for the response times for implementing hotdesking and virtual extensions when requested by a user.

Call failure rates

The SLA should provide for the customer's requirements in relation to successful calls and call failure rates. It should provide something like:

> The Supplier shall provide a grade of service of 1:100 from the handset to any PSTN number between the required maintenance cover times for all category A sites across the countries [or sites] covered by the Agreement.

The service level 1:100 means that in busy hours not more than one call in 100 is not available. It is sometimes described as PO1. Therefore, PO2 would mean that two out of 100 calls are not available in busy hours.

Data integrity

The SLA should provide for the procedures and processes that the supplier should follow in order to maintain integrity of voice and data carried across the network. This should include maintaining operational surveillance of the network and undertaking appropriate diagnostic and analytical software scans.

4.4.2   Technology platform

Although the main concern of a customer in a telecoms outsourcing is with the quality of the service (and not the platform by which it is delivered), sometimes the customer may want certain minimum safeguards in relation to the platform or network used to deliver the service. This may be because the nature of the platform may affect the resilience of the service or because the customer is concerned about ensuring that it remains sufficiently generic (this is helpful when the service is brought back in house or sent to another supplier).

Imposing certain minimum criteria in relation to the technology platform used also safeguards against a downgrading of the platform later in the life of the outsourcing (to drive down costs) and against interconnection arrangements with suppliers of inferior network platforms. The following clause is an example:

> The Network shall comply with the performance standards, specifications and other criteria set out in the Network Specification.
>
> The Supplier shall repair, replace or modify the Network (and any parts of it) to ensure such compliance in accordance with the time frames set out in the Service Level Agreement.

Sometimes all the customer will need in relation to the platform used is a requirement that the platform will comply with certain minimum, generally applicable industry standards, such as BS 7799 and other industry standards in relation to the choice of network components, protocols and interoperability.

4.4.3   Carriage in other countries

The supplier is unlikely to have an operating presence in all countries covered by the outsourcing agreement. It will want to use local carriers in those countries on a subcontracted basis. Sometimes local regulation requires the contract of carriage to be between the local telecoms carrier and the customer (or it may require the customer to give its explicit consent to the carriage of traffic in that country), limiting the benefits the customer is trying to achieve in having a one-stop shop outsourcing arrangement with the supplier. Various contractual provisions can be used to limit such problems:

> If the Supplier wishes to use local carriers to carry traffic in any country:
>
> (1)   the Supplier shall, unless prevented from doing so by regulations or laws applying in the country in question, contract with such local carrier as prime contractor and not as agent of the Customer for the carriage of such traffic;
>
> (2)   the Customer shall give such reasonable notifications of consent to the local carrier as are required by the regulations or laws of the country in question to enable the local carrier to carry its traffic (the Customer shall be entitled to withhold such consent where the requirements of the consent include giving indemnities to the local carrier or any other provisions not brought to the

Customer's attention by the Supplier prior to placing the order to which the local carriage relates);

(3) if such regulations or laws require that the Supplier contract with the local carrier as the Customer's agent or require that the Customer enter into some other direct contractual relationship with the local carrier:

(i) the Supplier shall use all reasonable endeavours to notify the Customer that the Supplier is required to contract with the local carrier as agent or that the Customer is required to enter into the direct contractual relationship with the local carrier; and

(ii) if the Customer was notified of this requirement by the Supplier prior to placing the order, the Customer shall enter into such reasonable letters of agency or other documents reasonably required by the local carrier or the regulations or laws applicable in the country in question to enable the local carrier to carry the traffic.

4.4.4 Local exchange carriers

The supplier will not be the local exchange carrier of traffic across the local loop in most (if not all) countries in which it contracts to provide a pan-European or global service. The supplier may therefore wish to provide for various exclusions arising out of its use of local exchange carriers carrying traffic across the local loop.

The supplier will, for example, seek to excuse itself from failure to comply with the SLA where this arises from carriage failure across the local loop. The supplier will argue for this exemption on the basis that it has no control over the local exchange carrier and that the customer would have faced the same disruption had it contracted with the local exchange carrier directly. An example of such an exclusion is as follows:

The Supplier shall not be regarded as having failed to provide the Services in accordance with the Service Level Agreement in relation to Excluded Countries to the extent that such failure arises in such Excluded Countries as a result of a failure occurring between the Supplier's POP and the egress point at the Service Termination Point.

In this clause:

'Excluded Countries' mean countries listed in schedule [ ];

'POP' means a physical location where the Supplier as inter-exchange carrier has installed equipment to interconnect with a local exchange carrier (for carriage of traffic across the local loop from POP to the Service Termination Point);

'Service Termination Point' means the physical connector at the Customer-facing local area network port on each router.

4.4.5 Authority to act as telecommunications service provider

An outsourced telecoms service provider running a telecommunications system (other than a purely domestic network not connected to another network) requires a licence to do so. The licensing provisions in the UK are subject to the implementation in the UK of the EU Licensing Directive (97/13/EC) and to various reforms envisaged at EU and domestic level in relation to licensing.

A customer-centric clause that deals with this issue is:

The Supplier warrants that it has (and will maintain) all permissions, Licences and consents (including all necessary interconnection agreements with third party network providers, and compliance with the requirements of the applicable regulatory authority in each country) necessary to:

(1) enable the Supplier to supply the Services using the Network;
(2) act as a telecommunications service provider in relation to this Agreement and the Services; and
(3) supply the Services on the terms and conditions of this Agreement.

'Act' means legislation and regulations regulating the provision and operation of telecommunications services in any country that apply to telecommunications systems (including the Network) operated or used by the Supplier.

'Licence' means any licences issued under the Act that authorise the provision of telecommunications services using telecommunications systems (including the Network).

'Network' means the part of the network or networks (including systems) provided or procured by the Supplier to provide the Services. The Network may include parts of third party systems.

However, in some outsourcings the customer may retain certain infrastructure (such as its in-house network), which may require it to have its own licence. The supplier may not legally be able to provide the service if the customer loses its own licence. Here the supplier may insist on a clause dealing with licensing that is of mutual effect:

The Supplier shall comply with the terms of its Licence, the Act and all other laws and regulations in the provision of the Services.

The Customer shall use its Equipment and the Services in accordance with the Act and any licence granted under the Act that governs the running of a telecommunications system by the Customer, and in accordance with all other applicable laws and regulations.

The Customer may wish to receive advance warning if any regulatory changes are likely to affect the outsourced service:

The Supplier shall keep the Customer informed of all regulatory changes (including those under its Licence and those to be implemented by the applicable regulatory authority in each country) that impact upon the level of Services or the Service Charges.

What should the outsourcing agreement provide for where one or other of the parties loses its licence? Customers will argue for immediate termination rights but these are resisted by suppliers. Instead suppliers will argue for a grace period and the right to implement a replacement service under a new licence:

If the Supplier loses its Licence:

(1)   the parties will attempt in good faith to develop within [ten] days a mutually acceptable workaround solution that conforms to all applicable regulatory requirements;

(2)   if the Supplier is able to provide functionally equivalent Services that:

(i)   materially comply with the requirements of this Agreement;

(ii)   are no less comprehensive than the previous Services, and whose terms and conditions are no more onerous on the Customer;

(iii)   in respect of which the Service Charges are no greater;

(iv)   are, in the reasonable opinion of the Customer, compatible with the Systems used by the Customer; and

(v)   do not require the Customer to incur additional costs in the operation of its own Systems or in relation to the interfacing with the Services,

('Equivalent Services'), then the Supplier shall be entitled to replace the affected Services with such Equivalent Services; and

if:

(vi)   the parties are unable to agree the workaround solution; or

(vii) the Supplier is unable to provide Equivalent Services,

within [ten] days of the loss of Licence, the Customer may by notice to Supplier terminate the affected Services.

The supplier itself will normally want a termination right if it loses its licence or the customer loses its own licence:

The Supplier may by notice to the Customer terminate this Agreement if:

(1)   the licence under which the Customer has a right to run its telecommunications system and connect it to the Network is revoked or otherwise ceases to be valid and such licence is not immediately replaced by another licence conferring similar rights (and the Supplier may immediately suspend provision of the Services until such licence has been reinstated or replaced by another licence conferring similar rights);

(2)   the Licence under which the Services are provided expires or is revoked (by reason other than the act or omission of the Supplier) and the Licence is not immediately replaced by another licence required for the provision of the Services. The Supplier shall give the Customer reasonable warning by notice if there is a risk, to its knowledge, that the Supplier has to rely on this provision to terminate the Agreement (and the Supplier shall also give the Customer the maximum period of notice of termination practicable in the circumstances).

A prudent customer will include a right to terminate if its own licence terminates. It is not unusual for the customer to seek indemnification if the supplier loses its licence if the agreement is brought to an end as a result. Suppliers will vigorously resist such provisions.

4.4.6   Restrictions on use of services

The supplier's own licence or the regulations that apply to it will usually place restrictions on what its own network can carry. Such restrictions must in turn be placed on the customer in the outsourcing agreement, as illustrated in the clause that follows (the words appearing in square brackets below are words that can be added to make the clauses more customer-biased):

The Customer shall not use the Services:

(1)   for the transmission of any material that is defamatory, offensive or abusive or of an obscene or menacing character; or
(2)   in a manner which [to the best of its knowledge, information and belief] constitutes an infringement of the Intellectual Property Rights of any person.

The Customer shall take all reasonable steps to ensure that its use of the Services, and its content carried through the use of the Services, comply with:

(1)   all applicable laws and regulations; and
(2)   any written and electronic instructions for use of the Services given by the Supplier.

If:

(1)   the Customer's use of the Services or the content does not comply with the requirements of this clause set out above; or
(2)   such use or content interferes (at a technical level in relation to System functionality, but not including interference arising from capacity or bandwidth demands of traffic) with the Supplier's ability to provide:

(i)   Services to the Customer; or
(ii)   any other services to the Supplier's other customers,

(each a 'Prohibited Use'), the Supplier may:

(1)   give the Customer notice of the Prohibited Use, giving it a reasonable opportunity to cease such Prohibited Use; and
(2)   if such Prohibited Use does not end within [5 (five)] Business Days after the notice is given, suspend provision of the affected Services until the Customer ends the Prohibited Use. [On receipt of notice from the Customer that the Prohibited use has ended, the Supplier shall immediately resume provision of the affected Services.]

As discussed below in more detail, many customers resist the right of suppliers to suspend services, even if there is a prohibited use. However, the supplier must not allow itself to be put in a position where what it carries causes it to be in breach of its own licence or regulations applying to it.

4.4.7   Attaching customer equipment to the network

Where the service is not end-to-end, or where the outsourcing agreement gives the customer the right to attach its own equipment to the network, the outsourcing agreement will need to deal with the customer's legal obligations in attaching such equipment. The classes of equipment (e.g. fax machines, answer phones, modems and similar end user equipment) that the customer may attach should be agreed in a schedule to the outsourcing agreement, with the customer having an obligation to seek the permission of the supplier if it wishes to attach any other type of equipment.

> The Customer may connect Customer Equipment to the Network (but no other equipment without the written consent of the Supplier).

> The Customer shall, if required to do so by any licence granted under the Act, notify, or obtain any necessary permission of, a public telecommunications operator or other relevant person for the connection of the Customer Equipment to the Network. The Supplier shall provide the Customer with such reasonable assistance in giving such notices or in obtaining such permission.

> The Customer shall ensure that the Customer Equipment is approved for connection to other telecommunications systems under section 22 of the Telecommunications Act 1984 and the Customer shall comply with the conditions of such approval.

> The Supplier may disconnect any Customer Equipment from the Network:

> (1) where the Customer does not comply with its obligations in this clause;
> (2) if in the reasonable opinion of the Supplier, the Customer Equipment is liable to cause the death of, or personal injury to, or damage to property of, the Supplier or its personnel;
> (3) if the Customer Equipment is likely materially to impair the quality of any services provided using the Network to the Customer or the Supplier's other customers.

> 'Customer Equipment' means any equipment at Customer sites used by the Customer in order to obtain or enhance the benefit of the Services, as specified in Schedule [ ].

4.4.8 Security

Access codes

Some types of services (particularly data network services) will require the supplier to provide the customer with access codes, allowing the customer to have access to the network.

> The Supplier shall allocate Access Codes to the Customer to allow it to access the Network.

> Access Codes are confidential information, and the Customer shall safeguard the Access Codes against unauthorised disclosure in accordance with clause [ ] (Confidential Information).

> The Customer shall:

> (1) use the Access Codes in accordance with the reasonable instructions of the Supplier;
> (2) notify the Supplier where the Customer believes that any unauthorised person has had access to, or is making use of, the Access Codes without the permission of the Customer or Supplier.

The Supplier may withdraw or change any Access Code if the Supplier reasonably believes that the Access Codes have been disclosed to, or used by, an unauthorised person.

'Access Code' means an authorisation code required in order to access the Network.

Hacking

Hacking into voice and data networks is both a security issue and a cost issue. The customer ought not to bear the cost of carrying unauthorised traffic unless the unauthorised access is in some way attributable to it:

If the Network is accessed, or use of the Network is made, by anyone other than the Customer or persons authorised by it ('Unauthorised User', and 'Unauthorised Use' shall have a corresponding meaning), the Customer shall not be liable to pay for Network Usage Charges associated with the Unauthorised Use unless such Unauthorised Use results from:

(1) the negligence, fraud or failure by the Customer to keep any Supplier Equipment or Customer Equipment located on the Customer's premises physically secure from Unauthorised Use; or

(2) disclosure by the Customer of Access Codes supplied to it by the Supplier for accessing the Network; or

(3) Personnel (or former Personnel) of the Customer making Unauthorised Use of the Network as a result of information or access obtained from the Customer relating to Network access or use.

Network security

Security of the customer's systems is an issue that grows in importance on an outsourcing, given the customer's loss of control over the day-to-day operations of those systems. Accordingly, the customer will need certain assurances in relation to the ongoing security of its retained systems:

The Supplier shall:

(1) not impede access to any part of the Network located on the Customer's premises by Personnel of the Customer carrying out their normal duties, safety officers of the Customer or by any third party providing the Customer with any IT services;

(2) comply with the Customer's IT policies set out in Schedule [ ] (and any replacement policies agreed in writing between the parties from time to time) in relation to remote access to, and use of, the Customer's systems, e-mail and the Internet;

(3) take all necessary steps in accordance with best industry practice to prevent any viruses being introduced on to the Network, into any of the Customer's systems or into any other information technology or systems (including computer hardware) used by the Supplier to provide the Services;

(4) except where contemplated by this Agreement or the Services, not access (or attempt to access) the Customer's systems without the written consent of the Customer; and

(5) indemnify the Customer for all costs, losses, claims, damages, expenses or proceedings incurred or suffered by it as a result of a breach of this clause.

Data security

The outsourcing agreement should also provide for the security of the data carried by the supplier. A customer-biased example of such a clause follows:

The Supplier shall:

(1) procure that no unauthorised third party will, as a result of any act or omission of the Supplier, obtain access to any Customer Data or any information of the Customer carried on the Network as part of the Services;

(2) apply security procedures in accordance with best industry practice to guard against the loss, destruction, corruption or alteration of Customer Data in the possession or control of, or accessed by, the Supplier;

(3) ensure that it and its Personnel do not deliberately or negligently corrupt or erase Customer Data on the Customer's systems or on the Network;

(4) in accordance with best industry practice, maintain appropriate physical and logical security over the Network;

(5) if it stores any Customer Data in order to provide the Services, keep such Customer Data physically and logically separate from the data of its other customers, and (where practicable) identify it as the confidential information of the Customer;

(6) not disclose Access Codes supplied to or by the Customer to access the Network or the Customer's systems to any person other than its Personnel with a need to know;

(7) immediately notify the Customer of any breach in relation to such Access Codes; and

(8) indemnify the Customer for all costs, losses, claims, damages, expenses or proceedings reasonably incurred or suffered by it as a result of a breach of this clause.

Auditing security

Recent emphasis on applying principles of good corporate governance in the outsourcing arena has resulted in customers asking for audit rights in relation to the security measures undertaken by the supplier. Suppliers usually vigorously resist such rights. The sample clause below shows what a customer might typically ask for:

The Customer may, by [24] hours notice at any time, require the Supplier to give the Customer and its Personnel access to the Network and the Supplier's systems in order to:

(1) enable it to audit the security and integrity of the Network and the Supplier's systems used to provide the Services; and

(2) establish whether there has been compliance with the provisions of clauses [   ] (Network Security) and [   ] (Data Security).

On receipt of such notice, the Supplier shall provide such access and all other assistance necessary to enable the Customer to undertake such audit.

The Customer shall in conducting such audit:

(1) take reasonable steps to minimise disruption to the Supplier's business operations;

(2) not be entitled to access any market-sensitive or confidential information of the Supplier;

(3) if requested by the Supplier, do so with the participation of the Supplier or its Personnel; and

(4) if requested by the Supplier, procure that its Personnel undertaking the audit sign reasonable confidentiality undertakings in favour of the Supplier.

4.4.9 Access to supplier systems

In conjunction with security audit rights, the customer might want to be able remotely to interrogate certain systems operated by the supplier from time to time. Suppliers invariably try to resist such rights. In the sample clause that follows the words in square brackets might be requested by a supplier to make the clause less customer-biased:

The Supplier shall provide the Customer with remote electronic access to the following systems:

(1) the troubleshooting and support systems;

(2) the database (if any); and

(3) all diagnostic systems relating to the Network used in providing the Services,

[(but only if the Supplier makes access to such database or systems available to its other customers as a standard service offering in relation to those types of services)].

4.4.10 Technology compatibility

Systems used by the supplier invariably will be updated and modified by it over time. The supplier may not wish to be constrained by having to use the change control procedure every time it wishes to do this. On the other hand, for the customer the issue is whether the changes made by the supplier will adversely affect the service, result in an increase in the service charges or result in the customer itself having to spend money in order for its systems to remain compatible with the new systems of the supplier.

The customer will also want the supplier's systems to be as generic as possible, so that transition back in house or to another supplier at the end of the agreement is not made more difficult. Accordingly the customer might want the supplier to use certain specified systems unless, in relation to a particular case, the customer agrees otherwise.

A customer-biased clause capturing these issues is set out below. The words in square brackets are often requested by a supplier:

The Supplier shall:

(1) consult with the Customer on all questions of telecommunications strategy and policy affecting the Customer in relation to the Services provided under

the Agreement. If the Supplier wishes to use any systems or equipment other than those specified in Schedule [ ] ('Technology Changes'), such change may only be implemented in accordance with the Change Control Procedure. Unless agreed in writing between the parties, the Supplier shall not be entitled to increase the Service Charges as a result of any Technology Change; and

(2) ensure that the Network used by it to provide the Services is compatible for use with, works in combination with, and interfaces with (together 'Compatibility') the systems used by the Customer.

If the Supplier makes changes to its Network or other systems resulting in the Customer having to make changes to its own systems in order to achieve Compatibility between the Network and systems used by the Supplier to provide the Services and the systems used by the Customer, the Supplier shall reimburse the costs reasonably incurred by the Customer in achieving Compatibility. [The obligation to reimburse shall not apply to changes required to comply with industry-wide changes, including changes required by law or regulation.]

Suppliers might, however, argue that they need the flexibility to make changes to the network. A supplier-biased clause providing for such flexibility is as follows:

The Supplier may modify, change, add to or replace parts of the Network (including systems) or the Supplier Equipment ('Technology Changes'), provided that such Technology Changes:

(1) do not result in an increase in Service Charges;
(2) do not materially detract from, reduce or impair the overall performance of the Services, the Supplier Equipment or the Network;
(3) do not result in the Supplier Equipment or the Network failing to comply with their specifications;
(4) do not result in the Services failing to comply with the Service Level Agreement;
(5) do not result in the Customer having to make material changes to the physical interfaces or protocols used by it to receive the Services.

4.4.11 Technology refresh

Technology refresh is particularly problematic in telecoms outsourcings. The supplier will have made an initial capital investment and it will be unlikely to be willing to implement later improvements to the technology unless this will result in cost savings to it or the cost is to be borne by the customer.

The difficulty with technology refresh is how to prescribe pricing mechanisms for it that will remain workable later in the life of the outsourcing agreement.[12] Various options are possible – for example: (1) agree the price for refresh at the start of the outsourcing agreement and index it to the date when the refresh is to take place; (2) price the refresh on a cost-plus margin basis; (3) set the price by benchmarking/market testing at the time the refresh is required; or (4) create an incentivised gain-sharing mechanism to share the cost savings of the refresh.

Providing for technology refresh in telecoms outsourcings requires three areas to be dealt with:

- being kept informed about new developments in the industry as a whole;
- dealing with a specific refresh that the parties know on signature will be required later in the life of the outsourcing agreement;
- dealing with other changes when the need arises.

Being kept informed

Recognising that technological developments in the telecommunications industry can quickly make existing technology obsolete, the parties agree that it will be necessary for the Customer to be kept up to date about such developments as far as they relate to the Network and the Services. Accordingly at least once every [6] months (or earlier, if requested by the Customer) the Supplier shall supply the Customer with information about:

(1) new equipment that might enhance the enjoyment or use of the Services (including equipment with enhanced functionality); and
(2) new functionality available as part of the Services or Network,

(together, 'Future Functionality'). The Supplier shall make the Future Functionality available under this Agreement to the Customer when it makes such Future Functionality available to its other customers generally, at such cost and on such other terms and conditions as may be agreed between the parties under the relevant Order at the time of supply.

Specific refresh projects

The customer might know at the time of entering the outsourcing agreement that it will want to migrate, say, its video conferencing facilities to IP over time. A sample clause dealing with this is:

As at the Commencement Date, the Supplier shall provide the Services via the integrated services digital network ('ISDN') Platform described in the Technical Specification.

The parties acknowledge that their preferred connection and transport protocol for the Services is the Customer's Internet Protocol ('IP') network. Accordingly, the parties envisage that, during the Term, a migration of the Services from the ISDN Platform to the IP network will occur.

The parties shall comply with the requirements and procedures set out in the Migration Plan in implementing such migration, and the cost of such migration shall be as calculated in accordance with the pricing mechanism set out in Schedule [ ].

Other changes

The Supplier and the Customer acknowledge that it is in the interests of both parties to take advantage of potential improvements in technology that will improve the quality and timeliness of the Services or reduce the cost of providing such Services. Accordingly either party may use the Change Control Procedure to propose any changes or improvements in the technology used to provide the Services.

The supplier may refuse to undertake a refresh in technology under the change control procedure, or agree to do so but at a price that is not acceptable to the customer. The customer might therefore push for a provision that allows it to source the refresh from another supplier in such circumstances, and require the supplier to co-operate in that external sourcing.

4.4.12   Pricing

There are numerous pricing mechanisms that can apply in the context of telecoms outsourcings. Which is appropriate may depend on the nature of the service and the underlying economic drivers for the outsourcing. However, there are two themes in pricing for telecoms outsourcings that are common. They are the prevalence of volume-based discounts and minimum spend commitments.

Typically a supplier will be prepared to provide discounts (and increase the level of discount the greater the volume of traffic). However, the supplier will be concerned to ensure that its initial capital outlay (plus a margin) is recovered – there is a risk that this will not occur if there is little traffic (resulting in low charges) or the service is otherwise underutilised. Accordingly the supplier will often insist on a minimum spend commitment to cover its fixed costs.

Yearly minimums

Set out below is an example of a clause that provides for a yearly minimum payment, regardless of the amount of traffic actually carried:

'Yearly Minimum' means the monetary sum specified in Schedule [ ] as changed from time to time by agreement in writing between the parties or in accordance with this clause.

If in any successive twelve-month period the volume of traffic does not result in the Customer being invoiced (after deduction of Service Credits and erroneously invoiced sums) for Service Charges for that twelve-month period an amount equal to or in excess of the then current Yearly Minimum ('Yearly Invoice Total'), then the Supplier shall be entitled to issue the Customer an invoice for the difference between the Yearly Invoice Total and the Yearly Minimum (a 'Shortfall Payment').

Economic downturn and downsizing

A customer locking itself into a spend commitment needs to consider what circumstances should excuse it from that commitment. Examples are as follows:

The Supplier's right to invoice the Customer for a Shortfall Payment is subject to the following:

(1) if there is a decrease in the Customer's use of Services which reflects a decrease in use of similar services in the economy generally, then the Yearly Minimum shall be reduced by a percentage equal to such percentage decrease in use of similar services in the economy generally over the previous year;

(2) if the number of Customer Personnel ('Users') has decreased over the relevant period, then the Yearly Minimum shall be reduced by a percentage equating to the percentage decrease in Users;

(3) if the failure by the Customer to meet the Yearly Minimum is due to the unavailability of the Service (for whatever reason) then the Yearly Minimum shall be reduced by a percentage equal to the percentage of time for which the Service was unavailable over the period in question;

(4) if the failure by the Customer to meet the Yearly Minimum is due to the termination for breach or expiry of a Service then the Yearly Minimum shall be reduced by a percentage equal to the value of the Services terminated or expired (in terms of Service Charges) taken as a proportion of the value of the Services (in terms of Service Charges) prior to the termination or expiry;

(5) if the failure by the Customer to meet the Yearly Minimum is due to non-payment by the Customer of any bona fide disputed invoices, then the Yearly Minimum shall be reduced by the amount of those disputed invoices.

If Service Charges for a Service are reduced in accordance with the Benchmarking Procedure, the Yearly Minimum shall be reduced by the same percentage as the reduction in the Service Charges for that Service.

4.4.13 Benchmarking

There are many possible benchmarking mechanisms against which out-sourced telecoms services are measured for value for money and price competitiveness. The appropriate mechanism may depend on the type of service at issue. Some forms of benchmarking may involve merely an internal review. Others may involve an independent assessment by a third party or market testing. Benchmarking is dealt with in more detail in Chapter 8.

Mobile telephony

There are many ways to benchmark charges for mobile telephony. A common mechanism is to require the supplier to maintain the most cost-effective tariff per user. A sample clause providing for this is set out below.

The Supplier shall ensure that each User is on the most Cost-Effective Tariff, and for this purpose the Supplier shall:

(1) monitor on a continuous basis the Network routing of Users' calls and monitor whether they are on the most Cost-Effective Tariff;

(2) advise Users on a [monthly] basis who are not on the most Cost-Effective Tariff of that fact and ask them whether they would like to move to the most Cost-Effective Tariff; and

(3)   promptly move Users (who request to be moved to the most Cost-Effective Tariff) to such tariff.

In this clause:

(1)   a 'Cost-Effective Tariff' for a User means meeting the User's user requirements notified by the User to the Supplier from time to time by routing the User's calls through the most appropriate Network to achieve the most inexpensive combination of Call Charges and Line Rental Charges for that User;

(2)   'Call Charges' mean the airtime charges applicable when a User accesses the Network to make a call using the handset. The Call Charges are specified in Schedule [   ];

(3)   'Line Rental Charges' mean [monthly] subscription charges applicable in relation to each handset for providing connectivity to the Network. The Line Rental Charges are set out in Schedule [   ].

PSTN

A typical benchmarking for fixed voice services would be twice yearly. The purpose of such benchmarking is to provide a means to review the PSTN tariff rate element of usage charges. Often no other element of the usage charges or any other charges (such as management charges) will be the subject of benchmarking.

The benchmarking will involve comparing the PSTN tariff rates as a whole with PSTN tariff rates in the marketplace provided by suppliers of a similar basket of services at similar service levels. In many respects the procedural elements of the benchmarking process for PSTN are similar to those for data networks (see below) and so are not repeated here.

Data networks

A sample benchmarking procedure for data networks is as follows:

THE INITIATION PROCESS

The Customer may request a benchmarking of the Service Charges:

(1)   once every [six (6)] months; or

(2)   whenever the Customer determines that the Supplier's Service Charges for Services are not commercially competitive due to market rate fluctuations,

(each, a 'Rate Issue').

The following process shall apply if there is a Rate Issue:

(1)   the Customer shall notify the Supplier in writing of the Rate Issue (including reasonable supporting information and materials) and specify that it is exercising the Benchmarking Procedure;

(2)   within [thirty (30)] days the Supplier will present to the Customer a formal written proposal with respect to pricing in relation to the Service Charges for all Services ('Supplier Baseline Proposal') for the remainder of the term for all Services.

APPOINTMENT OF INDEPENDENT THIRD PARTY

Within [fifteen (15)] days after the Customer has received the Supplier Baseline Proposal, the Customer may request benchmarking review by an independent third party, in which case:

(1) the Supplier will nominate [three (3)] independent benchmarking consultants. These must be recognised world-class experts at undertaking benchmarkings in the global communications sector;

(2) the Customer may choose one of these consultants in its sole discretion to perform the benchmarking or may require the Supplier to nominate an alternative independent benchmarking consultant (who must also be a recognised world-class expert at undertaking benchmarkings in the global communications sector) (the 'Third Party Consultant').

The Third Party Consultant shall:

(1) if requested by either party, be required to execute a non-disclosure agreement in a form mutually agreed to by the Supplier and the Customer;

(2) evaluate the Supplier Baseline Proposal on an overall comparative basis (i.e. on a 'like for like' basis), applying the Benchmarking Criteria (as defined below);

(3) complete its analysis within [thirty (30)] days (and it shall present its comparison in a written report (the 'Report') to each of the Supplier and the Customer).

THE BENCHMARKING CRITERIA TO BE APPLIED

In undertaking the benchmarking, the parties shall instruct the Third Party Consultant to apply the following criteria and procedures ('Benchmarking Criteria'):

(1) in determining what is 'like for like', the Third Party Consultant shall take into account:

    (i) the full range of countries in which the Services are provided;

    (ii) the quality metrics to which the Supplier has contracted (together with Service Credits);

    (iii) the precise functionality of such Services on a per country basis;

    (iv) the need to compare services (equivalent to the Services) supplied to similarly sized organisations conducting a similar type of business as the Customer;

(2) the total value of the Services provided under the Agreement;

(3) the Third Party Consultant shall consider what the market would quote in a fair open market competitive procurement situation (which, for the avoidance of doubt, shall not include a situation where a competitor to the Supplier is seeking to buy the business at below the rate which would constitute prudent business practice in the normal course of events) ('Competitive Bid'). The Third Party Consultant need not necessarily test the market by way of seeking Competitive Bids if it has objective market information available to it to enable it to undertake the benchmarking. However, if it seeks Competitive Bids from the market, it shall seek these from the Relevant Suppliers (as defined below);

(4) the identity of the suppliers to be considered in undertaking the benchmarking ('Relevant Suppliers') agreed by the Customer and the Supplier. If the parties cannot themselves agree the identity of the Relevant Suppliers, the

Third Party Consultant shall determine the Relevant Suppliers to be considered, and in such a case the Third Party Consultant shall choose (as a minimum) between three Relevant Suppliers who are recognised by global market share to be leaders in the provision of services similar to the relevant Services being benchmarked.

RESULTS AND ADJUSTMENTS

If the Service Charges contained in the Supplier Baseline Proposal are, as a whole, at least [5] per cent higher than the charges recommended by the Third Party Consultant in its Report as a result of its review, then:

(1) subject to paragraph (2) below, the Supplier will, by written notice to the Customer given within [ten (10)] days of the date of the Report, adjust its Service Charges to be within [5] % of the charges recommended by the Third Party Consultant (for the remainder of the Service term) for the reviewed Services; or

(2) if the Supplier is unwilling to adjust its Service Charges as is provided in (1) immediately above, the Customer may by notice to the Supplier terminate the Services under this Agreement which were subject to the benchmarking.

EXPENSES IN RELATION TO THE PROCEDURE

If the Service Charges in the Supplier Baseline Proposal are, as a whole:

(1) less than [5] % higher than the rates recommended by the Third Party Consultant in its Report, the Customer shall bear all fees and costs charged by the Third Party Consultant;

(2) [5] % or more higher than the rates, as a whole, recommended by the Third Party Consultant in its Report , then:

    (i) if the Supplier adjusts the Service Charges to fall below such [5] % threshold, the Supplier will be required to credit the Customer for [50] % of the Third Party Consultant's fees and costs directly incurred as a result of the benchmarking;

    (ii) if the Supplier declines to adjust the Service Charges to fall below such [5] % threshold, the Supplier will be required to credit the Customer for [100] % of the Third Party Consultant's fees and costs directly incurred as a result of the benchmarking (even if the Customer decides to continue with the Services and not terminate them in accordance with this schedule).

INCREASING SERVICE CHARGES

[Some benchmarking procedures contemplate that the procedure may result in increases in price as well as decreases (it is important to be explicit about this either way).]

If the Third Party Consultant's Report concludes that the total Service Charges then being charged to the Customer by the Supplier would increase in a competitive procurement by more than [5] %, then there shall be a corresponding increase in the Service Charges, but such increase shall be capped at the higher of the following:

(1) [5] %;
(2) the increase in the Index in the [twelve (12)] month period to which the bench-marking relates. The 'Index' shall be [   ] or any index that replaces it.

4.4.14 Reporting requirements

While the general reporting provisions applicable to any other kind of technology outsourcing are also appropriate for a telecoms outsourcing, there are also some specific reporting obligations that should be provided for in a telecoms outsourcing. The sample clause below shows suggested reporting items.

The Supplier shall provide the Customer with the following written reports:

(1) an annual report of global Network capacity requirements. The purpose of such report shall be to identify opportunities to optimise the performance and cost at each site as well as across the entire Network;
(2) a monthly activity report in relation to data traffic and use of the Network;
(3) an annual optimisation study of the Network and the Services; and
(4) an annual inventory in relation to all parts of the Network and each item of Supplier Equipment.

The Supplier shall, once in each month, report to the Customer about any new Service Charge options (including data traffic and PSTN rates) and Service options that become available and that might be of interest to the Customer under this Agreement.

4.4.15 Undisrupted service

Despite suppliers pushing for rights to suspend the services for non-payment and prohibited use, customers for whom telecoms services are critical to their business may argue that the supplier must not *in any circumstances* suspend the service (at least for a defined period of time).

Set out below is a sample clause giving the supplier a right of suspension for non-payment:

The Supplier may cancel or suspend any or all Services or part of any Services by serving [seven (7)] days' written notice on the Customer if the Customer does not pay any sums payable within the time provided under this Agreement.

However, a customer might be successful in arguing that the supplier must continue to provide the service for a period, even if it alleges breach by the customer:

Because of the critical importance of the Services to the operation of the Customer's business and the substantial reliance by the Customer on the Supplier for the provision of those Services, if requested by the Customer the Supplier shall continue supplying the Services and performing its obligations under this Agreement for a period of [180] days regardless of any dispute between the Customer and the Supplier regarding a claim by the Supplier that the Customer may have materially breached its obligations under this Agreement (including by non-payment).

4.4.16 Insolvency and telecoms outsourcing suppliers

In the current state of the telecoms market, the risk of the supplier becoming insolvent needs to be addressed in the outsourcing agreement. Having transferred its infrastructure to the supplier, the customer must address the problem of ending up with an insolvent supplier who can no longer supply the services and with no right to call for the retransfer of the infrastructure (to take back in house or to transfer to a replacement supplier). The various mechanisms discussed below address how to avoid disruptions to the services in such circumstances.

Performance bonds

While not strictly a mechanism to avoid disruption, a performance bond is designed to compensate the customer if such disruption occurs. In essence, the supplier procures a bank or other financial institution to enter into a deed with the customer under which the bank will release a specified sum to the customer if certain release events occur (such as insolvency or sustained disruption to the services).

Parent company guarantees

Telecoms suppliers try to 'house' their liability by using local shell operating companies as the contracting party. It is essential to conduct a due diligence on the financial standing and asset base of the supplier contracting entity. If it is merely an operating shell, the customer should seek to contract with the parent company.

In any event, customers should try to limit their exposure for a failure by the supplier by requiring an asset-rich company within the supplier's group to guarantee the performance and liability of the supplier under the outsourcing agreement, or to be jointly and severally liable for such performance and liability.

Termination rights

The outsourcing agreement should provide for the customer's immediate right to terminate the outsourcing agreement on the insolvency of the supplier.

Step-in rights

The outsourcing agreement should also provide for the right of the customer to insist upon the introduction of a temporary service provider to address problems with disrupted service if certain trigger events occur. Such trigger events might include insolvency, force majeure, persistent breach, catastrophic failures and other similar events.

The step-in rights clause will need to deal with to what extent (if at all) the supplier is entitled to receive payment during a period of step-in.

Assignment and novation rights

The customer should consider whether it wishes the outsourcing agreement to provide that the customer may, on insolvency, call for the supplier to be replaced by one of the supplier's subcontractors (or some other supplier nominated by the customer) and for a right to require the supplier to enter into an assignment or novation agreement with such replacement supplier.

The customer might also want the automatic transfer back to the customer (or to a replacement supplier) of the infrastructure used by the supplier to provide the services on the insolvency of the supplier.

Such arrangements may need to be put in place at the start of the outsourcing (so that they are extant rights at the time of the insolvency event). In all cases appropriate advice from an insolvency practitioner on the enforceability of such rights against the liquidator should be sought when advising clients.

4.4.17   Exit management

The supplier should be obliged, at the customer's request, to undertake an inventory of all handsets, switches, leased lines and other equipment used by it to provide the services. It should also be required to provide the existing numbering plan, fault resolution records, database of switch and network configurations and all other documents and process maps used by it to provide the services.

NOTES

1. The author would like to acknowledge Tom Wheadon, telecoms partner at Simmons & Simmons, for his helpful comments in relation to the content of this chapter. However, the views expressed in this chapter are those of the author, and do not necessarily represent those of Simmons & Simmons.
2. The transfer of telecoms infrastructure to the supplier raises issues analogous to those that arise on the sale of a technology business – see Michael Sinclair, 'Providing for Information Technology on Sale of a Business' (1997) 13 *Computer Law & Security Report* 331.

3. See, generally, Michael Sinclair *et al.*, 'Telecommunications Outsourcing', in *Outsourcing Practice Manual* (Sweet & Maxwell, 1998); Michael Sinclair, 'IT and Telecoms Outsourcing in Europe and the Law', in *The Strategic Guide to Outsource IT and Telecoms* (World Trade Magazines, 1992), p.42; and Michael Sinclair, 'Telecommunications Contracts: Outsourcing', in *Telecommunications Law* (Oxford University Press, 2001).

4. See Michael Sinclair *et al.*, 'Telecommunications Outsourcing', in *Outsourcing Practice Manual* (Sweet & Maxwell, 1998); Michael Sinclair, 'A New European Communications Services Regulatory Package: An Overview' [2001] CTLR 156; Michael Sinclair *et al.*, 'The European Communications Services Regulatory Package: An Update' [2002] CTLR 97.

5. See Michael Sinclair, 'Global Data Networks and Convergence – the Emerging Issues' (2003) 5(1) *Electronic Business Law* 7.

6. The 1984 Act will shortly be replaced by a new Communications Act (currently in the form of the Communications Bill).

7. The proposed Directive would extend the scope of the existing Telecommunications Data Protection Directive (97/66/EC) in the protection of personal data in the electronic communications sector.

8. See Michael Sinclair, 'A New European Communications Services Regulatory Package: An Overview' [2001] CTLR 156 and Michael Sinclair *et al.*, 'The European Communications Services Regulatory Package: An Update' [2002] CTLR 97 for a summary of the proposed directive.

9. For further discussion of the legal and operational requirements in relation to call centres, see Michael Sinclair, 'Customer Service Centre Outsourcings: Managing Risk for Good Corporate Governance' (2002) 23 BLR 194.

10. See Michael Sinclair, 'Is Technological Neutrality an Achievable Goal' (2000) 2(5) *Electronic Business Law* 11 (June) 11; Michael Sinclair, 'A New European Communications Services Regulatory Package: An Overview' [2001] CTLR 156 and Michael Sinclair *et al.*, 'The European Communications Services Regulatory Package: An Update' [2002] CTLR 97.

11. For detailed analysis of the legal and commercial challenges presented by data network convergence solutions, see Michael Sinclair, 'Global Data Networks and Convergence – the Emerging Issues' (2003) 5(1) *Electronic Business Law* 7.

12. See Mark Turner and Adam Smith, 'The Challenge of Changing Technology in IT Outsourcing Agreements' (2002) 18 *Computer Law & Security Report* 181.

CHAPTER 5

Website hosting

Chris Holder

5.1 INTRODUCTION

Customers who enter into website hosting agreements with suppliers will usually wish to receive a fully managed service for a number of years.

The service that customers typically wish to receive involves the supplier providing a physical location, the hardware and operating system software and the telecommunications network to enable the customers' website to be accessible to users. This may include a variety of different services, the provision of which should be made clear within the agreement between the parties and further details of which are set out later in section 5.4.

The web hosting agreement, therefore, must provide for all of these requirements from day one, and also provide the customer with the flexibility for change over the term of the agreement. Agreements typically run for a number of rolling annual periods or for fixed periods of, for example, three years.

This chapter will set out those various legal and commercial issues that a customer typically comes face to face with when choosing a supplier and negotiating a suitable agreement.

5.2 SELECTION OF SUPPLIERS

As with any procurement activity, a customer should be prepared to undertake a selection process that will provide it with the best chance of receiving the service that it requires. In this regard, a customer should prepare a detailed invitation to tender (ITT), which will be circulated to prospective suppliers.

The drafting of an ITT is key to determining the sort of response that a supplier will provide and the following sets out the key elements that should be contained within an ITT:

- *Customer history*: the ITT should provide a brief description of the customer's business, which will provide useful background material for any supplier.

189

- *Objectives*: the ITT should set out in full the reasons why the customer wishes to receive a website hosting service and how it envisages utilising the website in the future as part of its business strategy. The importance of this is, for example, if the website is to be used as a customer's prime interface with its customers and suppliers – in which case the resilience of the system and its availability for productive use will be of paramount importance.
- *Rules of engagement*: the ITT should spell out exactly how the supplier should interact with the customer during the procurement process. For example, who within the customer will be the prime contact; how should responses be provided and in what format; information contained in the ITT must remain confidential to the customer; a supplier's response will not in itself lead to any award of the business; a customer may use any part of the response in order to request additional information from another supplier; and unless specifically commented upon, a supplier will be deemed to have accepted any requirements set out in the ITT.
- *Evaluation criteria*: the ITT should set out precise details as to how the customer intends to evaluate a supplier's response. Particular emphasis should be given to any area of the service that is especially important to the customer – for example, where a customer requires a supplier to provide a helpdesk facility to end users of the website experiencing difficulties or where the website's ability to deal with a certain volume of traffic is required.
- *Scope of services*: the ITT must set out exactly what it is that the customer actually wants. In order to receive a meaningful response from a supplier, the details of the required service should be made very clear – otherwise a supplier will set out its generic service offering, which may or may not meet a customer's requirements. The more bespoke a service required by a customer, the more important it is that these requirements are fully articulated within the ITT.
- *Key terms and conditions:* a customer should set out within the ITT those key terms and conditions that it wishes to enter into, for example, details of specific warranties or indemnities, limits of liability, confidentiality and intellectual property should be set out and the supplier encouraged to agree to these. These terms should not be set out as fully drafted clauses, as set out and discussed in Chapter 2, but rather set out more in a 'term sheet' style, which sets out the principles that a customer requires compliance with. These will, of course, be part of the overall evaluation of a supplier's response. By way of example, set out below are details of certain key terms and conditions that should be included.

Term

The Agreement will commence on date of signature or the date of commencement of the services, whichever is the earlier.

The Agreement will continue for an initial period of [ ] years and shall be renewed annually thereafter at the customer's sole option.

Services

The hosting services shall meet the customer's stated requirements as set out in the ITT, be free of viruses and be currency and date compliant.

Supplier will obtain and maintain throughout the term of the Agreement at its own cost, all consents and licences that are necessary for supplier to provide the services and for the customer to receive the services.

The customer may reduce or increase the volume/scope of the services provided by supplier in the event that the customer's business requirements change during the term of the Agreement.

Service Levels

Supplier shall meet the minimum service level requirements set out in the ITT and as otherwise communicated to supplier by the customer.

Without prejudice to its other rights and remedies under the Agreement or at law, which include termination and the right to damages, the customer may accept service credits as a remedy for failure to meet service levels.

Charges

All charges for the services shall be fixed and shall be inclusive of all applicable taxes. Supplier's charges will not be subject to or contingent upon any due diligence to be performed after the commencement of the Agreement and all elements of supplier's financial proposal must be validated and agreed by the parties before contract execution.

Supplier will state any proposed additional charges or price increases during the term of the Agreement in its response to the ITT.

Any new services will be provided at a fixed price, such price to be agreed between the parties.

Payment

Properly submitted invoices will be due and payable by the customer within [ ] days from the date of receipt.

The customer will have the right to deduct sums that supplier is obligated to pay or credit to it.

The customer may withhold payment of all or part of any invoice that it disputes in good faith.

Contract Management

Each party shall nominate a contract manager and all communications between the parties shall be between the contract managers in the first instance.

The contract managers shall meet at least once a week to discuss any issues arising from the Agreement, including, without limitation, the performance of the hosting services.

Subcontractors

In all cases where supplier intends to subcontract or buy in any element of the services to be provided, this must be clearly stated in supplier's response to the ITT.

Supplier will not delegate or subcontract any of its obligations under the Agreement without the customer's prior written approval and consent.

Benchmarking

At the customer's request, the customer and supplier will establish a continuous benchmark programme to evaluate quality and delivery of service against best practice.

The customer shall have the right, annually, to have the performance of the hosting services and the related charges reviewed by an independent organisation with demonstrated benchmarking expertise in order to evaluate the efficiency, effectiveness and productivity of the services and whether the charges are competitive in the marketplace.

Supplier will automatically adjust any pricing or service levels as a result of the benchmarker's recommendation.

Quality Assurance and Audit

Upon notice from the customer, supplier will provide it, its auditors and/or inspectors with reasonable access to supplier's facilities during normal business days and hours in order to perform audits. Supplier shall provide such auditors and inspectors with any assistance that they may reasonably require.

Supplier shall provide the customer with access to such records and documentation as may be reasonably necessary for the customer to determine the accuracy of supplier's charges and service level performance.

Intellectual Property Rights

The customer will own all right, title and interest in and to any software developed by supplier as part of the services that is not a modification to supplier's pre-existing software or third party software provided by supplier.

The services will not infringe or violate any intellectual property rights, trade secrets, or rights in proprietary information, nor any contractual, employment or property rights, duties of non-disclosure or other rights of any third parties.

Representations and Warranties

Supplier will warrant, represent and undertake that:

- it will provide the services promptly and with all due skill, care and diligence, in a good and workmanlike manner and otherwise in line with best practice within its industry;
- supplier's personnel will possess the qualifications, professional competence and experience to carry out the services;
- it has full capacity and authority to enter into the Agreement and that it has or will obtain prior to the commencement date, any necessary licences, consents, and permits required of it for the performance of the services; and
- it will comply with all applicable laws, regulations and rules that relate to its obligations under the Agreement.

Indemnities

Supplier will indemnify the customer in full from any and all damages, costs, expenses, claims or demands ('Claims') arising from or in connection with the following:

- any claim by a third party in respect of the negligent or otherwise wrongful act or acts or omission of supplier or any of its personnel or subcontractors;
- any claim that the services, or any supplier software, equipment, tools, material, deliverable or any other resource provided or used by supplier (or by any third party on behalf of supplier) in performing the services, or the use, reproduction or exploitation of any of the same by or on behalf of the customer or any end user in the intended manner, infringes a third party's intellectual property rights or rights in respect of confidential information;
- any claim that any material provided by the customer (whether belonging to the customer or a third party) infringes a third party's intellectual property rights, if the claim is based on or attributable to the fact that supplier (or a third party, at supplier's request) has modified such material or has used, reproduced or exploited such material in contravention of any term or condition that the customer has disclosed to supplier;
- death or bodily injury caused by the tortious conduct of supplier or its personnel;
- loss or damage to personal property for which supplier is legally liable or responsible; and
- supplier's breach of its confidentiality obligations.

Confidentiality

Supplier will keep confidential the confidential information disclosed to it by the customer and will use such confidential information solely for purposes contemplated by the ITT.

Termination

The customer can terminate the Agreement in the following circumstances:

- if supplier commits a material breach of the Agreement not cured within [   ] days of notice by the customer;
- if the material breach is not capable of being cured;
- if supplier becomes insolvent;
- for convenience, at any time during the term of the Agreement, on [   ] days' notice.

Supplier can terminate the Agreement in the following circumstances:

- the customer fails to pay valid invoices within [   ] days of the due date, upon further written notice from the supplier; or
- the customer becomes insolvent.

In the event the customer breaches any other of its obligations, supplier cannot terminate the Agreement but will be excused from its performance of the relevant services, where appropriate, or can demand reimbursement of additional costs caused as a result of the customer's failure to perform its obligations.

Consequences of Termination

Supplier agrees to provide up to [   ] months' termination assistance in accordance with a mutually agreed termination assistance plan upon termination or expiry of the Agreement for whatever reason. This will include all information and assistance necessary to ensure a smooth transition of the services to the customer or another supplier.

Supplier will return all customer equipment, data and material (including any software developed by supplier for the customer).

Assignment

Supplier shall not assign or novate the Agreement to any third party without the customer's prior written consent.

The customer may assign or novate the Agreement at its discretion.

Force Majeure

Neither party will be liable for default or delay in the performance of its obligations under the Agreement due to a Force Majeure Event and the non-performing party will be excused from further performance or observance of the affected obligation(s) for as long as the Force Majeure Event prevails provided that the party will recommence performance or observance whenever and to whatever extent possible without delay.

If a Force Majeure Event substantially prevents, hinders or delays performance of the services necessary for the performance of functions reasonably identified by the customer as critical for more than [   ] consecutive days, then at the customer's option, it may procure those services from an alternate source, and supplier will be responsible for payment of any incremental charges for these services from the alternate source for so long as the delay in performance continues.

Disaster Recovery

Supplier will provide details of its disaster recovery plan as part of its response to the RFP. At a minimum, supplier will operate a secondary site, physically located at a distance from the primary site, which will automatically become operational in the event that the primary site fails for whatever reason.

Governing Law and Jurisdiction

The Agreement will be governed by and construed in accordance with the laws of England and Wales and shall be subject to the exclusive jurisdiction of the High Court of England and Wales.

Once the responses from suppliers have been received and evaluated, a customer must choose which supplier it wishes to use. In making this choice, a customer may wish to run a competitive procurement exercise with two suppliers, which would involve parallel negotiation on a fully drafted agreement.

Given the fact, however, that the ITT process should have pulled out any areas where suppliers have not agreed with a customer's requirements and these differences will either have been negotiated to the satisfaction of the customer or not, as the case may be, there should not be a need for a full-scale parallel negotiation.

However, customers should always bear in mind that such parallel negotiations do require a great deal of time and planning and certainly for large-scale transactions, may be extremely useful when it comes to obtaining the best deal possible. Negotiation leverage is maintained by customers during parallel negotiations, and indeed, through the ITT process set out above, which should be to a customer's advantage.

5.3 TERMS AND CONDITIONS OF THE WEB HOSTING AGREEMENT

5.3.1 Term

A typical initial term for a web hosting agreement is between one and three years, with automatic renewal at the end of the term (sometimes known as 'evergreen' clauses). Alternatively, the contract can contain an option to extend the term if the customer is happy with the supplier's performance. Evergreen clauses are the industry norm, and much easier to administer for both customer and supplier, as otherwise there is a risk that the parties will neglect to renew the contract and the customer's website could be suddenly disconnected.

5.3.2 Charges

The charges for website hosting agreements are usually fixed-price charges for a year, subject to increases based on a mutually agreed index if the agreement continues thereafter. However, fixed-price transactions for periods up to three years are not uncommon for hosting services.

Suppliers calculate these charges by a variety of methods: some are calculated on the square footage of floor space that a server actually takes up. Whatever the method of calculation, however, the charges should include the cost of the location, provision of hardware and software (although it may exclude certain applications software specific to a customer), telecommunications, heat, light, power and other environmental requirements such as air conditioning.

It is important to check whether all the services requested by a customer are included within a quoted price. It is not uncommon to find that disaster recovery is not included, for example, or helpdesk services.

Further, the level of monitoring and the maintenance and support services that are required to ensure the hosting service operates to the standards required in the service levels should also be included within the price.

5.3.3 Benchmarking

In order for a customer to ensure that it is receiving an efficient service over the duration of an agreement, a benchmarking clause can be included in the agreement.

It should be noted, however, that because of the nature of the web hosting service, complex and time consuming benchmarking provisions may prove too costly or complicated to administer and so would not be appropriate.

If one is required, then it is best to keep it as simple as possible and therefore such provisions should cover the following:

- the parties should agree on a number of benchmarkers up-front and then allow the customer to choose any of the benchmarkers to perform the benchmark at certain points throughout the term of the agreement;
- the benchmarker will carry out the benchmark against similar providers of similar services and will take into account the cost of the provision of the services and the service levels to which they are being performed;
- after the benchmarker has produced its report, the supplier should automatically be obliged to reduce prices to reflect those prices prevalent in the marketplace;
- the cost of the benchmarking exercise should be split equally between the customer and the supplier;
- the parties should limit the number of benchmarkers to a maximum of one per year during the term of the agreement.

5.3.4 Audit

The customer should have a number of audit rights during the term of the agreement, which will enable it to ensure that the services are being performed to the service levels, that the supplier is providing a secure environment for the customer's data and other intellectual property and that the supplier is generally performing the services in accordance with its obligations set out in the agreement.

As hosting services are most commonly provided remotely, this right to audit should include a right to visit the service provider's premises, rather than rely on audit information provided by the service provider.

Further, the supplier may want certain audit rights in order to ensure that it is being paid for the services provided. This, of course, depends upon the type of payment structure agreed between the parties but if the parties agree that the supplier is to be paid on the number of transactions or hits then the supplier will need to satisfy itself that such records are, indeed, accurate.

5.3.5 Data protection

Whenever data that are capable of identifying a living person are obtained, data protection laws, including the Data Protection Act 1998 (DPA), will apply. Such personal data might be obtained via a website through the use of cookies or because visitors to the site provide their personal details, e.g. they sign up for e-mail bulletins.

For the purposes of the DPA, the customer will be the data controller in respect of this personal data, and has primary liability under the DPA even where it delegates the actual data processing to a supplier providing hosting services. Processing is a very widely defined term, which covers almost any use of the personal data, including retrieval, disclosure, transmission or other dissemination.

The customer needs to ensure within the web hosting contract itself that the supplier is obliged to comply with the DPA and it is good practice to include an indemnity against breaches of data protection laws in case the supplier fails to comply.

The DPA lists eight data protection principles with which the parties will need to comply. In the context of a website, the seventh principle is particularly important as it requires appropriate technical and organisational measures to be taken against unauthorised or unlawful processing of personal data and against accidental loss, destruction or damage of such data.

What is an appropriate measure is dependent to large extent on the nature of the personal data. Sensitive personal data (such as details of people's credit history, their medical details, religious beliefs, sexual preferences and the like) require far more stringent measures to be taken.

Appropriate technological measures to prevent unauthorised or unlawful processing could include passwords and encryption to help prevent hackers and other unauthorised individuals accessing personal data. Likewise, having a backup facility at a secondary site would be an appropriate technological measure against accidental loss, destruction or damage of personal data, as would ensuring that the most up-to-date anti-virus protection is used.

Appropriate organisational measures include establishing a data protection policy and appointing a particular person or department to ensure that this policy is adhered to. The policy could include requirements as to passwords to access encrypted personal data, and who should have access to these passwords, how often should they be changed and so on. A procedure should be put in place to ensure data are kept up to date and retained or disposed of in accordance with the terms of the DPA. The website should be constantly monitored to ensure that security has not been breached.

British Standards BS 7799 and ISO/IEC Standard 17799 are codes of practice for information security management, and it is not uncommon to see data protection clauses containing an obligation on a supplier to comply with these standards.

5.3.6 Termination and termination assistance

Aside from the usual termination permission regarding material breach or insolvency, there are two areas that need to be included in the web hosting agreement.

The first deals with a customer's ability to terminate the agreement for its convenience. This may result in certain termination charges being applied by the supplier, especially if the supplier has made specific capital investment in setting up the service for the customer, so these charges need to be set out in the agreement prior to signature. It is important to note that no element of future profit to the supplier should be included in these sums.

The second deals with the ability to terminate for material breach itself. As the provision of the service is arguably more important to the customer than the revenue stream is to the supplier, the effect of termination of the agreement is not equal as between the parties. Therefore, termination clauses should be drafted in such a way as to make it clear that the supplier may only terminate if the customer fails to pay such proper invoices as have been delivered for a certain period of time – and cannot terminate for any other reason. The rationale is that for any other breach of the agreement by the customer, the supplier is relieved of its obligations to perform the services to the service levels, where the breach impacts upon a supplier's delivery capabilities, or has the right to sue for damages for breaches that are not service delivery related.

As regards termination or expiration assistance, at the expiration or termination of an agreement the customer has three options: to continue the service with the same supplier, to bring the service in house or to contract for a similar service from a third party.

In the last two examples, the customer will require the initial supplier to provide assistance during the termination/expiration phase. The customer should provide in the agreement that the supplier continues to license all the supplier's commercially available software on reasonable terms and conditions, should use reasonable efforts to obtain licences and consents from third parties allowing for assignment either to the customer or its new supplier and should be obliged to continue to perform the services to the service levels during this period.

Further, provisions dealing with the transfer or destruction of the other party's confidential information should be included.

5.3.7 Force majeure and disaster recovery

A web hosting contract must contain a force majeure clause, as with any other contract. However, the customer should consider carefully what the contract deems to be a force majeure event. The host is expected to have the facilities to deal with certain events that are usually deemed to be force majeure events, such as power failures or surges – perhaps by way of a secondary site located at a certain distance from the primary site, with all materials backed up to this site so that in the event that it cannot perform the services out of the first site, it can switch over to the secondary site and thus provide continuity of service.

5.3.8 Acceptable use policies

Customers should be aware of the supplier's acceptable use policies and other rules and regulations that may be incorporated into the contract by reference. Frequently, a supplier will reserve the right to amend these as and when necessary, and it may not be obliged to notify the customer when this occurs, thus obliging the customer to regularly check the supplier's own website so as to be aware when changes are made. As the supplier has a unilateral right to change the terms of these policies, without the agreement or even necessarily the knowledge of the customer, they could become far more onerous than at the date of signature but the customer will still be bound to abide by them.

5.4   STATEMENT OF WORK

The statement of work or scope of services will set out exactly what the supplier will be providing to the customer.

As well as setting out the necessary hardware, software, telecommunications and network and hosting services, a supplier may also be required to provide additional services to a customer.

These may include the provision of website design services, training, consultancy, helpdesk facilities and content management services, all of which should be clearly defined in the agreement.

Each statement of work should be drafted so as to describe fully those services that will be particular to the customer's requirements. It may begin with the requirement of the service provider to obtain and register a domain name for the use of the website and continue through the provision of security services, helpdesk services, content update services, software and hardware maintenance, technology refresh and end with order fulfilment and business process services.

While the agreement should make every effort to be as detailed as possible about the services to be provided, sweep-up clauses should also be included to cover incidental and ancillary services – this is particularly the case if the fees relate to specific services rather than being on a time and materials basis, as services that fall outside the scope of the specific services will cost extra.

The following sets out a non-exhaustive list of the types of services that should be provided by suppliers to customers and that will require detailed input from a customer's technical team:

- provision of dedicated servers (or, if not dedicated, then subject to suitable security requirements);
- hardware support services for servers and other equipment;
- software support services – for operating systems, applications and database support;
- network connectivity and monitoring services;
- monitoring services in order to monitor the availability and performance of the hardware and software;
- upgrade services – if volume increase or quality increases are required, then hardware and software will require upgrading;
- disaster recovery services;
- backup and restore services;

- reporting services;
- security services;
- helpdesk, fault resolution and problem management services;
- facilities management services – for the provision of heat, light, power, cooling, etc.; and
- maintenance planning services – which will require scheduling of any planned maintenance.

5.5   SERVICE LEVELS

Service levels are an important part of a web hosting and as such these need to be set out in the agreement in as detailed a fashion as possible.

This section contains a non-exhaustive list of those major elements of a web hosting service that should have specific contractual performance targets set against them.

5.5.1   Hardware

Server availability is a key requirement and an appropriate service level is required in order for the customer to be satisfied that the supplier can provide a robust solution.

The availability of a server is normally defined as the period of time that a server is fully operational, the software residing on the server is functioning properly and the customer has the ability to access all of its data. This period of availability excludes any scheduled maintenance periods and measurements should be taken on a daily basis.

The level of availability of an individual server is usually in the order of 99.5–99.9 per cent of the time. Therefore, if the supplier is willing to agree to a server availability service level of 99.7 per cent, the parties have agreed that, during a 30-day month and excluding scheduled maintenance periods, the server will be unavailable for use for a period of 2.16 hours per month.

This service level may be difficult for groups of servers in one location or servers split across several locations. Suppliers are more willing to provide a higher availability service level across a number of servers than for individual servers, as an element of redundancy is built into such networked servers. Therefore, service levels of 99.9 per cent and 99.99 per cent are more realistic targets that customers should be requesting.

Another service level that customers should request is the problem response and resolution service level. These service levels relate to the period that a customer must wait before any problem is properly fixed by a supplier.

There are normally different service levels for different problems, referred to typically as Severity 1, Severity 2, Severity 3, etc. Severity 1 problems are typically defined as those that cause a server or group of servers to be down and therefore the end users are unable to access the website. Severity 2 problems are normally those where the actual server is working but there is a particular application failure, so the level of use of the website is affected. Severity 3 problems are normally those that result in a degradation of performance of the server or application and a Severity 4 problem is usually one requiring assistance for rebooting or requesting scheduled maintenance.

The response times to the various problems are all different and are based on the severity levels. So, for example, a response time for a Severity 1 problem is typically 15 minutes and a maximum fix time is measured as the number of Severity 1 problems fixed within a certain period, for example 90 per cent of Severity 1 problems are fixed within 90 minutes.

Response times to Severity 4 problems are consequently a little longer, between 8 and 48 hours, with maximum fix times varying, so that 80–90 per cent of Severity 4 problems are resolved within 2–8 hours.

5.5.2 Software

The ongoing provision of a website service will require the supplier to provide the necessary level of software support and functionality to meet a customer's requirements.

As most commercial websites require access to information held in a customer's databases, database administration is an obligation that should be made subject to a specific service level.

A supplier should be expected to perform physical and logical database functions including data modelling, database design, tailoring and monitoring of database software products, database support, timing, backup and recovery and the monitoring of data volumes in order for the customer and the supplier to perform capacity planning. All these obligations need to be recorded and the levels of performance agreed between the parties prior to the start of the agreement.

Data storage management is also of key concern. The data generated by hits on a website, the areas of a website searched and the nature of any transactions entered into is very useful information for any enterprise and the management and storage of such data will be of interest for future company marketing and promotions.

The supplier will also have to provide application maintenance and support, especially for the portal software, and break/fix times, upgrades and helpdesk activities will require development for inclusion within the agreement.

5.5.3 Capacity

In order to ascertain the capacity of the servers and the website itself, the customer must provide the supplier with appropriate capacity projections. These projections will affect all areas of the infrastructure, from the network to the server to the memory storage capacity and unless a degree of flexibility has been built into the design of the system, system performance may suffer as a result of overusage.

The service level must, therefore, provide for a certain capacity of server, network and memory to be provided by the supplier and this capacity should grow in line with projected traffic over time.

Most suppliers will provide a range of service levels in this regard, with higher capacities being more expensive than lower capacities. For example, a supplier may offer a bronze, silver, gold service whereby each tier of service varies accordingly. Bronze service may contain 100mb of space within a server configuration and allow for 5gb of data traffic per month. A gold service would provide for 300mb of space and 100gb of traffic per month.

Certain baselines based upon usage should be developed that will provide the supplier and the supplier with the flexibility that they will need and around which pricing models can be constructed.

The service level should also contain references to the various methods and tools that are to be used by the parties in order to measure and report usage. These are vital to ensuring that the parties have a common set of parameters around which to operate and which will not result in dispute between them over the results of measurement.

5.5.4 Network

The network service levels are the most problematical given the nature of the hosting services, particularly with regard to transmissions across the Internet where the network is, by definition, not a private network.

A customer should always seek a high availability service level from its supplier. The more experienced the supplier, the higher the availability percentage of the network over time, as the supplier should be able to demonstrate that it has a better quality of infrastructure than its competitors. This may be the result of the supplier having the infrastructure itself or because the supplier has entered into agreements with data carriers itself for the provision of data traffic.

Another area that requires attention is that relating to network response times. A customer will lose business if end users experience delays in the accessing of information or delays in the performance of transactions across the Internet.

The ability to measure the round trip of a specific packet of information between the routers at each end of a network will provide both parties with valuable information as to the network response times. The level of expected network performance needs to be built into the service levels and this can also be used to measure the performance of the supplier's network against those of other suppliers.

Packet discard rates or packet loss levels are equally important, as this tracks the number of packets of information that are lost during transmission. At its simplest level, a packet of information would be an e-mail that enters the network via the sender's web browser and fails to arrive at the recipient's server. It is important, therefore, that a reliability service level is developed that can provide the customer with comfort as to the nature of the service to be provided.

Most hosting suppliers will not have the capability to provide their own network infrastructure and therefore the customer will have to rely on the supplier's subcontractor, who will invariably be a specialist telecoms provider like UUNet.

The supplier will, in turn, have arrangements with local public telephone and telegraph (PTT) services for the renting of bandwidth across PTT telecommunication infrastructures and it is this bandwidth that will dictate, to a large extent, the functionality of the website. It is, therefore, important for a customer to understand its functionality requirements before entering into negotiations with a supplier in order that the necessary bandwidth is provided.

Further, a supplier should be requested to provide details of the service levels that it has entered into with third parties in order to ascertain the level of service to be provided.

5.6 SERVICE CREDITS

A service credit regime should be developed by the customer in order to provide the supplier with a clear indication as to which service levels are important to the customer.

A service credit is not a penalty payment or a liquidated damage and a service credit regime should not be seen by a customer as a vehicle to make money out of a supplier. Rather, a service credit regime should be designed to motivate a supplier to achieve the service levels, and if it fails to do so, the level of the service credit should be set so as to reflect the fact that the customer has received a lesser service than the one that it contractually agreed to pay for.

Each service level should be weighted in such a fashion as to reflect its relative importance to another. This can be achieved by applying a percentage value to each service level, which can then be used to work out actual service credits.

There are a number of ways to set up a service credit regime and set out below is one example:

Service credit $= A \times B \times C$

Where $A =$ the percentage allocated to a particular service level

$B =$ the percentage allocated to any particular category of service levels

$C = [15-20\%]$ of the total monthly charges in respect of the hosting services.

The way in which this works is as follows. If there are a number of service levels, then they will be set out in categories. For example, there may be an availability category that will have a number of service levels within it. The category will have a percentage allocated to it, and then the service levels thereunder will each have 100 per cent of the category amount to divide up between themselves and weighted accordingly.

The number of categories do not have to share a figure equal to 100 per cent. In most cases, this figure will be higher, for example 350 per cent, so that, when the calculation set out above is made, the amount of service credits will quickly escalate to the maximum amount allowed for any month, which will be typically 15–20 per cent of the monthly charge.

The reason that this is set out in this way is that, if a customer limited the category percentage to 100 per cent of the maximum monthly amount (15–20 per cent of the monthly charge), then the supplier would have to fail all of the service levels in order to have the maximum amount at risk. Such an occurrence would represent a material failure to perform the services, which in itself would have far greater consequences to a customer's business than could be rectified by a maximum service credit.

Therefore, the 350 per cent category percentage has the effect of accelerating credits to the maximum level so, if one or two important service levels are not reached, the service credit reflects more closely the associated degradation in service provision.

Table 5.1 is a service level table that illustrates the various categories, types of service levels and percentages that may be applied.

One further point to raise in relation to service credits is that they are not designed to be the sole and exclusive remedy for a failure by a supplier to reach any particular service level. Therefore, it should be made clear that all other rights that a customer may have are reserved.

5.7 CONCLUSION

Web hosting agreements are becoming increasingly more common as enterprises deal with the requirement to implement technology solutions, keep up with competition, focus on core business strategies, reduce capital tied up in infrastructure and communicate more effectively with customers and suppliers.

Table 5.1 Service levels

Performance category	Service level	Measurement period	Reporting period	Service credit allocation percentage	Allocation of category percentage
Availability					200
	The network is fully operational and available for use during the measurement period no less frequently than 99.99% of the time	Monthly	Monthly	40	
	The hardware is fully operational and available for use during the measurement period no less frequently than 99.9% of the time	Monthly	Monthly	30	
	The software application is fully operational and is available for use during the measurement period no less frequently than 95% of the time	Monthly	Monthly	30	
Latency of the network					50
	The network response time between any two points within the network will be no greater than 15 milliseconds	Monthly	Monthly	50	
Packet loss	Packet loss shall not exceed 1% during the measurement period	Monthly	Monthly	50	

Continued

205

Table 5.1 Continued

Performance category	Service level	Measurement period	Reporting period	Service credit allocation percentage	Allocation of category percentage
Fault restoration					100
	100% of all calls to the helpdesk are answered in less than ten (10) seconds by a person	Daily	Monthly	20	
	The provision of service updates via the helpdesk on average within thirty (30) minutes	Daily	Monthly	10	
	The provision of service updates via the helpdesk for critical faults on average every thirty (30) minutes until the fault is resolved	[Daily]	Monthly	10	
	All critical faults with the network are resolved within five (5) business hours	Monthly	Monthly	20	
	All other faults with the network are resolved within twelve (12) business hours	Monthly	Monthly	20	
	No fault or problem reoccurs within twenty four (24) hours after being resolved	Monthly	Monthly	20	

The issues discussed above have obvious parallels with those discussed in other chapters relating to the outsourcing contract and ASP and the techniques used to draft, negotiate and implement web hosting agreements have largely developed out of these related areas.

This is an area that has suffered more than most in recent years but as customers and suppliers get used to dealing more through the Internet, the greater the reliance on secure, reliable web-based applications, including websites, there will be.

CHAPTER 6

Business process outsourcing

Sandra Honess

6.1 INTRODUCTION

This chapter is devoted to business process outsourcing (BPO). The starting point is a brief description of BPO, an analysis of the key differences between BPO and more well established forms of outsourcing (such as IS outsourcing), followed by a description of the key characteristics of the BPO market. The range of BPO services is broad, but this chapter will focus on four main types of BPO services, each of which is described in turn in section 6.5, which goes on to look at key contract clauses that are typically found in BPO contracts but may not be relevant in the non-BPO context. Finally, section 6.7 looks at new developments in the BPO market, such as the emergence of business service provision (BSP) as a service delivery model.

6.2 WHAT IS BUSINESS PROCESS OUTSOURCING?

The economic downturn and increasing competition are putting pressure on organisations to reduce costs and maximise efficiency. This may involve focusing on core business operations and passing the operation of non-core functions to a third party service provider. BPO, as its name suggests, is the outsourcing of their non-core or 'back office' business processes. Usually those processes are IS enabled (or should be IS enabled) and hence can be transformed by the use of a new or improved technology platform. The appeal of BPO is that (at least in the ideal world) it therefore involves a new support services model involving cost effective, scaleable, efficient services.

The growth in demand for BPO has also seen an expansion in the range of business process services being provided by suppliers. While there is some debate as to what is truly a business process (for instance, should cleaning services be included in this definition?), the core BPO services currently available in the marketplace are usually considered to include the following.

- *Finance and accounting*: the management of finance and accounting department functions; financial planning and budgeting; financial accounting and reporting; general ledger; accounts payable and receivable; payroll administration; treasury functions; and cash management.

- *Procurement*: the management of the procurement function to improve supplier service and quality, to reduce the cost of purchased goods and services and to optimise business performance.
- *Human resources*: the management of HR programmes including actuarial and insurance arrangements; compensation and benefits packages; payroll administration; pension plans; recruitment, claims processing and administration.
- *Real estate*: the management of corporate real estate to improve facilities planning; property usage; occupancy rates; asset management; capital programmes; portfolio optimisation and administration.

This list is certainly not exhaustive – many other business processes are being outsourced including logistics, warehouse management and parts of the sales and marketing function (such as call centre management, database marketing, telesales and telemarketing). However, for the purposes of this chapter we have concentrated on the four principal areas of outsourcing listed above. Indeed, in the interests of simplicity, the section that deals with key contract clauses focuses almost exclusively on finance and accounting outsourcing, although the majority of the principles apply to all types of BPO deals.

However, there are complications that follow from this simplified approach. One other service is often included within the BPO umbrella: applications process outsourcing (APO). This involves the management of enterprise resource planning systems, such as SAP, PeopleSoft and Oracle, as well as individual software applications and customised solutions that support business processes. However, as APO is essentially information systems (IS)-based, this particular BPO service is dealt with in the context of IS outsourcing in Chapter 3.

Another complication is the categorisation of payroll services. These services are often included within the scope of finance and accounting services, but could also come within a human resources transaction. However, for the purposes of this book, payroll processing is considered to be a stand-alone function. This chapter therefore deals with payroll services only briefly.

6.3 KEY DIFFERENCES BETWEEN BPO AND IS OUTSOURCING

While the fundamental approach to a BPO deal is the same as in the more traditional IS (or other) outsourcings, there are some differences that are worth mentioning at this stage. Most of these issues are then dealt with in more detail in the following sections of this chapter. The key differences include the following.

- *Supplier–customer interface*: in traditional IS outsourcing (ISO) there are not usually extensive obligations on the client in terms of assistance with service delivery. The client is simply the recipient of the services. However, in the BPO environment, the client will often have to play a more involved role and, for instance, provide the supplier with the raw data needed to produce the reports that are one of the usual deliverables in a finance and accountancy outsourcing. This can cause complications as there is less of a clear dividing line between the responsibilities of the customer and supplier. A client would traditionally expect to pass over all responsibility for provision of the outsourced service to the supplier, but this is much more difficult to achieve in relation to some BPO services.
- *Technology*: traditional outsourcings tended to be very IS intensive, and ISO in particular would often coincide with the phasing out of legacy systems and the introduction of a new technology platform. A major component of an outsourcing was the initial systems transfer – with the likelihood that a similar transfer would need to take place at the end of the transaction. BPO tends not to be so technology sensitive. Suppliers will probably be using a fairly standard desktop set-up and the services will be provided using standard issue PCs running packaged software. Suppliers providing services to a number of clients from a shared services centre will clearly want to use the same technology for each client, so it is less likely than in the traditional outsourcing that there will be any transfer of software or hardware at the start of the contract. Thus, it is likely that some of the well publicised problems faced in ISOs (of third party software vendors charging excessive sums before consenting to the transfer of the software licence or an extension of the terms of the licence) will be avoided. However, although BPO tends not to be as technology sensitive as more traditional outsourcing, it is the application of this IS to the previously unautomated processes that provides one of the key business drivers for a BPO transaction.
- *Service definition*: although each transaction is different and generalisation can therefore be dangerous, it is often the case that in an ISO the client will have made some attempt to define the internal service levels prior to the outsourcing. Indeed, on some occasions, full service level agreements (SLAs) will be in existence long before any services are transferred to a supplier. Largely because of the nature of the services, this is less likely to have happened in a BPO transaction. Accordingly, the first task for a supplier in a BPO transaction is often to produce the SLAs. This can be quite a time consuming process and provisions need to be included in the contract to deal with the process to be followed, including what happens if the SLAs are produced late, or are not satisfactory to the client. There is also considerable expense involved in the production of the SLAs and there may be a need for some negotiation over who should bear the resulting costs.

- *Deal sponsorship*: the decision to outsource in the BPO environment tends to be taken by the top level management as the BPO decision-making process is complex. By contrast IS outsourcers traditionally target IS managers. This difference can lead to long lead times on BPO deals. However, one advantage of this approach is that building good client relationships at such a high level and at such an early stage can lead to improved client–supplier relationships down the track. Much has been written about partnering between organisations, but strong relationships (at the right level) can greatly enhance the effectiveness of a BPO transaction.
- *Savings profile*: although it is difficult to produce definitive proof, it is often said that there is a greater prize in a BPO (as opposed to an ISO) deal. Suppliers are often prepared to strip out considerable costs from the processes transferred (figures of up to 30 per cent have been quoted). By contrast an ISO provider would be aiming for only 10–20 per cent cost savings. As most companies spend more on their business processes than on IS (perhaps in the region of 1–3 per cent on IS and 4–5 per cent on BPO), this can make the cost saving profile of a BPO transaction very appealing.

6.4 THE BPO MARKET

The continuing drive towards the globalisation of business provides new opportunities for the BPO service providers. Some foreign markets are harder to enter than others, but none are likely to be entirely straightforward. Expanding overseas can therefore be quite a challenge and an outsourcing provider may be able to provide valuable assistance to facilitate the process. For example, if a company wants to commence operations in a new territory, management will need to handle human resources programmes that will encompass recruitment, training, compensation and benefits, payroll and expatriate administration. Each element is likely to vary for expatriates and nationals. The correct technological infrastructure must be selected to underpin the new processes. In addition, everything from software to training manuals must deal with the language issue and accommodate currencies, social customs and local business practices. Companies choosing to deal with all these issues internally are likely to have to commit considerably more resources than those who obtain the services of an already established BPO supplier. Outsourcing suppliers would also argue that a BPO deal is a more advantageous way of learning a new culture and business environment, which is necessary before setting up efficient back office services. A BPO service provider will usually already be operating in the target country and will therefore have the required knowledge of the HR requirements and the regulatory framework that underpin most BPO services.

One of the fundamental drivers towards outsourcing is that the provision of these vital support functions by an external service provider should free up the organisation to concentrate on its core activities. As an aside, it is interesting to note that businesses' views of what is a core and non-core function has also been changing. It is now far more common to outsource what would previously have been viewed as part of the core competence of an organisation. A recent report by PricewaterhouseCoopers (PwC) states that, typically, companies think that 90 per cent of what they do is core to the business and only 10 per cent can be outsourced. The PwC report states that the reverse is true and that most companies have only a handful of core competencies that enable them to provide higher calibre products and services than competitors.

These drivers (along with the continuing drive towards profitability, plus the related pressure on costs and the need to introduce new business models and to adapt to a changing business environment) have fuelled a significant growth in the BPO market, which is the fastest growing segment of the European services market. As in other markets, BPO is experiencing the effect of the recent terrorist attacks and the economic downturn. However, the BPO market has proved itself more counter cyclical than, for instance, the IT services market and while the pace of growth has slowed substantially from previous projections, the market is still expanding.

In the Dataquest Report entitled *European Business Process Outsourcing Trends, 2001* (Gartner Group Inc., 19 February 2002) the Gartner Group points to strong growth in the market despite the economic downturn, with European BPO services expected to grow from US$32.4 billion in 2000 to US$64.2 billion in 2005, at a compound annual growth rate of 14.7 per cent.

Within the European market there are geographical differences. The Gartner survey indicates that the BPO market is more developed in countries such as the UK, Ireland and the Netherlands. By contrast demand for BPO in countries such as France, Italy and Spain is limited because of legislative constraints. The differing HR legislation across Europe can certainly make some BPO opportunities far more appealing than others. It is also anticipated that demand for BPO in northern Europe – especially Sweden – will increase as multinationals penetrate their country markets and as strong local companies begin to optimise their operations, with an emphasis on cutting costs. In addition, Eastern European countries are becoming increasingly popular, both as the site for low cost BPO centres and for domestic BPO opportunities.

It is, however, interesting to note that there is a different take-up of BPO services in different industries, and that the profile is different from ISO. A recent Morgan Chambers study indicated that the BPO market is dominated by three sectors, which together account for 82 per cent of the market. The banking market represents over one-third of the BPO contracts, closely followed by oil and gas (which account for just over one-third), jointly accounting for over two-thirds of such contracts. The remaining sectors account for the residual 18 per cent of the market comprising (among other things) life assurance, transport and food and drugs retailers. This indicates that there is still scope for growth in the BPO market as at least some of the sectors, which have not currently outsourced, are likely to consider this route in the future.

6.5 THE RANGE OF BPO SERVICES

6.5.1 Finance and accounting

The finance and accounting (F&A) function of an organisation will include a number of different functions and processes. Companies may have differing views on which of these functions and processes should be outsourced. While the scope issue has to be resolved on a case-by-case basis, the functions usually outsourced include the process-driven functions, such as accounts payable/receivable, financial accounting and reporting, fixed asset accounting, general ledger, credit and collections, customer invoicing, expense accounting and cash management. On the other hand, more complex areas such as treasury are often retained as this is viewed as a fundamental part of the organisation's finance management and control. In addition, the risks to an outsourcing supplier in taking over this function and, for instance, making investment decisions or hedging are probably greater than those usually costed into an outsourcing proposal. Such functions may therefore be beyond the comfort zone of most suppliers. There seems, however, to be no reason why a supplier would not take over more routine tasks – for example, such things as depositing funds overnight – as long as the parameters are sufficiently defined. Indeed, some suppliers offer more far-reaching F&A services including capital investment, financial planning, cost management and financial analysis. However, it is the process-driven services that are usually considered to be the most appropriate to outsource.

6.5.2 Human resources

In the early days of outsourcing, companies were likely to outsource payroll alone, but now suppliers have extended the range of available services (partly as a result of advances in technology) and it is feasible to outsource far more of the human resources (HR) function. HR outsourcing arrangements typically cover a range of services, including recruitment, payroll, training and development, administration, transfers and relocation, expatriate assignments and benefits administration. With the advancement of globalisation, companies need an infrastructure capable of handling hiring, executive succession, benefits, pension plans and other employee services on a global basis. In addition, new enterprise-wide technology provides a standardised platform for information so that HR can bring such diverse data as payroll, benefits,

213

training and personnel records into an integrated, unified system. Such integration should also provide the tools needed to analyse all aspects of the HR function and to provide management access to better decision-making areas like recruitment. Thus, using an outsourcing provider with extensive data management systems, an executive at a global company who needs to hire a manager is able to access personnel files, performance records and all the information needed for a worldwide search. As a result, the process should become less time consuming and more efficient.

Integrated systems should also be an advantage for other HR programmes such as training. If a single management system is used, regardless of the number of different training providers, the system should be able to give management up-to-date information about what training is being done, what it costs and how effective it is. At the same time, employees can access the system to register for training courses online. The result should be that the company has the ability to manage the training programme and make informed decisions about training requirements.

As a general rule, the majority of an HR department's time and budget is spent on routine transactions, with a relatively small percentage being spent on planning, strategy and design. The BPO concept is for HR departments to be able to concentrate on key issues, such as developing a creative compensation package, which would lead to a lower rate of staff turnover, rather than dealing with all the time consuming background processes.

It is often the case that a company will have multiple suppliers of HR services. But in an outsourced environment there should be only one point of entry to the entire system. This should result in record keeping being more accurate, avoiding duplication and providing easy access to information for both the company and the employees. The outsourcing supplier will also manage all the different HR service providers, such as the financial institutions providing savings and retirement schemes, and the providers of medical, dental, life and health insurance plans.

Ideally, HR executives need access to fast, reliable information when assessing such key issues as recruitment costs, turnover rates (and reasons), the cost of the deployment of employees, revenue per employee, and training effectiveness – all critical issues for companies today. The rationale behind outsourcing the more process-driven HR tasks is that HR executives can then spend more of their time on planning, strategy and design, which are particularly important as HR programmes grow more sophisticated.

The other side of the coin is the perceived benefit for employees. Employees who are now used to being able to bank and shop electronically 24 hours a day are demanding higher service levels in the workplace environment. Employees want quick responses to their inquiries and self-service access to their information. For instance, employees with children who want to update health benefits or access childcare information will want to make only one set of inquiries to get the information they need and to update their records. This improved service may be one of the benefits offered by an outsourcing supplier.

6.5.3 Procurement

The procurement department of a business is generally responsible for purchasing a wide range of goods and services. As with all outsourcings, a key issue is scope. In the context of a procurement outsourcing, it is necessary to clarify which particular procurement functions will be outsourced. Large-scale capital asset procurement projects may not be within the core competence of the majority of outsourcing suppliers, but the more process-driven functions certainly are. To date, most procurement outsourcings have centred on the procurement of basic office supplies, such as stationery, but it is likely that the range of goods and services available will expand rapidly. Suppliers are already offering procurement services in relation to a wide range of goods and services including computers, telecommunications and airline travel.

An outsourcing supplier will argue that there are two main benefits from a procurement outsourcing:

- *Strategic sourcing*: as part of the arrangement, a supplier will develop relationships with new and existing suppliers to improve their performance in terms of service and quality, while generating significant savings. It is anticipated that, by centralising the procurement process and ensuring that only a limited number of suppliers are involved, considerable discounts can be negotiated. In organisations without rigorous controls on the procurement process, where individuals purchase goods and services from a variety of sources, no benefit is received from the overall volume of purchases made and no attempt is made to improve the terms on which the goods or services are provided.
- *Process efficiency*: suppliers will also enhance the procurement process by improving efficiency in terms of people, processes and systems. With a totally integrated system it should be possible to increase the efficiency of all parts of the procurement process.

The procurement process is particularly well suited to the application of e-business solutions and many suppliers are now offering e-procurement services. This aspect of procurement outsourcing is dealt with in more detail in paragraph 6.7.2.

6.5.4 Real estate management

Office space, manufacturing plants, warehouses and retail space, typical components of a company's real estate portfolio represent substantial capital outlays for a business. In addition, significant cost can be incurred in relation to the operation and management of the real estate function, including personnel and technology costs and service contract charges. The bottom line costs of real estate can therefore be divided into two categories:

- the operating expenditures of the real estate itself, such as rent, maintenance and security; and
- the internal costs of running a property division, including staff and technology costs.

Many companies find it difficult to measure the true cost of their real estate portfolios. They can calculate the rent they pay and they may know their depreciation costs, but they do not know what percentage of operating expenditure is represented by real estate.

Observers have estimated that over 50 per cent of the cost of real estate is directly tied to the decision of whether to lease or own, the amount of space per person and the location of the space. It is important to ensure that these key decisions are also linked to a company's business needs. So, for instance, there is a trade-off between a company taking short-term lets (to gain flexibility) and the added cost (as short-term leases are not usually as cost effective as long-term leases). If a company has access to detailed information showing past usage patterns it may be possible to work out the optimal length of any lease, or indeed if the best approach is to buy rather than rent.

Spurred by the need to control costs and to concentrate on core activities, companies began to outsource real estate operations in the early 1960s. Since then, real estate outsourcing has grown rapidly. As with the rest of the outsourcing market, there are a number of possible approaches to outsourcing. For instance, companies can simply contract with an outsourcing company to provide a particular service, such as maintenance, security or lease management, at a lower cost than the company anticipates it is paying internally. The outsourcing suppliers will argue that, while the cost reduction may be real, the result is a range of different services provided by multiple providers – thereby negating one of the key benefits of outsourcing.

However, while there are a number of different possible approaches, the areas of real estate management usually outsourced include property management, lease administration, accounts receivable/payable, procurement of building materials and office equipment, and the management of third party contractors. This list also illustrates the areas of overlap sometimes found in BPO transactions, which leads to fairly fluid boundaries between the different BPO services. Thus office equipment purchasing can fall within a real estate BPO deal or within a procurement outsourcing; similarly, accounts receivable/payable may be within a real estate or an F&A transaction.

Whatever the type of categorisation used, performance measurement is as important in real estate outsourcing as in the other types of outsourcing. In relation to real estate, typical performance measures include real estate costs as a percentage of total operating costs, return on capital, portfolio efficiency and customer service measures. Real estate is an area where it is relatively easy to link the supplier's compensation to performance measures, and it is not unusual to see relatively aggressive cost-reduction commitments in the outsourcing contract.

6.6 KEY CONTRACT CLAUSES

Previous chapters have dealt with the provisions that are likely to be generic to all outsourcing transactions. The aim of this chapter is to concentrate on those issues that are peculiar to BPO transactions. Clearly it is only possible to generalise to a certain extent since each transaction is different. However, it is worth considering those issues that differentiate BPO transactions or that need to be addressed only in BPO deals.

In the interests of consistency, most of the examples of key contract clauses are taken from F&A transactions. The principles are similar in other BPO outsourcings, although the details may vary. For instance paragraph 6.6.3 deals with the regulatory issues, and in the F&A context the accounting and audit requirements are the prime concern. However, in an HR outsourcing the regulatory issues would be centred on issues such as compliance with the employment protection legislation, including the Sex Discrimination Act 1975, the Race Relations Act 1976, the Disability Discrimination Act 1995, and all the employment rights (such as unfair dismissal) granted under the Employment Rights Act 1996.

6.6.1 Roles and responsibilities

As previously mentioned, BPO is different from other types of outsourcing in that there is frequently a division of responsibilities between the supplier and the customer. Not only will there be a description of the services to be provided by the supplier – normally expanded into a full SLA – but the obligations of the customer will also need to be documented. These obligations are often documented in an operating level agreement (OLA), which is seldom found, for instance, in an IT outsourcing agreement, where there is little interplay between the supplier and the customer and where the customer simply receives a service. In the BPO environment the customer is likely to have a role to play in relation to the service provision.

By way of example, for a supplier in an F&A outsourcing to be able to produce management accounts, it will be necessary for the customer to provide the supplier with all the necessary raw financial data. Over time these data will need to be updated. The time frame within which this information is to be provided to the supplier must be set out in the contract. It is because of the need for the customer to produce certain information and fulfil its other responsibilities that suppliers often seek to define their performance targets (for instance, in terms of producing a report) as a specified number of days after receipt of the relevant information from the supplier, rather than expressing the obligation in absolute terms.

Responsibility for the accuracy of the data also needs to be addressed, and a supplier will not want to accept responsibility for the accuracy, timeliness or completeness of the customer data. Equally, the customer will expect that the supplier take full responsibility for the processing of such raw data once they have been made available to the supplier, although not for any inherent flaws or omissions in the data. A supplier may request that the customer gives some form of warranty or other assurance as to the accuracy and completeness of the data. The customer may resist this since it would not wish to find itself being sued by its own supplier. The manner in which issues such as accuracy and completeness are addressed in the contract can therefore lead to some interesting debates between the supplier and customer. One suggestion, which leads to a fairly clean division of responsibilities, is to include a provision making it clear that the responsibility for the raw customer data remains with the customer and that the supplier is not responsible for any errors or omissions in the deliverables that result from such errors or omissions. However, errors or omissions resulting from processing mistakes (such as miscalculations) are the responsibility of the supplier.

It is also worth clarifying what will happen if it subsequently becomes clear that there was an error in the input data, which needs to be corrected. This can lead to certain reconciliations or processes being repeated or new versions of reports or accounts produced. The supplier will want to be paid for such additional effort, but a customer may resist the payment of any additional fee – particularly if the work can be carried out by existing resources within the supplier team.

It is also important to assign responsibility for the accounting policies to be followed when providing the services and for ensuring compliance with the regulatory and tax requirements. This is dealt with in more detail later in this chapter, but it is important that ownership of this role is clearly set out.

6.6.2   Operating level/service level agreements

The need for an operating level agreement (OLA) stems from the concerns about the allocation of roles and responsibilities referred to above. It is necessary to document the customer's obligations and it often makes sense to do this in a document that mirrors the SLA. This is the document that is often referred to as an OLA, but different terminology may be used by different suppliers. Some suppliers also prefer to adopt a more generic approach and include in the contract a more general description of the customer's responsibilities. This differs from an OLA, which will mirror the SLA line by line and describe what the customer needs to do to enable the supplier to fulfil its obligations under the SLA. These obligations on the customer usually include providing information or checking interim reports or accounts.

As with the clauses in the contract dealing with roles and responsibilities, it is important to clarify the consequences of the customer failing to fulfil its obligations under the OLA. Suppliers will often ask that customers give warranties and assurances similar to those given by the supplier in relation to the SLAs. The suppliers argue that, if the OLAs are not complied with, they will not be able to provide the services, and contracts are often structured so that a supplier can only bill for services actually provided. The supplier may even argue that it should have the right to terminate the contract if there is a repeated breach that prevents it from fulfilling its obligations under the contract. Both of these requests are likely to be resisted by a customer, who will want it made clear that the only consequence of a failure on its part to perform in accordance with the OLA is that the supplier is absolved from any resulting failure to comply with the SLA.

6.6.3 Regulatory issues

The particular regulatory issues of concern will vary depending on the type of outsourcing, so it is not feasible to deal with all the relevant regulatory issues in detail in this chapter. A brief description of the regulatory environment in relation to F&A transactions should, however, provide an indication of the effect of the regulatory environment on BPO transactions. The basic obligation on companies to keep accounting records is contained in the Companies Act 1985, as amended by the Companies Act 1989 (the Companies Acts). The Companies Acts require the production of a balance sheet and profit and loss account each year within a specified time frame. Schedule A to the Companies Acts also sets out detailed requirements for the form and content of the accounts. In addition, the Accounting Standards Board produces Financial Reporting Standards (FRSs), which are gradually updating and superseding Statements of Standard Accounting Practices (SSAPs). The Companies Acts require that, with exceptions for small and medium-sized companies, accounts must state whether they have been prepared in accordance with those accounting standards. Various accountancy bodies also provide and ensure compliance with FRSs and SSAPs. In addition, listed companies must comply with the Listing Rules produced by the Stock Exchange (the *Yellow Book*). These Rules require compliance with the SSAPs and FRSs (as well as, among other things, requiring the production of interim accounts and setting out different timing requirements for public companies).

The key point to note is that, particularly in the context of F&A outsourcings, the client and the supplier will be operating in a well regulated environment and it is important that both parties are aware of this and that responsibility for regulatory compliance is clearly set out. While a supplier may accept that it is part of its responsibility to produce an SLA that sets out the precise nature of the services, it may not want to accept responsibility for ensuring that compliance with the SLA leads to the production of the requisite accounts within the time frame, or for fulfilling the content requirements as set out in the relevant legislation and related rules.

6.6.4 Scope

Clarifying the scope of the services to be outsourced is always critical to the success of an outsourcing project, and BPO transactions are no different. Any doubt about which services are in scope and covered by the specified charges and those that will only be addressed via the change control procedure is likely to lead to disillusionment and dispute. Clarification is therefore required. The first step is to clarify which services are included and which will be retained by the customer. This can be quite a difficult issue in the context of a BPO outsourcing. For instance, in an F&A outsourcing, it is necessary to allocate responsibility for the formulation of the client's accounting policies and procedures. Some clients will want to retain responsibility for these issues as they will be viewed as part of the core function of the client organisation. However, clients taking a more radical approach may want to include more senior management within the scope of the outsourcing and to transfer responsibility for these management issues. The approach taken will reflect the client's view of outsourcing. Some organisations view outsourcing simply as a way of contracting out certain stand-alone, non-core services. Others have a different philosophical approach and feel that a supplier can add more value if it can take over all the processes in an entire business unit (such as the finance function), rather than just certain services provided by that unit.

In addition to the accounting policies and procedures, it is necessary to allocate responsibility for compliance with the regulatory environment, including changes to the accounting and taxation requirements. Thus, a supplier may simply be obligated to produce SLAs and OLAs detailing the services to be provided, with the client ensuring that these agreements are in accordance with the various regulatory requirements. Alternatively, the customer may expect the supplier to take responsibility for the regulatory issues. In an F&A outsourcing there are statutory timing requirements for the production of the various in-scope accounts. Who is to be responsible for ensuring that those deadlines are met? In addition, there are often fines or other penalties for missing the deadlines, and it must be clear in which circumstances these fines will be paid by the supplier and when the cost will be borne by the client.

The regulatory issues can be complex, particularly in the context of an outsourcing that covers more than one country. If suppliers take over responsibility for services in a number of different countries and centralise the service provision in one country, they will have to find staff in that country who are familiar with the relevant regulatory requirements in a number of overseas jurisdictions. It can be difficult to find staff with these skill sets, and it will affect the cost if there is a greater percentage of relatively senior staff as opposed to more junior clerks. All these issues need to be taken into account when deciding on the scope of the outsourcing.

Having clarified the scope issue, the second stage is to produce a good service level agreement as this can help assuage many of the potential scoping problems. The key issues in relation to the production of service level agreements are dealt with in Chapter 2 and will not be repeated here.

6.6.5 Liabilities

Negotiating appropriate limits on liability is never an easy task in any outsourcing. One approach is to look at the different layers or types of liability that could be incurred and see how each should be addressed.

The first layer of liability is found in the service credit regime, if there is one. The purpose of a service credit regime is to encourage the supplier to perform in accordance with an agreed set of service levels. If the specified elements of the SLA are not met, a specific financial payment is due in the form of a reduction in the level of the service charge. Setting the level of the payment (and triggering event) is difficult. It needs to be a level that penalises the supplier, but still leaves the supplier with an incentive to continue with the service delivery (by not eating into the supplier's underlying cost base). The regime also needs to be well thought out and not overly complex, or disproportionate amounts of time and therefore money may be spent on monitoring and operating the regime. These considerations apply equally to BPO as to the other forms of outsourcing.

Similarly it will be necessary to decide whether it is appropriate for the supplier to exclude or in some way limit its liability for consequential loss. While it used to be standard to argue that such an exclusion should be included, it is now not unusual for such a clause to be the subject of lengthy debate. This raises the issue of the categorisation of different types of loss. In the F&A scenario the potential losses can be considerable as the supplier will usually be responsible for, among other things, cash management and accounts payable.

Payments could go astray and be sent to the wrong destination, or overpayments may be made. Similarly, if accounts are filed late there is the possibility of fines levied by the regulatory authorities. Who is to be responsible for such fines or erroneous payments? Rather than relying on standard form allocations of liability for direct and consequential loss, it is often advisable to deal specifically with the allocation of responsibility for these particular types of loss.

6.6.6   Termination

While outsourcing deals tend to be relatively long term (with most running for between three and seven years), all deals come to an end at some stage. Indeed some surveys have indicated that a relatively high percentage of deals fail each year. Figures in the region of 20–25 per cent have been quoted. Accordingly, termination is a key concern in any outsourcing. Clients are reluctant to commit to transferring to a supplier their staff and the other assets they need to provide a service themselves unless there are clearly defined arrangements to minimise any disruption caused by a subsequent termination. This is a complex area as the contractual consequences of termination should vary depending on the cause of the termination. For example, it would be unreasonable to expect the customer to pay an early termination payment if it had to terminate the agreement as a result of the supplier's persistent breach of contract. All of these issues are just as relevant to BPO as to non-BPO outsourcings.

However, one area where BPO is often quite different from the more traditional IS or telecommunications outsourcings is the relative absence of concern as to the technological solution used by the supplier. As discussed in section 6.3, it is unlikely that a BPO transaction will have involved significant system transfers at the start of the contract. Similarly, it is less likely that a client will want to call for the transfer of any software or hardware at the end of the contract, preferring to purchase or use its own systems. As a consequence, it may be possible to simplify the often detailed termination provisions (such as those specifying which systems the client can purchase and the method of valuing the relevant assets). While the client may decide that it still wants the option to require the transfer of the supplier's systems, this section of the termination arrangements is often omitted.

Another issue to consider on termination is the ownership of the various deliverables and the underlying know-how. In the BPO context, these issues are often of more significance than the technological issues. It is usually accepted that the actual deliverables (for instance, the reports produced in an F&A outsourcing), as well as the underlying raw data, are owned by the client. However, the supplier will be keen to ensure that it has protected its methodologies and processes and will want to ensure that the client is not in a position to pass these on to a successor supplier on termination. This can lead to some interesting debates regarding, for instance, the ownership of the intellectual property rights in the SLAs. Both the client and the supplier have legitimate concerns, but it is usually possible to find a compromise that addresses both parties' concerns. One approach is to make it clear that the supplier retains the rights to the methodology underpinning the SLA (and indeed the standard form SLA), thereby ensuring that it is not required to reinvent the wheel for each new transaction. However, the customer takes ownership of the customised version of the SLA produced in the context of the particular outsourcing deal, which will be particularly valuable on termination.

6.6.7 Data protection

Data protection is an important issue for any company that processes data (particularly as the Data Protection Act 1998 extends the field of legislative protection to manual records). A detailed analysis of the legislation is beyond the scope of this chapter, but it is important to note that, particularly in relation to human resources outsourcings, the data protection compliance issues may be extensive and will need to be addressed in detail in the contract. It may be advisable to go beyond the standard clauses seen in many contracts where it is simply acknowledged that both parties will comply with their obligations under the relevant legislation. Indeed, in the context of an HR outsourcing, a customer may want the supplier to take over responsibility for production of a data protection policy, which may need to be incorporated into employees' terms and conditions of employment. In any event, it is useful if the contract can draw specific attention to, for instance, any sensitive data (as defined in the Data Protection Act) to be processed as part of the outsourcing, as well as containing a clear delineation of responsibilities for complying with the legislative requirements in relation to such data.

6.6.8 Taxation

Taxation is an issue that needs to be addressed in all outsourcings. This chapter is not the right place to deal with the intricacies of taxation (see Chapter 11) but it is worth highlighting one major concern: VAT. VAT is almost irrelevant for many kinds of organisation but is a real cost for others (such as financial institutions, public administrations and companies that do not invoice clients for their goods or services). For companies in the financial services sector, outsourcing can involve an unpleasant additional charge. This is because, by outsourcing, such organisations go from a position where VAT only impacts on part of the IS budget (such as hardware or software) to a position where VAT is paid on every cost element (including staffing and the vendor's overheads and margins). This can eradicate the majority of the anticipated cost reduction from the outsourcing, which in turn can substantially undermine the business case for doing the deal.

Thus it is in the best interests of both the supplier and customer to find a way of minimising the effect of VAT. Clearly it is important to remember the distinction between tax avoidance and tax evasion, but there are ways of structuring deals to try to minimise unwanted tax charges. Frequently these structuring issues will centre around the use of some form of joint venture. As previously mentioned, this chapter is not the place to discuss these arrangements in detail (specific advice should be taken from a taxation expert on each particular transaction). Suffice it to say that the tax savings from such arrangements can be sufficient to outweigh the additional cost of setting up and operating a joint venture entity.

It is also worth pointing out that there can be unexpected taxation consequences of siting shared service centres in particular locations. Locations
such as the Netherlands and Eire are chosen for their beneficial taxation
regimes, but some of the less well known locations where suppliers are considering setting up shared service centres can have unexpected tax consequences. It is always advisable to run the arrangements past a tax expert at an
early stage to ascertain if there will be any hidden costs as a result of the
application of a particular tax regime.

6.6.9 Record retention

Owing to the nature of the services being provided in an F&A outsourcing
and the nature of the information being processed, it is important not only
that robust confidentiality and data ownership clauses are included in the
contract, but also that the record retention issue is addressed. There are legislative requirements in relation to record retention. In addition to these legal
requirements, companies will frequently have their own record retention
policies (reflecting the statutory requirements but sometimes going further).
Suppliers may need to revise their record retention policies to ensure compliance with the customer's policy, and this can be costly and difficult to
administer if the customers of the supplier all have different policies.

6.6.10 Interfaces

Even though technological issues are likely to be less important in a BPO
outsourcing, there may be various interfaces between the client and supplier
systems. For instance, the supplier may need to access the client's enterprise
resource planning systems to access certain raw data. It is important to
consider all such interfaces and to ensure that the appropriate consents
and licences have been obtained. It is also necessary to ensure that these
arrangements terminate at the end of the contract.

6.7 BPO DEVELOPMENTS

6.7.1 The joint venture approach

Joint ventures (JVs) are not a new feature in the business world; however,
what is relatively new is the use of joint ventures in the BPO environment.
Typically this involves the setting up of a corporate joint venture between the
client and a JV partner, usually either a consultancy firm (with sufficient
process or outsourcing knowledge) or an existing outsourcing supplier. A
shareholders' agreement will usually be entered into by the joint venture
partners, setting out the arrangements in relation to, among other things,

funding, management structure, dividend policy, exit and transfer of shares. The JV company will then supply BPO services to the customer (who is also a shareholder in the JV company) pursuant to an outsourcing agreement between the customer and the JV company.

So why add this extra tier? Why create an additional company as part of the outsourcing arrangement? In the previous section we briefly touched on the possible benefits from a taxation perspective of using some form of JV entity, but there is another reason. A new JV company may be formed if it is intended to use the company as the delivery vehicle for providing outsourcing services to third parties. If successful, the JV will gain and manage new clients and new services, producing economies of scale and leveraging as much as possible on the initial client's resources and assets. One danger for the initial client is that, in a successful JV, it tends no longer to be the preferred client. When a JV grows in scale, especially in highly competitive markets where prices are falling, existing and captive clients are very important in terms of economic stability. The JV will make every effort to keep prices high for existing clients so that it can provide lower prices to new clients. This is not likely to be beneficial for the original client and this can lead to tensions in the JV. However, if the pricing arrangements can be resolved in a mutually satisfactory manner, it should be possible to overcome this hurdle.

The use of the joint venture approach in relation to BPO deals is not extensive, but a number of the largest deals have gone down this route. It is therefore worth considering if the economics of a particular deal would be more beneficial if a joint venture vehicle were to be introduced.

6.7.2   E-business

Much has been written about the e-business revolution and such a broad topic is outside the scope of this book. However, it is interesting to note that the BPO market is well placed to take advantage of the changes in methods of doing business that are often an integral part of e-business. One of the keys to e-business is improved connectivity. An e-business offering may provide connectivity between and across business, as well as between businesses and their customers and suppliers, in ways that improve service, reduce costs and open new channels to new markets.

The possibilities for BPO are probably most apparent in relation to procurement outsourcing. Many suppliers point to the considerable volume discounts that can be produced by centralising and controlling the procurement process. This would be the case whether the procurement took place in an electronic or a non-electronic environment, but the efficiencies are likely to be more quickly realised in an electronic trading environment. The procurement process can be rendered completely paperless, with goods being selected from an electronic catalogue, online orders being sent direct to the manufacturer/logistics provider and order confirmation and despatch notices sent electronically. Payment is always a difficult issue and there are still concerns over the security of the various electronic methods of payment and communication, but developments in encryption technology and the use of trusted third parties are gradually allaying some of these fears.

E-business provides direct access to a business's customer base (via the Internet or, in the future, wireless application protocol (WAP) and other such technologies), thereby providing opportunities for supply chain re-engineering. As a result businesses should be able to remove certain middlemen from their supply networks. Again the procurement process is a good example of the opportunities for such re-engineering. An electronic procurement process, with direct access to the manufacturer via an electronic catalogue, means there is no need for any form of retailer or distributor, although the manufacturer will still need some form of fulfilment or delivery capability. This should keep prices low (good for the customer), but raise the manufacturer's margin as the profit no longer needs to be shared with other members of the supply chain (good for the manufacturer). It should also lead to greater efficiencies in the supply chain as, for example, suppliers have greater awareness of customers' demand cycles (through the use of various planning tools and software) and customers can place orders more quickly, both of which should enable suppliers to eliminate or greatly reduce inventory and hence cost.

However, the finance function should also be able to benefit from the application of e-business. E-business has the potential to reduce transaction processing costs, and the associated open standards should offer improved customer service capabilities as clients can access detailed transactional and reporting information online via the Web rather than using higher cost, less flexible dedicated interfaces between the client and the supplier. Potential e-business applications could include:

- online transaction review and approval for accounts payables, updating and establishing customer credit limits, accessing payroll information, travel and entertainment exception reports and customer billing information; and
- online reporting and controls for continuously updated cash forecasting, supplier performance reporting, contract administration, current transaction pricing and volumes and general status reporting.

Similarly, e-business offerings may play a part in the overall HR outsourcing strategy by enabling:

- *Integrated HR service delivery*: full integration of information, technology, people and processes should result in streamlined HR activities and cost-effective solutions.

- *State of the-art self-service applications*: advances in technology enable the implementation of employee self-service applications in the form of voice response units, Internet and Intranet websites and kiosks. This technology provides extended hours of access, provides the employee with more control over those changes, while reducing the overall cost of service delivery. Workflow technologies should also reduce the required manual interaction for common HR administration activities such as staffing and performance management.
- *The provision of a knowledge management system*: enabling knowledge about corporate policy, procedures, benefits and compensation plans to be available to employees, managers and call centre representatives whenever required.

In the real estate field, e-business may also be able to add value to a traditional BPO transaction by facilitating:

- the disposal of vacant space or premises, either internally through an Intranet or externally, potentially removing the need to pay a transaction fee; and
- leveraging information access for online measurement and reporting, contract administration and sharing information with related departments such as legal, F&A and insurance.

It is also possible that a BPO transaction will give customers the opportunity to benefit from advances in technology that would not be available to them individually, but are possible because of the scale of the service centre set up by the supplier. Thus the supplier, with a number of different customers, has the economies of scale that make it cost-effective to introduce initiatives that would not be feasible on a more limited scale. A useful side effect of BPO may be that a customer stays at the forefront of advancing e-business technology and applications.

6.7.3 ASP/BSP

Until relatively recently application service provision (ASP) was the new big thing. There was almost as much hyperbole written about ASP as about the e-business revolution – and both have failed to live up to expectations, at least in the short term.

ASP involves the delivery of a preconfigured template software from a remote location over an IP network. The ASP proposition is based on payment for a service rather than software products and professional services, and utilises a pay-as-you-go model rather than a traditional software licensing model. The aim was to use a standard or vanilla application that could be used by a variety of clients, rather than using heavily (and expensively) customised applications on a client-by-client basis. The assumption was that this would be particularly appealing to small and medium-sized businesses, which would be able to access high grade applications (such as enterprise resource planning (ERP) systems) without extensive up-front investment and while retaining flexibility (as ASP deals tended not to follow the long-term, BPO approach). However, although the business benefits of the ASP model are clear (predictable pricing, lack of up-front capital expenditure and the ability to rapidly deploy), expectations set by ASPs have been plagued by poor service delivery and inadequate infrastructure. There was also considerable oversupply in the market which, combined with the general economic slowdown, led to a number of suppliers failing. However the general consensus seems to be that the underlying ASP delivery model and value proportion are sound and that in time, the ASP market will undergo steady growth and increased market acceptance.

Why is this relevant to the BPO market? The answer is because of the convergence of ASP and BPO to produce business service provision (BSP). This involves BPO providers simplifying their service delivery from a complex, highly customised model to a standardised business service. It is anticipated that this will lead to new opportunities for BPO providers in the middle market and enable the introduction of increased flexibility into BPO pricing methodology. BSP services are preconfigured and purchased on a rental basis, and therefore require minimal development and implementation.

BSP pricing is typically characterised around the output of the services provided, for example, a credit checking BSP may charge a fee per credit report provided. While output pricing plays a part in some BPO deals, it is not often a key component of the pricing mechanism.

Currently only a handful of processes are provided through a BSP solution approach (procurement, HR and finance for example). However, it is anticipated that many more processes will emerge as the BSP model matures, although it is too early to tell whether the BSP market will be beset by the same difficulties that made the early years of ASP such a challenge.

6.7.4 Key issues for a successful BPO contract

1. If acting for the customer, ensure your client has analysed its processes and costs and can determine the cost consequences of outsourcing over a specific time period.
2. Define roles and responsibilities so that both parties understand what is expected of them, and include a clear, precise definition of services in and out of scope.
3. Include measurable performance objectives and set out performance incentives (both rewards and penalties) for meeting those objectives.
4. Include a detailed transition plan, or a process for finalising such a plan to ensure a smooth handover.

5. Include a clear dispute resolution process to handle issues as they arise. Some form of escalation process can often help to resolve issues by forcing senior management to intervene.
6. Provide a means of monitoring the services for continuous improvement.

CHAPTER 7

Public sector outsourcing

Lucille Hughes

7.1 INTRODUCTION

It has been argued that in the modern era the capabilities of government are increasingly determined and affected by the distinctive characteristics of their information and communications technology (ICT) systems.[1] As evidence of this, there has been a steady growth in the outsourcing of government ICT functions since the mid 1980s, a growth that has been further sustained in the UK through the setting of e-government targets for both central and local government. The setting of these targets has been part of the latest Labour government's general push for the modernisation and improvement of public services.[2] In addition to ICT outsourcing, a very wide range of other outsourcing transactions are also being undertaken by the public sector including small-scale packages of blue-collar (e.g. building maintenance services, cleaning, grounds maintenance) and white-collar (e.g. accountancy, payroll, human resources) services, as well as larger scale private finance initiative (PFI) projects, property outsourcing and business process outsourcing projects.

In the UK, market testing initiatives and the introduction of compulsory competitive tendering (CCT) for local government by the Conservative government in the late 1980s and early 1990s acted as a catalyst for many public sector outsourcing projects. The intention of those initiatives was to challenge traditional practices for in-house provision of services and at the time, this was in tune with developments in new public management theories throughout most liberal democracies. Such ideas espoused a new ethos of tight corporate management focusing on financial bottom lines, competition, incentivisation and a belief that it was not government's role to be involved in activities where it was not the best in the world.

Since the late 1980s numerous public sector activities have been outsourced to the private sector and some of the larger scale outsourcings have been undertaken by the Inland Revenue, the Department for Work and Pensions, the Ministry of Defence and the Home Office.[3] There have also been numerous smaller scale outsourcings of a whole range of white- and blue-collar functions such as ICT, catering, building management and security. Despite recent economic slowdown, the growth in public sector outsourcing continues. In addition there have been a number of property-based outsourcing projects involving the transfer of ownership of property from public sector bodies to a private sector provider in return for the provision of services. For instance, the outsourcing of many residential care functions by local authorities has also been accompanied by the transfer of either freehold or leasehold interests in local authority property. A very high profile property outsourcing project was undertaken by the Department of Social Security in 1998 – the PRIME (Private Sector Resource Initiative for Management of Estate) project saw the transfer of 700 offices in 350 towns and cities throughout the UK under a 20-year contract.

Consideration of outsourcing in a public sector context requires an understanding of the unique factors and legal and regulatory frameworks that affect government and that do not necessarily apply to private sector outsourcing. Although there are many similarities in the way in which the private and public sectors approach outsourcing, there are a number of key differences such as:

- the existence of a legislative procurement regime for the award of contracts;
- common law principles relating to *vires*;
- statutory provisions that govern what types of services can be contracted out as well as statutory provisions that can affect the terms of an outsourcing transaction;
- the need to meet objectives set by a wide range of stakeholders such as politicians, members of the public and government staff and unions;
- a difficulty in defining the business benefits arising from outsourcing because they are not always financially driven; and
- the impact the political dimension can have on an outsourcing transaction.

Finally, caution should be exercised when examining public sector outsourcing as a topic as this implies a homogeneity between the practices of different public sector bodies that is not strictly correct. Although there are often calls for greater standardisation in the procurement practices of UK public sector bodies, the reality is that even within the obligatory legal parameters, there are many different procurement and outsourcing practices that exist between central and local government, universities and the NHS for instance. It is also important to appreciate the wide range of outsourcing transactions that can be undertaken by the public sector, each of which possesses its own unique risk factors and key issues.

7.2 DRIVERS FOR PUBLIC SECTOR OUTSOURCING

Outsourcing in the public sector is an arrangement, underpinned by a commercial contract, whereby an external third party provider (usually a private sector company) provides services that typically or historically have been provided from within the contracting authority.[4] It is almost always undertaken through a competitive tendering exercise and will often also involve the transfer of staff and assets that the contracting authority had previously used to provide the service now being outsourced.

Governments have always historically purchased goods and services from third parties. However, the last two decades have seen the growth in competitive tendering and outsourcing by contracting authorities to the point where it has been observed that public sector outsourcing is now at roughly twice the level it is within the private sector.[5] This growth in public sector outsourcing has been driven partly by budgetary pressures requiring reduced government spending and partly by the influence of economic theories about public administration. Policies on outsourcing and in particular the private finance initiative (PFI) (which shall be discussed further below) have been adopted at central and local government levels and have been espoused by both Labour and Conservative governments as preferred methods of service delivery and improvement.

Before embarking on an outsourcing project, most contracting authorities will have gone through market testing activities as well as the construction of a business case quantifying the pros and cons of the proposed transaction. Generally a contracting authority will focus on asking itself: 'What outcomes do we expect to achieve through outsourcing?'; 'What problems is the outsourcing intended to solve?'; 'Do suppliers in the marketplace have solutions to these problems?'. Ultimately, there will be several factors in combination that influence public sector decisions to outsource activities and the most commonly cited examples are as follows:

- *Cost savings*: it has been argued that outsourcing can reduce both fixed and recurrent costs. It is also argued that outsourcing suppliers are in a better position to reap economies of scale that may not necessarily be available to a contracting authority alone.
- *Focus on core business*: it has been argued that outsourcing can free up the public sector to focus on its core business, which is to provide the public with a range of public services. For instance it is often cited that ICT systems development and maintenance are not part of government's core line of business.
- *Access to skills*: it has been argued that through outsourcing activities, the public sector can gain access to highly specialised skills as and when they are required. Highly specialised consultancy skills (for example relating to business process re-engineering) and skills in ICT systems integration and development are often regarded as falling into this category.
- *Access to technology*: many public sector bodies find keeping up with technical developments in ICT difficult and there may be a lack of in-depth knowledge of the full range of technical options available to assist a con-

tracting authority in the carrying out of its functions. It is argued that outsourcing can help resolve this and also save the contracting authority the expense of having to invest and then maintain ICT systems that are rapidly changing.

- *Increased accountability*: the process of formalising service specifications and performance indicators as part an outsourcing procurement process can have the effect of clarifying responsibilities and of sharpening management focus on service quality and key deliverables.

In addition to the benefits associated with outsourcing there are also some potential costs that need to be considered before the decision to outsource is made. These costs can include:

- *Transaction costs*: considerable resources need to be devoted to the administration and conduct of the procurement process as well as the ongoing monitoring and management of the resulting contract.
- *Lack of flexibility and lock-in vulnerability*: entering into a long-term contract for 10–15 years may prove to be a disadvantage when changing political, business or technological circumstances necessitate a change to an alternative solution. For example, a contracting authority may find itself locked into a particular suppliers' ICT system, for instance, and may find it extremely difficult if not impossible to rebuild ICT capability from scratch.
- *Human resource issues*: the extent of staff and trade union resistance to outsourcing can impact upon the success of the project.

The decisions as to what kinds of government services should be outsourced have been influenced by practical as well as political considerations. Practical considerations include consideration of desired costs savings and improvements in service quality that may be achieved. Political considerations can involve posing the question: 'To what extent should the private sector be involved in the provision of government services?' as well as using concepts such as 'non-core' and 'inherently governmental' to frame outsourcing initiatives.

The debates regarding public sector outsourcing are currently at their most intense, and sharp focus on outsourcing strategies is inevitable as the latest Labour administration aims to make significant improvements in the quality and accessibility of services in key areas such as health, education and transport. To assist in achieving this aim, extensive use of the PFI has been made in the UK since 1997 and as a measure of the PFI's prominence, there have been no fewer than eight reports published by the National Audit Office on PFI projects. However, there is widespread recognition that the results to date for public sector outsourcing projects are mixed and there have been some notable reports that focus upon high profile failures and seek to understand the reasons behind the failures.[6] Coming under particular scrutiny has been the ability of the public sector to project manage large outsourcing projects. It has been observed that the public sector will often initiate projects that are too complex, often to timescales that are unrealistic, having been set for political reasons rather than from sound project management principles. It has also been observed that there has often been a lack of clear ownership of projects especially when organisational boundary issues are encountered and a perceived inability to discontinue a project when it is clearly running into insurmountable difficulties. Having said this, it is also widely recognised that outsourcing failures are not just confined to the public sector and that project failures are just as widespread throughout the private sector. However, in the public sector much anecdotal and empirical experience of project failures has prompted the production and promotion of various project management techniques for outsourcing and complex procurements, including the use of gateway-type processes to enable the public sector to minimise the occurrence of problems.[7]

7.3 PUBLIC LAW CONSTRAINTS ON OUTSOURCING

Consideration of outsourcing in the public sector context would not be complete without an understanding of the general limitations in English law on the ability of public bodies to enter into outsourcing arrangements. This requires examination of several areas such as the legal capacity of public sector bodies to enter into outsourcing contracts, whether the individuals who have negotiated the outsourcing transaction have the authority to enter into the contract on behalf of the public sector body as well as the legal constraints affecting the actual procurement and contract award process.

7.3.1 Capacity to contract and the *vires* doctrine

Most public sector bodies that are not Crown agents[8] have been created by statute and are usually given corporate identity. Since the growth and development of corporations in the nineteenth century, the English courts have developed the doctrine of *vires*, such that the powers of these statutory corporations are strictly limited to those matters that Parliament has by statute authorised them to perform.

The term *ultra vires* therefore, refers to acts that are undertaken outside the powers conferred on a particular public sector body. A large body of case law has developed concerning *ultra vires* actions and from this case law we can distinguish key elements of the *ultra vires* principle as being:

- *Illegality*: namely acting outside of the terms or scope of the relevant legislation or an abuse of the purpose of the legislation.

- *Irrationality*: a breach of the principles required for proper and rational application of statutory powers.
- *Procedural impropriety*: the abuse of the statutory or other requirements applicable to action under the legislation or the process required by its terms; and
- *Fiduciary duty*: the duty to have regard to conflicting interests but in particular where expenditure is involved, the interests of those who will be required to fund the expenditure.

The effect of a ruling by a court that a decision of a public sector body is *ultra vires* may in many cases result in a finding that the relevant decision is void and of no effect in law. In the context of an outsourcing transaction this could result in either the restraint of the public sector body from entering into the relevant contract or, where a contract has already been entered into, a declaration that the contract is unlawful and therefore unenforceable by the parties. However, the courts do have a discretion to give effect to an *ultra vires* decision notwithstanding a finding by it that the decision was *ultra vires*.

Particularly in the local government context, the doctrine of *vires* has been responsible for striking down a number of transactions that attempted to utilise innovative ways of contracting with the private sector, but that also sought to circumvent the legislative restrictions placed on local authorities' ability to finance large capital projects.

- In *Credit Suisse* v. *Allerdale Borough Council* [1997] QB 306, [1996] 4 All ER 129, CA, the council formulated a scheme to provide a new swimming pool complex financed by a timeshare development. In order to avoid the restrictive borrowing controls on local authorities, the Council carried out the scheme through a newly formed company whose directors were Council officers. The company borrowed £5 million from Credit Suisse Bank for the construction of the pool complex and the timeshare apartments, and the Council guaranteed the loan. Unfortunately the company was unable to sell the apartments and was consequently unable to repay the loan. The Court of Appeal held that the establishment of the company and the guarantee provided by the Council went beyond the Council's powers with the result that the loan agreement and the guarantee provided by the Council were both void.
- In *Burgoine* v. *Waltham Forest London Borough Council* [1997] BCC 347 a company was established by the Council to develop a water leisure park. The requisite capital was loaned by a bank to the company on the security of the Council's guarantee. The guarantee was held to be *ultra vires* as was the indemnity provided by the Council to the Council officers who were directors of the company. The court held that the formation of the company and all related transactions were *ultra vires* with the result that the bank could not recover the loan from either the company or the Council.

235

As a consequence of those cases, private sector confidence in the viability of public sector projects was severely tested and even despite recent developments that have lessened the impact of the *vires* doctrine on a transaction, it is still common for private sector providers and their funders to carry out extensive due diligence examination of a public sector body's decision-making process and the procedures under which it purports to act.

However, since those cases, in the local government context legislation has been enacted to minimise the impact that the *vires* doctrine can have on transactions and this has been particularly significant within the context of outsourcing and PFI transactions. First, the Local Government (Contracts) Act 1997 was enacted to provide a process for the certification of service provision contracts in excess of five years' length. The effect of certification is to provide partial protection against proceedings alleging that a contract is *ultra vires* as well as providing protection where a finding of *ultra vires* is in fact made by the courts. Second, the enactment of the Local Government Act 2000, s.2(1) introduced a source of potentially very wide *vires* for local authorities to do anything that they consider is likely to achieve the promotion or the improvement of the economic, social and/or environmental well-being of their area.

7.3.2 Authority to contract

Although a public sector body may have the capacity to enter into an outsourcing contract, it is still necessary to confirm whether a particular person or persons who purport to conclude the contract on behalf of the public sector body have the authority to do so. As with the question of *vires*, it is essential that any private sector provider contemplating entering into an outsourcing contract, conduct a thorough investigation of all documentation that purports to confer express authority to conclude the contract. In the local government context this will often consist of minutes of executive or committee meetings, which need to be scrutinised carefully to understand the scope of the authority as well as the constitution of the local authority, which will govern delegation of power by persons having authority to make such delegations.

7.3.3 Limitations on ability to contract out government functions

Another constraint upon the ability of a public sector body to carry out an outsourcing transaction is the possibility that the outsourcing of a particular function is prohibited either expressly or impliedly by statute. For example, in the local government context such limitations apply in relation to some council tax and housing benefits administrative functions.

However, the Deregulation and Contracting Out Act 1994 was enacted to remove these legal obstacles by permitting a ministerial order to be made authorising the contracting out in part, in whole or subject to certain conditions, many public functions. However, there are certain functions that are wholly excluded from the possibility of contracting out under these provisions and these are functions where for policy reasons it is thought appropriate that full control and responsibility for performance of the function must be retained in house. These excluded functions are set out in section 71 of the Act and include those functions where the exercise or failure to exercise the function would necessarily interfere with or affect the liberty of an individual.

Contracts that purport to contract out or outsource functions under the Act's provisions must be limited to a period of 10 years and the contract period must always be specified (s.69(5)(a)). The Act also provides that the contract may be rescinded at any time by the public authority letting the contract; however, in such a case, or where the Minister himself revokes the order authorising the function to be contracted out, the authority is to be treated as repudiating the contract (ss.69(5)(b) and 70(4)). This in effect affirms the provider's private law rights to sue for damages for non-performance of the contract by the public body following a decision to override the contract in the public interest (s.73(2)).

7.3.4 EU public procurement regulations

At the heart of public procurement law is the concept of competitive tendering. Generally, tendering exercises are governed by the EU procurement regulations, but even where these principles do not apply, most contracting authorities have internal rules that require a competition of some sort as a means of demonstrating fairness, accountability and value for money – these rules and procedures for competitive tendering are normally found in the contract standing orders of a public sector body.

The use of a competitive tendering process is generally viewed as an effective tool for obtaining the best from suppliers in terms of price as well as the terms and conditions upon which the public sector contracts with the private sector. In the local government context it is seen as one of the ways to achieve best value or value for money (VFM).[9] If utilised correctly, the competitive tendering exercise can encourage suppliers to provide detailed tender submissions and best and final offers. However, there has been much press coverage recently concerning the excessive length of the procurement process particularly in the context of PFI projects. Suppliers will often incur very high bid costs the longer a procurement process carries on, which can make losing out on a particular contract a very costly exercise. This can also have the result of forcing suppliers to become more selective about the types of contracts they are prepared to tender for with the result that contracting authorities could be faced with a shrinking market of suppliers in some areas, thus undermining the attempt to gain maximum leverage through maintaining competitive pressure between several suppliers.

The public procurement regulations[10] apply whenever a contracting authority seeks offers from suppliers in relation to a proposed public works, supply or service contract, the value of which exceeds certain financial thresholds. The definition of what constitutes a contracting authority is set out in regulation 3 of each of the works, services and supplies regulations, and broadly covers any government entity, regional or local authority or any body governed by public law or associations formed by regional or local authorities. Central, regional and local government authorities are all covered as well as most universities.

The regulations set out specific rules for maintaining a level playing field between suppliers, and make provision for advertising of public sector contracts and the conduct of tendering exercises as well as imposing penalties upon contracting authorities for non-compliance. In the outsourcing context, the regulations most likely to apply are the Public Services Contracts Regulations 1993, SI 1993/3228, which govern a very wide range of service categories most of which are likely to be the subject of a public sector outsourcing transaction.[11]

The public procurement rules are only relevant where the estimated contract value (excluding VAT) exceeds the specified contract threshold. Different financial thresholds will apply depending on the nature of the public sector organisation and these thresholds apply to the aggregate amounts likely to be paid under the entire contract, not simply to the annual contract value. These thresholds are illustrated by Tables 7.1–7.3.

The UK regulations provide for three types of award procedure that contracting authorities can use in any particular instance:

- *Open procedure*: in which all interested suppliers, contractors or service providers may submit tenders.
- *Restricted procedure*: a two-stage tendering procedure in which only those suppliers, contractors or service providers invited by the contracting authority may submit tenders.
- *Negotiated procedure*: in which the contracting authority consults suppliers, contractors or service providers of its choice and negotiates the terms of the contract with one or more of them.

Table 7.1 Public procurement contract value – thresholds for local authorities and other contracting authorities: 1 January 2002 to 31 December 2003

	Supplies	Services	Works
Aggregate contract values	£154,477	£154,477	£3,861,932
PIN threshold	£464,024	£464,024	£3,861,932
Small lots	Not applicable	£49,496	£618,698

Table 7.2 Public procurement contract value – thresholds for central government and other entities in Schedule 1: 1 January 2002 to 31 December 2003

	Supplies	Services	Works
Aggregate contract values	£100,410	£100,410	£3,861,932
PIN threshold	£464,024	£464,024	£3,861,932
Small lots	Not applicable	£49,496	£618,698

Table 7.3 Public procurement contract value – thresholds for utilities: 1 January 2002 to 31 December 2003

	Supplies	Services	Works
Aggregate contract values	£308,954	£308,954	£3,861,932
PIN threshold	£464,024	£464,024	£3,861,932
Small lots	Not applicable	Not applicable	£618,698

The negotiated procedure is the most flexible of the three procedures and in the case of complex and large-scale procurements arguably the most appropriate. Much value is to be gained from a process whereby the public authority and the private sector provider engage in precontractual dialogue that clarifies clearly the terms of the contract, the ethos of the respective organisations and the goals and outcomes that each expects to achieve from the process. Depending on the scope and nature of a particular outsourcing contract, public sector bodies will often favour the use of the negotiated procedure where the procurement rules permit. However, public authorities that are subject to the public procurement regime are required to use the open procedure or the restricted procedure unless they can establish that they fall within one of the exemptions that permits the use of the negotiated procedure and in accordance with case law, these exemptions are interpreted restrictively (regs 10 and 13). The use of the negotiated tendering procedure has been widespread for PFI transactions. Such use, however, is not without its problems, as evidenced by the issue of a Reasoned Opinion by the European Commission in July 2000 against the United Kingdom. The Reasoned Opinion concerned the award of a PFI contract for the redevelopment of the Pimlico School in Westminster. The contracting authority had used the negotiated tendering procedure and it was the view of the European Commission that the use of this procedure was not properly justified in the circumstances and that the UK had infringed the EU procurement Directives.

In May 2000, the European Commission put forward a package of amendments designed to simplify and consolidate the current legislation and to modernise the regime of EU public procurement Directives to take into account liberalisation in the marketplace, new methods of procurement and the use of electronic tendering. A similar proposal was put forward in respect of the Utilities Directive. The Directive is expected to be adopted in 2003 and member states will then have 21 months to implement changes into national legislation. One of the proposed changes is the introduction of a new competitive dialogue procedure, which will replace the existing negotiated procedure and allow scope for increased negotiation and discussion in complex procurements such as high technology contracts, contracts involving complicated financing arrangements and arguably high value, large-scope outsourcing projects.

Under the proposed new negotiated procedure the emphasis and focus of negotiations is shifted to the technical specifications prior to the issue of the invitation to submit a tender. The competitive dialogue, therefore, is intended to permit a contracting authority to seek proposals from suppliers regarding technical solutions to the authority's needs and then for the authority to decide, on the basis of these proposals, what its final technical specification will be. Concerns regarding the misappropriation by an authority of a supplier's know-how and intellectual property are acknowledged by the European Commission in the Explanatory Memorandum to the draft Directive,[12] However, it is difficult to see how the Commission can reconcile an obligation for a contracting authority not to disclose proposed solutions or other confidential information received through the competitive dialogue phase, with an apparent freedom to take the best of the solutions offered to form the basis of a technical specification, or indeed, to combine one or more of the solutions presented.

The UK regulations also contain compliance procedures applicable to a breach of the regulations. These provisions introduce specific remedies into UK law that enable aggrieved tenderers to enforce the provisions of the UK regulations against non-compliant contracting authorities. Aggrieved tenderers can elect to issue proceedings in the High Court or make a complaint to the European Commission, depending upon the stage at which the application is made. Any court action must be commenced promptly and, in any event, within three months of the date when the grounds for the action first arose. The remedy for an enforcement action is either the suspension of a procurement process or the award of damages for loss suffered as a result of non-compliance with the procurement regime. Importantly, a procurement process can only be halted if the action is brought, and an injunction sought, before the contract is awarded. Once a particular contract is awarded, however defective the procurement process, then the aggrieved service provider's remedy is in damages alone. However, if an aggrieved service provider can bring an action before the contract is awarded, then a court may elect to award an injunction preventing the award of the contract if it feels that there is a serious issue to be tried, that damages may not be an adequate remedy at final trial and the 'balance of convenience' favours the award of the injunction.

7.4 THE PRIVATE FINANCE INITIATIVE

The PFI deserves a special section on its own in discussing outsourcing, as it is a high profile initiative initially proposed by the Conservative government but now embraced by the current Labour government administration. The PFI is a contractual model whereby the desired outcome is typically either the construction of a new building or the substantial refurbishment of an existing building, together with the provision of services, including services for the ongoing maintenance and management of the newly constructed or refurbished facilities. Payment for the capital investment is made over the lifetime of the PFI contract in the form of a service charge and the transaction is structured in such a way that in accounting terms the contracting authority's expenditure is considered to be off balance sheet.

Faced with the need to upgrade public infrastructure and improve the quality of public services, the PFI model was seen as a way of achieving this without having to increase the public sector borrowing requirement, increase taxation or juggle competing demands on public sector expenditure. Now the PFI is established as a major form of public sector procurement. It is estimated that there are over 400 PFI contracts in force committing government departments to future expenditure of around £100 billion.[13]

PFI has been used in central government to procure a variety of large infrastructure projects including roads, office accommodation, museums, ICT systems and prisons. In the health sector, the PFI has been embraced by the Department of Health as the primary means of procurement for new hospitals and the NHS Local Improvement Finance Trust (LIFT) programme is applying PFI-style procurement to new primary health care facilities in the community.

In local government, PFI has been applied primarily to schools but also to roads, libraries, magistrates' courts, police stations, sea defences, civic accommodation, street lighting, social housing, residential homes for the elderly, waste management and leisure centres.

The creation and promotion of some standard contract terms and guidance for all PFI projects in all parts of the public sector has been vigorously pursued, first by the government's Treasury Taskforce, and latterly by the Office of Government Commerce (OGC). The government's Treasury Taskforce first issued guidance on the standardisation of PFI contracts in July 1999. This has now been superseded by guidance produced by the OGC (Butterworths, 2002) drafts of which were sent out for consultation with the private and public sectors. The aims of this guidance are to:

- promote a common understanding as to some of the risks that are encountered in a standard PFI contract;
- promote consistency of approach and price across a range of similar products; and

- reduce the transaction times and costs by enabling all parties concerned to agree a range of areas that can follow the standard approach set out in the guidance without extended negotiations.

In addition, sector-specific guidance has also been published in the following areas:

- Department for Education and Skills (DfES) guidance for the standardisation of schools PFI contracts;
- guidance for leisure projects published by the local government project procurement agency, known as the public private partnerships programme (4Ps);
- guidance of standardisation of PFI contracts in the National Health Service published by the Department of Health in December 1999; and
- 4Ps guidance for standardisation of housing PFI contracts.

Anecdotal experience suggests that the standard position, as set out in the various guidance above, has focused the debate on certain issues such as termination, compensation payable on termination, force majeure, changes in law and some other areas that were previously subject to extensive negotiation between the public sector, private sector consortia and their funders.

Having said that however, it cannot necessarily be assumed that a PFI contract could be completed entirely on standard terms as inevitably the government body's own circumstances, the funding and subcontracting arrangements of the private sector, changes to prevailing market conditions and not least the operational details of the particular scheme will require some adaptation and expansion of the standard terms. The OGC has recognised this and has since issued correspondence (March 2003) confirming that the standardisation of PFI guidance is not intended to represent an exhaustive standard to be adhered to word for word. The OGC is maintaining a watching brief to monitor any industry or public sector concerns regarding the implementation of the guidance. However, care needs to be taken to ensure that terms do not deviate too widely from the OGC guidance as this may need to be justified in order to ensure continuing eligibility for PFI credits from the Treasury.

7.5 COMMERCIAL AND CONTRACTUAL ISSUES IN PUBLIC SECTOR OUTSOURCING

It is difficult to draw generalised conclusions about the commercial and contractual issues that will tend to dominate a public sector outsourcing project. Much will depend upon the type of outsourcing project, the value of the overall package and the particular culture and ethos, commercial experience and goals of the public sector body. Any discussion about contractual issues arising in the context of public sector outsourcing therefore needs to be caveated by an appreciation that there is not necessarily one standard approach (putting aside PFI contracts, which were discussed earlier) to contract drafting or contract negotiation.

The extent to which the use of standard terms and conditions of contract is commonplace in the public sector also varies greatly between the different tiers of government, between departments within government, and, in particular, between different types of outsourcing transactions. While standard terms and conditions are extremely useful and are commonly used in relation to the purchase of routine goods, caution needs to be exercised in using standard terms and conditions in an outsourcing context as each transaction will have its unique aims and the range of services to be outsourced can vary considerably. This latter factor affects the possibility of producing standardised service specifications for instance, which will feature as one of the most important schedules to the contract.

However, there have been some attempts to promote standardisation of contracts driven by much the same motives discussed earlier in relation to OGC guidance for PFI contracts. The OGC for instance promotes the use of model contracts for works and consultancy services in a construction context as well as model contracts for the supply and support of ICT hardware and software.[14] The NHS also encourages use of standardised forms of contract particularly in ICT procurements (see www.nhs.gov.uk/pasa). The Central Computer and Telecommunications Agency (CCTA) (formerly the government's IT procurement agency, now subsumed into the OGC) has also promoted the use of standard terms and conditions in ICT procurements having engaged with industry representatives to produce forms of contract that purport to represent an even playing field for both the public and private sectors. However, despite this, it is widely acknowledged that these model forms of contract do not suit all outsourcing transactions and will need to be tailored to fit the particular transaction. It also needs to be remembered that many of the longer and more complex outsourcing projects will be conducted using the negotiated tendering procedure and the resultant terms of contract will largely be influenced by these negotiations. Nonetheless it is possible to identify general contractual issues that will often be of particular significance in public sector outsourcing projects and these are discussed below.

7.5.1 Term and duration

One of the features of public sector outsourcing transactions about which it is extremely difficult to generalise is the typical or standard duration and what is legally permissible under the EU procurement regulations, competition law and as mentioned previously, the Deregulation and Contracting Out Act 1994. Until recently, public sector outsourcing contracts tended to be awarded for terms in the range of five to seven years, with longer contracts being used occasionally where particular circumstances demanded. It was felt that a contract for five to seven years' duration maximised the benefits available for outsourcing while complying with public procurement rules and avoiding long-term irrevocable commitments that were potentially susceptible to change upon a change of government.

However, in certain cases (for example, the mid-1990s outsourcing of the information technology office of the Inland Revenue), it has been decided that a longer duration would be necessary in order to secure best value for money and allow bidders to obtain the best return on their investment. Accordingly, bidders have been asked to bid on a variety of longer terms and, ultimately, contract terms as long as 25 years or more have been selected for serviced building construction and management contracts. In the local government context there has been an increase in the length of outsourcing contracts up to periods of 10 years or more.

The advent of the PFI has enhanced the trend towards longer-term contracts as bidders are being asked to make greater investments in order to provide services and therefore require longer durations in order to recover that investment. On a number of significant IT outsourcing contracts made under the PFI, bidders have argued very strongly (and with success) that they require up to five years or more to recoup their initial investment, with only the later years of the contract being profitable. The trend towards longer-term deals has therefore increased the focus in public sector outsourcing transactions on the issues of technology refreshment and exit management.

7.5.2 Technology refreshment

Technology refreshment has always been a key issue in outsourcing transactions. This obviously affects IT outsourcing more than other forms but it is a significant issue in any outsourcing contract involving a technology-driven services delivery platform. As contracts are being awarded for longer terms, it is important for public sector bodies to attempt to anticipate changes in technology or, at the very least, set in place a mechanism by which technology refreshment can be factored into the transaction.

Public sector bodies undertaking outsourcing projects are not dissimilar to the private sector in that they are seeking to ensure the maximum level of predictability in forecasting of cost and forecasting of future technology movements. In many public sector outsourcing transactions, thought has been given to setting out a baseline for technology refreshment or, at the very least, a basis for costing of technology refreshment initiatives. This may involve asking private sector bidders to bid in advance a minimum level of annual investment on technology refreshment schemes. If such an annual fund can be established, it enables the public sector body to call off against that fund in relation to mutually agreed refresh initiatives. At the very least, this gives the public sector predictability of spend as well as greater certainty that the technology used in the provision of the outsourced services will remain up to date and efficient throughout the life of the contract. It does, however, put the onus on the public sector to ensure that it gets maximum value for money, since, of course, the private sector will have costed into its bid the extent of the annual fund as amortised over the life of the contract.

7.5.3 Exit management

Exit management arises in all outsourcing transactions regardless of their shape or size. It is essential to consider the prospect of divorce at the point of marriage, that is, to anticipate and forward plan for the management of exit arrangements in the event of early termination or expiry of the contractual relationship. It is now regular practice in the outsourcing contracts to include an exit plan schedule the objective of which is to ensure:

- a smooth transition of service provision from the existing contractor to a new contractor;
- that the responsibilities with respect to exit arrangements are clearly defined;
- that all relevant assets that the contracting authority may require are transferred;
- that any transfer payment in respect of transferring assets is correctly calculated. The calculation of this payment can be complex and will be influenced by factors such as the point in time at which the contract comes to an end, the valuation of the payments made by the contracting authority towards the assets through the service payment and the terms on which and the consideration paid for any contracting authority assets transferred to the contractor at the start of the contract.

The types of matters commonly dealt with in an exit plan include transfer of assets, licences and any authority owned data. The transfer of data back to a contracting authority is of particular significance and this schedule would also make provision for the delivery of inventories of data, the definitions of data structures (data dictionaries) and proposed methods for testing the integrity and completeness of data to be transferred.

7.5.4 Employment issues

The application of the Transfer of Undertakings (Protection of Employment) Regulations 1981 (TUPE), SI 1981/1794, to outsourcing projects has undoubtedly been an area of much debate and can give rise to protracted negotiations as both the private and public sectors seek to minimise their exposure to staff-related liabilities. Many public sector outsourcing projects will involve the transfer of staff from the public sector body to the private sector provider who will provide the outsourced services back to the contracting authority. TUPE imposes obligations to consult with affected staff as well as to protect the terms and conditions on which staff are to be employed post transfer. In January 2000, the Cabinet Office issued a *Statement of Practice on Staff Transfers in the Public Sector*,[15] which is intended to set out a clear and consistent policy for the treatment of transferring staff, including making appropriate arrangements to protect occupational pensions, redundancy and severance terms. It is not surprising therefore that suitable clauses will be found in contracts apportioning staff liabilities between the private and public sectors depending on whether they arise pre-transfer (to be borne by the public sector) or post transfer (to be borne by the private sector).

Perhaps of all the contractual issues that can arise in a public sector outsourcing transaction, TUPE has the potential to generate the most uncertainty and instability, given the potential involvement of trade unions that may oppose the basis of an outsourcing. Recent developments in this area include the release of a new Code of Practice by the Offices of the Deputy Prime Minister in February 2003, dealing with the issue of the two-tier workforce in local government. The Code has proved to be controversial and at the time of writing still potentially subject to revision. The Code is primarily aimed at the treatment of new recruits and aims to ensure that new recruits are engaged on terms that are overall no less favourable than the terms on which local government staff who had previously transferred to the private sector provide.

7.5.5 Corrupt gifts

A corrupt gifts clause is an example of a clause over which individual contracting authorities have little discretion. It is commonplace in UK public sector outsourcing (and other) situations to impose obligations upon private sector bodies in relation to the acceptance of corrupt gifts or the commission of other so-called prohibited acts. Depending on how widely these clauses are drawn they may appear draconian if they reserve the right for the contracting authority to terminate the agreement for any breach of these obligations regardless of the scale of the alleged corrupt act. For instance, query whether on a strict interpretation of a clause, the purchase of a drink for a public sector official after a late night negotiating session could lead to the termination of the contract!

The Treasury Taskforce has recognised the severity of the authority's ultimate sanction to terminate the contract in response to one of these prohibited acts, and they go on to recommend an approach whereby the contractor should have the opportunity to avoid termination where the act has been carried out by a subcontractor or employees acting on their own. Thus, if a breach is a result of an act of an employee acting independently, then the contractor should terminate that person's employment and procure a replacement. If this is not done, then the contract can be terminated. Similar principles apply for prohibited acts committed by a contractor's subcontractors. It is virtually certain that no contracting authority would accept the obligation to pay compensation to a contractor (except, perhaps, compensation to senior debt funders in the case of PFI contracts) in cases where termination occurs because of the commission of a prohibited act.

7.5.6 Intellectual property rights

It has been appreciated for some time that intellectual property rights (IPR) are a commercially valuable asset and their prominence as a contract issue has been guaranteed as a result of the modernising government agenda and e-government targets that are shifting the focus to the use of technology to automate and improve business processes. One approach has been to require contractors to assign all IPR that may be developed during the course of provision of the outsourced services to the public sector body. The public sector organisation would then, typically, grant back to the private sector outsourcing services provider a licence to use the IPR, although in many cases this grant-back licence was limited to the extent of the services contract. However, one issue that has arisen from this approach is that having insisted on this assignment, public sector bodies do little, or indeed are not permitted, to exploit the rights for which they have paid so much and the investment would in effect go to waste. For instance it is often pointed out that public sector bodies do not have the skill or capacity to market, distribute and sell software and that this is best left to the ICT industry. Nonetheless, with the increased emphasis on joined-up working between different tiers of government it could be argued that retention of IPR ownership by the public sector can facilitate distribution of software solutions that have the capacity to apply across a range of public sector organisations thus generating public sector economies of scale.

An alternative approach in public sector outsourcing transactions is to permit private sector bodies to retain all IPR but to require the grant of a very wide licence to the authority to use the intellectual property, perhaps at a discounted price to take into account the contribution of the public sector body to the cost of the development.

Given the constraints upon the public sector on being able to commercially exploit IPR, perhaps what should be given greater focus rather than the ownership of IPR is the issue of continuity of service provision and therefore the extent to which guaranteed continued use of the licensed software is essential to continuity of service. In addition, the focus should be on ensuring that, if necessary, at any point in time the public sector body can pull the outsourced services back in house or re-outsource to a different provider and that the IPR clauses and any associated licensing provisions are sufficiently flexible to deal with such an eventuality. The public sector user will also be focused on avoiding supplier dependency (i.e. lock-in to one particular supplier). The deposit of software (both source code and object code and documentation) in escrow is another potential safeguard to ensure continuity of use.

Typically in public sector outsourcing contracts, the government body will want to ensure that use of licensed software is permitted by necessary third parties. For instance in the local government context, this may include public bodies it provides services to (for example payroll services) under the Local Authority (Goods and Services) Act 1970.

In any discussions on this subject the private sector is extremely keen to ensure that a clear distinction is made between those rights that are pre-existing and that predate the outsourcing arrangement and those rights that are specifically created as a result of the arrangement. In many cases this can be difficult. However, notwithstanding this difficulty, the public sector is keen to identify a dividing line where possible and, if something has been specifically funded by it, to ensure that rewards for subsequent exploitation of that item are flowed back to the public sector in terms of a reduced licensing price or future royalty or lump sum payments. It can be very difficult for the parties to agree on what the scale of benefit may be. However, most central government entities would not deny the benefits of a rebate on the contract price.

In some projects, the extent of a commercial exploitation arrangement for results of the outsourcing has been an item that is taken into account at the evaluation stage of a procurement process and is factored into a separate partnership schedule. This is actually a relatively neat solution to the dilemma, which allows the private sector the ability to propose the extent of joint commercial exploitation and for the public sector to take account of the distinguishing features between different bidders.

7.5.7 Warranties

All outsourcing contracts, whether public sector or not, will contain a set of warranties. Many of the warranties will depend upon the nature of the services being outsourced but typically the most common relate to capacity to enter into the contract and the nature and extent of the services themselves.

In many situations it will be a commercial necessity to agree that the warranties expressly set out in the contract replace those that may be implied at law.

Observers point to an imbalance between the warranties that the public sector expects from the private sector as opposed to the warranties it is prepared to give. This can often give rise to difficulties in the area of asset transfer where authorities might refuse to warrant the condition, fitness for purpose or any other matter relating to the assets. However, unlimited access and assistance will often be provided to the private sector to carry out sufficient due diligence investigations to satisfy itself that such a warranty is not necessary and the terms under which assets are transferred (particularly the consideration provided) may be favourable such that the private sector may be prepared to carry this risk. In reality however, private sector providers may find themselves unwilling to engage in expensive and time consuming asset audits to ascertain the condition of the assets – this is particularly so in large outsourcing transactions involving a large volume of existing ICT infrastructure such as networks, voice and telephony, servers, desktops and a range of software applications. They may also have concerns regarding the impact that defective or poor condition assets have on their contractual obligations to provide services to agreed service levels and the potential impact this could have on their payment stream. Another approach of the private sector when faced with a public sector body reluctant to provide warranties is to negotiate into the contract a specific obligation on the public sector body to perform obligations set out in a separate schedule of the contract.

7.5.8 Audit

The extent of an audit clause will depend upon the nature of the charging basis and whether it incorporates elements of open book verification (which primarily relates to the cost-plus basis of charging) and as to whether the authority has sought to reserve rights to verify prices in some kind of benchmarking exercise (see Chapter 8).

In addition, most audit clauses will require wider audit rights for general government purposes. This specifically means rights of audit access for bodies such as the National Audit Office (NAO) (for central government departments) or the Audit Commission for other local authority and non-Crown bodies.

Many private sector contractors in the outsourcing field are aware of the rationale underlying NAO and Audit Commission access rights and the need for them and generally consent to access rights (potentially negotiating additional confidentiality provisions or the like to resolve any lingering concerns).

7.5.9 Benchmarking

The NHS Benchmarking Club defines the process of benchmarking as 'using structured comparisons to define and implement good practice'. The NHS, central and local government, police and fire authorities all use benchmarking practices to some degree (and to various degrees of success). Many outsourcing contracts will contain clauses that require a contractor to carry out benchmarking exercises. In the local authority context, such benchmarking exercises are designed to assist an authority in the implementation of its best value improvement plan, and are important in enabling an authority to compare performances with other organisations.

There are a large number of benchmarking groups in the NHS and local government, and the Cabinet Office has promoted the use of the European Foundation for Quality Management (EFQM) Excellence Model and the European Union Common Assessment Framework (CAF). These models score performance not just on results, but on service enablers such as leadership and people management. However, one potential limitation of both of these scoring models is that the scores are often based on self-assessment. The Cabinet Office in partnership with HM Customs and Excise have also established the Public Sector Benchmarking Service, which can be accessed at www.benchmarking.gov.uk. This service aims to provide practical advice and information on benchmarking and a mechanism for sharing knowledge and good practice on benchmarking.

The results from public sector benchmarking efforts are mixed, with some good results, but a higher proportion of benchmarking practices failing to achieve tangible benefits. A survey conducted by the Audit Commission of local authorities found that at the time, only 12 per cent of authorities considered that their benchmarking activity was successful.[16] At the time, a similar survey carried out by HM Customs and Excise of directors and managers of 50 blue chip companies revealed that the recommendations of about a quarter of benchmarking projects were not implemented at all, and many more were only partially implemented.[17]

7.5.10 Break option

The approach to break options in public sector outsourcing contracts is closely linked to the trend towards longer-term deals. Typically, a break option consists of the right of the contracting authority to elect to terminate the contract for convenience. This right can be contrasted with the right to terminate for default, insolvency or some other fault-based reason.

The inclusion of a termination for convenience or break option is a classic example of the balance between risk and price in an outsourcing arrangement. The explanation often proffered in support of including a break option is the possible need to deal with changing of government policy or, indeed, a change in government itself, which may result in the reversal of policy. It is also argued that government discretion cannot be fettered in any way, including through contractual means.

Invariably, inclusion of a break option will come at a price for the contracting authority and may involve the payment of compensation for lost revenue and/or costs and expenses that would result directly from the exercise of the break option. The amount of compensation will depend on factors such as when the break option is exercised and the level of capital investment required of the contractor and the extent to which this is financed by third parties.

Contractors will often try to resist the inclusion of a break option clause on the basis that an outsourcing project involves a large amount of third party-financed investment, and the period during which the return on this investment is received should remain fixed.

7.5.11 Change in government policy

The issue of which party accepts liability for different aspects of legislative change is one that needs to be considered as part of the overall risk transfer assessment. In the past, it has been assumed by the private sector that any change in legislation would be a change control issue necessitating an adjustment to the contract price. However, there has been a shift away from this traditional assumption. Under the auspices of the Office of Government Commerce, there has been a trend to transfer a significant amount of the risk of legislative change on to the private sector supplier. Particular care should be taken by both parties to address the different types of potential for legislative change. For example, in relation to the outsourcing of payroll and accounts services possible areas of legislative change include health and safety, taxation rates and methods of collection of taxation.

If legislative change occurs that specifically affects only the particular type of project in question, then it is recognised that this should be borne by the public sector contracting authority on the basis that such changes are not reasonably forseeable. In *Standardisation of PFI Contracts*[18] this is referred to as a 'discriminatory change in law'. Other types of risk that affect the contractor's method of approach or general health and safety issues (which could include, for example, a new EU requirement on operating in the office environment) will fall on the private sector on the basis that they are reasonably foreseeable to a prudent commercial organisation offering services in a particular sector. Another possibility is to agree a sharing of costs in different proportions depending on the amount of the cost of change in law to the contractor.

7.5.12 Transfer and assignment

Generally in most public sector outsourcing transactions no transfer or assignment (or, indeed, subcontracting) is permitted without the consent of the contracting authority and this does not differ from the approach taken in private sector contract terms. Some contracts also make provision for the termination of the contract in the event of any involuntary change of control such as on a merger or consolidation.

In relation to subcontracting, many contracting authorities will compromise on the level of control required and will only retain control over principal subcontractors or the extent to which the subcontracting of key activities takes place, excluding subcontracts awarded for the general operation of the contractor's business.

In contrast to the tight control exercised over potential assignments by the contractor, a public sector body will often seek to ensure that it has the flexibility to organise itself in whatever way is possible. This will include reserving the right to undertake transfers or assignments of its contractual rights, typically to other contracting authorities, but also to other third parties. This gives many contractors a problem if they believe that a public sector body could exercise its rights in order to put the contractor in a contractual relationship with, potentially, one of its principal competitors. However, this is highly unlikely to eventuate.

7.5.13 Limitation of liability

The issue of limitation of liability for defaults by the private sector provider under the outsourcing contract is a classic trade-off between cost and risk. It is virtually a given that in large-scale transactions, the private sector provider will seek to limit its liability and in return it will offer a competitive reduction in price to take into account the acceptance of risk by the contracting authority. If a contracting authority adopts a negotiating stance of insisting on unlimited liability or very high limits of liability, there will be an inevitable upward increase in the price offered by the provider, which may not necessarily offer value for money.

There is no hard and fast rule about how an authority should quantify the best limit of liability to agree to; however, authorities are best advised to make a realistic assessment of the potential likelihood of loss and the potential scale of loss before settling on a limit on liability. Officers from a public sector body's insurance department will often undertake this risk assessment exercise in conjunction with heads of service who have a thorough understanding of the particular risks attached to a particular service. The private sector provider will of course be taking on board the risk that any limit of liability clause will be struck down as being unreasonable under the Unfair Contract Terms Act.

It is important that public sector bodies do not request limits of liability out of all proportion to the scale of loss that could be suffered. The most appropriate limit of liability is one that takes maximum advantage of the contractor's existing insurance protection in relation to its defaults but does not cause the contractor to take out additional insurance that could lead to increased service charges as a result of additional insurance premiums being included in the contractor's overheads.

Most limit of liability clauses will draw a distinction between damage to property (i.e. buildings, equipment, etc.) and non-property loss (for example, the cost of procuring replacement services, the administrative costs of a failure to provide the services or the necessary overtime or additional staffing costs of providing services in an alternative fashion). This has arisen because it is easier for a private sector contractor to insure its property-based loss and, as a result, higher limits of liability tend to be included in outsourcing contracts in relation to property-based loss.

Contracting authorities will also typically make a decision as to whether they wish the limit on liability to be expressed in terms of a per event cap, a per contract year cap or an aggregate lifetime cap. As far as the contractors are concerned, the aggregate lifetime cap is likely to be the most acceptable since it puts a predefined limit on the potential exposure over the lifetime of the contract. Conversely, as far as contracting authorities are concerned, it may be better to set a per event cap in order to maximise the ability to claim in respect of multiple event loss. However, this may not always be the case as, for example, it is extremely unlikely that the contractor would make multiple significant defaults – the rationale being that the authority would be likely to terminate the contract after the first, or possibly the second, major event of default and therefore it is almost irrelevant for the authority to reserve the right to make multiple claims in respect of multiple events of loss since the authority would never let the situation deteriorate so far.

7.6 CRITICAL SUCCESS FACTORS

One significant difference between the public and private sectors' perceptions of success in an outsourcing transaction is the absence of the profit motive from the public sector. Public sector organisations are obviously not in the business of making a profit; they are in the business of service delivery. Accordingly, the overall assessment of the benefits in outsourcing tends to focus more on overall value for money (meaning cost savings and improved service delivery) than on the bottom line of overall company performance and enhancement of shareholder value. Therefore, in public sector outsourcing projects, the attainment and measurement of the standards as expressed by the key performance indicators (KPIs) assumes a central role. Collating and prioritising KPIs can itself be a daunting task as public sector bodies try to sift through the plethora of performance measurement indices that currently abound. It is essential for public sector bodies to distinguish between those indicators that are of such crucial importance that failure to achieve them (or indeed success in exceeding them) will impact upon the deduction or bonus regime of the payment mechanism, as opposed to those indicators that are collected primarily for information purposes only.

The key tests therefore for critical success in public sector outsourcing are whether the project will result in a better service to the public in a more cost-effective fashion. In the local government context, critical success will be measured through an external scrutiny and review of service provision by the Audit Commission and other inspectorates. The recently developed Comprehensive Performance Assessment (CPA) framework introduced by the Audit Commission effectively seeks to publicly rank local authorities into one of the following categories: excellent, good, fair, weak or poor.

It will be interesting to see whether the CPA framework has any significant impact upon the decisions of local authorities to outsource the provision of services.

From the point of view of the public sector there are a number of factors that can assist in ensuring that the outsourcing transaction achieves its twin goals of improving service delivery in a more cost-effective fashion. These critical success factors can include:

1. *Establish clear objectives from the outset*: the contracting authority needs to have considered in great detail before it commences the procurement process what it hopes to achieve as a result of the outsourcing transaction. Although ideally it would hope to achieve the twin outcomes of saving money and improving a service, it needs to determine which of these is of higher priority, as it will not always be the case that both these outcomes can be achieved simultaneously within an immediate period of time.

2. *Obtain support from key stakeholders*: support from, for example, politicians, senior management, staff and trade unions is vital not only to bolster the perception held by the private sector that there is commitment to the project, but also to minimise the risk that a transaction will be aborted owing to external political pressures such as trade union opposition. It is important that the contracting authority has a clear and effective communication strategy that enables it to consult and communicate with the key stakeholders in a meaningful and effective way. Such support obviously needs to be maintained throughout the lifetime of the outsourcing contract.

3. *Pre-procurement preparation*: it is essential to undertake preparation such as soft market testing, the collation of baseline data that measure existing volumes and service standards as well as the cost of current service delivery, the collation of due diligence material such as asset registers (of assets likely to transfer, their condition and their value) and contract registers (of contracts likely to be assigned and whether consent is required for assignment) and prioritisation of key performance indicators that are agreed by the authority and the authority's members. Collation of the baseline data is essential in the construction of a public sector comparator by which the authority can measure value for money in a meaningful way when comparing the cost of service provision by the private sector. Authorities should resist the urge to commence a procurement process without having laid the foundations as they will find themselves ill prepared to face the many issues that arise on the outsourcing of key services.

4. *Settle public law issues*: this should be done as far as possible, at the beginning of a transaction. That is, establish that a public sector body is acting *intra vires*, is compliant with public procurement laws and that officers purporting to negotiate on behalf of the public sector body have the authority to do so. Maintaining a written audit trail with respect to these matters is of vital importance, particularly in the event of a challenge by a tenderer or in the event of investigation by a body's internal or external auditors and is vital to assuring a private sector provider that the risk of the transaction becoming null and void is minimised.

5. *Conduct a competitive tendering exercise*: do this in order to obtain the best terms from outsourcing suppliers in terms of price, risk transference and the terms and conditions that will apply to the project. This will require a contracting authority to have fully prepared its tendering documentation (in particular, the contract and the specifications) in order to maintain a competitive advantage and to be tactical in not down-selecting to a preferred supplier too soon in the competitive process.

6. *Appoint a project manager who is empowered*: the project's main sponsors should control project management. In some instances a neutral third party that is not an employee of the contracting authority can be more effective. Where an outsourcing project is heavily underpinned by ICT investment, particular additional risks apply to these types of projects and care needs to be taken with respect to project management of these procurements, typically using the PRINCE (Projects in a Controlled Environment) 2 project management methodology and the 'gateway process' in order to minimise the risk of failure.

7. *Ensure sufficient resources are allocated to the project*: it is vitally important that contracting authorities have project teams dedicated to an outsourcing project whose members are able to devote enough time to the project and do not have to juggle the demands of their day jobs. It is also critical that these individuals are given sufficient administrative support.

8. *Provide suppliers with as much information as possible*: it is important that contracting authorities are as open as possible with suppliers about the existing position and what cost savings or organisational change it requires in order to improve the status quo. Equally, contracting authorities need to be robust in their interrogation of submissions from suppliers to ensure that they can better the status quo and to ensure that they fully understand and have costed the contracting authority's requirements.

9. *Plan for transition carefully*: contracting authorities need to ensure that attention is given to phasing in the new supplier, particularly with respect to asset transfer and transfer of third party contracts. The aim should be to achieve a seamless transition with minimal interruption to service delivery. Equal attention should be devoted to exit and handover arrangements in the event of early termination or expiry of the outsourcing contract.

NOTES

1. For an article discussing this see Patrick Dunleavy *et al., Policy Learning and Public Sector Information Technology – Contractual and E-Government Changes in the UK, Australia and New Zealand*, London School of Economics and University College London Paper for the American Political Science Association's Annual Conference 2001.

2. The e-government targets require central and local government to make all services available electronically by December 2005. The impetus for this came from the White Paper *Modernising Government* (CM4310) (March 1999) and the Office of the Deputy Prime Minister's consultation paper *e-gov@local: towards a national strategy for local e-government* (April 2002).

3. The Inland Revenue has strategic partnering arrangements with EDS for the provision of IT services for tax activities and with Accenture for National Insurance contributions work. The Ministry of Defence has signed over £2.3 billion worth of private sector investment into defence. Recent examples include seven training simulator projects, the provision of accommodation for families of service personnel and the provision of generator sets to support operational electrical requirements in the field. The National Probation Service, which is part of the Home Office, has outsourced its facilities and estates management services. Regional police forces have also outsourced services such as crime scene security.

4. Throughout this chapter public sector bodies will be referred to as contracting authorities, which are defined in the Public Works Contracts Regulations 1991, SI 1991/2680, the Public Contracts Regulations 1993, SI 1993/3228 and the Public Supply Contracts Regulations 1995, SI 1995/201 as covering central government departments, Crown bodies, local authorities and other bodies governed by public law, such as fire authorities, police authorities and education boards.

5. *Cf* Richard Meeks IDPM, University of Manchester, *Reinventing Government in the Information Age: Explaining Success and Failure* (July 1998).

6. With respect to ICT projects see in particular, the Central IT Unit's Report (also known as the *McCarthy Report*) entitled *Successful IT: Modernising Government In Action*.

7. The Office of Government Commerce (OGC) has created a 'gateway' process that is compulsory for all high value central government procurements. In local government, the Improvement and Development Agency (IDeA) has also developed a gateway review process for local government projects, which can be found at www.idea.gov.uk.

8. The unlimited capacity of the Crown's ability to contract is generally accepted as is the capacity of agents acting on behalf of the Crown, although there is much academic debate about the source of Crown agent capacity.

9. See also local authorities' best value duties in the Local Government Act 1999. These require local authorities to compare, challenge, compete and consult with respect to the provision of services.

10. The Public Works Contracts Regulations 1991, SI 1991/2680, Public Supply Contracts Regulations 1995, SI 1995/201 and the Public Services Contracts Regulations 1993, SI 1993/3228.

11. The UK regulations distinguish between core or Part A services and residual or Part B services. Part A services are subject to the full procurement regime whereas Part B services are less fully regulated and are subject only to a few of the less onerous regulations.

12. See pages 9 and 10 of the Explanatory Memorandum of the 'Proposal for a directive of the European Parliament and of the Council on the co-ordination of procedures for the award of public supply contracts, public service contracts and public works contracts' (COM (2000) 275).

13. These figures come from the *Forty Second Report of the Committee of Public Accounts* (HC460, session 2051–2, TSO-11) and include all central government PFI contracts and those let by local authorities where there has been financial support from central government.

14. See www.ogc.gov.uk for these as well as the *Successful Delivery Toolkit*, which is a best practice toolkit aimed at improving the speed and outcomes of central government procurement.

15. See www.cabinet-office.gov.uk/civilservice/2000/tupe/stafftransfers.pdf

16. This survey was done in 1999; *cf Getting Better All The Time; Making Benchmarking Work*, Audit Commission Report (16 November 2000), p.4.

17. *Ibid.*

18. Guidance produced by the Office of Government Commerce and Butterworths, issue No.3, September 2002.

CHAPTER 8

Benchmarking

Robert Morgan

8.1 INTRODUCTION

Benchmarking is an overused and hackneyed phrase in today's outsourcing and sourcing environments. However, while degraded to some extent by familiarity and overuse, the technique – when applied subtly and practically – has many uses in ensuring best value and understanding based upon market comparison.

The techniques of benchmarking can be applied at any point during the life of a contract. As the majority of outsourcing deals are unique, benchmarking will provide a market comparison and an objective understanding of the cost/time/quality paradigm.

The major uses of benchmarking in the current climate are centred on the commodity elements of IT/IS or other tools/technologies-delivered services. In fact, any service that has a low level of variability, a maturity of specification and a strong market for competitive supply can be simply benchmarked against a market comparison – which is the basis for consumer surveys, price indices and ultimately metric or research-based benchmarking.

In a VNU publication in April 1996 Janice McGinn, Caroline Gabriel and Nicolas King wrote:

> Benchmarking studies have revealed variations of up to 300 per cent in the IT costs of companies with similar operations. If there's one message from the traditional IT benchmarking studies it is that, in terms of bangs for your bucks, you don't get what you deserve, you don't even get what your corporate muscle might entitle you to. In IT you get what you negotiate – and the secret to good negotiation is information.

This is still true today. Just because the service provider's costs are less than the client's does not mean that the client is receiving a fair deal, and it is certainly not exploiting the potential of best-of-breed costs or a single sourced approach.

This chapter is designed to provide the reader with a high level overview of the different evolving approaches to benchmarking, the importance of its initial timing and ongoing use, what it facilitates and the key benefits it attracts to the management and running of outsourcing contracts. Annex 8A contains an overview of very simple commodity benchmarking techniques within telecommunications.

8.2 WHAT IS BENCHMARKING?

Benchmarking is about objective analysis of processes to measure the gap between industry best practice and current performance. It can be used prior to outsourcing to act as the measure against which the service provider must perform, or as the post-deal measure to show over the lifetime of the contract how well the service provider is performing relative to accepted norms or indices.

Benchmarking can also be a tool of business process re-engineering, contained within and as part of, an outsourcing programme. Comparing processes before and after re-engineering, it must ultimately be compared to best practice. Best practice in this context is the most appropriate cost/performance for the objective in hand – which may be lowest cost, stripped out/slimmed down services, or high contribution services centred on business contribution and/or innovation. In this instance it is about step change, not incremental change.

8.2.1 A definition of benchmarking

Benchmarking within any business support service is a set of processes, options and procedures that generate confidence for the customer that the supplier is meeting the service objectives at a performance and cost consistent with market best practice.

8.2.2 Types of benchmarking

Commercially available benchmarking falls into two major categories:

- metrics and research-based benchmarking;
- commercial benchmarking.

Metrics and research-based benchmarking

This form of study is done against a basket of remote and abstract research into those elements of the service that can be delivered as commodity. Commonly such basket benchmarking compares clients within the same industry sector and therefore reflects aspects such as buying power and commercial savvy rather than the value derived from services, although it is not uncommon for clients to be compared with companies from other industries in different countries and even different continents.

Even those that compare service delivery mechanisms and work practices (manning levels, degrees of automation, etc.) within the competitor basket do not satisfy the outsourcing-related question of how does supplier X compare in similar circumstances with supplier Y or Z?

A key question to ask is how much of these data are actually European or indeed UK based – the bulk of such research using US-generated information. The main conventional benchmarking companies are still American, for example Meta, Gartner, Compass, Yankee Group, etc. It is vital to understand that outsourcing is undertaken and delivered against fundamentally different business objectives in the US. Classic bottom-line cost reductions and matching quarterly Wall Street reporting requirements are very different from the UK and European requirement for sustainable cost reductions over the long term, matched with efficiency and effectiveness gains contained within sophisticated continuous improvement programmes (CIPs). In addition, risk–reward issues are really only just beginning in the Americas and commercial transparency (such as open book) are not comparable with the less sophisticated cost-plus models in the US.

Commercial benchmarking

This is an alternative form of study that looks in detail at the specifics of the supplied services in the context of both the service objectives and the market for supply. Not abstract or research led, it therefore requires specific practitioner knowledge and experience to achieve value.

Businesses operating in two entirely different sectors will still have common processes. In outsourcing the question should not be about how much better the client is in comparison to its competitors; rather, it ought to be about how its service provider(s) compare with their competitors for similar services, i.e. vendor-on-vendor analysis. However, in those client-led situations prior to contract letting, where the client does not have any truly indicative idea of how its services compare, a practical service audit is advisable. This is to understand how to challenge the service provider(s) to deliver meaningful service level agreements (SLAs) that are not just an improvement on internal standards to date but that really approach best practice. Improved and measurable services are often a key business driver and objective for outsourcing in the first place. Understanding current practice and the gap is important to fuel expectations for the user community within the client. Too often deals are considered not to have worked when the user community expects a Rolls Royce service while paying for a Mondeo service. Benchmarking on a regular basis can then be used as part of a CIP process to chart the progress from one level of service to another.

The dimension of commercial benchmarking, while new five years ago, is now entirely possible and affords the client the best opportunity to view the quality and performance of any service against the capability of its service provider and the market. In an ideal world, the objective must be to identify best practice, to measure the gap between it and your supplier's performance, and then to replicate those practices that will lead to such best practice.

More usually clients default to client-on-client industry comparisons that are easier to quantify but may allow the service provider to make undue profits, owing to its buying power, work practices, degrees of automation, methods of service delivery, consolidated helpdesk functions, etc. This is, of course, quite acceptable where commercial transparency is part of the contract and elements such as risk–reward are in place to balance out any excessive service provider profiteering.

In addition to value for money comparisons, commercial benchmarking should look at the service management performance and stakeholder satisfaction to provide a view of the entire agreement.

Service management performance should look at aspects of the service such as:

- service delivery management (efficiency of the role holder);
- management reports (accuracy and timeliness of reports);
- problem management;
- change management;
- service desk (knowledge, helpfulness, etc.);
- invoicing (accuracy of information);
- third party management (flow of data between parties).

Stakeholder satisfaction normally consists of the supplier undertaking a survey of key client business stakeholders.

Specialist consultancies have emerged to undertake this form of commercial benchmarking.

The contract should stipulate the frequency and the charging mechanisms for benchmarking during the life of the contract.

8.2.3 Other benchmarking approaches – market testing

A classic but rudimentary form of benchmarking is undertaken when a client goes to the market with a competitive tender for the supply of particular services. This at best fixes a price in time, but it does not take into account:

- the physical time and costs of undertaking the project for the client or the potential supplier(s);
- that predatory pricing in certain market conditions might not be sustainable in the medium to longer term;
- the risk to the business of transferring to an external supplier (or from one supplier to another);

- the staff costs, TUPE legislative considerations, etc.;
- the cost of introducing sophisticated value add services such as continuous improvement programmes, risk–reward, etc.

Market testing is still important and clearly has its place. However, a detailed view of commercial benchmarking (set out below) will allow the reader to understand why market testing is a fairly unsophisticated and rudimentary form of benchmarking in comparison.

Throughout the lifetime of a services contract, there is a time for different types of benchmarking: research based for commodities, commercially based for strategic review and relationship check pointing – the two things that provide a successful business responsive service. Therefore, provision for changing the benchmarking method should be allowed for in the setting up of any contract to allow for the dynamics of:

- rapid change in the delivery of services;
- the outsourcing industry generally;
- the changing relationships between customers and their suppliers;
- significant business change on the client's side (i.e. can the contract continue to be fit for purpose?).

While benchmarking is an essential tool for a client, there are a number of issues that should be raised with any potential benchmarking supplier. These include:

- *Data availability/compatibility*: ensure that the supplier has access to sufficient data to allow meaningful comparisons to be made.
- *Commercial sensitivity*: as each outsourcing deal is unique, any benchmarking reports should have (suitably anonymous) details of any exceptional commercial peculiarities.
- *Risk/commercial benchmarking*: the objectives and success factors of the benchmarking exercise should be agreed at the outset between the client and the benchmarker to avoid any false expectations.

The contract should stipulate the frequency and the charging mechanisms for benchmarking during the life of the contract. Annex 8B contains sample wording for the benchmarking schedule.

8.3   WHY WOULD YOU BENCHMARK?

8.3.1   What benchmarking facilitates

Benchmarking facilitates:

- ongoing processes for a continuous improvement programme (CIP);
- identifying improvement areas that will make a significant difference to

key areas of the service, the business' agility or even the speed to react to new market forces;

- setting and aligning standards for those key indicators that make up prevailing and accepted best practice;
- establishing how the best companies and service providers meet these standards;
- adapting and implementing these lessons and ideas to meet and exceed these standards;
- discussion around (with caution) contract negotiations;
- the client avoiding confrontations with service providers simply because they have the acquired knowledge of benchmarking to ease resolutions;
- the setting of prices for new services added to an existing contract.

8.3.2   The benefits of benchmarking

Benchmarking:

- allows re-alignment of services to suit cost and quality drivers;
- increases awareness of the need to query work practices, methods of delivery, manning levels, etc.;
- leads to more effective management;
- provides credible targets;
- identifies what to change and why;
- removes blinkers and 'not invented here' (NIH) attitudes;
- provides external focus;
- enables organisation to learn from outside;
- if used prior to outsourcing, can allow cost correction and reduction before inviting in the professional service providers who will further decrease costs;
- challenges assumptions on both sides and maintains flexibility in long-term outsourcing relationships;
- allows an assessment of the desirability of renewing a contract.

8.4   THE BENCHMARKING PROCESS

Without going into an unnecessary level of detail, the process of benchmarking traditionally follows four stages:

- Organisation and planning:
  - select subject area;
  - define process to be benchmarked;
  - identify potential benchmarking partners;
  - identify data required, sources and appropriate methods of collection.

- Data analysis:

  - select benchmarking partners;
  - collect the data;
  - determine the performance gap (cost–quality);
  - establish the difference in the process;
  - target future performance.

- Action:

  - communication and commitment;
  - adjust targets and develop the improvement plan;
  - implement and monitor.

- Review:

  - review progress and recalibrate.

8.5 WHAT IS BEST PRACTICE?

This is about doing things in the most effective manner and is usually focused on the mission-critical business processes, e.g. supplier management, design, infrastructure management. Any organisation can learn how other companies operate even from someone entirely out of sector. This need not be IT related but could be business process related.

The service provider works with a myriad of clients and thus they should bring translatable concepts to the table that facilitate a world-class approach – the price (physical and cultural) needs to be balanced with the achievable or perceived benefits. World-class organisations must have a strong customer focus, retain flexibility, and aim for continuous improvement.

8.6 CONTEXT AND WHERE TO INCLUDE BENCHMARKING

Benchmarks are useful to understand some key drivers and opportunities within the client's current environment from a market perspective. Benchmarking is a process of measurement to agreed standards and levels of understanding, not necessarily requiring an external comparison. Given the above, it is obvious that:

- ideally no contract would be finalised without the client having either viewed or reviewed their internal service very carefully prior to externalisation;
- the rights to benchmarking the services must be secure with the client at the time of striking the deal;
- benchmarking is a useful tool, not a panacea or silver bullet and must be used with discretion;

- choice of action following a benchmark must be with the client;
- benchmarking can be stressful, costly and time consuming and must, therefore, be done at intervals in manageable/logical pieces;
- the more complete the data, the better the results; however, do not underestimate the effort involved in compiling the data;
- in using metrics-based benchmarking, there is a need to review the companies within the basket to ensure that a valid comparison can be made;
- at the very least, services should be formally benchmarked prior to any contractual breakpoint or formal extension to the contract or competitive reletting.

8.6.1   Positioning for benchmarking

Benchmarking should be encouraged and almost mechanical these days. Contracts should assume benchmarking as the norm and allow for at least annual partial or complete testing of the service. If this is not seen as normal and to be expected, when a client eventually does decide to go for benchmarking, the service provider can become quite resistant, seeing this as a threat, as abnormal and as a prelude to potential conflict or loss of the contract.

Co-operation and openness is to be encouraged and checking the service provider's attitude to routine benchmarking is a key cultural indicator to be tested and monitored in the selection or shortlisting of potential service providers in the request for proposal (RFP) stage. Both parties will benefit from the open debate and actions that result from benchmark research.

8.6.2   Practical uses of different types of benchmarking

These include the following.

- *Value for money [VFM]*: validation of a sole source bid prior to contract signing, i.e. where the client decides against a competitive procurement because of factors such as speed, the stakeholders of the company will demand to understand that there is value in this approach.
- *Health check/service audit*: during the lifetime of the contract the client will need to validate the supplier performance against outsourcing norms. This is not a full market test benchmark; it is used where the amount of change in the client (and consequently their services) demands validation on the approach and/or costings, for example after the divestiture of a subsidiary or the bringing in of more service volumes as a result of merger and acquisition activities.
- *Sourcing strategy reviews*: validating the incumbent solutions and pricing structures against future strategic thinking and anticipated business change.

- *Introduction of a balanced scorecard system*: this can obviate the need for more formal benchmarking processes, and can introduce soft skill analysis as opposed to technical and technology-driven metrics. This is particularly useful in measuring business perception of the service provider's contributions.
- *Development of business metrics*: in a competitive world, clients need to understand their costs and efficiencies in a non-technical format. This can be a very useful business planning and development tool. For example, an insurance company may want to determine what the average administration cost per policy is, or the average number of support staff per policy and how this compares in the overall insurance sector.

8.7 WHAT A METRICS-BASED BENCHMARK SHOULD COVER AND DELIVER

Typically the indicators should be shown against the companies within the peer group, the client, the average for the peer group and the average for all clients of the benchmarking partner. It should show comparable indicators including the following (not exhaustive) list.

- Efficiency indicators:

  - cost per user;
  - cost per client device;
  - users per device;
  - cost per support staff;
  - support staff per number of users, etc.

- Performance indicators:

  - helpdesk speed to answer, abandonment rates, etc.;
  - first time fixes;
  - response times;
  - equipment/applications/change failure rates;
  - service availability (uptime), etc.

- Volumetrics

  - system utilisation rates;
  - bandwidth per user;
  - MIPS and DASD (machine storage quotient) per user, etc.

8.8 WHAT A COMMERCIAL BENCHMARK SHOULD COVER AND DELIVER

It is important to distinguish between commercial benchmarking undertaken as a prelude to an outsourcing arrangement and commercial benchmarking during the life of the outsourcing contract. Undertaking such an exercise prior to committing too much commercial data to the potential service provider(s) is the ideal situation, for the following reasons:

- Service providers should not be supplied with detailed costs prior to understanding how effective the in-house service truly is. Classically, service providers will offer to guarantee 20 per cent savings where cost is seen by the client as a business objective. This offer is made in order to accelerate the client's decision-making process and to ensure that the process will not be competitive.
- Savings can be made, or at least pointed to, prior to challenging the service providers to compete. Thus, if the client accepts service delivery changes ahead of compiling the RFP, these savings belong to the client ahead of other innovation that the service providers can and will make. For example, accepting that a helpdesk does not have to be in house and on site means that it can be very efficiently rolled up into the service provider's infrastructure and low cost base. This can typically take a 10-person team and allow it to be run by only three full-time employees. Not only that, but the office space is freed up, infrastructure and software licences, etc. are also saved.

Without a precontract commercial benchmark, all these savings belong to the winning service provider. Costs can be significantly cut merely by identifying how the professional service provider will seek to change the methods of delivering the service and then challenging them, within the RFP, to go further. The investment in any identified change does not have to take place prior to letting a contract; it is part of the transition to the service provider.

Once a contract has been let, commercial benchmarking is undertaken to ensure that value for money is consistently being achieved. Remember that the outsourcing market is changing very rapidly and commoditisation is extremely quick. It will certainly change beyond recognition in the usual three- to four-year contract span. Benchmarking ensures that service reflects change in the client's needs, the service provider's capabilities and the dynamics within the outsourcing market generally.

8.9 CHECKLIST

What is covered in the checklist below need not apply to all contracts but it is a typical list of considerations:

- Areas of cost savings:
  - *Hardware*: consolidation/replacement/location.
  - *Software*: consolidation/standardisation/elimination.

- *Staffing levels*: full-time employees v. headcount/peak handling/centres of expertise.
- *Comms/networks*: resilience v. cost/integration/current commerciality.
- *Disaster recovery*: block discounts/testing.
- *Procurement*: buying power and services.
- *Security*: shared partitions and data networks.
- *Transition strategies*: aimed at reducing costs.
- *Retained organisation costs*:

  - commercial;
  - service/contract management;
  - IT strategy and planning.

- Cultural and communication impact costs.

- Financial aspects:

  - Treatment of assets.
  - Future capital costs.
  - Costs of money and amortised costs that may be distorting service charges.
  - Provisions for risk and penalties, etc.
  - Supplier/customer transition cost handling.

- Metrics and audit reviews:

  - Building a process improvement index with:

    - quality;
    - performance;
    - delivery;
    - customer commitment quotient.

  - Best-in-class market reviews.

- Best practice approaches:

  - Technological currency/refresh/total cost of ownership.
  - Unit pricing/cost per seat.
  - Cost transparency/risk–reward.
  - Business linked pricing.

ANNEX 8A

Example of a benchmarking approach

The main part of the chapter was deliberately designed to be high level and not to delve into undue detail. In order to illustrate how complex a world benchmarking can be, below is a very simple overview of benchmarking techniques for telecommunications.

It is considered simple because of the commodity nature of these services and the relative ease of finding published data to support the comparisons. Telecoms, while still dynamic and suffering from being semi-regulated, is a very mature market and served well by many industry indices and analysts.

This will be as easy for certain IT/IS services and, in some cases, not be possible at all for business process outsourcing where metrics are simply not available (for example, how do you measure the cost base and effectiveness of maintaining insurance policies via different third parties, or the proactivity and efficiency/effectiveness of suppliers of building facilities management?), whereas the uptake and relative maturity of services such as claims management, debt collection and human resource management are now becoming measurable.

INDEXATION AND BENCHMARKING OF TELECOMS SERVICES – AN OVERVIEW OF BENCHMARKING TECHNIQUES
Barry Eliades – Morgan Chambers plc

What is indexation?

Perhaps the most widely understood definition of an index is that which is used by the investment and financial institutions to monitor trends in share prices.

An index is an indicator of the cost or price of a service, commodity or entity that is monitored on a regular and consistent basis. It is used to monitor change and trends rather than as a discrete measure taken at any one moment. Quite often the index is a composite of several elements that are measured, and the value of the index does not represent the specific price of an item.

Telecommunications indexation

Indexation can be applied to the telecommunications market in a number of ways. It is possible to monitor:

- prices of specific services;
- aggregated prices of several services that reflect the needs of particular applications;
- costs of providing specific services (future prices of that service are then governed by the output of the indexation formula which combines costs of labour, materials and other factors in the calculation of an overall index);
- share prices of telecommunications suppliers and operators;

269

- financial ratios of the telecoms industry (such as turnover per capita or R & D investment per subscriber).

Types of indexation service

There are at least two approaches to indexation in telecommunications.

- *A basket-based price index*: the basket-based approach is designed to monitor different telecoms services and specific profiles of use. This method can be used to track price trends of telecoms services, so that price variations of specific telecoms contracts, over time, can be compared with general trends. This type of indexation can help maintain price differentials (discounted prices), especially in fully deregulated mature markets.
- *A formula-driven price index*: the formula-based price index brings together a number of factors that have a direct and indirect bearing on the cost of a service. This method is best used in situations where there are no other competing services, and is normally used to control tariffs for services from a specific supplier.

Indexing methodologies

The two principal indexation methods are described below in a little more detail. As this annex is to be used as a starting point for more detailed discussions on benchmarking and indexation, it is not the intention here to present a definitive methodology. The correct approach is to always have a full understanding of the client's requirements before prescribing any specific methodology.

Basket-based price index

The basket indexation process is based upon the concept of a portfolio of scenarios whose prices are regularly monitored. Over time, a picture emerges of the price trend for each type of portfolio or basket.

Baskets are formulated to represent a particular mix of services. For example, one can monitor the following types of basket.

- International VPN.
- Digital mobile.
- Leased line configurations (national and/or international).
- National ISDN services.
- PSTN calls.
- International frame relay.
- Toll free services.
- General voice services (mix of VPN, PSTN and toll free) national and/or international.

An example of the presentation of indexation values is shown in Figures 8.1a and 8.1b. The data shown in the examples are only given as an illustration and do not represent actual costs.

The basket-based approach can use several categories for indexation. For example, baskets can represent typical applications (such as a large call centre scenario) or generic services (such as international voice or high speed data services). Specific services or classes or service can also be indexed (such as PSTN, frame relay or national ISDN).

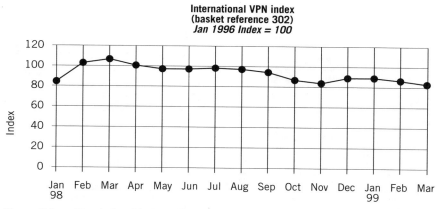

Figure 8.1a   Example of indexation results

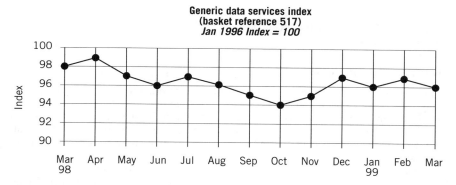

Figure 8.1b   Example of indexation results

The application basket can comprise a group of different services that are used in relation to a particular application. Several types of application can be indexed and they can be defined for a specific country, a region or many countries. The size of the application can also vary to represent different scales of activity.

Figure 8.2 shows how applications may have different combinations and proportions of services.

This service basket can focus more on a specific type of service. The basket can be specified for just one profile of use or configuration. However, it can also comprise several scenarios, each representing a particular element of the business, such as a large international organisation with local factories or offices, regional offices, data and call centres and a main headquarters.

271

Application-based baskets	PSTN	Free phone	VPN	64K Line	ISDN2	ISDN3	2Mb Line	X25	Frame Relay	Mobile	ATM	SMDS
1 Application #1	15%			30%	30%			25%				
2 Application #2				35%		25%	15%	5%	20%			
3 Application #3	85%	10%	5%									
4 Application #4				10%	90%							
5 Application #5	50%		30%		5%					5%		
6 Application #6	65%	5%	10%		10%				5%	5%		

Figure 8.2 Application-based example baskets

Figure 8.3 shows how the PSTN, leased circuits and VPN baskets could comprise different scenarios.

Formula-driven price index

This approach uses a complex formula combining external and internal factors that may influence the cost of service provision. It is used in cases where the contract for services allows for the price list to be revised by the supplier within the variation of the formula-based price index. A formula can be developed for an overall price catalogue or, more appropriately, specific formulas can regulate price changes of a particular service.

This method is not so influenced by market prices. It is more closely linked to the supplier's costs and is effective in the circumstances where there are no equivalent services in the market.

Elements included in these types of formula include:

- labour costs;
- material costs;
- telecoms prices;
- other overhead costs (transport, depreciation, property).

In addition, the formula may allow for continuing productivity improvements so that the supplier is expected to make efficiency improvements.

In a long-term contract it is advisable to agree a rebalancing schedule that will enable changes to be made to the weightings of the elements in the formula. This is necessary to allow for disproportionate changes in costs that may affect the different elements during the life of the contract.

A typical indexation formula would, in general, look like this:

$$Icurrent = Ibaseline + \frac{Mw}{100} \times \left(\frac{Mc - Mo}{Mo}\right) + \frac{Lw}{100} \times \left(\frac{Lc - Lo}{Lo}\right) \times \left(\frac{100 - P}{100}\right) + \frac{Tw}{100} \times \left(\frac{Tc - To}{To}\right)$$

Where:

Icurrent	is the current price index (as a percentage)
Ibaseline	is the baseline price index (as a percentage)
Mw	is the materials weighting factor (as a percentage)
Mc	is the current materials index
Mo	is the original baseline materials index
Lw	is the labour weighting factor (as a percentage)
Lc	is the current labour index
Lo	is the original baseline labour index
P	is the productivity factor (as a percentage)
Tw	is the telecoms weighting factor (as a percentage)
Tc	is the current telecoms service index
To	is the original baseline telecoms service index

and:

$$Mw + Lw + Tw = 100$$

VPN	Configuration type		
Basket elements	A	B	C
Total VPN sites	300	50	20
Total VPN extensions	6,000	5,000	6,000
Total VPN calls	100,000	200,000	150,000
On-net call minutes	3,000,000	2,000,000	3,000,000
National call minutes	1,000,000	800,000	150,000
UK call minutes	30,000	65,000	10,000
USA call minutes	5,000	25,000	10,000
			20
			3yrs

PSTN	Configuration type		
Basket elements	A	B	C
No. of exchange lines	5,000	150	20
Number of locations	200	10	2
Total calls	30,000,000	1,500,000	150,000
Call minutes-local	62,000,000	3,000,000	300,000
Call minutes-national	25,000,000	1,500,000	150,000

Leased circuits	Configuration type		
Basket elements	A	B	C
9.6 kbit/s circuits @ 5km	0	0	0
9.6 kbit/s circuits @ 50km	0	0	0
9.6 kbit/s circuits @ 200km	0	0	0
64 kbit/s circuits @ 5km	30	2	1
64 kbit/s circuits @50km	100	8	1
64 kbit/s circuits @ 200km	30	2	0
2 Mbit/s circuits @ 5km	50	1	0
2 Mbit/s circuits @ 50km	20	0	0
Contract length	5 yrs	3 yrs	3 yrs

Figure 8.3   Service-based example baskets

273

The labour and materials indices can be derived from a number of sources and, in particular, monthly government statistics reports. The telecoms index would be derived from a basket of services that are grouped for a specific service indexation formula.

Indexation and benchmarking

In many situations there is a need for several indices so that it is possible to carry out comparisons in several different ways – for example on a service-by-service basis, for specific countries or applications. It may also be required that an overall, global picture is examined. In these cases consolidation can bring together individual indices into one overall benchmark index.

In outsourcing cases, for example, when the contract is agreed and prices finalised, a baseline index can be derived from a combination of suitable control scenarios (baskets) that are a close match to services that may be provided under the outsourcing agreement. Figure 8.4 shows how basket indexation can be applied for regular service benchmarking.

The basket indices can be monitored as often as once a month. In carrying out the calculation of the index, an appropriate method for price adjustment should be used (such as purchasing power parity) to allow for normalised year-on-year comparisons.

Figure 8.4 suggests the use of indexation on an annual basis and shows how the index can be used to control contact prices.

The shaded bars are the index value for the basket that is closest to the actual services being benchmarked. The unshaded bars represent the value of the actual service units being benchmarked. In Year 0 the index is set to a nominal value of 100 and the service unit price is aligned with the index. In subsequent years, the index varies and one can see how the service unit prices can be benchmarked against the index. One can introduce a variation tolerance to allow for margins of error and provide some leeway in price negotiations between customer and supplier.

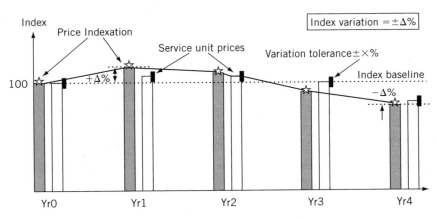

Figure 8.4 Service benchmarking using basket indexation

ANNEX 8B

Benchmarking schedule

PURPOSE OF THE SCHEDULE

This schedule defines the approach regarding commercial and performance benchmarking for the services as described in the services schedule of the agreement.

SCOPE

Annually, on or after the anniversary of the commencement date, the company shall inform the supplier that it wishes to conduct a benchmarking exercise of the services.

The company shall give the supplier one month's prior written notice of the intention to carry out a benchmarking exercise, which shall include details of access requirements to the supplier's premises. The supplier shall use reasonable endeavours to provide access at the requested times or provide a suitable alternative to the company. This exercise shall, if required by the company, additionally include technical aspects of the services and pricing versus objective standards, such as Gartner, Compass, Meta Group or any other mutually agreed objective third party. The purpose of the complete exercise shall be agreed prior to its commencement.

The benchmarking exercise shall be conducted during business hours.

INVOCATION

Both the company and the supplier shall share equally the costs arising as a result of the benchmarking exercise up to a maximum of £[ ] each. Each party shall take all reasonable steps to minimise all costs incurred by it as a consequence of such an exercise.

In the event that the company requires a third party to be involved in the benchmarking exercise, this shall be subject to the agreement of the supplier prior to the appointment and signing by the third party of a confidentiality agreement, the terms of which are to be agreed between the parties.

Where a third party is engaged to undertake a benchmarking exercise at the supplier's premises, the supplier shall reasonably co-operate with the agreed third party. The company and the third party will endeavour to ensure that the supplier's normal operation is not unduly disrupted during the course of such a benchmarking exercise.

REVIEW PROCESS

Following completion of the benchmarking exercise, the company and the supplier shall jointly review the findings with a view to identifying any significant difference between current industry pricing/standards, as identified in the benchmarking exercise, and those currently being provided by the supplier.

Where significant differences in price performance are identified, both parties will agree how these will be addressed. In a case where performance is shown to be below the industry norm, the service improvement plan will be adjusted and agreed to bring it in line with industry standards.

Where a significant commercial difference against the industry norm has been identified, both parties will negotiate to agree a revised charge for such a commodity.

CHAPTER 9

Employment issues

Malcolm Sargeant and Ricky Vassell

9.1 INTRODUCTION

An important aspect of European Union social policy has been how to help the process of change that has occurred, and will continue to occur, in all member states as a result of the development of the single market. The EU has always assumed, with some justification, that the demands of the single market would lead to considerable structural change as business became more EU orientated, rather than nationally based. The result of this structural change would be increased levels of mergers and acquisitions and, perhaps consequently, increased numbers of insolvencies and redundancies. This has been a concern since the European Community's first Social Action Programme launched in 1974 and subsequent programmes launched periodically since then.

This has given rise to a number of measures designed to provide some protection for the workers involved in this process, in order to make that process more acceptable. It has become clear that part of the structural change that has, and is, taking place is an important increase in the use of outsourcing. This has been especially true in the UK and is becoming increasingly true in other member states of the EU. Two such protection measures that may have a direct effect on the process of outsourcing are the Acquired Rights Directive (Directive 77/187/EEC amended by Directive 98/50/EC; consolidated into Directive 2001/23/EC OJ L 82/16) transposed into national law by the Transfer of Undertakings (Protection of Employment) Regulations 1981 (TUPE), SI 1981/1794; and the Collective Redundancies Directive (now Directive 98/59/EC on the approximation of the laws of the member states relating to collective redundancies), transposed into national law in Part IV of the Trade Union and Labour Relations (Consolidation) Act 1992.

9.2 EMPLOYMENT PROTECTION IN OUTSOURCING

TUPE and the Acquired Rights Directive have been the source of much litigation in attempting to decide on their applicability to outsourcing. Simply stated, the effect of TUPE, where a relevant transfer has taken place, is to transfer an employee's contract of employment from the transferor employer to the transferee employer. It is as if the employee had entered into the original contract of employment with the new (outsourced) employer and means, for example, that length of service and seniority is transferred as well as the rights, liabilities and obligations attaching to the contract.

At a basic level the Directive and TUPE operate when there is a transfer of an undertaking (or part of one). What constitutes an undertaking and how the Directive and TUPE define a transfer is of critical importance. When TUPE applies, as well as operating to transfer the contracts of employment of particular staff it provides other protections to employees. These include the right not to be dismissed simply because a qualifying transfer is taking place (save in particular circumstances) and to be informed and consulted about the transfer process and its consequences.

In this chapter we trace the developments of the law in respect of the Directive and TUPE and examine their practical effect on the management of outsourcings. It is clearly not possible to cover all of the material case developments in this chapter and it therefore concentrates on well established principles in respect of the application of the Directive and TUPE.

9.3   WHEN IS A TRANSFER A 'TRANSFER OF AN UNDERTAKING'?

There are a number of issues that affect the employment aspects of outsourcings in the context of the Directive and TUPE. The main question is in what circumstances the transfer of a function from an in-house operation to a third party service provider (a first generation transfer) or a subsequent change of service provider, as a result of a re-tendering (a second generation transfer) will constitute a relevant transfer of an undertaking.

The question, put in another way, is: what is meant by a transfer of an undertaking in the context of an outsourcing?

9.4   THE DIRECTIVE

In *Berg and Busschers* v. *Besselsen* (C-145/87) [1989] IRLR 447, ECJ, the European Court of Justice held that the Directive applied as soon as a 'change occurs of the natural or legal person operating the undertaking who, in that capacity, has obligations *vis-à-vis* the employees employed in the undertaking, and that it is of no importance whether the ownership of the undertaking has been transferred'. The test, therefore, is whether there has been a change in the natural or legal person running the operation, as would normally take place in an outsourcing situation. Actual ownership is not important, so merely transferring shares will not be enough. However a transfer of shares followed by a

278

hiving off of the business to a group company or special purpose vehicle may well trigger the application of TUPE.

In the seminal case on this topic the European Court of Justice, in *Spijkers* v. *Gebroeders Benedik Abbatoir CV* (C-24/85) [1986] ECR 1119, defined a transfer of an undertaking as the transfer of an economic entity that retained its identity. The case concerned an abattoir, which was sold by a company that then became insolvent. The abattoir was closed for a period and Mr Spijkers was not employed by the new owners. The European Court of Justice looked at the purpose of the Directive and concluded that its purpose was to ensure the continuity of existing employment relationships. It then stated the approach that has been followed extensively in subsequent decisions in the European Court of Justice and in the UK courts: 'it follows that the decisive criterion for establishing the existence of a transfer within the meaning of the Directive is whether the entity in question retains its identity'.

Thus, if the operation that is transferred is an identifiable entity before and after the transfer then a relevant transfer is likely to have taken place. The Court of Justice then gave further guidance as to factors that would help in the decision as to whether a transfer had taken place. It was necessary to take all the factual circumstances of the transaction into account, including:

- the type of undertaking or business in question;
- the transfer or otherwise of tangible assets such as buildings and stocks;
- the value of intangible assets at the date of transfer;
- whether the majority of staff are taken over by the new employer;
- the transfer or otherwise of customers;
- the degree of similarity between activities before and after the transfer; and
- the duration of any interruption in those activities.

The Court stated that each of these factors was only part of the assessment. One had to examine what existed before the transfer and then examine the entity after the change in order to decide whether the operation was continued. This helpful clarification proved to be a stepping stone to a series of cases that further defined and expanded the applicability of the Directive, especially in relation to outsourcing (see *Rask and Christensen* v. *ISS Kantineservice* (C-209/91) [1993] IRLR 133, ECJ), and concluded that transfers resulting from outsourcing, including labour-only contracts, could be relevant transfers of undertakings (see *Schmidt* v. *Spar-und Leikhasse der Fruheren Amter Bordesholm* (C-392/92) [1994] ECR I-1311).

9.5 TUPE

In the UK this approach by the European Court of Justice resulted in the courts finding that outsourcing could amount to a relevant transfer for the purposes of TUPE. *Kenny* v. *South Manchester College* [1993] IRLR 265, for example, concerned the provision of education services at a young offenders' institution. After a tendering exercise the contract was won by South Manchester College. The question was whether the undertaking had retained its identity. The High Court stated that:

> The prisoners and young offenders who attend, say, a carpentry class next Thursday will, save those released from the institution, be likely in the main to be the same as those who attended the same class in the same classroom the day before and will doubtless be using exactly the same tools and machinery.

This was followed by *Wren* v. *Eastbourne District Council* [1993] ICR 955, where the outsourcing of a local authority refuse collection contract was held to be a relevant transfer; and *Dines* v. *Initial Health Care Services and Pall Mall Services Group Ltd* [1994] IRLR 336, which was an important case regarding the applicability of TUPE to compulsory competitive tendering. This was because it involved the moving of a hospital cleaning contract from one contractor to another, establishing the applicability of TUPE to second generation transfers.

The result was that the application of TUPE removed the possibility of saving significant amounts of money, when taking over a contract, by reducing the wages payable to employees.

A number of the cases referred to above involved labour-intensive operations (e.g. operations with few assets other than the workforce). In such cases the examination of which assets transferred was thought to be unhelpful. Instead a more purposive approach was taken and where the same activity was carried on after the transfer (even though no tangible assets transferred) TUPE was found to apply.

It was then that the European Court of Justice appeared to have second thoughts about its approach, in *Süzen* v. *Zehnacker Gebaudereinigung* (C-13/95) [1997] IRLR 255, ECJ. The Court distinguished between the transfer of an entity and the transfer of an activity. The Court held that:

> an entity cannot be reduced to the activity entrusted to it. Its identity also emerges from other factors, such as its workforce, its management staff, the way in which its work is organised, its operating methods or, indeed, where appropriate, the operational resources available to it.

Süzen set limits on the applicability of the Directive in mainly labour-intensive scenarios (e.g. cleaning contracts) by seeking to define in clearer terms the need for a transfer of some significant part of the undertaking before the Directive would apply. In other words, if the main assets of an entity (even where this was just staff) were not being transferred, there might not be a transfer. There has been confusion as to where these limits apply and the real difference between an entity and an activity.

Süzen led to two contradictory decisions of the Court of Appeal in respect of TUPE. *Betts* v. *Brintel Helicopters* [1997] IRLR 361, CA, concerned the transfer of a helicopter ferrying contract to and from oil rigs in the North Sea. Brintel Helicopters had all three of the contracts that were in existence. When they came up for renewal, Shell decided that no single company should hold all three contracts. Subsequently Brintel won two of the contracts and lost the one that serviced the southern sector of the North Sea. This was won by another contractor, KLM Helicopters, who carried out the contract from a completely different part of the United Kingdom. None of the individuals employed by Brintel on the contract were recruited by KLM. The Court of Appeal considered *Süzen* and concluded that the contract was not a labour-intensive activity and, as a result of no other tangible or intangible assets transferring, it held that there was not a relevant transfer in accordance with TUPE.

In contrast to *Betts* the Court of Appeal held, in *ECM (Vehicle Delivery Service) Ltd* v. *Cox* [1998] ICR 631, CA, that a relevant transfer took place in somewhat similar circumstances. ECM won one of two contracts, during a re-tendering exercise, delivering VWs and Audis to dealers or local delivery centres. In carrying out the contract, the location for operations was to be changed as would the mode of working. The new contractor refused to employ any of the old contracting staff, apparently because they had threatened to take unfair dismissal proceedings if not taken on. Many of the characteristics of *Betts* are contained in this case, namely the lack of a transfer of any assets or employees and the reorganisation and carrying on of the work at another location. As a result, ECM Ltd argued that all that was transferred was an activity and not any assets or employees. A transfer of an activity, it was argued, was an essential prerequisite for there to be a relevant transfer, but it is not sufficient in itself. The Court of Appeal concluded that a relevant transfer might have taken place if the staff had transferred, so the employer's motivation in failing to take on these staff could be questioned and be a reason for a relevant transfer. Thus if an employer refuses to take on the employees in order to avoid TUPE, then this can be a relevant factor. (This was a factor for the Court of Session, which chose to follow *ECM*, in *Lightways (Contractors Ltd)* v. *Associated Holdings Ltd* [2000] IRLR 247.) This has become known as the ECM point and the issue of the transferee's motivation is now one that needs to be considered in each relevant situation (see *Adi (UK) Ltd* v. *Willer* [2001] IRLR 542 and *RCO Support Services* v. *UNISON* [2002] IRLR 401, CA).

It is the distinction between an entity and an activity, proposed in *Süzen*, that has led the European Court of Justice into a situation where it needs to distinguish between groups of workers who may or may not be entitled to the protection of the Directive. Having accepted that more than an activity is required to create a protected transfer, the Court is faced with drawing the dividing line between what constitutes an activity and what constitutes an entity. It has also weakened the Directive's potential effect by creating circumstances where employers can avoid its effect by manipulating what is or is not transferred. It was this problem that was recognised by the Court of Appeal in *ECM* v. *Cox* (see above) when it took into account the transferee employer's motivation in not transferring staff or assets as a factor in deciding whether a relevant transfer had taken place or not. See also *RCO Support Services* v. *UNISON* [2002] IRLR 401, CA, where the employers were held not to have attempted to avoid TUPE, but there were sufficient indicators to suggest that a hospital cleaning operation retained its identity to qualify as a relevant transfer for the purposes of TUPE.

9.5.1 Legal summary

Based on the case authorities there is no doubt that TUPE is capable of applying to both first and second generation outsourcings provided that the necessary tests are satisfied. When looking at the question in practice there is a sensible distinction to be made between labour-intensive services and more asset-based operations.

In labour-intensive cases there should be a focus first of all on whether there is in fact what is best referred to as a stable economic entity (*Rask and Christensen* v. *ISS Kantineservice* (C-209/91) [1993] IRLR 133, ECJ). This, in most outsourcing cases, is answered in the affirmative. It is then a case of examining what proposals are being advanced in respect of the workforce and why.

In more asset-based operations, a careful examination of what is being transferred is necessary. This includes, but should not exclusively focus on, proposals for staff. However, even if the majority of staff assigned to the operation are taken on by the new provider a transfer may still not have taken place (*Oy Liikenne AB* v. *Liskojärvi and Juntenen* (C-172/99) [2001] IRLR 171, ECJ).

9.5.2 Practical steps

In outsourcings from the public to the private sector the need for a definitive assessment of the application of TUPE has been reduced by the prescriptive nature of the Cabinet Office guidance in respect of business transfers (see section 9.12). Contractors and government departments/agencies are required to proceed on the basis that TUPE applies save in exceptional circumstances (i.e. where the non-application of TUPE is clear cut). Tenders, whether on a first or second generation basis, must also comply with the government's best value requirements. This means tenders are assessed using a number of factors, including the need for the relevant department/agency to examine closely the proposals put forward by the contractor in relation to staff issues.[1] Private sector contractors in reality have little option but to work within the government guidance and assume that TUPE will apply in most cases. There is nonetheless ample scope for negotiation with government departments/agencies around the specifics of how the guidance will be implemented in practice, particularly around issues such as pensions and redundancy terms.

In the private sector matters are less clear cut. The application of TUPE is, in most cases, likely to be explored between the parties. It is advisable, therefore, for outsourcers to give an early indication of the basis on which tenders should be submitted and in particular whether charging and service level proposals should take account of the possible application of TUPE. The aim should be to ensure that contractors focus on the costs and management issues that flow from the possible application of TUPE. Employment costs and the processes TUPE imposes are often a significant overhead of an outsourced operation and so it is important that the impact of TUPE is given considerable thought at the outset of the process.

The parties must have adequate information to enable them to make a sensible judgement about the application of TUPE. Tender processes are generally sophisticated and contractors are provided with substantial information as part of the tender process. Information is normally easy to come by at the first generation stage as the outsourcer is in control of the necessary information. The outsourcing entity will however also need to have one eye to the future and the possibility of a subsequent transfer. It will need to be in a position to secure accurate information about the operation once it has transferred.

While general audit provisions in outsourcing contracts may provide some of the necessary information, they tend not to cover employment matters in detail. A requirement for a contractor to provide at the re-tendering stage specific employment-related information should be considered. This will enable the outsourcer to provide relevant information in its re-tender documentation and sufficient due diligence material to potential new contractors.

Contractors are of course keen to ensure confidentiality of their business operations and may well require restrictions on the use of the information supplied to the outsourcer. This is understandable given the information provided is likely to end up in the hands of a direct competitor.

Whether TUPE regulations are presumed to apply or not, there should always be substantial debate about the scope of the liabilities that the parties are prepared to assume. In that sense the ambiguity in respect of TUPE can be a positive commercial advantage, allowing a party to negotiate a position that might otherwise be difficult to secure if the application of TUPE could be established without question.

9.6 OUTSOURCING SURVEY

In 1999, 12 member companies of the Business Services Association (BSA)[2] were interviewed to identify problems that they had experienced with TUPE and what changes they would like to see made.[3] The interviews were carried out between July and November 1999 (the BSA survey). The participants were all companies concerned with a variety of outsourcing businesses. Their size, stage of development and the type of work that they undertook was varied. The range of work on outsourcing contracts ranged from that carried out by highly skilled and scarce technical employees, at one end of the spectrum, to part-time unskilled employees at the other end. The companies employed over 130,000 contract staff between them, working on some 10,000 outsourced contracts. Total turnover on these contracts amounted to over £3 billion per annum. There was a mixture of work from the public and the private sectors.

A number of potential issues were identified. First, there was a lack of clarity as to when TUPE applied. All the participating companies mentioned the uncertainty that had occurred since the *Süzen* case in the European Court of Justice. There was a unanimous desire for clarification. Examples of problems caused by the uncertainty included disagreements between contractors that resulted in the transferor refusing to make employees redundant because they had transferred, while the potential transferee denied that TUPE applied and refused to transfer the employees concerned. The result was that the employees were left in a state of limbo with both the transferor and the transferee denying that they were the employers. There was concern that contracting companies would be left with potentially large liabilities for redundancy and notice payments if it was decided finally that TUPE would not apply to second generation transfers. One member company, for example, thought that it might have been exposed to potential payments of over £30 million if such a situation was reached; the potential liabilities in some contracts could affect the decision as to whether to tender. If there are a significant number of long-term older employees, then some companies may not have tendered because of the potential risk.

Three companies stated that it was too simplistic to talk merely in terms of first and second generation contracts. Sometimes a customer could change the nature of a contract between the initial outsourcing and subsequent re-tendering, e.g. one company related the story of one contract being broken up into a large number of smaller contracts designed, in the contractor's view, to exclude TUPE and leave the contractor with important liabilities. Another company described the reverse process of a number of smaller contracts being brought together to form one contract. The participating companies had differing experiences as to which sector was most at fault. Views expressed were that TUPE was always applied in the public sector; that it was not always applied; or that large private companies applied it and that the problem lay with smaller private businesses.

The overwhelming requirement from all the companies was a need for certainty of application and some relief from litigation, or the threat of it, with regard to TUPE.

9.7   THE AMENDED DIRECTIVE

The Acquired Rights Directive was amended in 1998 by Directive 98/50/EC and new TUPE regulations by the government are intended to end this uncertainty.

Article 1.1(*b*) of the amended Directive states that there is a transfer within the meaning of the Directive 'where there is a transfer of an economic entity which retains its identity, meaning an organised grouping of resources which has the objective of pursuing an economic activity . . .'

The issues for the government were: first, what is the entity that constitutes a transfer of an undertaking; second, does TUPE apply to second generation contracts (i.e. the transfer of an outsourced contract from one contractor to another following a competitive tender); and, third, does TUPE apply when the work to be performed is taken back in house?

The proposed test is to be based on the concept of service provision changes. Outsourcing, second generation transfers and taking work back in house are all defined, in so far as they are ongoing (rather than one-off) arrangements, as service provision changes. There are two questions to be asked. These are: first: is there a service provision change, such as those above, to take place? Second, were there, prior to the change and relying upon the Directive, employees assigned to an organised grouping, the principal purpose of which was to perform the service activities in question specifically on behalf of the client concerned? If the answer to these questions is yes, then two things follow. First, the employees assigned to the organised grouping must then be treated in the same way as where TUPE does apply. Second, the party with the responsibility for the provision of the service before the change is the transferor and the party responsible for the provision after the change is the transferee.

9.7.1   Legal summary

If adopted, while the government's proposals will result in a measure of certainty, they may go further than is necessary. In essence, provided there is service provision change, employees will transfer without any further consideration of whether there is a genuine transfer of an undertaking. This, in effect, would reinstate the pre-*Süzen* position and give the parties more limited scope to make savings based on the fact that TUPE does not apply.

9.8 WHO IS PROTECTED BY TUPE?

9.8.1 Which type of personnel are transferred?

Regulation 5 of TUPE states that a relevant transfer shall not operate so as to terminate the contract of employment of any person employed by the transferor in the undertaking or part transferred. This is in contrast to the amended Acquired Rights Directive, which refers, in Article 3, to obligations arising out of the contract of employment or from an employment relationship. In the UK interpretation has been strict, so that only those with a contract of employment are transferred. Those working under any other sort of contract, such as a contract to provide services, do not receive any protection from the Directive or TUPE.

The European Court of Justice removed any doubts as to who should be protected by stating that the Directive was only aimed at the partial harmonisation of the laws of the member states. This meant that there was no intention to adopt the same approach in each country, but merely to extend existing national laws that provide protection to include transfer situations. In *Mikkelsen (Foreningen Arbejdsledere I Danmark)* v. *Danmols Inventar A/S* (C-105/84) [1985] ECR 2639 the European Court of Justice stated:

> It follows that Directive 77/187 may be relied upon only by persons who are, in one way or another, protected as employees under the laws of the member state concerned. If they are so protected, the Directive ensures that their rights arising from a contract of employment or an employment relationship are not diminished as a result of the transfer.

The amended Directive explicitly ensures that this protection is extended to certain individuals on 'non-standard' contracts of employment. It ensures that individuals should not be discriminated against solely because of the number of hours that they work, or because they are on fixed-term contracts, or because they are temporary agency employees.

The result is that only those individuals who are employees with contracts of employment are eligible for protection. If such an employee is dismissed for a reason connected to a relevant transfer, then by virtue of regulation 8 the dismissal will be automatically unfair. The only way to avoid such a finding is if the dismissal falls within a category of specified exemptions, i.e. an economic, technical or organisation reason entailing a change in the workforce (see below).

9.8.2 Who is employed in the undertaking?

The next problem occurs in deciding who works for the 'part transferred', when only part of an organisation is transferred to a new employer. This is commonly the case in outsourcing situations, where non-core businesses are contracted out. There are likely to be a number of employees, such as those in human resources, who work in the parts remaining, but whose jobs consisted of servicing those parts transferred. This may be the entire content of their jobs or only a part.

The leading European case is *Botzen* v. *Rotterdamsche Droogdork Maatschappij BV* (C-186/83) [1985] ECR 519, which states the employee will need to be 'wholly engaged' in the part of the business that is transferred in order to gain protection. As can be seen the test is general and has been applied in a variety of ways in different cases under TUPE.

The issue was considered in *Michael Peters Ltd* v. *(1) Farnfield and (2) Michael Peters Group plc* [1995] IRLR 190. This concerned a group of companies that were in financial difficulties, resulting in the sale of four of them (out of 25). The EAT considered two questions. One was whether the transfer of subsidiaries by a group entitled the group company to be regarded as the transferor and the second was whether the group chief executive could claim to be part of the companies transferred and, therefore, entitled to the protection of the Directive and TUPE.

The EAT decided that it was wrong to regard the group as a single economic unit for employment protection matters. The EAT allowed that there would be occasions when this approach would not be correct, but, in this case, their decision was not to regard the group as the transferor. They then rejected the employee's claim that he spent the majority of his time on the four companies and concluded that he was a group employee working on group matters.

Some clarification came from another case, *Duncan Web Offset (Maidstone) Ltd* v. *Cooper* [1995] IRLR 633. This concerned three employees who worked at the company's Maidstone office, but spent some of their time working at other offices that were part of the same group. Occasionally this meant a significant amount of time away from their office. When the business of the Maidstone office was sold by the receivers these three were not transferred. All three had spent at least 80 per cent of their time on work connected with the Maidstone office. The EAT concluded that the whole of the Maidstone business had been transferred and the employees were, therefore, held to be protected by TUPE. The EAT did point out, however, that if they had been employed by Maidstone to solely or predominantly carry out the business of the group at other locations, then the result might have been different.

The cases under TUPE have not resulted in a single formulation of the *Botzen* test that can be used by employment tribunals or practitioners to decide when a person is assigned to an undertaking and when they are not. This is essentially a question of fact to be determined in each case and so far the EAT has taken the view that it can give only limited guidance because facts may vary markedly from case to case.

The EAT in the *Duncan Web Offset* case accepted that a number of indicators may well help future consideration by tribunals. These were:

- the amount of time spent on one part of the business or another;
- the amount of value given to each part by the employee;
- the terms of the contract of employment showing what the employee could be required to do; and
- how the cost to the employer of the employee's services had been allocated between the different parts of the business.

9.8.3   Who is employed at the time of the transfer?

The issue of whether it is possible to reorganise and reduce employment levels prior to a transfer are discussed below. The concern here is that it is those employed at the time of the transfer who are protected. It is only, according to Article 3(1) of the consolidated Directive, the obligations arising from a contract of employment on the date of the transfer that are transferred to the transferee. The same issues arise under regulation 5 of TUPE.

There is, therefore, an issue about whether it is possible to dismiss individuals before the date of the transfer and then argue that they were not protected because they were not employed on the date on which the transfer took place. The matter was settled by the House of Lords in *Litster* v. *Forth Dry Dock & Engineering Ltd* [1989] IRLR 161. In this case the old owners agreed with the prospective owners to dismiss the workforce one hour before the transfer took place, so that they were not employed at the time of the transfer. The Court found this argument unconvincing and relied upon the case of *Bork International A/S* v. *Foreningen af Arbejdsledere i Danmark* (C-101/87) [1988] ECR 3071 at the European Court of Justice. In that case the Court considered the closing and subsequent reopening of a factory. There was a gap of eight days between the closure and reopening. Despite this gap the Court concluded that the dismissals were still by reason of the transfer, with the result that their contracts of employment transferred to the new organisation. In *Litster* the House of Lords followed this approach and construed TUPE as applying:

> to a person employed immediately before the transfer or who would have been so employed if he had not been unfairly dismissed before the transfer for a reason connected with the transfer.

This purposive construction of the Directive and TUPE appeared to mean that any dismissals in connection with a transfer, which would be automatically unfair dismissals, would be effectively void if the result was to stop the contracts of employment transferring.

The question of the effectiveness of precontractual dismissals was considered again by the House of Lords in *Wilson* v. *St Helens Borough Council; British Fuels* v. *Baxendale* [1998] IRLR 706. The conclusion was that the concept of nullifying a dismissal that had already taken place was unknown in English law. The effect of TUPE was to ensure that certain obligations passed to the transferee. In the case of dismissal, this would mean that any claims for unfair dismissal or redundancy payments would transfer (see below).

9.8.4 Employees who choose not to transfer

In *Foreningen af Arbejdsledere i Danmark* v. *Daddy's Dance Hall* (C-324/86) [1988] ECR 739 the European Court of Justice concluded that the rights given by the Directive were a matter of public policy and not subject to the wishes of the parties concerned. The Court held that the workers did not have the option to waive the rights conferred on them by the Directive. In the later case of *Katsikas* v. *Konstantidis* (C-132/91) [1992] ECR I-6577, this decision was considerably weakened. The Court pointed out that in *Daddy's Dance Hall* there had been no intention to undermine 'the fundamental rights of the employee who must be free to choose his employer'. The case of *Katsikas* concerned the transfer of a restaurant with a cook who refused to work for the new employer. The transferor then dismissed the employee, allegedly at the request of the transferee. The Court concluded that an employee could object to being transferred and then it was up to the member states to decide the fate of the contract of employment in such a situation.

The matter was settled in the UK by an amendment to TUPE introduced by section 33(4) of the Trade Union Reform and Employment Rights Act 1993. This provided that the rules on transferring obligations arising out of the contract of employment do not transfer if the employee objects to becoming employed by the transferee. The effect of this, however, is to terminate the contract of employment with the transferor without it being regarded as a dismissal by the transferor. This means employees exercising the right to object will not be entitled to claim unfair dismissal or a redundancy payment when their employment ends (*Hay* v. *George Hanson (Building Contractors) Ltd* [1996] IRLR 427).

9.8.5 Legal summary

The following issues need to be considered in order to decide who receives protection from TUPE.

- Only those individuals who are employees with contracts of employment are eligible for protection. The new TUPE regulations, once implemented, are likely to mean that those on part-time, fixed-term and temporary contracts should be treated in the same way as full-time permanent employees.
- Factors that assist in deciding which employees are assigned are the amount of time spent on the part of the business transferred, the amount of value given to each part by the employee, the terms of the contract of employment showing what the employee could be required to do, and how the cost to the employer of the employee's services had been allocated between the different parts of the business.

- The purpose of the Directive is to transfer the existing employment relationship and contract of employment from the transferor to the transferee. If the individual is treated as an employee for employment protection purposes under national law, then that protection is extended to include TUPE. The government's ongoing examination of the area of employee rights and who should have those rights may therefore have a significant impact on the scope of protection under TUPE.
- It is only persons employed at the time of the transfer who are protected, but liability for pre-transfer dismissals by reason of the transfer are likely to pass to the transferee.
- The rules on transferring obligations arising out of the contract of employment do not transfer if the employee objects to becoming employed by the transferee. The effect of this, however, is to terminate the contract of employment with the transferor without it being regarded as a dismissal by the transferor.

9.8.6 Practical steps

The identification of the pool of transferring staff is a key stage of the outsourcing process. It has a direct impact on cost for both contractor and outsourcer. Early due diligence is essential if this issue is not to become contentious. The following issues should be considered.

- The parties should agree at the outset of the process (based on the legal principles set out above) a basis for identifying which employees are assigned to the undertaking and agreeing a list on that basis.
- The list should take account of potential recruitment and termination issues where service provision will not commence immediately on completion of the outsourcing agreement. This is common in IT outsourcings where there is often a need for an implementation period to test the systems before the operational commencement date.
- What action will be taken in the case of borderline employees who fall outside the pool of transferring employees and who will bear the costs associated with this category of employees? This should include, in the case of decisions to dismiss staff, whether this should take place prior to or following the transfer. The answer to this question is likely to be dependent upon which party is liable in the outsourcing contract for the termination costs and potential claims that may result.
- How will claims from those excluded from the pool of transferring staff (whether consciously or because they were not identified) be dealt with and who will bear the cost of any claims?
- How will self-employed staff be dealt with pre-transfer and who will bear the cost of any claims?
- Mechanisms should be agreed for the provision of information about which of the contractor's employees are assigned to the undertaking

during the term of the agreement. Alternatively, there should be a mechanism for agreeing which of the contractor's employees and workers are assigned to the services at the time when the outsourcing contract ends and another provider is appointed.

- The apportionment of liabilities on termination in respect of staff assigned to the undertaking needs to be decided. It may be wise to make a distinction between situations in which TUPE (or any similar successor legislation) applies and does not apply.

The practical effect of agreeing a list of employees and moving forward on this basis is that it will crystallise many of the primary issues in respect of who is an employee and who is assigned to the undertaking. Additionally, by requiring a defined number of identified staff to transfer, practical issues such as migration to a different payroll system, removal from benefits scheme, etc. become easier to manage.

While those in the list of transferring staff may not, in law, be the definitive legal transferring employees, the practical consequence of the list being inaccurate is generally a legal claim. The resulting costs need to be dealt with by way of indemnity or adjustments to pricing. Contractors should consider obtaining a warranty about the accuracy of the list of transferring staff to plug any potential holes in their due diligence.

Management of these issues on termination of the agreement is also important. Careful apportionment of liabilities may reduce the risk that a potential contractor will have to take on significant employee liabilities at the start of a second generation contract. A lack of clarity concerning the employment costs on termination of an outsourcing contract can act as a disincentive to potential bidders or may result in lengthy negotiations to work through the maze of potential liabilities. Issues on termination should therefore be provided for expressly in both first and second generation outsourcings agreements.

9.9   WHAT IS TRANSFERRED?

9.9.1   General liabilities

Regulation 5(1) of TUPE provides that a relevant transfer shall not operate so as to terminate the contract of employment of any person involved in the transfer. Regulation 5(2) then describes what is actually transferred. This includes all liabilities and responsibilities, arising from the contract of employment, existing at the time of the transfer. It is as if the contract of employment was originally made between the transferee and the employee and as if the transferor never existed.

A significant aspect of TUPE is that it has been established for some time that variations to the terms and conditions of transferring staff (whether before or after the transfer) introduced by reason of the transfer are void (*Foreningen Arbejdsledere I Danmark* v. *Daddy's Dance Hall* (C-324/86) [1988] ECR 739). This means that even where employees agree to changes in their terms and conditions it is arguable that they can be set aside at a later date as being attempts to contract out of the statutory novation of terms and conditions of employment that existed at the time of the transfer. This is one of the principal reasons why the nature of the obligations that transfer are so important as the contractor will have limited scope to make legally effective changes to the terms of employment of transferring staff. It should be noted that nothing in TUPE would prevent a contractor from changing terms of employment for a reason unconnected with the transfer.

One of the principal protections that TUPE offers to transferring employees is protection against unfair dismissal. The case of *Litster* established that where employees would otherwise have transferred but for their dismissal for a transfer-related reason, liability for the dismissal will transfer to the transferee. In the context of an outsourcing, this is an important point, on the basis that contractors frequently have their own ways and methods of working and it may be unclear as to what extent the existing staff have the requisite skills to satisfy the rigours of the service level agreement.

While there is some limited scope to dismiss staff prior to the transfer the law in the area is extremely complex. This issue is examined in more detail in the next section of this chapter, but it is important to note here the possibility of liability for an automatically unfair dismissal under TUPE to transfer from an outsourcer or first generation contractor to the incoming contractor. This often means that the contractor will be forced to accept employees whom it might otherwise have asked the outsourcer to dismiss.

In *Wilson* v. *West Cumbria Health Authority* [1995] PIQR P38, a county court considered the position of three porters who had been injured in accidents at work during 1992. Their contracts of employment were transferred from the West Cumbria Health Authority to the West Cumbria Healthcare NHS Trust. The porters claimed that their action in support of their claims also transferred. The new NHS Trust applied to strike out the claim, saying that its liabilities only arose from a breach of contract. The judge held that if the cause of action arose out of the contract of employment, then these claims were transferred. As a result, liability, whether in tort or contract, was transferred because of TUPE.

In *DJM International Ltd* v. *Nicholas* [1996] IRLR 76 the EAT held that liability for an act of alleged sexual discrimination transferred from the transferor to the transferee. It concluded, applying regulation 5(2)(*b*), that what was done to her by the transferor was deemed to have been done to her by the transferee, and that, therefore, the transferee would be liable if the claim were successful. The claimant had been dismissed on reaching the age of 60 years. She had subsequently been re-employed on a part-time basis. It was argued that the alleged act of discrimination had occurred during the first, full-time, contract and that it was the second, part-time, contract that existed at the time of the transfer and had been transferred. The EAT supported the view of the employment tribunal, which was that regulation 5(2)(*b*) applied not only to acts done in respect of a contract, but also to acts done in relation to a person employed in the undertaking at the time of the transfer. This has obviously been an issue of concern for employers, perhaps especially in relation to outsourcing when tenderers may take over contracts and discover previously unknown liabilities.

The general liability of transferees was limited in *Tsangacos* v. *Amalgamated Chemicals* [1997] IRLR 4, where an ex-employee of the transferor had a claim for unfair dismissal and unlawful discrimination against the transferor. The problem for the claimant was that the transferor went into liquidation some four months after his dismissal. The business was taken over by another undertaking and an attempt was made to transfer this claim. The EAT stressed that only liabilities related to those employed at the time of the transfer were transferred, unless they had been dismissed for reasons connected to the transfer. As this complainant was not employed at the time of the transfer and had not been dismissed by reason of the transfer, then liability did not transfer to the transferee. The alternative, as the EAT pointed out, was to consider claims arising out of events that took place years before the transfer as potential liabilities. This was not deemed to be a sensible approach.

9.9.2 Specific liabilities

Restrictive covenants

Restrictive covenants, incorporated into the contract of employment, can also be transferred. In *Morris Angel & Son* v. *Hollande* [1993] IRLR 169, a covenant not to do business with a company's clients for one year was considered. The clients concerned were those that had been dealt with in the previous 12 months. As a result of a transfer, the contract of employment, including the restrictive covenant, was deemed to have been concluded with the transferee. The restriction could, therefore, be enforced by the transferee. There was a limitation, however, in that the restriction could only apply to the transferor's clients, not those of the transferee.

The rule only applies to restrictive covenants existing at the time of the transfer. There have been situations where the potential transferee has persuaded employees of the transferor to sign agreements restricting their ability to work for competitors, in exchange for payment (see *Credit Suisse First Boston (Europe) Ltd* v. *Lister* [1998] IRLR 700 and *Credit Suisse First Boston (Europe) Ltd* v. *Padiachy* [1998] IRLR 504). These could not be relied upon using TUPE because the agreements were not part of their original contracts of employment with the transferor and constituted variations to their existing terms of employment, which were void under TUPE (see below).

Pensions

The right to continuing membership of an occupational pension scheme was excluded in the original Directive and it has been an issue of great concern to those involved in outsourcing, both employers and employees. Pensions matters are considered in Chapter 10.

Collective agreements

Regulation 6 of TUPE provides that where a collective agreement exists at the time of the transfer between the transferor and a trade union recognised for the purposes of representing individuals transferred, then that agreement is deemed to have been reached between the transferee and the trade union concerned.

It is possible for an employer to end, or lapse, a collective agreement after the transfer, assuming that it is not a legally enforceable agreement. Such a decision may be limited if the terms of the agreement have become incorporated into the individual contract of employment. If they are incorporated, then the terms of the collective agreement will transfer regardless of whether the trade union is recognised or not. Thus a unilateral repudiation of the collective agreement will not necessarily remove the terms of a collective agreement that has become part of the individual contract of employment.

The issue is illustrated in *Whent* v. *T. Cartledge* [1997] IRLR 153. This concerned the outsourcing of street-lighting services by the London Borough of Brent. The contractor took over the activity and then, 10 days later, wrote to the trade union and withdrew recognition. It also stated that any collective agreements transferred from Brent would no longer have effect. Prior to the transfer the contracts of employment of the employees expressly stated that their remuneration and other terms and conditions would be in accordance with the agreement. This was a collective agreement made between an employer's association and trade unions. The repudiation of this agreement was seen as a way of freezing the pay levels of the transferred employees. If the national agreement were to remain incorporated in the individual contracts, then the employees would be entitled to the annual pay increases negotiated by the national body. The EAT held that such incorporation could not be revoked by unilaterally ending a collective agreement.

Employers' liability compulsory insurance

One of the more surprising court decisions, concerning the transfer of liabilities, took place in *Bernadone* v. *Pall Mall Services Group* [2000] IRLR 487, CA. The Court of Appeal confirmed that in the event of a transfer of a liability claim to a transferee employer, the benefit of the transferor's liability insurance also transferred. The result is that a transferee employer can make a claim against a policy arranged between the transferor and their insurance company.[4] This windfall protection is certainly useful in the private sector but might have more limited application in the public sector. (Government departments and agencies often self-insure and it is unclear as to what extent a private sector contractor could call upon such insurance in the case of an employer's compulsory liability situation.)

Working conditions

Regulation 5(5) provides that TUPE does not prejudice an employee's ability to terminate the contract of employment without notice 'if a substantial change is made in his working conditions to his detriment'. An employee cannot, however, claim that the identity of the new employer is such a reason. If an employer has a reputation for low standards, for example, this will not be a sufficient reason for leaving and still claiming the protection of TUPE. It is also difficult for an employee to resign and claim constructive dismissal as a result of a deterioration in working conditions. There will still be a need to show that there has been a repudiatory breach of contract (see *Rossiter* v. *Pendragon plc* [2002] IRLR 483, CA).

Merckx and Neuhuys v. *Ford Motor Co Belgium SA* (C-171/94) [1996] ECR I-1253 concerned the transfer of a car dealership. The European Court of Justice held that:

> Article 4(2) provides that if the contract of employment or the employment relationship is terminated because the transfer within Article 1(1) involves a substantial change in the working conditions to the detriment of the employee, the employer is to be regarded as having been responsible for the termination.

The European Court of Justice described a change in the level of remuneration as a substantial change in working conditions, even where remuneration is linked to sales. In *Sita (GB) Ltd* v. *Burton* [1998] ICR 17 the European Court of Justice referred to other situations:

> We cannot exclude the case that in the context of transfers of undertakings the consequences of the proposed transfer, as known by the transferor, to his employees are so dire, whether in health and safety terms or otherwise, that the proposal on the part of the employer to go ahead with the transfer could so undermine the confidence relationship with his employees as to defeat it.

It does indicate that the potential changes that need to take place are likely to be significant and that the provisions may be treated quite narrowly.

The importance of regulation 5(5) is that where the employee employs its use effectively the claim for unfair dismissal will not transfer to the incoming contractor but will remain with the outsourcer or first generation contractor. This means that an outsourcer or first generation contractor who is being replaced will need to have careful regard to the proposals being put forward by the incoming contractor so that it can examine its exposure to claims of this type (see *University of Oxford* v. *Humphreys* [2000] IRLR 183, CA).

Share entitlements

The EAT has also concluded that regulation 5(2) need not be treated literally. In *Mitie Managed Services Ltd* v. *French* [2002] IRLR 512, for example, the issue was whether a profit share scheme transferred. The scheme included a share allocation to employees. The transferee employer was unable to make share allocations in the transferor employer's undertaking. In these circumstances what was required was an opportunity for the transferred employees to participate in a scheme of 'substantial equivalence'.

9.9.3 Statutory confirmation of term and conditions?

Article 3(2) of the amended Directive states that:

> Member States may adopt appropriate measures to ensure that the transferor notifies the transferee of all the rights and obligations which will be transferred to the transferee under this Article, so far as those rights and obligations are or ought to have been known to the transferor at the time of the transfer.

The problem for outsourced organisations is that the discovery of unknown liabilities related to transferred employees can seriously damage the profitability of a particular contract.

The government is likely to take advantage of this option and introduce a number of simple rules in the new TUPE regulations:

- first, the transferor in a prospective transfer is to be required to give the transferee written notification of all the rights and obligations in relation to employees to be transferred;
- second, if any of these rights and obligations change before the transfer, then there must be written notification of the changes;
- third, notification may be given in more than one instalment, but it must be given in good time before the transfer; and
- finally, if special circumstances make this not reasonably practicable, then it must be done as soon as is reasonably practicable, but no later than the completion of the transfer.

These measures will help enormously, although they still do seem to leave open potential loopholes. For example, will contractors be able to change their pricing if there are late notified changes to the employees' terms and conditions?

The favoured remedy for failure to notify is likely to be the ability of the transferee to make the transferor party to any proceedings and for the court to apportion liability between the transferor and the transferee on a just and equitable basis, having regard to the damage suffered by the employee and the relative contributions of the parties to that damage. This would enable the court to allocate, if it wished, 100 per cent liability to the transferor. The problem with this approach, as the consultation document accepted, is that it relies upon one or more employees making a complaint. There are anecdotal stories of employers, who have lost contracts, giving large pay rises to affected employees just prior to the date of the transfer. In such cases the employees are unlikely to make a complaint about their treatment, yet the transferee employer may be seriously damaged by such an action. There needs to be some provision whereby transferors can be made liable for payment of undisclosed liabilities, so that the transferee employer will be able to take some action against them. The consultation document suggests a defence for the transferor, namely that the rights and obligations in question were not ones that it knew about or should have known about at the time of the transfer. This defence would be unaffected by the proposal for transferor liability as suggested here.

9.9.4 Legal summary

The following issues need to be considered in deciding what is transferred by TUPE.

- Regulation 5(2) provides that all liabilities and responsibilities, arising from the contract of employment, existing at the time of the transfer are transferred. The contractor will assume responsibility for all debts related to the transferred contracts of employment as if the transferee had incurred them in the first place.
- The new TUPE regulations are likely to ensure that the contractor is notified of the contractual rights and obligations that will be transferred with the employees assigned to the undertaking.
- TUPE provides that where a collective agreement exists at the time of the transfer between the transferor and a trade union recognised for the purposes of representing individuals transferred, then that agreement is deemed to have been reached between the transferee and the trade union concerned.
- Regulation 5(5) provides that TUPE does not prejudice an employee's ability to terminate the contract of employment without notice 'if a substantial change is made in his working conditions to his detriment'.

9.9.5 Practical steps

The need for contractors to examine carefully the terms of employment and working practices of staff who may potentially transfer is going to be a significant part of its due diligence, in particular:

- The contractor will need to satisfy itself as to the transferring employees' terms and conditions; in particular, the issues arising out of existing pension arrangements, share option or share save entitlements, discretionary bonus arrangements, etc. While it is customary to obtain a warranty as to the accuracy of the due diligence materials provided as part of the outsourcing process, this merely gives the contractor an action in damages in the event that the warranty is breached. The same is likely to be true of any statutory obligation to identify the rights and obligations that will transfer. The contractor needs to be sure that it has covered all of the bases and where there are gaps should press the outsourcer for further information.
- The parties need to agree what indemnities will be given in relation to potential claims that flow from the contractor's proposals for the business going forward. In most cases, it is not possible for the contractor to replicate each of the benefits the transferring employees receive. There will inevitably be some variations and these have to be introduced with the minimum of disruption to service provision and in a way that limits legal risk. Consultation is likely to play a pivotal role in getting employee buy-in.
- There will need to be an apportionment of liabilities for pre-transfer and post-transfer matters. Given the liabilities that the incoming contractor will inherit, it is very likely that it will seek assurances that will not have to be financially responsible for the misdemeanours of the current employer of the transferring employees and the same will be true for the outsourcer or outgoing contractor in respect of the period after the transfer.
- It is advisable to make sure that in the run up to the termination of the outsourcing agreement, the outsourcer has an opportunity to restrict the ability of the incumbent contractor to make changes to employee terms and conditions as well as other aspects of the operation, e.g. dismiss or redeploy staff. This is an important aspect of arrangements that needs to be built in to deal with a change of contractor.

In short, the incoming contractor will wish to make sure of its access to all necessary documents to decide what its liabilities are (even with the comfort of a warranty as to its liabilities from the outsourcer) and the outsourcer will wish to make sure that in the run up to the change of any contractor it can ensure there is clarity and stability in relation to the terms on which the outgoing contractor has employed its staff.

9.10   REORGANISATIONS

There has been a lack of clarity concerning the ability of employers to engage in reorganisations of the workforce both prior to and subsequent to a transfer.

It is not always the case that an employer wishes to employ all the relevant staff of the transferor or bring employees into an organisation on terms and conditions that are out of step with its own workforce. There have been difficulties for employers in distinguishing actions that are related directly to the transfer and actions that merely take place at or near the time of the transfer.

9.10.1 Economic, technical or organisational reasons

Article 4(1) of the amended Directive states that:

> The transfer of an undertaking, business or part of the undertaking or business shall not in itself constitute grounds for dismissal by the transferor or the transferee. This provision shall not stand in the way of dismissals that may take place for economic, technical or organisational reasons entailing changes in the workforce.

The words 'economic, technical or organisational reasons entailing changes in the workforce' are repeated verbatim in regulation 8 of TUPE. There is no clear definition or guide as to the meaning of this phrase.

The case of *Berriman* v. *Delabole Slate Ltd* [1985] ICR 546 concerned a quarryman in Cornwall working in a quarry that was transferred to a new employer. He was offered continuing employment at a reduced rate of pay, in order to bring his earnings into line with other employees. The Court of Appeal subsequently held that standardisation of pay rates was not an economic, technical or organisational (ETO) reason entailing changes in the workforce. The objective needed to be to achieve changes in the workforce, rather than merely the standardisation of pay. There was further clarification in *Wheeler* v. *Patel* [1987] ICR 631. Mrs Wheeler was dismissed by the transferor and not employed by the transferee. The dismissal was held to have taken place in order to achieve a better price for the business being sold. It was claimed therefore that there was an economic reason for the change. The EAT did not accept this because it held that the terms economic, technical or organisational should be considered together, rather than being able to take one out and using that as justification. A more relaxed approach was taken in *Trafford* v. *Sharpe and Fisher* [1994] IRLR 325, where an individual was dismissed because the new employer wished to reduce numbers. The dismissal was held to be an economic reason entailing changes in the workforce. The EAT stated that the

> Rights of workers not to be dismissed on the transfer of an undertaking must not stand in the way of dismissals which take place for economic reasons entailing changes in the workforce. In such cases the rights of workers may be outweighed by the economic reasons.

The EAT has further held that, when looking at the reasons for the dismissals, one needed to look at them at the time they took place (see *BSG Property Services* v. *Tuck* [1996] IRLR 134). There may be a subsequent reorganisation, but at the time of the dismissals, the question was whether the dismissal was related to the transfer itself.

In *Whitehouse* v. *Charles A Blatchford & Sons Ltd* [1999] IRLR 492 the EAT again considered the meaning of economic, technical or organisational and concluded that the reason must be connected with the future conduct of the business as a going concern. In this case a contractor was obliged by the customer, when tendering for a contract, to reduce the number of technicians working on the contract from 13 to 12. This was held to be for an ETO reason as it was concerned with future conduct. The transfer was merely the occasion of the dismissal and not the reason for it (see also *Thompson* v. *SCS Consulting Ltd* [2001] IRLR 801).

9.10.2   Variations in contracts of employment

The ability to vary contracts of employment, even with the consent of the employees, was considered by the House of Lords in the joined cases of *Wilson* v. *St Helens Borough Council* and *British Fuels Ltd* v. *Baxendale* [1998] IRLR 706. The first case concerned the transfer of a community home from Lancashire County Council to St Helens Borough Council. The county council had decided that it could no longer afford to run the home and, as a result, gave the trustees of the home two years' notice that it would cease to be involved. St Helens agreed to take it over, but only after substantial reorganisation. The result was a reduction in the size of the home and the number of staff needed to run it. Negotiations took place with the trade union concerned and staffing levels were reduced from 162 to 72. In addition, some of the 72 who transferred did so on reduced terms and conditions. All were dismissed for reasons of redundancy by the county council prior to the move. Subsequently the employees claimed that TUPE applied and that they should have been transferred on the same terms and conditions that they enjoyed when employed by Lancashire County Council.

The House of Lords concluded that 'the transfer of the undertaking did not constitute the reason for the variation'. The transfer itself was not the reason for the variation, although deciding when a variation in terms is as a result of a transfer and when it is not seems a difficult question. Lord Slynn, in delivering judgment, stated that:

> It may be difficult to decide whether the variation is due to the transfer or attributable to some separate cause. If, however, the variation is not due to the transfer itself it can in my opinion, on the basis of the authorities to which I have referred, validly be made.

In the *British Fuels* case, an existing subsidiary company was merged with a newly acquired organisation. The employees concerned were dismissed because of redundancy by the old company and taken on by the newly set up business. They were offered a new contract of employment, which was accepted. The problem for the new enterprise was that the terms and conditions of the two sets of employees were different and the new employer wished to rationalise them. The employees subsequently claimed that their terms and conditions should have been protected. The House of Lords held that their original dismissals had been effective and could not be regarded as a nullity.

It is possible, therefore, to reorganise provided that the reason for the dismissal or variation is not connected with the transfer. It is not always easy to separate the reasons for the dismissals in order to show that they were for another reason. The dismissals themselves are, however, effective, although the employees might have a claim for unfair dismissal. In *Warner* v. *Adnet Ltd* [1998] IRLR 394 the appointment of joint receivers resulted in the dismissal of all the employees. After the transfer they were all re-employed with the exception of four people. Previously there had been a report advising that four people be made redundant. The EAT held that TUPE regulation 8(1) and 8(2) (dismissals because of a transfer and ETO reasons) should be considered as a whole, not exclusively from each other. If there are ETO reasons then these might disapply reasons connected with the transfer. The real reasons may be a combination of transfer-related and ETO reasons, which are difficult to separate.

The government has proposed changes to TUPE that would make clear some of the circumstances in which employers could legitimately amend terms and conditions of employment without falling foul of the regulations. It proposes that it would be permissible for there to be changes in terms and conditions where it could be shown that these were for a reason unconnected with the transfer or where connected they were for an economic, technical or organisational reason entailing a change in the workforce.

Looking at this suggestion in the round, it falls short of the mark for a number of reasons. First and foremost there is a lack of clarity about what constitutes an economic, technical or organisational reason entailing a change in the workforce. Second, for the most part, the need to change terms and conditions will not necessarily result in a change in the workforce. There could be an economic-based reason (e.g. a change in shift patterns), which could have a great impact on service delivery but would not mean a change in the number of employees or the type of work carried out by the workforce.

9.10.3 Post-transfer reorganisations

It is not clear whether there is a limit to the length of time that TUPE is applicable after a transfer. Presumably, it will be more difficult to show that dismissals and changes to terms and conditions are as a result of a transfer the further one gets away from the transfer date. The Acquired Rights Directive does provide, in Article 3(3), that member states may limit the period for observing terms in transferred collective agreements to one year. There are, however, no such limitations in TUPE.

It is, of course, possible to reorganise a workforce after a transfer, provided that it is for an ETO reason entailing a change in the workforce. In *Crawford* v. *Swinton Insurance Brokers* [1990] IRLR 42 the EAT held that what had to be looked at, when considering whether there were such reasons entailing a change in the workforce, was:

> Is the workforce as an entity, that is to say, as a whole, separate from the individuals who make it up. It then has to be seen whether the reason in question is one that involves a change in the workforce, strength or establishment.

This can include changing the contents of jobs, or occupations, as happened in this case.

9.10.4 Legal summary

- It is possible to dismiss employees for economic, technical or organisational reasons entailing a change in the workforce. This needs to be connected with the future conduct of the business as a going concern.
- It may be difficult to decide whether a variation of a contract of employment is due to the transfer or attributable to some separate cause. It is important to ensure that any variation is not attributable to the transfer unless it is for an ETO reason.
- Post-transfer reorganisations may not be related to the transfer, unless for an ETO reason.

9.10.5 Practical steps

The issues of dismissals and pre-transfer and post-transfer reorganisations are difficult to navigate from a legal perspective because of the lack of certainty. What the parties must aim to achieve, therefore, is a measure of certainty in the way in which they deal with these issues as part of the outsourcing agreement. Clearly any fundamental proposals to reorganise service delivery must be fed through to the outsourcer and into the information and consultation process that will be conducted in respect of staff who are affected by the transfer.

Where there needs to be a significant change in the terms and conditions of employment the possibility of dismissing employees and re-engaging them on new terms and conditions may have to be considered. However, it is very likely that these terminations will result in automatically unfair dismissals that will involve significant risk to the parties. The pragmatic option may be to pursue a negotiated change in terms through the consultation process. Although, depending on the reason for the change, it may not be effective in law, the employees may be less likely to challenge the variations where they have been involved in negotiating them.

It may be sensible to consider whether the outsourcer or incumbent contractor should dismiss pre-transfer staff who will be redundant following the transfer. These terminations may be managed more effectively by their existing employers with whom the employees are familiar and in whom they are likely to place greater trust. That having been said, this may be something that an outsourcer or incumbent contractor may be reluctant to do (even with the benefit of indemnities) preferring instead to leave that logistical headache to the incoming contractor.

9.11 CONSULTATION

Regulation 10 is concerned with the duty to inform and consult employee representatives and regulation 11 with the consequences of failing to do so. The requirements are that the appropriate representatives of all employees must be informed of:

- the fact that a relevant transfer is to take place;
- when the transfer is to take place;
- the reasons for the transfer;
- the legal, economic and social implications of the transfer for affected employees; and
- the measures that the employer envisages will be taken, in connection with the transfer, in relation to the affected employees or the fact that there are no new measures envisaged.

The information and consultation requirements apply to the affected employees of the transferor and the transferee. There is an obligation upon the transferor to inform affected employees of the measures that the transferee envisages will be taken in relation to those employees. There is also an obligation upon the transferee to provide the transferor with such information as they will need to carry out this duty. This information is to be given long enough before a relevant transfer in order to provide opportunities for consultation. If measures are envisaged, then the employer must consult the appropriate representatives of the affected employees with a view to seeking agreement to the measures to be taken. The employer is required to consider the representations made by the employee representatives and reply to them. If the employer does not accept the representations, then reasons must be given.

9.11.1 Appropriate representatives

The Collective Redundancy and Transfers of Undertakings (Protection of Employment) (Amendment) Regulations 1999, SI 1999/1925 introduced further rules concerning the election of employee representatives. The employer is given the responsibility for ensuring that the arrangements for the election are fair and for determining the number of representatives to be elected as well as their term of office. There are also requirements that candidates for election should be affected employees at the date of the election and that all affected employees may vote, having as many votes as there are representatives to be elected. If there are subsequent doubts as to whether the employee representatives were appropriate representatives for the purposes of the consultation, then the onus is on the employer to show that they had the necessary authority to represent the affected employees. Employees participating in the elections have the right not to suffer detriment or dismissal as a result of their participation. Elected employee representatives have the right to time off for carrying out their functions and to receive training.

9.11.2 When should consultation begin?

The obligation in TUPE is to begin the process long enough before a relevant transfer to enable consultation to take place. The High Court in *Institution of Professional Civil Servants* v. *Secretary of State for Defence* [1987] IRLR 373 held that these words meant as soon as the measures are envisaged and, if possible, long enough before the transfer. The case concerned the introduction of private management into the Royal Dockyards at Rosyth and Devonport, to which the trades unions were opposed. Before consultation could take place there needed to be some definite plans or proposals around which discussions could take place. There was a failure of consultation in this case because, according to the Court, the unions were so opposed to the introduction of commercial management into the dockyards that they failed to take the opportunities to negotiate. The Court commented that 'effective consultations cannot take place with those who do not wish to be consulted . . .'.

In *South Durham Health Authority* v. *UNISON* [1995] IRLR 407, the Health Authority started the process on 7 February, when it wrote to the trade union informing it of a transfer to trust status on the following 1 April. On 27 February the union replied, asking for more information and complaining that not enough time had been allowed to comply with TUPE. The employer replied on 11 March and suggested a meeting in the near future. The trade union presented an application to an employment tribunal on 16 March, that is, two weeks before the transfer date, complaining of a breach of (then) regulation 10. Regulation 11 provided that complaints must be made within three months of the date of the relevant transfer, or on another date if the tribunal agreed that this was not practicable. The Health Authority objected, but the EAT held that TUPE specified an end date for complaints, not a commencement date. This was also the case in *BIFU* v. *Barclays Bank* [1987] ICR 495, where the Court held that the transfer was not an essential element before a complaint could be made about the lack of consultation. It is, therefore, possible to complain about lack of consultation prior to a transfer.

The TUPE regulations provide a special circumstances defence for a failure to consult. Provided that an employer has taken all the steps that are reasonably practicable in the circumstances, then the employer may be able to claim that these special circumstances rendered consultation impossible. The courts have traditionally construed this exception, albeit in relation to other matters, very narrowly, for example in *Clarks of Hove* v. *Bakers Union* [1978] IRLR 366, a case concerning consultation in a redundancy situation, insolvency was held not to be a special circumstance. To be special, the circumstance is likely to be something that is quite unexpected.

A complaint may be made to an employment tribunal concerning the failure to consult. The tribunal will make a declaration and, if there has been a failure, award compensation to each of the affected employees, not exceeding 13 weeks' pay. One interesting aspect of awarding compensation for the failure to consult was whether the liability, for failing to consult, transferred to the transferee along with the contracts of employment. In *Alamo Group (Europe) Ltd* v. *Tucker* [2003] IRLR 266 the transferor failed to inform or consult the affected employees prior to a transfer. The EAT held, in this case, that the right to be informed and consulted arose out of the employment relationship and the subsequent obligation upon the employer therefore transferred with the employment relationship. Thus the transferee became liable for the transferor's failure to consult. This was in contrast to a previous EAT decision in *TGWU* v. *McKinnon* [2001] IRLR 597 where the EAT had held that the liability for failure to consult remained with the transferor.

9.11.3 Consultation about collective redundancies

Council Directive 98/59/EC on the approximation of the laws of the member states relating to collective redundancies is a consolidation directive. It consolidates Directive 75/129/EEC as amended by Directive 92/56/EEC on the same subject. The provisions are now contained in Part IV Chapter II of the Trade Union and Labour Relations Act 1992, which outlines the procedure for handling collective redundancies. The duty to consult rests upon an employer who is proposing to dismiss 20 or more employees at one establishment within a period of 90 days or less for reasons of redundancy. This consultation shall begin in good time and in any event at least 30 days before the first dismissal takes effect, or at least 90 days before the first dismissal takes effect if the employer is proposing to dismiss 100 or more employees at one establishment within a period of 90 days.

A debatable issue here, of course, is at what point in time the employer is proposing to dismiss. It is likely that, except perhaps in a disaster situation, there is a period of time over which the decision to dismiss employees by reason of redundancy is reached. There is, perhaps, first the decision in principle to dismiss employees. There may be a second stage where the parts of the organisation in which the redundancies are to take place are identified, followed by a further stage when particular employees are identified.

This issue was considered in *Hough* v. *Leyland DAF Ltd* [1991] IRLR 194.

This case concerned security staff at a number of the employer's premises. The security manager was asked to prepare a report on the possibility of contracting out the security function. The manager produced a report recommending that it should be contracted out. It was a further six months before the employer approached the trade union informing it of the employer's intention to contract out security services. The issue was at what stage the employers could be said to have been proposing to dismiss. The EAT held that this occurred at the time of the security manager making his report recommending the contracting out. The EAT then went on to state that it would not be more helpful to seek a more precise definition because of the large variety of situations that might arise. The correct point is when the employer has proposals to make, rather than when the employer is merely contemplating them as required by Article 2(1) of the Collective Redundancies Directive; see *MSF* v. *Refuge Assurance plc* [2002] IRLR 324.

Again, financial penalties exist for a failure to consult in respect of collective redundancies, which can result in deductions and an award of up to 90 days' pay for each affected employee.

9.11.4 Legal summary

- Information needs to be provided and consultation needs to take place, in transfer situations, about the fact that a relevant transfer is to take place, when the transfer is to take place, the reasons for the transfer, the legal, economic and social implications of the transfer for affected employees, and the measures the employer envisages will be taken, in connection with the transfer, in relation to the affected employees or the fact that there are no new measures envisaged.
- The obligation in TUPE is to begin the process long enough before a relevant transfer to enable consultation to take place. The High Court has held that these words mean as soon as the measures are envisaged and, if possible, long enough before the transfer.
- TUPE provides a special circumstances defence for a failure to consult. Providing that an employer has taken all the steps that are reasonably practicable in the circumstances, then the employer may be able to claim that these special circumstances rendered consultation impossible; these situations are likely to be very few and far between in outsourcing situations.
- Collective redundancy situations have rules requiring collective consultation at a point when the employer has proposals to make.

9.11.5 Practical steps

The obligations imposed by TUPE mean that an early discussion between the parties is required in order to establish the requirements to inform and, where necessary, consult with affected employees. The requirement is likely to be triggered when there is a firm proposal to outsource. It may not be possible to inform and consult in detail until the outsourcer has narrowed the potential field of contractors. It should be noted in public sector outsourcing that there is an expectation that any recognised trade union be provided with information as to the proposals made by potential contractors and asked for its input.

The outsourcer or incumbent contractor will need to give consideration to more than just the transferring employees. Outsourcings normally involve the hiving off of a particular part of the business. This will leave a part that must be managed by the remaining members of staff. This may involve changes to their terms and conditions of employment, including their patterns of working, the scope of their duties and the location from where they carry out those duties. These employees are therefore affected by the transfer and will require information about the fact that it is taking place and may also need to be consulted about the fact that their duties will change.

Consultation is a vital part of 'selling' the new employer to the transferring staff. Whether the organisations involved are large or small there needs to be a carefully organised and managed programme of information and consultation. This can include general information in the form of Q&As, consultation clinics, where employees can raise any concerns they have in person, and consultation meetings between the outsourcer, the incumbent contractor (if any) and the incoming contractor.

The outsourcer should also ensure that it has enough of a stick to compel the contractor to provide the necessary detail concerning its proposals for the business so that information about this can be given to the employees. This in practice is normally a straightforward process on the basis that the incoming contractor will need to work with the outsourcer going forward and that the terms on which it is to provide the service will be clarified as part of the outsourcing agreement generally.

A timetable for consultation should be drawn up and this should be part of any implementation plan that the parties sign up to in the lead up to the operational commencement date of the services. The outsourcing contract will need to apportion the liability by way of indemnity between the various parties concerning any failure to carry out their respective duties under TUPE.

9.12   THE PUBLIC SECTOR

Article 1.1(c) of the amended Directive includes public or private undertakings engaged in economic activities within its scope, but excludes administrative reorganisations of public administrative authorities or the transfer of administrative functions between such authorities. This is a continuation of the approach of the original Directive, and the fact that such transfers are capable of being outside the scope of the Directive was confirmed by the European Court of Justice in *Henke* v. *Gemeinde Schierke* (C-298/94) [1996] IRLR 701.

The government had clearly concluded that there was the potential for future problems. It has decided that employees in public sector organisations should be treated no less favourably than those in private sector organisations when they are part of an organised grouping of resources that is transferred between employers. The chosen methods of implementing this policy are to be the application of the Statement of Practice on *Staff Transfers in the Public Sector*.[5] This was issued by the Cabinet Office in January 2000 and is the current practice in the public sector.

The Statement of Practice is inextricably linked to government policies on public/private partnerships. The guiding principles to government policy, contained in the Statement, are, first, that the public sector should be a 'good employer and a model contractor and client'; second, that the approach to the provision of services is to be a pragmatic one, which can involve some services and functions being provided by the private sector; and, third, that there should be 'clarity and certainty about the treatment of staff'. There are a number of outcomes resulting from these principles. These are:

- that all contracting out exercises with the private and voluntary sector and all transfers between different parts of the public sector will be treated as if TUPE applies, unless there are exceptional reasons for not doing so;
- second generation transfers, i.e. when there is a change of contractor dealing with an outsourced public service and transfers back into the public sector are to be treated as being covered by TUPE; and
- there should be appropriate arrangements for the protection of occupational pensions, redundancy and severance payments to staff affected by these situations.

The Statement of Practice represents a willingness to apply TUPE generally throughout the public sector with the result that it will still be applied even if there is no change of employer, such as transfers of functions within the civil service.

NOTES

1. Cabinet Office (1998) *Better Quality Services*, Stationery Office Books.
2. The Business Services Association was an active participant in the informal preconsultation process that preceded the publication of the formal consultation document.

3. First discussed in Malcolm Sargeant, 'Transfers and Outsourcing' (2000) CLLR 282.
4. See Malcolm Sargeant 'Transferring liability for employee claims', *Journal of Business Law* (March 2000) 188–92.
5. See www.cabinet-office.gov.uk/civilservice/2000/tupe/stafftransfers.pdf.

CHAPTER 10

Pension considerations

Mark Catchpole

10.1 INTRODUCTION

Most outsourcing transactions will involve a transfer of employees from one entity to another. The employment law implications of such a transfer have been considered in Chapter 9. Although related to the general employment law position, the structure of occupational pension schemes, their unsettled relationship with the contract of employment and the exemption applicable to occupational pensions under TUPE means that they require separate consideration.

Most employees of medium to large employers (i.e. the type of employers who would usually consider outsourcing functions currently undertaken in house) will have access to a pension scheme as part of the benefit package offered by such employers to their employees. The type of pension arrangement in which the outsourced employee participates will affect how pensions are dealt with in the outsourcing process. Therefore, this chapter will start with a brief introduction to the structure of pension provision in the UK and the different types of occupational pension scheme provided by employers.

On a transfer of employees from one employer to another there will usually be a need to consider the impact of the transfer on those transferring employees' pension benefits. The key considerations will usually involve:

- the types of pension arrangement currently provided by transferor and transferee;
- the level of coverage to be sought or provided by warranty;
- the continued participation of the transferring employees in the transferor's scheme for a limited period;
- the basis on which benefits accrued for past service are to be transferred; and
- the level of the benefits to be offered by the transferee employer.

A further consideration for those involved in public sector outsourcing is the Treasury's guidance and, where relevant, admission of the transferee employer as an admitted body (i.e. participating employer) in the Local Government Pension Scheme (LGPS).

10.2   SOURCES OF PENSION PROVISION

The system of pension provision in the United Kingdom is a mixture of state and private provision.

The first tier of state provision is the basic state pension. All employees and the self-employed (except those earning below the lower earnings limit) pay compulsory National Insurance Contributions, which entitle them to the basic state pension. The Minimum Income Guarantee was introduced with effect from April 1999. It is not a replacement of the state basic pension but provides, through income support, a minimum pension to those who are not entitled to receive the basic pension.

Currently the second tier of state provision (up to April 2002) is the State Earnings-Related Pension Scheme (SERPS). SERPS is payable to employees (not the self-employed) provided sufficient National Insurance Contributions have been paid during a person's working life. Employees may contract out of SERPS and make alternative provision through a private scheme and the employee will, as a result, pay reduced rate National Insurance Contributions. In a two-stage process commencing in April 2002, SERPS is being replaced by the State Second Pension (S2P). S2P will provide defined pension benefits using accrual rates that will be dependent upon the band within which a person's earnings fall during their working life. The system is designed to favour those on lower earnings and, from 2007, it is intended that the benefit will cease to be earnings related for those earning below a certain level.

Private pensions, sometimes referred to as the third tier of pension provision, are provided through occupational and personal pension schemes. These schemes can take various forms:

- contracted in or contracted out defined benefit occupational pension schemes;
- contracted in or contracted out defined contribution occupational schemes;
- individual personal pension schemes;
- stakeholder pension schemes;
- grouped personal pension schemes.

There are also subcategories of the above, such as free-standing additional voluntary contribution schemes, self-invested personal pension schemes and small self-administered pension schemes.

All these arrangements will usually comply with the requirements laid down in legislation and applied by the Inland Revenue so that they qualify for tax relief. There is a separate tax regime for occupational schemes and personal pension schemes although a unified tax regime for defined contribution schemes was introduced with effect from 6 April 2001 and applies to those occupational schemes that opt to have the new regime apply. Generally, the tax regime that applies to occupational pension schemes is the same whether the scheme provides final salary or money purchase benefits.

10.3   DEFINED BENEFIT AND DEFINED CONTRIBUTION SCHEMES

As far as occupational pension schemes are concerned, there are two basic types:

- defined benefit (also referred to as final salary; these include career average schemes) pension schemes;
- defined contribution (also referred to as money purchase) pension schemes.

A defined benefit scheme provides a benefit that is specified in advance. The benefit will usually be determined by reference to the number of years an employee has been a member of the pension scheme and that employee's salary at the date of retirement or, if earlier, leaving the scheme. The benefit is commonly expressed as a rate of accrual: for example, if a member had 20 years of pensionable service (i.e. 20 years' full membership of the pension scheme) and his final pensionable salary (i.e. the rate of salary at retirement or, quite commonly, the average of the best three years' salary ending in the 10 years prior to retirement) is £30,000 and the accrual rate is 1/60th of final pensionable salary for each year of pensionable service, the member would be entitled at normal retirement age to a pension of 20/60ths (one-third) of final pensionable salary, i.e. £10,000. To complicate matters, members will usually be able to convert some of their pension to a lump sum on retirement. This is usually referred to as commutation and the option to commute will normally be taken to the full extent possible because the lump sum is not subject to tax but the pension payable is taxed at the recipient's marginal rate.

In contrast, under a defined contribution scheme there is no fixed level of benefit promised. The obligation on the employer is to pay a rate of contribution to the scheme. The rate of contribution is usually expressed as a percentage of salary. Many such schemes will require a minimum employee contribution before the employer is under any obligation to contribute. Some schemes have different categories of membership so that the employer contribution varies, subject to a ceiling, depending on the level of the rate of employee contribution. The number of schemes requiring no contribution at all from employees is decreasing. At retirement, a member of a defined contribution scheme receives a pension that is determined by what the accumulated contributions to the scheme can purchase by way of annuity, hence they are often referred to as money purchase schemes.

Under a defined contribution scheme there is no minimum level of benefit: the level of pension is subject to the vagaries of the stock market over the member's membership of the scheme and the state of the annuity market when a benefit becomes payable. The position has been improved by the ability to defer the buying of annuities and limited draw-down facility on any accumulated fund during deferment. The appeal to employers is that, in contrast to funding a defined benefit scheme (see below), the employer's obligation is limited to paying the contribution rate agreed. The appeal to members is that in theory defined contribution benefits are easier to transfer on a change of employer, because one transfers the member's account or money purchase pot. Defined contribution is also a much easier concept to convey than the accrual rates associated with defined benefit schemes. The downside for the member is, of course, that the level of the benefit that is to be paid cannot be ascertained with any certainty.

10.4 DEFINED BENEFIT SCHEMES AND FUNDING

In a defined benefit scheme there is not usually an identifiable part of the fund that is associated with a particular member. The member's entitlement is to a level of benefit. The ultimate responsibility for ensuring that there is enough money in the scheme to pay that benefit lies with the employer. While it is usual for the member to have a fixed proportion of salary deducted from pay and paid to the scheme, the employer's funding obligation is determined by reference to triennial actuarial valuations of the scheme. At these valuations the scheme actuary will assess the liabilities under the scheme and compare them with the assets of the scheme. In doing this, the actuary makes certain assumptions about such variables as future salary increases and investment returns. The actuary will also make assumptions about the future membership of the scheme and, as a consequence, the amount of contributions that will be paid into the scheme. If the assets exceed the liabilities on the basis of these assumptions, then the scheme is said to be in surplus. It follows that if the liabilities exceed the assets, then the scheme will be considered to be in deficit. It should be stressed that these deficits or surpluses are actuarial and are founded on the basis that the assumptions the actuary makes in valuation are borne out in practice. In the valuation, the actuary will recommend to the trustees the rate at which the employer should contribute until the next valuation is due.

If the scheme is in surplus, the actuary may recommend that the existing rate of employer contributions may be reduced or suspended (i.e. a contribution holiday).

10.5 THE REGULATORY STRUCTURE OF PENSIONS

Inland Revenue exempt approved pension schemes remain, for the moment at least, the most tax efficient form of saving available in the UK and the

Inland Revenue is concerned to ensure that these valuable tax breaks are not abused. As a consequence, there has, over the years, developed a large and complex body of Inland Revenue guidance that relates to exempt approved occupational pension schemes. Indeed, depending on when a member joined a scheme or when the scheme was established there are three main distinct sets of Inland Revenue limits that place a ceiling on the maximum benefit that may be obtained under an exempt approved scheme. However, these rules are currently under review and are due to be simplified in the next 12 months. In addition to the tax rules, there are regulations that govern the minimum level of benefits that may be obtained if a member leaves a scheme prior to retirement, often referred to as the preservation regulations.

A further layer of complexity is added when a scheme contracts out of SERPS, which is currently overseen by the Inland Revenue National Insurance Contributions Office. Again, with a new system of contracting out applicable from April 1997, there are now two systems of contracting out, which is further complicated by the various combinations that can arise in respect of a member with pre-April 1997 contracted out rights, especially where they are transferred to a scheme contracted out on the post-April 1997 basis.

The statute book also contains a vast raft of regulation that is Robert Maxwell's bequest to the pensions industry, such as: member nominated trustees; minimum funding requirements; statements of investment principles; debt on the employer regulations; internal dispute resolution processes. These requirements are regulated by another regulatory body: the Occupational Pensions Regulatory Authority (OPRA). There is also now a cheap and cheerful alternative to the Chancery Division of the High Court if a member is not entirely happy about how a scheme is operated: the Pensions Ombudsman. It is this panoply of regulation that makes pensions the complex area that it has become.

10.6 THE LEGAL STRUCTURE OF PENSION SCHEMES

It is a requirement of Inland Revenue exempt approved occupational pension schemes that they are set up under irrevocable trust. A scheme will have trustees who are responsible for the administration of the trust and the investment of the trust fund. Some schemes provide benefits in respect of employment with one employer and other schemes provide benefits for more than one employer. In the latter category there are two different types of arrangements: group schemes and industry-wide schemes. Group schemes allow for the participation of more than one employer within the same group of companies. An industry-wide scheme allows participation by employers that are not associated but may be involved in a similar industry or occupation. In industry-wide schemes there are normally subsections in the scheme in respect of each employer that participates in the scheme.

There are a number of legal relationships between those involved in a typical occupational pension scheme. There are essentially three parties: employer, trustees and beneficiary. In terms of trust law, the employer is the settlor of the trust, the trustees the administrators of the trust and the beneficiaries are the objects of the trust. The trustees will owe the beneficiaries a fiduciary duty to administer the trust in the best interests of all the beneficiaries. Contractually, there will be, or in the past there will have been, a contract of employment between the member and the settlor or participating employer. In addition, the employer will owe a duty of mutual trust and confidence (sometimes referred to as a duty of good faith) in relation to the exercise of any of its powers under the scheme, for example, the power of appointing or removing trustees.

10.7 PENSIONS AND CONTRACTS OF EMPLOYMENT

The question of whether pension benefits are contractual or not is relevant because it will affect whether the transferee employer has an obligation to continue to provide the benefit (see section 10.8 on pensions and TUPE).

One would have thought that there should be a reasonably straight answer to the rather central question: do an employee's pension benefits form part of the terms and conditions of employment? However, rather than a 'yes' or 'no' answer the best response to the question is, 'it depends'. The nature of the relationship between pensions law and employment law would probably provide sufficient material for a chapter in itself; however, there is space just to deal with some general points.

In some cases, and this is not the norm, a contract will provide that an employee is entitled to a particular level of benefit at retirement. If so, the employee can with some confidence claim a contractual entitlement to that level of benefit. Therefore, if for some reason the pension arrangement in which the employee participated failed to provide the promised level of benefit, the employee could enforce the benefit promise against the employer. In such cases, the pension benefit is clearly contractual. Indeed, where there is no separate scheme or arrangement to provide the promised benefit, the Inland Revenue takes the view that the promise itself constitutes a pension scheme. Whether that promise is funded or not will affect its tax treatment.

Although pension benefits are not usually an express contractual obligation, the position is changing. With the move from defined benefit pension arrangements to defined contribution pensions, employers increasingly do not provide pension benefits under occupational pension schemes but merely provide a promise to pay a stated level of contribution to a personal pension scheme, usually established on a grouped basis. If employers do provide an occupational pension scheme but on a defined contribution basis, the level of the employer's contribution obligation may well be contractual.

Traditionally, the approach has been to provide in contracts of employment that employees are eligible to participate in a specified scheme subject to its governing provisions. Those governing provisions will usually reserve to the employer and/or the trustees of the scheme a power to amend or wind up the scheme. Therefore, an employee who is eligible to join such an arrangement has no guarantee of being able to continue to participate in the scheme throughout the employment either at all, or on a particular level of benefit. It is on this basis that many employers are either amending the basis on which employees accrue benefits in the future or winding up such schemes completely.

While it may be possible to reduce or discontinue pension benefits for future service without the consent of the employee it is not possible to amend their terms and conditions of employment without employee consent. However, the distinction has become blurred as a result of the treatment of occupational pension schemes by the European Court of Justice. The Court has described the benefits provided by such schemes as deferred pay (*Barber* v. *Guardian Royal Exchange Assurance Society* (C-262/88) [1990] ECRI-1889) and has placed an obligation on the trustees of such schemes (*Re Coloroll Pension Trustees* v. *Russell* [1994] ECRI-4389) to comply with the requirements of EU law requiring male and female employees to receive equal pay for work of equal value.

As well as supporting a distinct treatment of pensions, the question of whether a pension benefit is provided by an occupational scheme or a personal scheme or whether the pension promise is contractual or not is important in the application of TUPE to pensions. Chapter 9 deals extensively with TUPE and the importance of TUPE to outsourcing transactions. TUPE is also an important factor in how one should deal with pension benefits on an outsourcing.

10.8 PENSIONS AND TUPE

Broadly, TUPE provides that where an employee transfers to another employer as part of an undertaking the terms and conditions of employment also transfer. As a result, the transferee employer has an obligation to provide at least the same the terms and conditions following the transfer. There is however an exemption in relation to the benefits provided under an occupational pension scheme.

It is worth setting out in full the key regulation (regulation 5) and the occupational pension schemes exemption in regulation 7 of TUPE:

5. Effect of relevant transfer on contracts of employment

    (1)   . . . a relevant transfer shall not operate so as to terminate the contract of employment of any person employed by the transferor in the undertaking or part transferred but any such contract which would oth-

316

erwise have been terminated by the transfer shall have effect after the transfer as if originally made between the person so employed and the transferee.

(2) Without prejudice to paragraph (1) above . . . on completion of a relevant transfer:

All the transferor's rights, powers, duties and liabilities under or in connection with such a contract shall be transferred by virtue of this regulation to the transferee; and,

Anything done before the transfer is completed by or in relation to the transferor in respect of that contract or a person employed in that undertaking or part shall be deemed to have been done by or in relation to the transferee . . .

7. Exclusion of occupational pension schemes

(1) Regulations 5 and 6 above shall not apply:

(a) to so much of a contract of employment or collective agreement as relates to an occupational pension scheme within the meaning of the Social Security Pensions Act 1975 . . . or

(b) To any rights, powers or duties or liabilities under or in connection with any such contract or subsisting by virtue of any such agreement and relating to such a scheme or otherwise arising in connection with that person's employment and relating to such a scheme.

(2) For the purposes of paragraph (1) above any provisions of an occupational pension scheme which do not relate to benefits for old age, invalidity or survivors shall be treated as not being part of the scheme.

The exact scope of the pensions exemption and whether it fully reflects the scope of the Acquired Rights Directive from which it is derived has been the subject of a number of cases. In *Walden Engineering Co Ltd* v. *Warrener* [1992] PLR 1, *Perry* v. *Intec* [1993] OPLR 1 and *Adams* v. *Lancashire CC and BET* [1998] OPLR 119 it was argued unsuccessfully that the Acquired Rights Directive required the transfer of pension rights in order to give effect to the purpose of the Directive, i.e. the protection of workers' benefits on a business transfer.

Rather than continue to attempt to neutralise the pensions exemption in its entirety, those seeking to undermine the exemption sought to restrict its ambit. In *Frankling* v. *BPS Public Sector Ltd* [1999] OPLR 295 it was argued unsuccessfully that a redundancy pension paid prior to normal retirement age under a statutory scheme would transfer under regulation 5 and would fall outside the exemption in regulation 7. The same issues in the *Frankling* case came up again in *Beckmann* v. *Dynamco Whicheloe Macfarlane Ltd* [2000] PLR 269 but despite the ruling in *Frankling* it was referred to the European Court of Justice. The European Court in *Beckmann* did not follow *Frankling* and, in short, determined that any entitlement to benefits payable from an age prior to normal retirement age fell outside the exemption because they 'do not relate to benefits for old age'.

The *Beckmann* ruling has had, and will continue to have, a profound effect on the way pensions are negotiated on business transfers and, particularly, outsourcing transactions. This is especially the case in the public sector, where enhanced early retirement benefits are more common. Some may seek to argue that the *Beckmann* case can be distinguished from most everyday situations and, therefore, its influence should be limited. While it is true that *Beckmann* involved an unfunded statutory scheme and a redundancy pension that was only paid until normal retirement, the ECJ's ruling is not qualified and the prudent course would be to assume that entitlement to early retirement or redundancy pensions (other than upon ill health) transfer to the transferee on a TUPE transfer. Therefore, transferees should check the transferor's pension arrangements for any *Beckmann*-type liabilities that will transfer and have to be provided by the transferee. Early retirement defined benefit pensions are costly to provide and the allocation of that cost between the transferor and transferee is likely to be a significant feature in the commercial negotiations.

10.9 THE PENSION ASPECTS OF AN OUTSOURCING TRANSACTION

In the introduction to this chapter, five main considerations were identified as likely to arise when dealing with pensions, particularly defined benefit pensions, on an outsourcing transaction:

- due diligence to ascertain current pension arrangements of the parties;
- warranty protection;
- interim periods of participation;
- transfer calculations (defined benefit only);
- future service provision.

10.9.1 Collating information

There is normally a tension between the willingness of the transferor to disclose information and the desire of the transferee to see as much as possible. There are three crucial factors affecting the provision of information:

- relevance;
- availability; and
- timing.

Relevance

Many advisers acting for the transferee will have a standard list of the pensions-related documentation they would like to see (for an example, see Annex 10A). Unfortunately, because the list is often an office standard it is sometimes sent out with little thought as to whether it is appropriate to the transaction. In addition, quite often the list is designed to be as comprehensive as possible and has been prepared on the assumption that the transferee will be assuming responsibility for the transferor's pension scheme. This very rarely happens in an outsourcing transaction because it is unusual for the transaction to take the form of a sale of shares of an operating company.

Therefore, the transferor may receive a request for pensions information that has not been tailored to the transaction contemplated between the parties. One option is to ignore the request and provide only that which the transferor considers relevant. The other is to ask the proposed transferee to reconsider its request. In any event, it is reasonable for the transferee to be able to have sufficient information to establish in some detail the pension arrangements applicable to the transferring employees.

As well as being asked to provide information on pensions, transferors are also often asked to warrant the accuracy of that information and/or to warrant that all the documents listed in the warranty have been disclosed. Warranties are dealt with separately at paragraph 10.9.2, but care should be taken when considering any warranty concerning the accuracy of documentation that in most cases has not been prepared by or for the transferor.

Where the transferor operates a defined benefit pension scheme, the transferee will also usually make a request to see at least the most recent actuarial valuation and any subsequent actuarial advice concerning the funding the transferor's scheme. Clearly, such a request is a valid one where the transferee is assuming responsibility for the transferor's pension scheme, i.e. the scheme is transferring to the transferor either because the principal employer of the scheme is being acquired as part of the transaction or the transferor is to be substituted as the principal employer of the scheme. However, as noted above, this is rare in outsourcing transactions. In the more usual circumstances where there is to be a negotiation concerning the amount of the assets to be transferred from the transferor's pension scheme to the transferee's scheme (see below), the transferee will want to see the actuarial valuation to assist in its negotiation of the transfer amount. As far as the transferor is concerned, if it accedes to the transferee's request it is likely to limit its negotiating position. For example, it becomes difficult for the transferor to negotiate a transfer calculation method if the assumptions it proposes are less generous than those used by the relevant scheme.

Availability

There can be quite a difference in the quality of documentation provided by or in respect of occupational pension schemes. Most self-administered occupational pension schemes will have a reasonably full set of documentation. The difficulties tend to arise with insurance company based products. Quite often the only document that might be available is a copy of the proposal form and a spreadsheet of how much the employer pays each month. As a result it is not always easy to identify the nature of the pension scheme and, consequently, the pension promise. In these circumstances, the transferee will need to place greater reliance on the strength of its warranty protection.

Timing

It is not unknown for pensions to be left to the last minute. Understandably, negotiation of the commercial transaction takes precedence and the more immediate concerns relating to a transfer of employees (such as consultation) take centre stage. However, pensions, particularly defined benefit pensions, are increasingly important to employees. A negotiation of the terms upon which future and past pensions are to be provided requires time and can involve significant financial consequences, particularly in the light of *Beckmann* (see section 10.8). Therefore, because disclosure of information is a precondition to any negotiation on pensions, disclosure should occur as soon as possible.

10.9.2   Warranties

The warranties given in Annex 10B are reasonably comprehensive. It will be evident from the notes that, if a transferee is acquiring an entire pension scheme as part of a transfer (which is highly unlikely), detailed warranties such as a funding warranty are required. However, where the transferee is acquiring just the transferring employees, not all the warranties may be appropriate.

The main warranties cover the following areas.

Standard and additional benefits

A general warranty should be provided that all pension or lump sum retirement benefits applicable to the transferring employees have been disclosed. A warranty should also be included to the effect that the transferor is not making any *ex gratia* payments to the employees and that no undertaking or assurance has been given to any employee in relation to the increase or improvement of any benefit that the transferee would then have a contractual obligation to implement or be pressured to provide in accordance with good industrial relations practice.

Compliance

A warranty is normally requested to the effect that the pension scheme has been administered in accordance with all appropriate legal requirements and no claims have been made or threatened in respect of any breach of any applicable requirement. This is a wide warranty, which the transferor should consider carefully before agreeing to. Often a transferor will try to limit such

320

a warranty to its awareness. Frequently a transferee will try to expand the warranty to the effect that no legal proceedings or complaints have been made to the Pensions Ombudsman and that no enforcement action has been taken by OPRA.

Payment of contributions and premiums

All contributions due should have been paid to the trustees within the prescribed period and by the due dates specified in the contributions.

10.9.3   Interim periods of participation

At the date of commencement of a contract the transferee may not be in a position to admit the transferring employees into its pension scheme. This can be for a number of reasons, including:

- the timescale of the transaction has not given the transferee time to set up or adapt appropriate pension arrangements for the transferring employees;
- the transferee does not have a pension scheme or has a pension scheme of a different type to that required;
- there may be a redundancy programme shortly following the commencement and it is agreed that this should be dealt with while the employees continue to participate in the transferor's pension scheme;
- the transferor may be enjoying a contribution holiday and as part of the commercial transaction it is agreed that the transferor can benefit from this for a limited period;
- it gives the parties time to offer the transferring employees membership in the transferor's scheme and to calculate and pay any transfer payment from the transferor's scheme to the transferee's scheme.

Whatever the reason, it is possible for an employer (the transferee) to participate in the occupational pension scheme of a non-associated employer (the transferor) for a limited period (generally, not exceeding 12 months).

If there is to be an interim period of participation, it will be necessary to negotiate a separate schedule to the agreement (an example is at Annex 10C, which assumes the transferor has both a defined contribution and a defined benefit section in its scheme) dealing with such participation and the basis on which any transfer between schemes is to be calculated (see section 10.10). The first part of the schedule is usually taken up setting out the obligations of the parties in respect of the period of participation. The transferor will usually agree:

- to continue to operate its pension scheme for at least the length of the period of participation;
- not to do anything to affect the exempt approved tax status of its scheme;

- if it is contracted out, to continue the scheme as a contracted out scheme;
- not to amend the scheme so as to increase the financial obligations of the transferee in respect of the transferring employees;
- to provide sufficient information to the transferee.

The transferee will normally agree:

- to pay the contributions due, usually at a rate specified in the agreement, such rate to include an allowance for costs of administration and life assurance costs;
- not to exercise any discretion or powers as a participating employer under the scheme without the consent of the transferor;
- to enter into a deed of adherence or participation, which is sometimes appended to the schedule as an agreed form document;
- not do anything to prejudice the exempt approved and, if appropriate, the contracted out status of the scheme;
- not to increase transferring employees' salaries over an agreed rate;
- before the end of the period of participation to offer membership of its scheme to the transferring employees on an agreed basis.

The areas that cause most discussion particularly in relation to defined benefit schemes are: the contribution rate; the exercise of discretion in relation to such matters as early retirement and the limit on salary increases, as they all have cost implications.

The simplest approach would be for the transferee to pay the same level of contributions as the transferor. However, if the transferor's scheme is a defined benefit scheme that is underfunded and those contributions contain an element to make up that underfunding, the transferee may take the view that it should not share responsibility for the past. If the transferee is taking on a significant group of young active members and the transferor's scheme is a mature scheme with a high proportion of pensioners, the transferee may argue that the transferor's contribution rate is inappropriate. Alternatively, the transferor may have a well funded scheme and be reluctant for the transferee to benefit from this through a lower contribution rate than the actuary's estimate of the long-term funding rate for the scheme. Transferors should also ensure that any contribution rate includes an allowance for administration costs and any costs of insuring the death in service benefit.

Many schemes give employers a discretion to allow employees to retire before their normal retirement age on a non-actuarially reduced pension. This can have a significant cost implications for a scheme if this discretion is exercised more than at the rate assumed by the actuary. Therefore, it is important for transferors to ensure that transferees do not have an unfettered discretion to retire employees early effectively at the cost of the transferor.

The other area where a transferee can dramatically increase the pension costs of the transferor's defined benefit pension scheme is by increasing salaries in the interim period where the transfer amount is calculated by reference to pensionable service and salary at the end of the interim period.

10.10   TRANSFER CALCULATIONS

Where the transferor's scheme is a defined benefit scheme the most important point to be negotiated is the calculation of the transfer amount. How this amount will be calculated will be a matter of negotiation between the parties, subject to members' statutory entitlements to a minimum of the cash equivalent of their accrued benefits. It may be agreed that the transfer amount is to be calculated using one of the following methods:

- as a share of the overall fund, i.e. in an overfunded scheme, the transfer payment would include a pro rata element of any surplus, and in an underfunded scheme, the transfer amount would be reduced proportionately according to the deficit in the scheme; or
- on a past service reserve basis: with this method the value of the benefits taken at the date of transfer or completion as agreed for the members and their dependants will make an allowance at an assumed rate for increases in pensionable salary to the normal retirement date, with possibly some additional allowance for future discretionary increases to pensions in payment; or
- as the transferring members' statutory cash equivalents.

Even where a method is agreed, there is still plenty of scope for dispute between the parties over the assumptions used by the actuaries to calculate the transfer amount. The main assumptions that need to be agreed tend to be:

- the rate of investment return;
- the rate of inflation; and
- the rate of salary increase.

Where the transferor's scheme is a defined contribution scheme, the position is much more straightforward because all that is transferred is the member's accrued money purchase pot. There is no need for actuaries to agree a method and assumptions for calculating the transfer amount. However, care should be taken to ensure that defined contribution benefits are actually what they profess to be. There are hybrid arrangements under which there is a target funding commitment on the transferor or a defined benefit underpin.

The schedule should also set out how the transfer amount is to be applied under the transferee's scheme. The transferor will want to be sure that the transfer value, when applied in the transferee's scheme, will be fully utilised for the benefit of the transferring members and that it will not be available for use in providing benefits for other members of the transferee's scheme and hence indirectly to reduce the contribution liability of the transferee. The transferor should ask the transferee to agree that the transfer value, once paid into its scheme, will be applied in providing past service benefits for the transferring employees in the transferee's scheme to the full value of the transfer amount.

The appropriate date by reference to which the transfer payment is to be calculated will need to be determined. The two alternatives are as follows:

- The transferring liabilities may be calculated by reference to the completion date, i.e. the beginning of the interim period of the transfer agreement. If this approach is adopted, a mechanism must be established for adjusting the transfer payment to cover the period between the completion date and the date of payment. The method of adjustment will either be by reference to base rate or by reference to the movement in a representative group of investments. If the transfer payment is to be calculated at completion, the contributions to the transferor's scheme during the interim period will normally be treated on a cash basis, but adjusted from the effective date of payment.
- Alternatively, the calculation of the transfer payment can take place immediately before the transferring employees join the new scheme, i.e. at the end of the interim period. Under this method, the transferor's scheme makes a profit on any leavers prior to the end of the interim period but the transferor will need to ensure that it is protected against the transferee increasing the contributions of the transferor's scheme during the interim period.

The parties must agree whether the transfer payment is to be paid in cash or a transfer of investments from the transferor's scheme or a combination of the two. If investments are being transferred, the transferee should ensure that it is able to refuse specific investments.

10.10.1 Shortfall clauses

Just because the transfer amount has been agreed between the transferor and the transferee, this does not mean that this is the amount that will be transferred by the trustees of the transferor's scheme. The trustees may take a different view of what is appropriate to transfer in the circumstances. For example, the parties may have agreed a service reserve but the trustees may be constrained to transfer a cash equivalent because of the funding provisions of the transferor's scheme. In practice this is unlikely because the actuary who advises the transferor in negotiations on the method of the transfer payment is usually the same actuary who advises the trustees on the appropriate amount to transfer. However, it is usual for the transferee to insist on a provision whereby the transferor agrees to make a cash payment (net of tax relief) to make up the inclusion of any shortfall between the transfer amount agreed between the parties and the amount actually transferred.

The clause should state that if the transferor's scheme does not pay cash equal to the full amount of the transfer amount agreed between the parties to the transferee's scheme on or before the due payment date, the transferor will pay an amount equal to the deficit to the transferee, i.e. by way of an adjustment to the price. In addition, it is usual to include a penal interest rate for late payment, for example compound interest calculated on a day-to-day basis with monthly rests on such amount for so long as it remains unpaid at x per cent above base rate.

The transferor may attempt to reduce its liability by including a deduction in respect of the rate of mainstream corporation tax, the argument being that the transferor will be able to obtain a corporation tax deduction in respect of a payment to the transferee's scheme.

10.11 FUTURE SERVICE OBLIGATIONS

A transferor will usually want to ensure that the transferee continues to provide a similar level of pension benefit in the future. Clearly, there are employee relations issues if a transferor is not seen to protect its employees outsourced to another employer. Failure to provide such protection is likely to undermine the acceptability of the outsourcing process. In contrast, transferees will wish to ensure that their labour costs are as small as possible. They may have quoted for the contract on the basis that they can make savings by offering less expensive pension benefits. In so far as a transferee has an obligation to continue to provide non-standard pension benefits under *Beckmann*, the transferee will want to receive consideration for the cost. It will be apparent that there is plenty of scope for negotiation.

10.12 THE PUBLIC SECTOR

10.12.1 The background

The treatment of pensions on outsourcing of public contracts including staff transfers caused by market testing as well as PFI and public/private partnerships has developed following the issue of guidance by the Treasury in June 1999 and the issue of the Local Government Pension Scheme (Amendment, etc.) Regulations 1999, SI 1999/3438. Previously, companies taking over an outsourced contract from a government department, NHS Trust or local authority were usually required to provide comparable pensions for employees of the contracting authority. This was because of the view taken by government on the potential for a claim for unfair dismissal against the contracting authority if the transferee did not provide comparable pensions.

10.12.2　Treasury guidance

The Treasury guidance (*Staff Transfers in the Public Sector: A Statement of Practice*) is an attempt to ensure that there is common practice within the public sector on the transfers of employees to the private sector. Annex A to the guidance on pensions is set out in Annex 10D of this chapter.

Broadly the guidance deals with two issues, the treatment of pension entitlements accrued in the public sector and the level of future accrual in the private sector. In relation to benefits accrued in the public sector, transferees will have the usual option to leave their benefit behind in the public sector scheme or transfer it to a new scheme, usually that of the new employer. The position before the guidance was that failure to propose a bulk transfer to the new employer's scheme would be considered as putting the bidder at a disadvantage. The effect of the guidance is to strengthen the existing approach by:

> making it a condition for the business transfer there will be a bulk transfer agreement under which the pension scheme of the new employer will provide day for day past service credits (or an equivalent recommended by the Government Actuary's Department as a suitable reflection of differences in benefit structures between the schemes) to staff choosing to transfer their accrued credits.

The guidance makes the point that it is now necessary to ensure pensions matters are settled at an early stage and that this is tied into the negotiation process. Staff should be given a three-month period after being informed of their pension options to decide whether to keep their accrued benefits in the public sector or transfer them on the bulk transfer terms to their new employer's scheme.

In relation to future service, the new employer should offer transferring employees membership of a pension scheme that provides benefits that are broadly comparable to the public sector scheme they are leaving. A broadly comparable scheme is one that:

> in the professional opinion of the actuary, satisfies the condition that there are no identifiable employees who will suffer material detriment overall in terms of their future accrual of pension benefits.

The guidance does provide that there may be exceptional circumstances where broad comparability may not be feasible. In those circumstances, appropriate compensation would have to be provided to employees.

The guidance sets out the process through which the bidder's proposed pension arrangements are effectively vetted. The process requires that:

- the Government Actuary's Department (GAD) certifies the broad comparability of any replacement pension arrangements before any contractual commitment is made;
- GAD advises on any compensation to be provided in exceptional circumstances;

- GAD follows its published paper setting out how it assesses broad comparability;
- GAD provides an analysis of the key differences between the public sector proposed replacement and the private sector arrangement that is made available to unions;
- after a reasonable period allowed for consideration, if areas of difference remain between the contractor and the unions, a direct approach may be made to the contracting authority;
- the transfer agreement must expressly require the implementation of the agreed arrangements.

Local government pension scheme

The guidance referred to above is not the only approach adopted to transfers of the private sector. The Local Government Pension Scheme (Amendment, etc.) Regulations 1999, SI 1999/3438 came into force in January 2000. The regulations amended the Local Government Pension Scheme Regulations 1997, SI 1997/1612 by widening the category of persons who may obtain admitted body status in the scheme. This allows private sector employees to participate in the Local Government Pension Scheme (LGPS) when they are awarded a contract. Instead of a transfer to a broadly comparable scheme, the employees remain in the public sector scheme so that their period of pensionable service remains unbroken by a series of successive transfers. There are attractions for both private sector employers and the public sector in this approach. The private sector does not have to go through the broadly comparable process referred to above and larger employers need not have a number of broadly comparable schemes or sections within schemes. The public sector is able to ensure continued pensionable service for its former employees, overcoming a major concern of employees moving into the private sector.

The Local Government Pensions Committee of the Department of the Environment, Transport and the Regions has issued guidance notes on the admission of private sector employers entitled *The Pensions Implications of Transferring Employees to an External Contractor*. This can be found on the Employer's Organisation website at www.lg-employers.gov.uk.

The basis on which a private contractor will be admitted to the LGPS will be governed by an admission agreement, which must contain certain provisions set out in a Schedule to the 1999 regulations. The more significant provisions, which are preconditions to admission, are required in order to protect the contracting authority against private admitted bodies failing to pay contributions to the scheme and going bankrupt. The major requirement, and one that would not normally be seen in commercial transfers, is the taking out of an approved indemnity or bond. The admission agreement must also contain a provision whereby the transferring public sector employer may set off against payments due to the transferee private sector employer an amount equal to any overdue pensions contributions owed to the scheme.

As private sector employers have been admitted to the LGPS since January 2000, experience has shown that the 1999 regulations have needed frequent amendment to deal with the issues that have arisen. This is likely to continue. Now that public sector employees can remain in the LGPS after their employment is transferred, employee representatives and the unions see continued participation as a key factor. Therefore, while entering into an admission agreement is just one way private sector employers can deal with pensions, and while employers who have been admitted may leave the LGPS with due notice, continued participation is likely to be the preferred route for employees, unions, the transferring employer, and the new employer seeking good employee relations.

ANNEX 10A

Due diligence enquiries – asset purchase

Pensions   **Comments**

1. In respect of each relevant pension scheme,
    please provide:

    (a) copies of all deeds, rules booklets, member
        announcements and staff handbooks;
    (b) copies of the latest trustees' report and
        audited accounts, the latest actuarial
        report and valuation, and any subsequent
        actuarial advice;
    (c) evidence of contracted out and exempt
        approved status;
    (d) full membership data, together with such
        information in respect of prospective
        members, and copies of scheme mem-
        bership provisions in employees' service
        contracts;
    (e) full details of contributions and benefits
        (and any recent changes), the practice in
        relation to benefit augmentations, and
        bulk transfers paid to or by the scheme;
    (f) full details of any non-compliance by or
        disputes relating to the scheme;

    together with full details of:

    (g) personal pensions;
    (h) any ex gratia or unapproved arrangements;
        and
    (i) sickness/disability/PHI benefits;

    which the seller is liable to provide and/or
    contribute to in respect of relevant employees.

Please also provide similar details in respect of any pension scheme in which the
transferring employees formerly participated.

ANNEX 10B

Pensions warranties

1. [Save for the Pension Scheme] the Company is not a party to nor participates in nor contributes to any scheme, arrangement or agreement (whether legally enforceable or not) for the provision of any pension, retirement, death, incapacity, sickness, disability, accident or other like benefits (including the payment of medical expenses) for any past or present employee or officer of the Company or of any predecessor to all or part of its business (each a 'Relevant Employee') or for the widow, widower, child or dependant of any Relevant Employee.[1]

2. Neither the Company nor any [of the Vendors] [member of the Vendor's Group] (i) has given any undertaking or assurance (whether legally enforceable or not) to any Relevant Employee or to any widow, widower, child or dependant of any Relevant Employee as to the continuance, introduction, improvement or increase of any benefit of a kind described in paragraph 1 above or (ii) is paying or has in the last two years paid any benefit of a kind described in paragraph 1 above to any Relevant Employee or to any widow, widower, child or dependant of any Relevant Employee.

3. All material details relating to the Pension Scheme are contained in or annexed to the Disclosure Letter including (without limitation) the following, namely (i) a true and complete copy of the [deed or other instrument by which the Pension Scheme was established and all deeds and other instruments supplemental thereto] [documentation containing the current provisions governing the Pension Scheme], (ii) a true and complete copy of all announcements, explanatory literature and the like of current effect that have been issued to any Relevant Employee in connection with the Pension Scheme, [(iii) a true and complete copy of the report on the last actuarial valuation of the Pension Scheme to be completed prior to Completion and of any subsequent written recommendations of an actuarial nature], (iv) a true and complete copy of the last audited accounts of the Pension Scheme to be completed prior to Completion and details of any material change in the investment policy of the Pension Scheme since the date as at which those accounts were made up, [(v) a true and complete copy of all investment management, nominee and custodian agreements (if any) of current effect to which the Pension Scheme is a party,] [(vi) a true and complete copy of all insurance policies (if any) and annuity contracts (if any) held for the purposes of the Pension Scheme and details of any such policies and contracts which the Pension Scheme has agreed to effect], [(vii) a true and complete copy of the memorandum and articles of association of any company that is a trustee of the Pension Scheme and the names and addresses of the directors and secretary of that company], [(viii) the names and addresses of the trustees of the Pension Scheme], (ix) details of all amendments (if any) to the Pension Scheme that have been announced or are proposed but have not yet been formally made, (x) details of all discretionary increases (if any) to pensions in payment or in deferment under the Pension Scheme that have been granted in the ten years prior to Completion or

are under consideration, (xi) details of all discretionary practices (if any) that may have led any person to expect additional benefits in a given set of circumstances (by way of example, but without limitation, on retirement at the behest of the Company or in the event of redundancy), and (xii) details of the rate at which and basis upon which the Company currently contributes to the Pension Scheme, any change to such rate and/or basis that is proposed or is under consideration and all contributions paid to the Pension Scheme by the Company in the three years prior to Completion.[2]

[4. No power under the Pension Scheme has been exercised in relation to any employee or officer of the Company or, since the date as at which the last actuarial valuation of the Pension Scheme to be completed prior to the Completion was undertaken, in respect of any other person, (i) to provide terms of membership of the Pension Scheme (whether as to benefits or contributions) that are different from those generally applicable to the members of the Pension Scheme, or (ii) to provide any benefits that would not but for the exercise of that power have been payable under the Pension Scheme, or (iii) to augment any benefits under the Pension Scheme.][3]

5. All benefits [(other than any refund of members' contributions with interest where appropriate)] [that are not money purchase benefits and that are] payable under the Pension Scheme on the death of any person while in employment to which the Pension Scheme relates are insured fully under a policy with an insurance company of good repute and there are no grounds on which that company might avoid liability under that policy. [All other benefits payable under the Pension Scheme are money purchase benefits. In this paragraph 5 'money purchase benefits' has the same meaning as in section 84(1) of the Social Security Act 1986.][4]

6. Contributions to the Pension Scheme are not paid in arrear and all contributions and other amounts that have fallen due for payment have been paid punctually. [No fee, charge or expense relating to or in connection with the Pension Scheme has been incurred but not paid. If any such fee, charge or expense has been paid by any person other than the Pension Scheme the Pension Scheme has reimbursed that person if and to the extent that the Pension Scheme is or may become liable so to do.] [The Company has (to the extent that it is required to do) discharged its liability (if any) to pay or reimburse (whether wholly or in part) anyone who has paid any costs, charges or expenses that have been incurred by or in connection with the Pension Scheme.][5]

7. The Company (i) has observed and performed those provisions of the Pension Scheme that apply to it; [and], may (without the consent of any person or further payment) terminate its liability to contribute to the Pension Scheme at any time subject only to giving such notice (if any) as is expressly provided for in the documentation containing the current provisions governing the Pension Scheme[.] [; and (iii) has at all material times held or been named in a contracting-out certificate (within the meaning of the Social Security Pensions Act 1975) referable to the Pension Scheme;] [,(iv) has been admitted to participate in the Pension Scheme on the same terms as apply generally to other employees participating in the Pension Scheme;] and [(v) is not indebted to the Pension Scheme by virtue of section 144 of the Pension Schemes Act 1993 or section 75 of the Pensions Act 1995.][6]

[8. The Company is the only employer for the time being participating in the Pension Scheme. No employer that has previously participated in the Pension Scheme has any claim under the Pension Scheme and in respect of any such employer the period of participation has been terminated and benefits have been provided in accordance with the provisions of the Pension Scheme.][7]

[9.   All documentation and records in respect of the Pension Scheme are up to date and so far as the Covenantors are aware complete and accurate in all material aspects.]

[10. [None of the assets of the Pension Scheme (i) is invested in or in any description of employer-related investments (within the meaning of section 57A of the Social Security Pensions Act 1975), or (ii) save for deposits with banks, building societies and other financial institutions and save for any instrument creating or acknowledging an indebtedness listed on any recognised stock exchange of repute, is loaned to any person, or (iii) is subject to any encumbrance or agreement or commitment to give or create any encumbrance.] [Save for any deposit with a bank or building society the only assets that the Pension Scheme has held are insurance policies and annuity contracts with insurance companies of good repute.][8]

[11. No payment to which section 601 of the Taxes Act applies has been made out of the funds that are or have been held for the purposes of the Pension Scheme.][9]

12.   The Pension Scheme (i) is an exempt approved scheme (within the meaning of section 592 of the Taxes Act), [(ii) has properly and punctually accounted to the Inland Revenue for all and any tax for which the Pension Scheme is liable or accountable;] [(iii) is not liable to taxation on any income from or capital gains on any of the funds that are or have been held for the purpose of the Pension Scheme;] and (iv) complies with and has at all times been administered in accordance with all applicable laws, regulations and requirements (including those of the Board of Inland Revenue and of trust law).[10]

13.   [The report dated [ ] of [ ] on the actuarial valuation of the Pension Scheme as at [ ] (the 'Valuation Date') (a true copy of which is annexed to the Disclosure Letter) shows a true and fair view of the respective actuarial values of the assets and liabilities of the Pension Scheme at the Valuation Date on the basis of the actuarial assumptions and method detailed in that report. Since the Valuation Date nothing has occurred, been done or been omitted to be done that may affect materially the level of funding of the benefits under the Pension Scheme.] [The date used for the purposes of the last actuarial valuation of the Pension Scheme to be completed prior to Completion was complete and accurate in all material respects and since the date as at which that valuation was undertaken nothing has occurred, been done or been omitted to be done that may affect materially the level of funding of the benefits under the Pension Scheme.][11]

14.   Neither the Pension Scheme nor the Company [nor any member of the Vendor's group] is engaged or involved in any proceedings that relate to or are in connection with the Pension Scheme or the benefits thereunder and no such proceedings are pending or threatened and so far as the Covenantors are aware there are no facts likely to give rise to any such proceedings. In this subsection 'proceedings' includes any litigation or arbitration and also includes any investigation or determination by the Pension Ombudsman.

[15. In relation to the Pension Scheme or funds that are or have been held for the purposes thereof neither the Company nor the trustees or administrator of the Pension Scheme has given an indemnity or guarantee to any person (other than in the case of the Company any general indemnity in favour of the trustee or administrator under the documentation governing the Pension Scheme).][12]

[For personal pension schemes only:]

[16. There is set out in the Disclosure Letter a statement of the basis on which the Company has undertaken to contribute to each scheme that has been disclosed and that is a Personal Pension Scheme (meaning any personal pension scheme approved or provisionally approved for the purposes of Chapter IV, Part XIV of the Taxes Act to which contributions have been made or are intended to be made pursuant to any agreement, arrangement, custom or practice) and the rate and the amount of the contributions in respect of each member of such scheme made in the last three years.

No assurance, promise or guarantee (whether oral or written) has been made or given to any member of any disclosed scheme which is a Personal Pension Scheme of any particular level or amount of benefits to be provided for in respect of him under such disclosed scheme on retirement, death or leaving service. The Company may terminate any obligation it may have to contribute to any such disclosed scheme being a Personal Pension Scheme without incurring any liability to any member of such scheme under any agreement or arrangement with the member.]

17. In determining the damages flowing from any breach of the Warranties contained in this section, the Company shall be deemed to be under a liability (i) to provide and to continue to provide any benefit of a kind referred to in that paragraph which is now provided or has been announced or is proposed, and (ii) to maintain and to continue to maintain (without benefits being reduced) the Pension Scheme and any other arrangements of a kind described in that paragraph which are now in existence or are proposed and any discretionary practices of a kind referred to in that paragraph which have hitherto been carried on.

NOTES

1. If the company does not have a pension scheme, incorporate only paragraph 1 but delete the words in square brackets.
2. There may not be an actuarial valuation report in the case of a money purchase scheme and consequently paragraph (iii) may be negated in the disclosure letter. Paragraph (v) will not apply in the case of a money purchase scheme. Paragraphs (v), (vi), (vii) and (viii) are not appropriate where the company participates in the vendor's group scheme.
3. Paragraph 4 will not be applicable in the case of a money purchase scheme.
4. Delete the wording in the second and third square brackets if the scheme is a defined benefits scheme as distinct from a money purchase scheme.
5. Use the second option where the company participates in the vendor's group scheme.
6. Paragraphs (iv) and (v) only apply where the company participates in the vendor's group scheme. Paragraph (v) will not apply if the group scheme is a money purchase scheme.
7. Paragraphs 8, 9, 10 and 11 do not apply where the company participates in the vendor's group scheme.
8. The first option is for use with a defined benefits scheme. The second option is for a money purchase scheme.
9. Paragraph 11 applies only to a defined benefits scheme.
10. Paragraph (iii) only applies in the case of a defined benefits scheme. Paragraphs (ii) and (iii) do not apply where the company participates in the vendor's group scheme.
11. Paragraph 13 is only relevant to a defined benefits scheme.
12. Paragraph 15 is only relevant to a defined benefits scheme and does not apply where the company participates in the vendor's group scheme.

ANNEX 10C

Pro forma pensions schedule

1 Definitions

1.1 In this Schedule [ ], references to Sections are to Sections of this Schedule [ ], and all capitalised terms shall have the meanings set out in Clause [ ] of the Agreement unless otherwise defined in this Schedule [ ].

'**Account Balance**' means the amount each member has accrued in the DC Section at the Account Balance Payment Date.

'**Account Balance Payment Date**' means the fourteenth day after the Membership Transfer Date.

'**Actuary's Letter**' means the letter from the Transferor's Actuary to the Transferee's Actuary a copy of which is attached hereto at Annexure 1.

'**Adjusted Transfer Payment**' means the Transfer Payment (agreed or determined in accordance with Section 4.2 or 4.3 as the case may be) adjusted in accordance with the Actuary's Letter for the period from and including the Membership Transfer Date to and excluding the DB Payment Date.

'**Transferor's Actuary**' means [ ] of [ ] or another actuary appointed by the Transferor for the purposes of this Schedule [ ].

'**Transferor's Scheme**' means the DB Section and the DC Section.

'**DB Section**' means the Transferor's Pension Scheme – Defined Benefit Section.

'**DB Payment Date**' means the date on which payment is due under Section 4.6.

'**DC Section**' means the Transferor's Defined Contribution Retirement Benefits Scheme section of the Transferor's Pension Scheme.

'**Membership Transfer Date**' means [ ], or another date agreed in writing by the Transferor and the Transferee.

'**Member**' means an Employee who is an active member of the Transferor's Scheme on the Contract Start Date.

'**Transferee's Scheme**' means, for members of the DB Section, the [ ] Scheme (the '**Transferee's DB Scheme**') or, for members of the DC Section, the [ ] Plan (the '**Transferee's DC Plan**').

'**Transferring Member**' means a Member who consents to a transfer of assets being made to the Transferee's Scheme under Section 2.3.

'**Transfer Payment**' means the actuarial value in respect of the Transferring Members of their benefits under the DB Section by reference to pensionable service in the DB Section up to the Membership Transfer Date, determined by the Transferor's Actuary and agreed by Transferee's Actuary in accordance with Section 4.2 or determined by an independent actuary in accordance with Section 4.3.

'**Transitional Period of Participation**' means the period from the Contract Start Date until the day before the Membership Transfer Date.

'**Transferee's Actuary**' means [ ] or another actuary appointed by the Transferee for the purpose of this Schedule [ ].

2　The Transferee's Scheme

2.1　The Transferee's DB Scheme is contracted out and an exempt approved scheme for the purposes of Chapter I Part XIV of the Income and Corporation Taxes Act 1988 and the Transferee's DC Plan is a non-contracted out exempt approved scheme for the purposes of Chapter I Part XIV of the Income and Corporation Taxes Act 1988.

2.2　The Transferee will, at least six weeks before the Membership Transfer Date, offer Members of the DB Section membership of the Transferee's DB Scheme (details of which are attached at Annexure 3) and offer members of the DC Section membership of the Transferee's DC Plan (details of which are attached at Annexure 2), both with effect from the Membership Transfer Date, subject to their continued employment by the Transferee.

2.3　The Transferee will ensure that, when invitations to join the Transferee's Scheme are given, each Member will be invited (subject to his continued employment by the Transferee at the Membership Transfer Date), in terms approved by the Transferee and the Transferor (such approval not to be unreasonably withheld or delayed), to consent within four weeks of the invitation to a transfer of assets being made to the Transferee's Scheme in respect of their accrued rights under the Transferor's Scheme.

3　Transitional Period of Participation

3.1　Subject to Inland Revenue approval, the Transferor will use its reasonable endeavours to ensure that the Transferee may participate in the Transferor's Scheme in respect of the Members during the Transitional Period of Participation. For this purpose the Transferee will enter into a Deed in the form reasonably required by the trustees and the principal employer of the Transferor's Scheme.

3.2　The Transferor and the Transferee will use their respective reasonable endeavours to enable Members to remain contracted out by reference to the Transferor's Scheme until the day before the Membership Transfer Date.

3.3　During the Transitional Period of Participation, the Transferee will:

3.3.1　pay contributions in respect of Members of the DB Section of the Transferor's Scheme at the rate of [ ] per cent of pensionable salary and at the rates specified in the trust deed and rules of the Transferor's Scheme in respect of Members of the DC Section, and will use reasonable endeavours to remit these contributions (together in each case with the Members' own contributions) to the trustees of the Transferor's Scheme by no later than the 14th day of the next following month and in any case shall remit them by no later than the 19th of the following month (and if any amount payable in accordance with this Section is paid later than the 19th of the following month for payment, the Transferee will in addition pay interest on the amount concerned at the rate of [ ] per cent over the Transferor's base rate from time to time from the 19th of the following month for payment until payment is made and any fines imposed by any Regulatory Authority in relation to such late payment);

3.3.2　comply with the reasonable requests of the Transferor in relation to Inland Revenue requirements and/or for the contracted out status of Members; and

3.3.3　observe and perform all the provisions of the Transferor's Scheme relevant to it as a Participating Employer including entering into a deed of participation in the form annexed.

3.4 The Transferee authorises the Transferor or such other person as the Transferor may nominate to exercise all powers, rights and discretions conferred on the Transferee under the Pensions Act 1995 by virtue of its participation in the Transferor's Scheme. The Transferee will take any reasonable steps required by the Transferor to give effect to this authorisation.

3.5 The Transferee will not without the Transferor's prior written consent (which may be made subject to conditions as set out below):

3.5.1 issue any notice or announcement to any of the Employees concerning any benefit payable from the Transferor's Scheme;

3.5.2 exercise any powers or discretions conferred on it by the Trust Deed and Rules of the Transferor's Scheme;

3.5.3 grant or consent to the redundancy or ill-health early retirement of any Member or allow early retirement in any other circumstances on an unreduced pension;

and if it nevertheless does so, and/or if it increases by more than [ ] per cent the total pensionable earnings of the Members of the Transferor's Scheme, the Transferee will pay to the trustees of the Transferor's Scheme such sum as shall be determined by the Transferor's Actuary and agreed by the Transferee's Actuary as being equal to the increased liabilities of the Transferor's Scheme, calculated in accordance with the assumptions set out in the Actuary's Letter (in respect of Sections 3.5.1 and 3.5.2) or those from time to time used by the Transferor's Scheme for such purpose (in respect of Section 3.5.3). In the event of disagreement between the actuaries, the determination of the required sum may be referred to an independent actuary in accordance with Section 9 below.

3.6 The Transferor undertakes that it will use its reasonable endeavours to procure that, save as may be necessary to comply with any statute, regulation or the requirements of governmental or any regulatory body or authority (and without prejudice to the generality of the foregoing, arising as a result of the Pensions Act 1995 and any regulations made under it) no amendment will be made to the Transferor's Scheme during the Transitional Period of Participation that would adversely affect the calculation or payment of the Transfer Payment or Account Balances and that any alteration (of whatever nature) that may be made to the level of contributions due to or the accrual of benefits under the Transferor's Scheme shall not apply to the Transferee and/or the Members without the prior consent of the Transferee.

4 The Transfer Payment from the Transferor's Scheme

4.1 The Transferee and the Transferor jointly undertake promptly to provide the Transferor's Actuary and Transferee's Actuary with such documents and information in their respective control or possession (including for the avoidance of doubt full details of the Employees) as the Transferor's Actuary and Transferee's Actuary may reasonably require in order to calculate the Transfer Payment. The Transferee and the Transferor each warrant that the documents and information that each of them supplies to the Transferor's Actuary or Transferee's Actuary as appropriate pursuant to this Section 4.1 will to the best of their knowledge and belief be true, complete and accurate in all material respects as at the Membership Transfer Date and shall contain no omission material to the calculation of the Transfer Payment or material for any other calculation for the purposes of this Schedule [ ].

4.2 Promptly after the Membership Transfer Date the Transferor and the Transferee shall respectively instruct the Transferor's Actuary and Transferee's Actuary to consult with a view to the Transferor's Actuary calculating the Transfer Payment in respect of Transferring Members in the DB Section of the Transferor's Scheme in accordance with the assumptions set out in the Actuary's Letter and providing such calculations to Transferee's Actuary within 30 days of the Membership Transfer Date (or, if later, the date when the Transferor's Actuary receives the data he requires in order to calculate the Transfer Payment) and the Transferee's Actuary agreeing to such calculations within 30 days of receipt of such calculations from the Transferor's Actuary or notifying him of the reasons why he is unable to agree the calculations.

4.3 If the Transferor's Actuary and Transferee's Actuary are unable to agree the Transfer Payment in accordance with Section 4.2 above the determination of the Transfer Payment may be referred to an independent actuary in accordance with Section 9 below.

4.4 The determination of the independent actuary under Section 9 below shall be final and binding upon the parties except where there has been manifest error.

4.5 Payment of the Adjusted Transfer Payment to the Transferee's Scheme will only be made if:

4.5.1 the Inland Revenue has consented to the payment (to the extent that its consent is required);

4.5.2 the Transferee has complied with all its obligations set out in Section 2;

4.5.3 the trustees of the Transferee's Scheme have confirmed that they will accept the payment on the terms set out in Section 5.

4.5.4 there is agreement of the Transfer Payment by the Transferor's Actuary and Transferee's Actuary under Section 4.2 or the determination of an independent actuary under Section 4.3.

4.6 Payment to the Transferee's Scheme is due on the later of the following:

4.6.1 [ ] days after the Membership Transfer Date; and

4.6.2 seven days after the date when the last of the conditions in Section 4.5 has been satisfied; or

4.6.3 such other date as may be agreed between the Transferor and the Transferee.

4.7 If the trustees of the Transferor's Scheme do not pay the Adjusted Transfer Payment in full on the DB Payment Date, the Transferor will within 28 days after receipt of a written demand from the Transferee pay or procure to be paid, as an adjustment to the consideration, an amount in cash to the Transferee (for immediate onward transmission to the trustees of the Transferee's Scheme) equal to the amount ('the Shortfall') by which the Adjusted Transfer Payment exceeds the amount transferred from the Transferor's Scheme to the Transferee's DB Scheme. The Shortfall shall be increased by the timing adjustment set out in the Actuary's Letter in respect of the period from and including the DB Payment Date to and excluding the date of final payment under this Section 4.7.

4.8 If, in error, the trustees of the Transferor's Scheme pay more than the Adjusted Transfer Payment calculated and adjusted in accordance with Section 4.2 (or, if applicable, as determined by an independent actuary under Section 4.3) on the DB Payment Date, the Transferee will within 28 days after receipt of a written demand from the Transferor pay or procure to be paid, as an adjustment to the consideration, an amount in cash to the Transferor (for immediate onward transmission to the trustees of the Transferor's Scheme) equal to the amount of the overpayment, increased by the timing adjustment set out in the Actuary's Letter in respect of the period from and including the DB Payment Date to and excluding the date of final payment under this Section 4.8.

4.9 If either the Transferee or the Transferor obtains any saving (whether by way of any payment, repayment, credit, set-off or otherwise) in corporation tax that would not have been made but for the receipt and payment to the Transferee's Scheme or the Transferor's Scheme referred to in Section 4.7 or 4.8 respectively, then the Transferee or the Transferor (as appropriate) will, within 28 days after the receipt of that saving, repay a like amount in cash to the party by whom the original payment was made.

4.10 Payment of the Adjusted Transfer Payment from the Transferor's Scheme to the Transferee's DB Scheme will be made in such assets of the Transferor's Scheme as the Transferor and the Transferee agree or, in default of agreement, in cash. Payment of the Account Balances from the Transferor's Scheme to the Transferee's DC Plan will be made in cash unless otherwise agreed by both the Transferor and Transferee.

4.11 The Transferor shall use best endeavours to procure that, on the Account Balance Payment Date, the Account Balances of the Transferring Members from the DC Section are paid to the trustees of the Transferee's DC Plan.

5 Benefits to be provided by the Transferee's Scheme in respect of service under the Transferor's Scheme

5.1 The Transferee will procure that subject to receipt of the Adjusted Transfer Payment (together with, if Section 4.7 applies, the shortfall payment due under that Section) benefits will be provided in accordance with Annexure 3 (subject to Inland Revenue Limits on benefits not being exceeded) for the Transferring Members in respect of pensionable service (qualifying under the provisions of the Transferor's Scheme) up to the day before the Membership Transfer Date on the basis that each of the Transferring Members will be credited with a period of pensionable service under the Transferee's DB Scheme that shall be determined in accordance with paragraph [ ] of the Actuary's Letter.

5.2 The Transferee will procure that, subject to receipt of the Account Balances, the trustees of the Transferee's DC Plan will credit to the [Member's Account] (as defined in the Transferee's Plan) of such Transferring Member the Account Balance received in respect of him.

6 Voluntary contributions

Nothing previously contained in this Schedule will apply to voluntary contributions or to benefits secured by them. However, the Transferor will use reasonable endeavours to ensure that the assets representing the Transferring Members' voluntary contributions will be transferred to the Transferee's DB Scheme, and the Transferee will use reasonable endeavours to ensure that in that event its scheme provides benefits for the members concerned equal in value to the assets transferred.

7 Debt on the employer

The Transferor shall from the Membership Transfer Date indemnify and keep indemnified the Transferee against all claims, actions, proceedings, costs, expenses, losses or damages whatsoever in relation to the Transferring Members (whether arising before, at or after the Membership Transfer Date) that arise from any liability of the Transferee to make any form of payment to the Transferor's Scheme that constitutes a debt under sections 60 or 75 of the Pensions Act 1995, save in so far as the same derives from any failure by the Transferee to make such payments to the Transferor's Scheme as are required under this Schedule [ ].

8 [Members returning to the Transferor

If during the period of [ ] years commencing on the Membership Transfer Date any of the Transferring Members who transferred their benefits from the DB Section to the Transferee's DB Scheme are re-employed by the Transferor under an agreed transfer to the Transferor (such agreement not to be unreasonably withheld), rejoin the DB Section and are invited to transfer their benefits from the Transferee's DB Scheme to the DB Section, the Transferee shall use its best endeavours to procure that the amount of the transfer payment made available by the Transferee's DB Scheme shall be calculated in accordance with the Actuary's Letter subject to such adjustments (if any) proposed by either the Transferee's Actuary or the Transferor's Actuary and agreed (such agreement not to be unreasonably withheld or delayed) to allow for changes in circumstances in the meantime. In the event of disagreement between the actuaries, the determination of the transfer payment may be referred to an independent actuary in accordance with Section 9 below.]

9 Resolving disagreements between actuaries

If the Transferor's Actuary and the Transferee's Actuary cannot agree on any matter that requires their agreement under this Schedule [ ], either the Transferor or the Transferee may require the matter to be determined by an independent actuary appointed jointly by the Transferor and the Transferee or if they are unable to agree on a joint appointment, by the President for the time being of the Institute of Actuaries. The determination of the independent actuary shall be final and binding upon the parties except where there has been a manifest error. Such actuary shall act as an expert and not as an arbitrator and his costs should be borne by the Transferor and the Transferee equally except to the extent that the independent actuary considers it fair and equitable for the costs to be borne by them otherwise than equally.

Annexure I

[Actuary's letter]

Annexure 2

[Summary of benefits for Transferring Members of the DC Section who become members of the section of the Transferee's DC Plan]

Type of benefit	Benefit to be provided

Annexure 3

[Summary of benefits for Transferring Members of the DB Section who become members of the Transferee's DB Scheme]

Type of benefit	Benefit to be provided

ANNEX 10D

Annex A to Treasury guidance:
Staff Transfers From Central Government:
A Fair Deal For Staff Pensions

[*Guidance to Departments and Agencies, H M Treasury, June 1999*]

INTRODUCTION

1. This paper sets out in general terms how pensions issues are to be handled in future when staff from central government Departments and Agencies are transferred to a new employer as part of a business transfer. The new approach set out here builds upon earlier guidance, and extends and strengthens its application in order to ensure that staff are treated fairly. It is mainly concerned with transfers between the Government and the private sector when contracts are awarded under public-private partnership (PPP) deals.

2. *Better Quality Services* gives guidance on the treatment of staff pensions in PFI and PPP deals, and there are also policy statements and guidance issued by the Treasury Task Force covering, for instance, the Government's continuing commitment to dialogue with staff and other interested parties about the way in which PPP projects are managed.

3. This new guidance should be reflected in procurement practice as soon as is practicable without disruption to projects which are already at an advanced stage. Detailed guidance will be issued to contracting authorities later this year.

Background

4. Pensions are often an important element in the overall remuneration of staff, particularly within the public services where there are occupational pension schemes offering a high quality of benefits. Sometimes public service schemes require very low employee contributions to earn pension benefits, such as in the Principal Civil Service Pension Scheme (PCSPS) where employee contributions are set at only 1½% of pay, and in these cases employee pay is somewhat lower than it would otherwise be, to reflect the value of the pension scheme.

5. If appropriate arrangements were not made for staff pensions as part of business transfers, the result could be disadvantageous to public service staff who were transferring to the new employer. Not only are pension arrangements an important subject, but they are complex and likely to cause confusion and apprehension if not handled openly and consistently by the contracting authority. It is not in the interests of the contracting authority, or the new employer, or the taxpayer, for staff to be alarmed about the prospects for their pensions in a business transfer which depends upon staff motivation for delivery of good quality public services.

6. Occupational pensions are not covered by the Transfer of Undertaking (Protection of Employment) Regulations 1981 (the TUPE regulations). The new EU Acquired Rights Directive gives Member States the option of including occupational pensions within the terms which are protected by national legislation when an undertaking transfers between employers, and the Government is reviewing whether and if so, how, to include pensions within new TUPE regulations.

7. Independently of the TUPE review, and without prejudice to its conclusions, this paper sets out the standard practices which the Government will follow when its own staff are transferred to other employers. Contracting authorities in other parts of the public sector will continue to make their own arrangements consistent with the law and good employment practice. It would be welcome if they adopted approaches comparable to those set out here. Separate consideration is being given to staff transfers from local government.

8. The principles which Government will apply as a contracting authority in relation to the pensions of transferring staff are:

- to treat staff fairly;
- to do so openly and transparently;
- to involve staff and their representatives fully in consultation about the process and its results; and
- to have clear accountability within Government for the results.

9. There are two separate but related aspects to treatment of pensions in a business transfer:

- first, staff should continue to have access after the transfer to a good quality occupational pension scheme under which they can continue to earn pension benefits through their future service;
- second, staff should be given options for the handling of the accrued benefits which they have already earned.

Each of these aspects is discussed, in turn, in the following sections.

FUTURE SERVICE

10. The focus of this guidance is upon those cases, likely to be in the majority, where a business transfer means that staff have to be 'early leavers' of the occupational pension scheme associated with their former employment. The Government has no plans to seek amendment to the Superannuation Act 1972 to broaden the categories of employees eligible for membership of the PCSPS. Where Civil Servants transfer to private sector employment they will therefore cease to be eligible for PCSPS membership, and their ability to earn further occupational pension benefits through future service will depend upon the occupational pension arrangements offered by the new employer.

11. Not all private sector employers offer occupational pension schemes which are as valuable to employees as the public service schemes, and where good quality pension schemes are offered they typically differ in major respects: for instance, the age of normal retirement, the rate of accrual of pension entitlements, provision of a lump sum on retirement, the degree of indexation of pensions increases, and so on. If care were not taken over staff pensions, the unintended upshot of a business transfer might be a detriment to staff pension benefits.

12. The terms of the business transfer should specifically protect staff pensions. The arrangements made to achieve this need to be considered within the overall context of the business transfer negotiations between the contracting authority and

prospective private sector partners and should not be so cumbersome or expensive to administer as to militate against finding a justifiable business solution.

13. To require that the new employer should offer transferring staff access to a pension scheme which is in all respects identical to the public service scheme which they are leaving would be unduly restrictive. It would add to administrative costs and it could hamper harmonisation of terms and conditions. In the case of the PCSPS it would be an unrealistic requirement, because a non-statutory scheme which was identical to the PCSPS would not qualify for tax exemption. A requirement for an identical scheme would also prevent employers from offering different benefit packages, more in line with private sector standards, which might overall be of greater value to many transferring employees.

14. The guiding principle should be that the new employer offers transferring staff membership of a pension scheme which though not identical is 'broadly comparable' to the public service pension scheme which they are leaving. To satisfy the criteria for broad comparability there must be a rigorous scrutiny of the alternative pension arrangements by a professionally qualified actuary which compares the alternative scheme with the public service scheme in detail. A broadly comparable scheme will be one which, in the professional opinion of the actuary, satisfies the condition that there are no identifiable employees who will suffer material detriment overall in terms of their future accrual of pension benefits under the alternative scheme. The PCSPS takes actuarial advice from the Government Actuary's Department, as do a number of other public service pension schemes.

15. There may be cases where although there are no identifiable classes of employee who would be materially worse off overall, transfer to the new scheme might be materially detrimental to a few individuals. In such cases it will be a matter of judgement whether the new scheme should be adjusted, or whether it would be better simply to make appropriate compensation arrangements to protect the disadvantaged individual(s).

16. Each case should be considered on its merits. There may be exceptional circumstances where there are special reasons for not providing a broadly comparable pension scheme. The strength of those reasons should be tested rigorously and it would then be necessary for the terms of the business transfer to ensure appropriate compensation for all the staff. Actuarial advice should be taken by the contracting authority on the calculation of any compensation in these exceptional circumstances if a broadly comparable scheme is not to be provided, or if there are identified individuals who would be materially worse off overall in the new scheme. In all cases the preference should be for the new employer to offer transferring staff membership of a broadly comparable scheme, and this should be a contract condition in the procurement. Only in exceptional circumstances should the combination of pension arrangements which are less than broadly comparable plus appropriate compensation for employees be accepted.

17. This principle is already being followed by the Government. Its practical application will now be strengthened, extended and made more open:

(i) for transfers of staff from Government Departments and Agencies it will continue to be a requirement for the Government Actuary's Department (GAD) to certify the broad comparability of specified alternative pension arrangements before any contractual commitment is made;

(ii) if for exceptional reasons the requirement for broad comparability is to be waived, GAD advice on appropriate compensation to staff must be followed;

(iii) GAD will follow a published Statement of Practice in certifying broad comparability [. . .]. This sets out clearly the principles which are already being followed. Publishing these principles in the form of this Statement for the first time will increase transparency and accountability;

(iv)   GAD will provide to the contracting authority an analysis of the key differences between the alternative pension scheme and the public service scheme, and the ways in which the differences balance out overall to satisfy the condition of no material detriment overall, by reference to the different groups of employees identified in the staff to be transferred;

(v)   the full GAD analysis will be made available to trades unions and staff representatives, and GAD will respond to any queries or observations which staff representatives have. A reasonable period will be allowed by the contracting authority for discussion, if requested, of any points arising from the GAD analysis;

(vi)   at the conclusion of this period, if any points of concern about the suitability of the proposed alternative pension arrangements remain which cannot be settled by discussion between staff representatives and the contracting authority, staff representatives may raise their concerns directly with a nominated Minister responsible for the affairs of the Department or Agency;

(vii)   no contractual commitments will be made whilst this process of review and consultation is underway, but a reasonable time limit may be set by the contracting authority;

(viii)   the contract for the business transfer must specifically require the implementation of the alternative pension arrangements which have been accepted.

18.   In practice this will mean that in order to avoid delay or having to retrace steps, contracting authorities will need to be satisfied about the broad comparability of alternative pension arrangements well in advance of moving a procurement to selection of short-listed bidders or a preferred bidder. Bidders will need to provide GAD with detailed specifications of their proposed pension arrangements in good time to allow the analysis required and, if necessary, subsequent discussion of it with staff representatives. Contracting authorities will have to reflect this in their procurement logistics. There can be no proper evaluation of options for public-private partnership without a full analysis of the future staff pension arrangements.

19.   Ministers will not authorise a procurement contract, and contractual commitments should not be made under delegated powers, if the conditions set out in paragraph 17 (above) have not been satisfied. This provides a guarantee to staff that the process of identifying acceptable alternative pension arrangements will be fair and open and carried out in full consultation with their representatives.

Subsequent transfers of staff

20.   Current practice restricts the contracting authority's concern about broad comparability to transfers from Government to another employer. Once staff have transferred to a new employer, they may be involved in subsequent business transfers. As a contracting authority, the Government will usually not be involved directly as a party to those arrangements. A contracting authority cannot take responsibility for the treatment of its former staff throughout the remainder of their working lives. But a contracting authority does take an interest in the conduct of business transfers which occur as the direct consequence of actions which it takes as a contracting authority.

21. Therefore:

    (i) where a contract for services is terminated and the work is given to another contractor, the contracting authority will require that pension arrangements are made for staff transferring from the first contractor to the second contractor which would at least be broadly comparable with the public service pension scheme which those staff were in originally. The requirement will be limited to staff originally transferred from the contracting authority, although employers may find it convenient to harmonise terms and conditions in the workforce; and

    (ii) where a primary contractor under a Government contract transfers staff whose work is integral to performance of the contract to a subcontractor in consequence of the terms of the primary contractor's obligations to the Government, it should be a condition of that subcontracting that broadly comparable pension arrangements are made for the transferring staff who were originally in the employ of the contracting authority.

ACCRUED BENEFITS

22. The treatment in procurement practice of the accrued pension benefits of transferring staff is more complex, but raises issues of equal importance. Regulations applicable to pension schemes require 'early leavers' to be given the option of 'preserving' their accrued benefits in the pension scheme which they are leaving, or transferring them to another pension arrangement. In the former case (preservation), the early leavers become 'deferred pensioners' of the scheme which they are leaving. The value of their benefits in that scheme will be uprated by price inflation until they come into payment at normal retirement age. This option may often be preferred by staff, especially those who are closer to retirement and do not expect significant future real earnings growth. In the latter case, where accrued benefits are transferred, the transferor scheme makes a transfer payment to the transferee scheme which extinguishes its liability to the early leaver; in return the new employer's scheme awards a past service credit to the individual. (If the transfer were made to a personal pension plan instead, it would be invested in the normal way.)

23. Regulations stipulate a basis for calculating a minimum transfer value where accrued credits are transferred. Typically this will not result in individuals securing full credits in the new employer's scheme in relation to the credits they are surrendering in the transferor scheme, unless there is a specific agreement between the two pension schemes that they should do so. Typically there is then a different basis for calculation of the transfer value involving the transferor scheme in making higher transfer payments. Such agreements between pension schemes are called 'bulk transfer agreements' (although they may in fact cover only a few members of staff, or just one). A bulk transfer agreement specifies the basis for calculating the transfer payment and the size of the transfer credits it will secure.

24. It is desirable where staff are obliged by a transfer of undertaking to be early leavers of a public service pension scheme for there to be bulk transfer agreements covering the award of past service credits by the new employer's pension scheme. Current practice, as set out in *Better Quality Services* is to treat the absence of a bulk transfer agreement as a significant disadvantage of a bid. In practice this means that bids should be unlikely to succeed unless there is a very good prospect of a bulk transfer agreement being concluded to cover transferring staff. But it is still possible for the business transfer to become dissociated

from negotiation of the bulk transfer agreement between the two pension schemes, leaving staff uncertain about the arrangements which will eventually be made.

25. The existing approach will therefore now be strengthened by making it a condition for the business transfer there will be a bulk transfer agreement under which the pension scheme of the new employer will provide day for day past service credits (or an equivalent recommended by the Government Actuary's Department as a suitable reflection of differences in benefit structures between the schemes) to staff choosing to transfer their accrued credits.

26. It will therefore be essential in future that negotiations between the public service pension scheme and the new employer's pension scheme are settled at a sufficiently early stage in the procurement. The contracting authority should then be able to explain to staff and their representatives what the terms for award of past service credits will be. Staff representatives will be able to discuss this with the contracting authority and GAD, and they will have a reasonable period in which to make any observations and, if necessary, to make representations directly to the Minister nominated as responsible for the project.

27. Only in exceptional circumstances should staff transfers be contemplated where the contract terms will not ensure appropriate bulk transfer terms. If there are exceptional circumstances justifying a waiver of this contract requirement, these should be explained and discussed with staff representatives at an early stage.

28. As in current practice, staff should normally be given a three month period following the issue to them of pension option forms in which to elect whether to preserve their accrued benefits or transfer them. Pension option forms should be issued as soon as practicable following the staff transfer.

29. Further guidance will be issued to contracting authorities concerning the mechanics of bulk transfer negotiations.

Subsequent transfers

30. Where a public service pension scheme associated with the public contracting authority is not a party to a bulk transfer agreement involving a further transfer of former public servants, the position is substantially more complicated. But appropriate bulk transfer terms should be sought for staff in transfers arising from second-round and subsequent contracting, and subcontracting. Further guidance will be issued to contracting authorities concerning appropriate contractual safeguards covering availability of bulk transfer terms in subsequent TUPE transfers involving staff who in initial transfers from the Government were the subject of bulk transfer payments by a public service pension scheme.

31. Making these reforms to procurement arrangements will ensure fair treatment of staff pensions in public-private partnerships. It will continue to be important to look at each case on its merits, and to allow contractual mechanisms to continue to evolve towards better practice. The new approaches described above will guide current practice and new developments to ensure that staff are treated consistently on terms which are fair and predictable, and that there is in every case an opportunity for staff to understand fully the implications for their pensions and to make any representations they wish to the responsible Minister *well before* a Government contracting authority makes final arrangements for a business transfer involving the transfer of staff.

32. The Government will be ready to consider any further reforms which may be needed to cope with developments. In addition, for the longer term, it will review

with representatives of employers and employees the scope for simplifying the administration of public-private partnerships, for instance by developing 'model schemes' or industry-wide multi-employer schemes which are broadly comparable with public service schemes and can facilitate transfers of staff between employers more easily as public-private partnership arrangements become more important to the delivery of public services.

ASSESSMENT OF BROAD COMPARABILITY OF PENSION RIGHTS: STATEMENT OF PRACTICE BY THE GOVERNMENT ACTUARY

The Government has issued a Code of Practice entitled *Transfers of Government Staff: A Fair Deal for Pensions,* describing the key steps which the Government is taking when staff are transferred within the public service, or from the public service to the private sector, with their work. Central to the process is the requirement for an assessment of whether pension arrangements being offered to employees by their new employer are 'broadly comparable' to those provided by their existing employers. This requirement relates only to the period of employment after the change of employer. Exceptionally, if comparability is not available, there is a requirement for the valuation of any detriment on pensions to be offset by elements of the remuneration package outside the pension scheme.

This Statement of Practice sets out the principles on which the Government Actuary's Department (GAD) undertakes its assessments of broad comparability.

Assessments may be commissioned by a public service employer, or by a contracting authority, on a one-off basis in relation to a specific group of staff. They may also be commissioned by a private sector employer with a view to obtaining a 'passport' that his pension scheme is broadly comparable to a specific public service scheme for any group of employees who may transfer from that scheme to his employment over a given period. In either case, the principles are the same. For a passport, where a specific group of employees cannot be identified, the tests are conducted using a very large range of employee profiles containing different characteristics affecting the value of pension rights, for example age, gender, salary level and service length.

Benefits against which assessment is made

The assessment will be made against those benefits provided as a right from the current employer's pension scheme, for which the employees are eligible, and the contributions which employees pay towards that scheme. The assessment will not take account of any benefits which are payable solely as a result of a member being declared redundant, either compulsorily or voluntarily, where those exceed the normal benefits available to an individual who resigns from employment at that time.

The assessment excludes the injury benefits payable by public service employers which provide a minimum income guarantee as a result of injury or death while in the service of the employer. It is recognised that there is uncertainty over the legal protection for benefits available on redundancy and injury within the Transfer of Undertakings (Protection of Employment) Regulations 1981. If so requested by a public service employer or contracting authority, an additional assessment of comparability of the arrangements being offered by the new employer against a base of those on offer with the existing public service employer will be undertaken.

General principles

The general principles on which the assessment of broad comparability is made on transfers from the public service to the private sector are set out below. Corresponding principles apply on other transfers. It must be recognised that there is a very wide range of possible remuneration packages, including pensions, and that some flexibility may need to be applied in the practical implementation of these principles.

Value

- The overall value of the new scheme should be equal to or greater than that of the current scheme.
- There will not be any identifiable group of individuals within the staff being transferred who, overall, are materially worse off.
- Value is assessed by calculating, on consistent assumptions and methods, the underlying employer costs, in excess of the employee's share of the cost, of providing the benefits under the scheme which will accrue over the remaining working life.
- Value is considered as that in the hands of the employee gross of any liability to tax.

Contributions

- Schemes with higher employee contributions, will not be deemed broadly comparable because of the implied reduction in net pay (unless a compensating pay rise is proposed).

Benefits

- The range of benefits provided under the new schemes must at least match that provided by the current scheme.
- Benefits must be available from the new scheme in respect of the same events and at the same time as would have arisen in the existing scheme.
- In some cases, the amount of benefit may be lower on a particular contingency than under the current scheme, but this will need to be balanced by better benefits on other contingencies.
- Normal retirement age – at which full unreduced retirement benefits are available without employer consent and at which deferred benefits are payable will be no greater than in current scheme.
- The initial rate of pension at normal retirement age should normally be no lower than that in the former scheme.
- Shortfalls in the level of pensions increases offered must be offset by better benefits elsewhere.
- In defined benefit schemes, benefits and contributions must be calculated on a definition of pensionable pay of at least the value of that applying in the current scheme.
- Under the arrangements for contracting-out of the State Earnings-Related Pension Scheme currently in place, schemes which are either contracted-out or not contracted-out will be considered for broad comparability
- Time spent with the current employer which would have counted towards qualification for benefits in the existing scheme will count in the new employer's scheme as qualifying service, regardless of whether or not accrued rights are transferred to the new scheme.

Membership

- All those eligible to participate in the current scheme will automatically be admitted to the new scheme from the date of transfer of employment without medical examination. This would not interfere with an employee exercising his/her right to choose to opt out of scheme membership.

Security

- It is recognised that the security of a private sector scheme cannot be provided in the same form as that applying in the public service, but specific safeguards will be sought in the following areas:

  - member representation on trustee bodies;
  - protection of accrued rights, on an on-going basis, on any rule change;
  - changes inspired by the employer, including loss of the contract, involving joining another pension scheme will trigger the offer of a bulk transfer payment or enhancement of benefits within the scheme, to a level commensurate with existing benefits.

Types of scheme

- Only defined benefit schemes will be certified as broadly comparable to defined benefit schemes; only defined contribution schemes will be certified as broadly comparable to defined contribution schemes.
- A test of adequacy of contribution (for a defined contribution scheme) or of benefit design where broad comparability cannot apply (for a defined benefit scheme) will be carried out with the aim, but not the certainty, of ensuring benefits of similar value are expected to emerge.
- When the transfer is between defined benefit and defined contribution schemes, (or vice versa), specific provision should be made for death benefits.

Certification

Pension proposals which satisfy my view of broad comparability will be certified as such. The onus, as set out in the certificate, will be on the current employer to ensure that the pension promises made by the prospective new employer are delivered for the staff concerned.

The certificate will detail the key design features of the proposed arrangement and any associated undertakings provided by the new employer. It will be written in plain English. It will be in a form which can be distributed to the employees and their representatives.

Where a passport application is being considered an interim certificate will be issued if the formal documentation and approvals from regulatory bodies are not in place.

C. D. Daykin   26 May 1999
Government Actuary
London

CHAPTER 11

Tax considerations

John Newman and John Voyez

By its very nature, the tax relating to any transaction is complicated and requires specialist attention. This chapter therefore highlights the areas that should be of concern to the practitioner rather than giving a detailed analysis of all the issues.

11.1   INTRODUCTION – WHY CONSIDER TAX?

Whatever the form of the contract used for technology outsourcing and whoever the parties are, it should be recognised that the government also will be an interested party in the transaction. In the UK, the corporate tax rate is 30 per cent; in the Netherlands it is currently 35 per cent; in Germany it is over 40 per cent, including state trade taxes. These taxes are levied on profits so that any concerned company should ensure that costs and payments in an outsourcing operation are deductible for tax purposes.

Governments in the European Union also levy value added tax (VAT) on the turnover of a business, with the UK rate of 17.5 per cent just below the average for member states. If VAT is not considered in advance of entering into an outsourcing venture, and there is a mismatch or disallowance of VAT, this can be severely harmful as the VAT is not related to profit but to turnover (see section 11.10 for a more detailed discussion of VAT).

Taxation also has an impact on payments that may be made in the context of an outsourcing contract. Withholding taxes can apply in cross-border, and indeed in domestic situations, to interest, royalties and payments that are deemed to be wages or similar. The tendency within the EU over the last few years has been to apply Pay As You Earn (or its European equivalent of wage withholding taxes) on payments that really consist of wages or fees for the services of individuals. Equally, National Insurance and similar social security charges can be charged within outsourcing operations. Unplanned, these charges can increase costs.

11.2   DEFINITIONS

There are various ways of structuring a technology outsourcing relationship, the most common being:

- *Joint ventures*: although these are most commonly utilised in the construction industry area, some are used for technology outsourcing where there is an element of sharing of risks and rewards but a partnership is avoided to prevent joint and several liability falling on the parties (see below);
- *Joint venture companies*: here, a separate company is formed to carry out the technology outsourcing, which is owned by the parties involved, usually two in number;
- *Consortium companies*: again, a separate company is formed, but usually there are three or four (or more) owners of the consortium company;
- *Contractual operations*: by this is meant the outsourcing is a supply of services under a contract. The supplier is commonly incentivised in some way: usually, there is a bonus payment related to savings/results rather than a straightforward price relating to units supplied/time spent under the contract;
- *(SPVs) Special purpose vehicle companies*: these usually fall within the categories of 'joint venture companies' or 'consortium companies' described above.

The above list does not include partnerships; they may be considered but after examination are usually disregarded. This is because the legal definition of a partnership, in an English context, is: 'The relation which subsists between persons carrying on a business in common with a view of profit' (section 1(1) of the Partnership Act 1890). Each partner has joint and several liability for the whole liability of the partnership, making it an unattractive proposition as a vehicle to be used.

In addition, the tax position for companies in partnership is that each corporation in the partnership starts up a separate and distinct trade, being the underlying trade of the partnership. Losses and profits in that partnership activity are relieved by set-off contemporaneously against other profit losses arising in the same company and group (the latter being achieved by group relief). If the partnership activity is loss-making, however, and the loss cannot be absorbed or relieved, then the carry forward or carry back set-off is restricted to profits arising from the same trade. This should be contrasted with the situation where the loss arises from an activity that is part of the corporation's main trade, and the loss can be carried forward to be offset against future profits from the same trade and set back against profits from that trade. There is no ring-fence around the particular business venture/partnership activity.

As a result, corporate partnerships, in practice, are very rarely seen. The term 'partnership' is used to denote relationships that are not partnerships for tax and legal purposes, such as 'public/private partnerships' in the context of London Underground Limited.

11.3   THE FOREIGN DIMENSION

The above categorisations are mainly relevant to domestic, i.e. wholly UK transactions. Where one of the parties is a non-UK corporation and the activity takes place outside the UK, particularly the European Union (or states that are attempting to become members), then the first consideration is whether that foreign state can levy tax on profits in some way.

The EU member states have a network of double tax treaties, which all follow a common model: that of the Organisation for Economic Co-operation and Development (OECD) (see www.oecd.org for more details). A UK company's activities will be charged on profits in a foreign state, if it has a 'permanent establishment' in that state.

Technical terms used in international (and domestic) taxation are never simply defined and the definition of permanent establishment is no exception. This is further complicated by the fact that the treaties were written before modern communications made technology outsourcing possible. To summarise, a permanent establishment is defined as a 'place of management, a branch, an office, a factory, a workshop and a mine or similar'. A building site or construction/installation project is a permanent establishment if it lasts for more than six months (or 12 months in some agreements). However, the use of premises for storage, display, purchasing or other auxiliary or preparatory matters does not constitute a permanent establishment.

A technology outsourcing contract that utilises a site outside the UK to carry out the process could be a permanent establishment of the business that was outsourcing. This applies if the premises or offices are owned/let/licensed by the business itself. To avoid this, the contractor should take care that all premises are legally occupied by the foreign local contractor and there is no licence to use specific offices/premises, etc.

Lastly, a permanent establishment will not be deemed to exist where a UK corporation has a broker or an independent agent; it will be, however, if the agent does not have independent status in that foreign state. In the context of technology outsourcing, the status of agents outside the UK is dealt with in more detail below, as well as possible withholding taxes on cross-border payments.

11.4   JOINT VENTURES

Under a joint venture agreement, each party has a share of turnover, expenses, assets and so on of the joint venture. The economic result of a joint venture where the parties share turnover and expenses 60/40 is exactly the same as a partnership sharing profits 60/40, except that legally the joint venture is not a partnership. The result is that the parties do not assume joint and several liability for the joint venture. For tax purposes, each party's share of income and expenses is included in its own main profit and loss account, along with other income and expenses. Unless the trade or business of the party is radically different from that being carried on before entry into the joint venture, no new trade is deemed to have started and accordingly a loss can be set off against the other activities of the corporation and carried back or forward in the normal way.

A retailer and a logistics company may work together to develop an advanced logistics ordering system from electronic point of sale (EPOS) technology. Their objectives would be to pool technology and knowledge to develop a working product that could be utilised by other companies in the supply chain as well as other retailers. A joint venture where costs were borne in a fixed ratio and income from third parties was shared in a fixed ratio would be a simple structure with no inherent corporation tax dangers.

11.4.1 Joint venture company or consortium company

A joint venture company usually involves two or three shareholders – the so-called joint venturers in a new company. A consortium company, on the other hand, is a term that is usually utilised to note a business partnership that is legally in fact a corporation, i.e. a company owned by the consortium members. The number of members in a consortium is usually three or more. A joint venture or consortium company shareholders agreement among the consortium members will be signed, which sets out the rules of the governance of the company, including issues of funding. It is usual to see these agreements matched by agreements between the consortium company and each shareholder relating to the supply of services (i.e. the outsourcing contract), equipment, premises and finance, particularly where the consortium company draws disproportionately on one party for, say, technological know-how or finance.

For tax purposes the joint venture or consortium company is a new corporate taxpayer, which will have to file a separate tax return just like any other taxpayer. Charges to and from the company will generally be taxable and tax deductible in the normal way. However, the start-up losses or ongoing losses of the company can be relieved against profits arising outside the joint venture if one of the following applies:

- One of the joint venture shareholders is a company and owns over 75 per cent of the ordinary share capital of the joint venture/consortium company. In that case, 100 per cent of any loss in that company may be offset under group relief against profits in the joint venture shareholders group of companies. No part of the loss could be relieved against profits in the minority shareholders group of companies.

- Over 75 per cent of the shareholders in the consortium/joint venture company are corporations resident in the UK, and own over 5 per cent each of the consortium/joint venture company. Each shareholder can claim up to its percentage share of the share capital of the loss under consortium group relief. This usually means that not all the losses in the consortium company are claimed. The amount unclaimed is either carried forward (or possibly carried back) for offset against future profits for tax purposes inside the consortium company.

11.5 OUTSOURCING CONTRACTS

The tax position of the contractual operations should be simple: each party (and there are usually only two involved) is taxable on its profit or loss. This position is achieved if both parties are profitable and the outsourcing contract works well. If the contract goes wrong then tax difficulties can result.

Sometimes, one party, typically the company providing the outsourced services, finds the contract loss making and wishes to be prudent and provide for future losses to the end of the contract term by setting up an appropriate provision at a balance sheet date. The Inland Revenue will try to disallow the provision and allow the future loss only when it is incurred, arguing that the provision is non-specific and, further, that the loss is not in accordance with accounting conventions. Furthermore, if the contractor decides to terminate the contract and make a lump sum payment to the other party, this can be non-deductible as a capital payment. The basis for this is a tax case concerning Granada Motorway Service Stations, where Granada paid a lump sum to the Department of Transport to reduce the lease payments on the motorway stations that were tied to retail turnover on sites. The payment was ruled to be non-deductible as capital (*Tucker (HM Inspector of Taxes)* v. *Granada Motorway Services Ltd* [1979] 53 TC 92).

The start (or the termination) of outsourcing contracts often involves the transfer on to one party's payroll of employees who were employed by the other party. This will usually mean that the transfer of an undertaking rules arising from European Union law apply. The result, in tax terms, is that the new contractor inherits the withholding tax liabilities (if any) of the predecessor on the payroll under PAYE. Further, there can be ongoing risks: if the outsourcing contract is, for example, fulfilled by specific employees processing data at the premises of the main contractor and the primary liability for PAYE is not met by the direct employer, the liability can fall on the 'innocent' party in the outsourcing contract, i.e. the main contractor.

11.6   AGENTS OUTSIDE THE UK

If an agreement with a foreign, non-resident company constitutes an agency that is not independent, the UK company concerned can be liable for the tax levied by the other country on the profits of the deemed branch or permanent establishment.

Whether an agent is independent or not is determined by:

- whether the agent has and habitually exercises the authority to conclude contracts in the name of the principal;
- if the agent has no such authority, whether a stock of goods/merchandise from which it delivers for the principal is maintained for the principal;
- whether the agent, although formally independent, devotes all or almost all of its activities to the principal's transactions.

In each case if the answer is affirmative, the agent is deemed dependent and the principal is taxable in the foreign country under the name, generally, of the agent.

The tax charge is restricted to that arising on income to the branch or agency acting notionally at arm's length to its head office. Because of the difficulty of attributing profit to a branch, foreign tax authorities tend to use a method by which profit is deemed to be some percentage of sales or expenses. In some circumstances this can be acceptable, but in others it may be advisable to incorporate a new subsidiary in the country concerned.

11.7   WITHHOLDING TAXES ON CROSS-BORDER PAYMENTS

This topic cannot be covered in the context of this book, but a few pointers can be given. In general, given cross-border transactions in a European Union context, the tax position will be dealt with by treaties conforming to the OECD model (see section 11.3). Payments that are characterised as royalties for patents/know-how/software will attract no withholding taxes but each case has to be looked at taking into account the relevant treaty and the definitions in the countries concerned: beware these can vary widely!

11.8   TRANSFER OF ASSETS

In the establishment of an outsourcing operation, the parties may wish to transfer assets that will be used in the new operation. The assets can range across items such as:

- *Plant and equipment*: the transferors may retain title in the plant and equipment that is used by the new joint venture. Capital allowances on such equipment, which can be claimed by owners, have to be considered: the company that does not own the assets would not be eligible to claim capital allowances unless contractually it had a right to buy the equipment akin to a hire purchase contract. If ownership is transferred, consideration should be given to the possibility of electing the value at which the assets are transferred.

- *Real estate land and buildings*: the ownership of these assets would normally stay with the contributor. Accordingly there would be no disposal for chargeable gains purposes. If the premises concerned are leased or licensed by the customer to the outsourcing supplier or contractor, then rent payments would be taxable in the customer's hands and deductible for the supplier or contractor. It would be difficult for the Inland Revenue to impute a market rent, so quite often a low licence fee is charged.
- *Intellectual property*: the position on intellectual property could range from allowing use under licence for a restricted period to outright sale. In most cases, the contributor would be liable to corporation tax as income on all amounts due in respect of transfers of intellectual property. It would be unlikely that these would be treated as chargeable gains: this depends on the status of the contributor and the impact of the intellectual property provisions of the Finance Act 2002, in which the revised code dealing with the sale and purchase of intellectual property is contained. For the recipient of the intellectual property, either the amount paid for the use of the intellectual property would be deductible, or if the transaction was treated as a capital acquisition, tax depreciable subject to the anti-avoidance provisions of the Finance Act 2002.

11.9   RESEARCH AND DEVELOPMENT

The Finance Act 2002 included favourable provisions for research and development (R&D) in the form of tax credits and enhanced capital allowances. Technology outsourcing works against the outsourcing party claiming either, though it will vary in specific cases depending on the nature of the R&D and the operation of the parties.

11.10   VALUE ADDED TAX

As has already been noted, one of the main reasons for outsourcing is the reduction of costs. Clearly, to the extent that any extra costs are generated, the advantages of outsourcing are reduced. It follows that as soon as third party suppliers are contracted to deliver the same services as those previously provided in-house, a new cost arises for which an invoice has to be issued. This then gives rise to the question of VAT: should VAT be charged or not?

The VAT legislation (consolidated within the VAT Act 1994) defines supplies that may be treated as either zero rated or exempt for VAT purposes. If the supply made is not within either of the Schedules for zero rating or exemption, then VAT is due at the standard rate (certain supplies may be treated as outside the scope of UK VAT). Outsourcing per se is not a service that is identified as a supply in its own right, and therefore it is necessary for VAT purposes to clarify exactly what service is to be supplied in order to agree the VAT liability.

11.10.1 Taxable business activities

Subject to the above, provided the business that has outsourced part of its activities is registered for VAT, and able to recover VAT in full, no material issues should arise. The third party outsourcer will simply invoice for the services and charge VAT at the appropriate rate. Where the standard rate applies, VAT will be recovered in full by the client. The only issue that may be worth some consideration is the timing of invoices to ensure cash flow is not impaired. Ideally invoices should be issued to coincide with the end of the VAT quarter of the client to allow recovery of VAT at the earliest possible opportunity. This may, however, clash with the objective of the outsourcer, who will wish to be paid the VAT by the client at an early date in its VAT period. Where both client and outsourcer are truly independent, it may not be possible to co-ordinate the timing of invoices in this manner.

It should be noted that where outsourcing involves government bodies and local authorities, such bodies generally have a special status for VAT purposes. Where costs are incurred for undertaking non-business activities, i.e. where the body has a statutory obligation to provide a service, the VAT on such costs should be fully recoverable. Where, however, such bodies are involved in business activities, the VAT treatment is the same as for other commercial enterprises. For the outsourcer, it is always worthwhile checking at a very early stage in the negotiations the VAT status of the customer.

11.10.2 Exempt business activities

It is where businesses are exempt from VAT on income received that most VAT problems arise. Typically this will apply to the financial services sector, but can have an impact in other areas such as health, welfare and education. As already noted, outsourcing will often generate a VAT charge in respect of services supplied that would not otherwise arise. Most commonly this will apply to the charge for salary and personnel costs. If the client is unable to recover VAT on these charges, then outsourcing is far less attractive. Some businesses may accept a standard rated VAT charge as being a necessary cost arising from outsourcing, but many clients will look to avoid irrecoverable VAT arising in this way.

However, in the world of financial services (or health, welfare and educa-tion) it is possible that the services supplied by the outsourcer may qualify to be treated as exempt from VAT if falling within the exemptions provided for in Schedule 9 to the VAT Act 1994 (as governed by Article 13 of the EC Sixth Directive on VAT). There is, however, considerable case law on the interpre-tation provided by the European Court and Customs and Excise on the exemptions found in the legislation, and this has developed over a number of years.

In the Danish case of *Sparekassernes Datacenter* v. *Skatteministeriet* (C-2/95) [1997] All ER (EC) 23 (SDC) an association of savings banks pro-vided outsourced operations comprising executions of transfers, advice and trade in securities, and management of deposits. It was claimed that these supplies to the bank were exempt from VAT. The decision in favour of SDC outlined a number of principles including;

- there is no distinction between the provision of services by electronic or manual means; it is the nature of the services that determines whether they qualify for exemption;
- it is not necessary to have a contractual relationship with the end user of the services in order for exemption to apply;
- the fact that a service is essential for completing an exempt transaction does not mean that the service is exempt;
- in order to be characterised as an exempt transaction, the service must have the effect of transferring funds and entail changes in the legal and financial situation;
- in order to qualify as exempt, the services, when viewed as a whole, must constitute a transaction listed in Article 13 of the EC Sixth Directive (77/388/EEC); it is not sufficient that a particular service is necessary to complete an exempt transaction.

In the case of *CSC Financial Services (formerly Continuum)* (C-235/00) [2002] 1 WLR 2200, CSC provided call centre and administration services to Royal Sun Life in respect of personal equity plans. The High Court referred a number of questions to the ECJ for clarification. The ECJ's responses to these were that:

- in order to qualify for exemption, the services must be distinct in charac-ter, specific to, and essential for exempt transactions;
- the services must have 'the effect of transferring funds and entail changes of a legal and financial character';
- the supply of a mere physical, technical or administrative service, which does not alter either the legal or financial position, would not be VAT exempt;
- the fact that a service is essential for completing an exempt transaction does not make the service exempt.

These tests are similar to the ground rules established by the ECJ in the *SDC* case as above.

Although CSC was unsuccessful in its claim at EU level, primarily because it did not actually issue or transfer units in the unit trust plans, the decision demonstrates that in certain cases in order to achieve exemption it may be necessary to go a step further in the tasks outsourced.

In the case of *Customs and Excise Commissioners* v. *FDR Ltd* [2000] EWCA Civ 216, the company acted as a clearing house for credit and debit card transactions, dealing with customer and retailer payments and transfers between issuing banks. Following the principles established in the *SDC* case, the Court of Appeal determined that FDR's principal supply was the processing of card transactions and the settling of liabilities, and that other administrative functions were ancillary to these services. Accordingly, the services were exempt.

In the case of *Electronic Data Systems Ltd* [2003] EWCA Civ 492, EDS administered personal loans for Lloyds Bank. EDS' services covered everything from receiving the application, validating it, releasing the funds on approval, calculating interest, dealing with queries, the production of statements and the closure of loans on repayment. Customs argued that EDS' services did not amount to the granting of credit (because it was the bank not EDS lending money) and instead could be characterised as credit management, administrative services, physical and technical supplies and the provision of financial information, all of which are taxable.

The Tribunal rejected Customs' approach, ruling that EDS performed a complete service of granting credit and carried out all the necessary operations for it to be effected. Following the *SDC*, *FDR* and *CSC* cases, the Tribunal decided that EDS effected the change in legal and financial arrangements between the bank and its customers, and its involvement was not merely ancillary or preparatory to these operations, but crucial and essential to their conclusion. Accordingly, EDS' services were exempt, and this has been confirmed in the Court of Appeal.

These are all prominent decisions in the financial services sector, but exemption may also cover activities such as outsourced health and welfare services, e.g. the provision of locums. It is however in the financial service world where the VAT guidelines have been most severely tested, and at the time of writing the legislation contained at Group 5 (Finance) of Schedule 9 to the VAT Act 1994 is the subject of consultation and will be amended. This follows Customs and Excise withdrawal of their appeals in the *Prudential Assurance Co Ltd* [2001] BVC 2201 and *Abbey National plc* [2002] BVC 2077 cases, concerning the management of unit trusts and open-ended investment companies (OEICs), and also the publication of a consultation paper on pensions.

A further aspect of this is that when providing the core outsource service, many other services may also be required and provided, e.g. an outsourced specialist insurance claims handling operation will, in addition to dealing with claims, provide accounting support plus a range of other activities as part of the contract. The VAT liability of a package of services was tested in the case of *Card Protection Plan Ltd* (CPP) (C-349/96) [2001] BVC 158, ECJ. CPP provided insurance cover for lost credit cards, together with a number of other services, which on their own would fall to be treated as standard rated. The ECJ established a number of important principles, including:

- there is a single supply where one or more elements of the services could be regarded as constituting the principal service, to which the other services are ancillary;
- the fact that a single price is charged is not decisive, although it might suggest that there is a single service;
- even if a single price is charged, if the customer intended to buy distinct services, apportionment would be required.

Where the core service is exempt from VAT, it is now accepted by Customs and Excise that all other activities that are simply ancillary to and supportive of the main supply should also be treated as part of a single exempt supply. However, when these other activities become an aim in themselves, and it is possible to identify separate supplies as being made, then these activities attract their own VAT liability, which will often result in a multiple supply part of which will be standard rated and part of which may be exempt.

Finally, the outsourcer should remember that where the supplies to be made are exempt, the corollary is that VAT on costs incurred in making these supplies will be irrecoverable. When a contract first starts up the take on costs may be significant, e.g. new computer systems. The outsourcer's irrecoverable VAT should be factored into the contract price.

11.10.3   VAT planning

Exempt businesses requiring outsourced services have in the past looked at structures that avoid generating irrecoverable VAT. In the past these have included the use of VAT group structures and offshore companies. However, legislation has been passed to block artificial arrangements, and Customs and Excise now has considerable powers particularly in the area of VAT groups (see Business Brief 01/2001, 10 January 2001 and most recently Business Brief 30/2002, 19 November 2002). At the time of writing, a number of high profile cases are proceeding through the courts on VAT avoidance.[1] Although they are not related to outsourcing, the principle of being able to defeat an arrangement that Customs and Excise considers to be avoidance, on the basis that it is not undertaken in the course or furtherance of an economic business activity, may create a dangerous precedent. Any party considering mitigation of VAT costs in an outsourcing arrangement will do well to review Customs and Excise policy in this area.

Other planning areas include the use of joint employment contracts where staff are employed by both the client and outsourcer with one paymaster, thus avoiding VAT on recharged salary costs. This should be acceptable to Customs and Excise, but unfortunately is rarely workable commercially, and often gives rise to employment law issues.

When considering outsourcing contracts, artificial attempts to wrap a bundle of separate standard rated supplies into a single core exempt supply, in order to obtain the benefit of exemption, need to be treated with caution if a confrontation with Customs and Excise is to be avoided. However, it may be that a business will need to outsource more of its activities, rather than less, in order to ensure that the service being received does qualify for exemption if this is necessary. Presentationally, where a package of services is to be supplied, if the core service is exempt, it is preferable for this to be clearly identified at the start of the agreement as being the principal activity for which the contract is being entered into. All other ancillary supporting services, e.g. the accounting function should be relegated to the appendices. The principles outlined in the *CPP* case above should be considered.

Finally, the consideration to be paid in any contract for the services should always be stated to be exclusive of VAT, which will be added where appropriate. This is for the protection of the supplier of the services in the event that Customs and Excise should be of the view that the service is standard rated and VAT has to be charged. Clearly the VAT exempt client may have different views on this. The reader will appreciate that it is imperative for both parties to a contract to be certain on the VAT position if the supplies are to be properly costed.

11.10.4 Transfer of assets

The above deals with the role of specialist outsourcing operators, but it may be that a business will decide to transfer out part of its operations to a 'Newco' established specifically for these purposes. This will often mean the transfer of fixtures, fittings, computers, buildings, personnel and possibly goodwill and intellectual property, depending on the exact nature of the activities being outsourced. In this case, where essentially the activity undertaken by Newco after the transfer is the same as that before the transfer, Customs and Excise should treat this as a supply of neither goods nor services, and such transfers of business and assets are made free of VAT. Newco will, however, need to consider VAT registration, and, if an election has been made to waive exemption in respect of any property transferred, then Newco must also waive exemption prior to the transfer.

However, depending on precisely what business and assets are transferred, it is possible that Customs and Excise will not accept a transfer of a going concern (TOGC) treatment and VAT will be chargeable on the consideration.

Newco will be able to recover the VAT, provided the future outsourcing activities will be fully taxable. There is, therefore, only a cash flow issue to consider. However, if either transferor and/or transferee are exempt or partially exempt, the charging of VAT on the transfer will have implications.

In the case of *Royal Bank of Scotland Group Plc* v. *Customs and Excise Commissioners* [2002] BVC 2213 (RBoS), following the purchase of NatWest Bank, RBoS sold the division of NatWest Bank that dealt with financial clearing services to EDS. The intention was that EDS would be contracted by RBoS to carry out all its clearing services. RBoS considered this to be a TOGC, which Customs and Excise challenged. The Tribunal ruled that a TOGC had taken place in that a part of the RBoS business had been transferred to EDS that was capable of separate operation, notwithstanding the retention by RBoS of certain contracts and assets, plus an option by the vendor to repurchase the operation at a later date.

Any contract for the transfer of all or part of the business and assets should contain standard TOGC clauses whereby both parties agree to treat the transaction as being a supply of neither goods nor services, and thus outside the scope of VAT (Article 5 of the VAT (Special Provisions) Order 1995, SI 1995/1268). However the transferor will wish to protect its position by ensuring that the right to charge VAT is retained in the event that Customs and Excise should take a different view.

11.11 CONCLUSIONS

Tax should be considered as a priority before entering into any outsourcing contract. The only way to do this is to be clear about both the commercial and tax objectives of the transaction, in terms not only of the responsibilities of each party, but also of which party is to bear the tax costs and tax risks, if any. It may not be possible to achieve the desired tax result but, given clear objectives, it is usually possible to plan for a less harmful position.

NOTE

1. For many years it has always been the case that a *Furniss* v. *Dawson* [1984] AC 474, attack did not apply to VAT as this is a transactional tax and the courts accepted that it was not permissible to stand back and take a global view of the arrangements. Each step in a chain of transactions had to be analysed, and if the step complies with the appropriate legislation, then the arrangements would work. This approach has changed with the advent of *Halifax* v. *Customs and Excise Commissioners* [2002] STC 402, which involved a sequence of transactions structured purely to obtain recovery of VAT which would otherwise have been irrecoverable.

Customs and Excise attacked the arrangements successfully in the court on the basis that the inserted steps were not for a business purpose, but existed purely as a mechanism to recover VAT. Subsequent cases have followed a similar line and Customs and Excise have in most cases been successful pursuing this line, which has been backed up by the European concept of 'abuse of rights'. The debate regarding whether businesses should be allowed to structure their activities so as to pay the least amount of tax continues, but the next stop for the *Halifax* case is the European Court and the outcome of this hearing (which is some way of at the time of writing) will be eagerly awaited.

Index

acceptable use policies
website hosting 198–9
access codes 174–5
accommodation 31
accounting
business process outsourcing (BPO)
208–9, 213, 219, 224
additional resources 95–6
agents
taxation and 355
application service provider (ASP)
agreements
business process outsourcing (BPO)
227–8
telecommunications outsourcing
157, 163–4
applications process outsourcing 209
arbitration 150
assets 29
exit management and 146, 147
taxation and transfer of assets
355–6, 361–2
see also **transfer of assets agreement**
assignment 187
public sector outsourcing 251–2
audio and video conferencing 155, 167
audit
auditing security 176–7
public sector outsourcing 249
rights 54–5, 105–6
skills 39
website hosting 196

backlogs 29
back-to-back structure 75
benchmarking 107–8, 258–76
best practice 264
checklist 267–8
commercial 260–1, 266–7
context 264–6
example 269–74
indexation 269–74, 275–6

information systems outsourcing
134–5
market testing 261–2
meaning 259
metrics based 259–60, 266
practical uses 265–6
process 263–4
public sector outsourcing 249–50
reasons for 262–3
telecommunications outsourcing
181–5
types 259–62
website hosting 195–6
bid process 16–17
overview 18–19, 20
bonuses 42
service debits 102
break option
public sector outsourcing 250–1
bribery 246–7
buffer zone 50
business changes 98
business drivers of outsourcing 2–3
building contract around 43–4
public sector 231–4
business process outsourcing (BPO) 1, 43,
208–29
application service provider (ASP)
agreements 227–8
comparison with IT outsourcing
209–11
data protection 223–4
developments 224–9
e-business 225–7
finance and accounting 208–9, 213,
219, 224
human resources 209, 213–15,
226–7
interfaces 224
joint venture approach 224–5
key contract clauses 217–24
liabilities 221

business process outsourcing (BPO)
  (*continued*)
    market for 211–13
    meaning 208–9
    operating level agreement (OLA)
      218–19
    procurement 209, 215
    range of services 213–17
    real estate management 209, 215–17
    record retention 224
    regulatory issues 219–20
    roles and responsibilities 217–18
    scope 220–1
    taxation 223–4
    termination 222

cabling and related infrastructure
    telecommunications outsourcing
      157, 166
Call Centre Association (CCA) 162
call centres 155, 160–3
Centre for Dispute Resolution (CDR) 150
change
    changing services 94–8
    of control 110
    control over cost of 49–50
    government policy and public
      sector outsourcing 251
    management 140
    types 95–8
charges 51
    information systems outsourcing
      135–8
    linkage of charging to delivery of
      benefits 52–3
    telecommunications outsourcing
      180–1
    website hosting 195
collective agreements
    transfer of undertakings 294
collective redundancies
    consultation on 305–6
co-location/hosting arrangements 157
commercial benchmarking 260–1, 266–7
communication 30
    disputes and 104–6
competitiveness
    outsourcing and 2, 3
**Computing Services and Software
  Association (CSSA)** 23, 33
confidentiality agreements 58
    specimen 62–3
consequential losses 101, 138

consortia 72, 78–80, 351, 353–4
consultation on transfer of undertakings
  303–7
    on collective redundancies 305–6
    commencement 304–5
    representatives 303–4
contract of employment
    pensions and 315–16
    variation 300–1
contract of outsourcing 66–112
    drivers for outsourcing and 43–4
    expiry 55–7
    information systems outsourcing
      114–17
    prime and subcontracts 72–4
    renewals 25
    services agreement 81, 83, 86–112
    structuring the contracts 80–3
    structuring the deal 66–80
    taxation and 354
    term (period) 116–17, 195, 243–5
    termination *see* **termination of
      contract**
    third party rights 74–7
    transfer of assets agreement 80–1,
      84–6
corruption 246–7
customers
    attaching customer equipment to
      network 173–4
    business process outsourcing 210
    dependency on 30
    due diligence exercise and 19, 23
    objectives 49–55
    procurement by *see* **procurement
      process**

damages
    liquidated 91, 99
data networks 154
    benchmarking 182–5
    convergence solution 164–6
    data security 176
    mobile data and WAP 155, 167
    network security 175–6
    traditional 164
data protection 31–2
    business process outsourcing (BPO)
      223–4
    information systems outsourcing
      141–2
    website hosting 196–7
day-to-day conversations 104

dedicated trading and information
exchanges 156
dependency 69
  on customers/suppliers 30
  rare skills dependency check 39
  in services agreement 92–3
desktop deals 113
development centre workshop 42
direct losses 101
disaster recovery
  website hosting 198
disputes
  communication and 104–6
  escalation 106, 149
  information systems outsourcing
    149–50
  resolution procedures 149–50
drivers *see* **business drivers of outsourcing**
due diligence 17–43, 81, 119
  barriers to 32–3
  benefits for customer and supplier
    19
  checklist of information needed
    24–5
  content 27
  customers and preparation for 23
  example areas 29–32
  formal 35–7
  format 27
  human resources 33–43
  informal 37–43
  methodology 33–43
  methods 26–9
  post-completion stage 28–9
  preparation 23, 26–7
  role 17, 19
  when undertaken 25–6

e-business
  business process outsourcing (BPO)
    225–7
  telecommunications outsourcing
    156–7
employers' liability insurance
  transfer of undertakings 294–5
employment *see* **human resources and**
  employment issues
encryption 156
escalation 100–4
  disputes 106, 149
European Union (EU) 277
  authority to act as

  telecommunications service
    provider and 171
  call centres and 162
  Directives on transfer of
    undertakings 277, 278–9, 285
  procurement process and 12,
    237–40
  taxation 352, 355
  telephone number portability and
    160
evergreen clauses 195
exclusion clauses 138
exclusivity 93
exit management
  information systems outsourcing
    144–8
  public sector outsourcing 245
  telecommunications outsourcing
    187
experts
  dispute resolution and 150

finance and accounting
  business process outsourcing (BPO)
    208–9, 213, 219, 224
financial services 163
fixed-term contracts 108
force majeure clauses 93
  website hosting 198
forecasting meetings 105

government sector *see* **public sector**
  outsourcing
guarantees
  parent companies 186

hacking 175
hardware
  changing hardware platform
    45–6
  voice telephony 158
  website hosting 200–1
health and safety issues 30, 41
holiday entitlements 41
hotdesking 158–9, 168
human resources and employment issues
  277–308
  business process outsourcing (BPO)
    209, 213–15, 226–7
  consultation 303–7
  due diligence methodology 33–43
  employment protection 277–8

human resources and employment issues
(*continued*)
    EU Directives on transfer of
      undertakings 277, 278–9, 285
    informal due diligence and 38–42
    outsourcing survey 283–4
    public sector outsourcing and 233,
      245–6, 307–8
    reorganisations 298–303
    transfer of undertaking and 277,
      278–308
    see also **skills; transfer of**
      undertakings

implementation of services 91
indemnity 101, 139
    letter 59–61, 64–5
Independent Committee for the
  Supervision of Standards for
  Information Services (ICSTIS) 162
indexation 107, 136–7
    benchmarking 269–74, 275–6
induction programmes 41
information exchanges 156
information systems outsourcing 113–51
    change management 140
    charges 135–8
    data issues 141–2
    dispute resolution procedures
      149–50
    exit management 144–8
    general warranties 148
    intellectual property rights 117–19
    liability 138–9
    operations management 125–6
    performance improvement 134–5
    production control 126–8
    service credits 132–4
    service level and service level
      agreement (SLA) 128–32
    technology services 123–8
    term (period) of contract 116–17
    termination 143–4
    transfer of third party software
      119–23
    typical contract terms 114–16
insolvency
    telecommunications outsourcing
      186–7
insurance *see* **employers' liability**
  insurance
intellectual property 30, 46–8, 356

information systems outsourcing
    117–19
    licences 85, 117–18
    public sector outsourcing 247–8
    transfer of assets agreement 85
intent
    letter 59–61, 64–5
investment
    protection 48–9
invitation to tender (ITT) 8, 44
    confidentiality agreements and 58
    contents 9–10
invoicing 32
IP tunnelling 156

joint priming 71–2
joint ventures 78–80, 351
    business process outsourcing (BPO)
      224–5
    taxation 352–4

letter of indemnity/letter of intent 59–61
    specimen 64–5
liability
    business process outsourcing (BPO)
      221
    information systems outsourcing
      138–9
    public sector outsourcing 252–3
licences
    exit management and 146
    intellectual property 85, 117–18
    loss 110
    transfer of third party software
      117–18, 119–23
liquidated damages 91, 99
local government pension scheme 327–8

maintenance
    telecommunications outsourcing
      155
mandatory changes 97–8
market testing 261–2
mediation 150
meetings 105
metrics based benchmarking 259–60, 266
mobile data and WAP 155, 167
mobile telephony 154–5, 181–2
most favoured nation/customer clauses
  94
multiple provider structures 71–4
    joint priming 71–2

prime and subcontracts 72–4
provider consortia 72

negative indexation 107
networks *see* **data networks**
novation rights 187
numbers
telephone 159–60

operations management
information systems outsourcing
125–6
outsourcing
appropriateness 3
preparation for 6–11
selective 4
simple outsourcing 67
size of market 1–2
strategy 1, 3–4
survey 283–4
value based approach 4
what to outsource 4
see also individual topics

parent companies 67–9
guarantees 186
partnerships 351
payroll deductions 39
pensions 38, 40, 310–49
contracts of employment and
315–16
defined benefit and defined
contribution schemes 312–13
documentation 318–20
future service obligations 325
interim periods of participation
321–3
legal structure 314–15
local government pension scheme
327–8
outsourcing transaction and 318–23
preliminary enquiries 329
public sector outsourcing 325–8
regulatory structure 313–14
shortfall clauses 324–5
sources of pension provision
311–12
taxation 313–14
transfer calculations 323–5
transfer of undertakings 294,
316–18
Treasury guidance 326–7, 341–9

warranties 320–1, 330–3
performance
payment and 53
performance bonds 186
service debits 102, 133
performance improvement
information systems outsourcing
134–5
Pimlico School project 12
plant and equipment 355–6
preferred supplier clauses 93
preparation
due diligence 23, 26–7
outsourcing 6–11
pricing *see* **charges**
Private Finance Initiative (PFI) 12, 230,
232, 233, 241–2
privity of contract 76
procurement process 11–16
business process outsourcing (BPO)
209, 215
cost model 12–13
financial/viability assessment 13
overview 14–16
qualitative model 13
production control
information systems outsourcing
126–8
proposals 17
checklist for 21–3
provider consortia 72
public sector outsourcing 230–57
assignment 251–2
audit 249
authority to contract 236
benchmarking 249–50
break option 250–1
capacity to contract 234–6
change in government policy and
251
commercial and contractual issues
242–53
corrupt gifts 246–7
critical success factors 253–5
drivers for 231–4
EC public procurement regulations
12, 237–40
exit management 245
human resources issues 233, 245–6,
307–8
intellectual property 247–8
liability 252–3

public sector outsourcing (*continued*)
limitations on 236–7
local government pension scheme
327–8
pensions 325–8
Private Finance Initiative (PFI) 12,
230, 232, 233, 241–2
public law constraints 234–40
technology refreshment 244–5
term (period) of contract 243–5
transfer of undertakings and 245–6,
307–8
ultra vires 234–6
warranties 248–9

quality systems 29–30

real property 84, 356
business process outsourcing (BPO)
209, 215–17
record retention
business process outsourcing (BPO)
224
reduced resources 95–6
redundancy 55, 56
consultation on 305–6
regulatory issues
business process outsourcing (BPO)
219–20
pensions 313–14
remedies 99–104
escalation 100–4
liquidated damages 91, 99
service credits 99–100, 132–4
reorganisations 298–303
economic, technical or
organisational reasons 299–300
post-transfer reorganisations 301–2
variation in contracts of
employment 300–1
reporting requirements
telecommunications outsourcing
185
representatives
contract negotiation 104–5
transfer of undertaking
consultation 303–4
request for proposal (RFP) 8, 44
confidentiality agreements and 58
contents 9–10
research and development
taxation 356

research based benchmarking 259–60
resources
additional or reduced 95–6
flexibility in allocation 51–2
restrictive covenants
transfer of undertakings 293
retendering 108–9
review meetings 105
reward
allocation 98–9
reward systems 52–3
service debits 102, 133
risk 3
allocation 98–9
mandatory changes and 97–8
run off services 145–6

security 31, 38, 54
access codes 174–5
auditing security 176–7
data security 176
hacking 175
network security 175–6
telecommunications outsourcing
174–7
selective outsourcing 4
**service level and service level agreement
(SLA)** 83, 87, 89
business process outsourcing (BPO)
218–19
conflict with service agreement 92
definition of service level 90
information systems outsourcing
128–32
measurement of service levels 90,
129
statement of work 199–200
telecommunications outsourcing
167–8
website hosting 200–3
services
changing 94–8
defining 86–90, 210
implementation 91
information systems outsourcing
123–8
level *see* **service level and service
level agreement (SLA)**
retaining control 54–5
service credits 99–100, 132–4, 203–4
service debits 102, 133
statement of work 199–200

services agreement 81, 83, 86–112
  allocating risk and reward 98–9
  changing the services 94–8
  communication and disputes
    104–6
  defining the services 86–90
  establishing dependencies and
    qualifications 92–3
  exclusivity and preferred
    supplier/most favoured nation
    clauses 93–4
  implementing the services 91
  remedies 99–104
  retendering and exit 108–12
  value for money 106–8
  website hosting 195–9
share entitlements
  transfer of undertakings 296
shortlists 26
simple outsourcing 67
skills
  access to new skills 44–5
  audit 39
  rare skills dependency check 39
  transfer 30
software
  locks 148
  transfer of third party software
    117–18, 119–23
  website hosting 201
special purpose vehicle companies 351
staff *see* **human resources**
state pension scheme 311
state sector *see* **public sector outsourcing**
statement of work
  website hosting 199–200
step in rights 186–7
strategy for outsourcing
  defining 3–4
  need for 1
subcontracting
  public sector outsourcing 251–2
subsidiary companies 67–9
suppliers
  access to supplier systems 177
  bid process *see* **bid process**
  business process outsourcing 210
  cost profile 11
  dependency on 30
  due diligence exercise and 19, 38
  objectives 44–9
  selection 189–94

tangible assets 84–5
taxation 350–62
  agents outside UK 355
  business process outsourcing (BPO)
    223–4
  contract of outsourcing 354
  foreign dimension 352
  joint ventures 352–4
  pensions and 313–14
  research and development 356
  transfer of assets 355–6, 361–2
  value added tax 350, 356–62
  withholding taxes on cross border
    payments 355
technology compatibility
  telecommunications outsourcing
    177–8
technology improvements 105
  public sector outsourcing 244–5
  telecommunications outsourcing
    178–80
technology outsourcing 4–5, 351
  charter for 7–8
  see also individual topics
technology platform
  telecommunications outsourcing
    167, 169
telecommunications outsourcing 152–88
  access to supplier systems 177
  application service provider (ASP)
    agreements 157, 163–4
  attaching customer equipment to
    network 173–4
  audio and video conferencing 155,
    167
  authority to act as
    telecommunications service
    provider 170–2
  benchmarking 181–5
  cabling and related infrastructure
    157, 166
  call centres 155, 160–3
  carriage in other countries 169–70
  co-location/hosting 157
  data networks 154, 164–6, 182–5
  e-business-related infrastructure
    156–7
  exit management 187
  insolvency 186–7
  local exchange carriers 170
  maintenance 155
  mobile data and WAP 155, 167

telecommunications outsourcing
(*continued*)
    mobile telephony 154–5, 181–2
    pricing 180–1
    reporting requirements 185
    restriction on use of services 173
    security 174–7
    service level agreement 167–8
    technology compatibility 177–8
    technology platform 167, 169
    technology refresh 178–80
    types 153–7
    undisrupted service 185
    voice telephony 153–4, 157–60, 182
    VOIP (voice using Internet
      protocols) 154
telephone numbers 159–60
term (period) of contract
    information systems outsourcing
      116–17
    public sector outsourcing 243–5
    website hosting 195
termination of contract 108–11
    business process outsourcing (BPO)
      222
    costs arising from 55–7
    exit management 144–8, 187, 245
    information systems outsourcing
      143–4
    termination rights 186
    website hosting 197–8
third parties
    contract rights 74–7
    third party agreements 31
    transfer of assets agreement and
      85–6
    transfer of third party software
      117–18, 119–23
trade unions 38–9
training 39
transfer of assets agreement 80–1, 84–6
    intellectual property 85
    other contracts with third parties
      85–6
    real property 84
    tangible assets 84–5
transfer of third party software 119–23
    intellectual property rights and
      117–18
transfer of undertakings 30, 34, 55–7,
    147, 277, 278–308
    collective agreements 294

    consultation 303–7
    employees who choose not to
      transfer 289
    employers' liability insurance 294–5
    EU Directives 277, 278–9, 285
    formal due diligence and 35
    general liabilities 291–3
    informal due diligence and 37, 42
    pensions 294, 316–18
    public sector outsourcing 245–6,
      307–8
    reorganisations after 298–303
    restrictive covenants 293
    share entitlements 296
    statutory confirmation of term and
      conditions 296–7
    survey on 283–4
    what is transferred 291–8
    who is protected 286–91
    working conditions 295–6
trust/agency structure 75

ultra vires 234–6
umbrella structure 75–6
unfair contract terms 139
user group structures 67–9

value added tax 350, 356–62
    exempt business activities 357–60
    planning 360–1
    taxable business activities 357
    transfer of assets 361–2
value based approach to outsourcing 4
value for money 106–8, 237, 265
variation in contracts of employment
    300–1
video conferencing 155, 167
virtual extensions 158–9, 168
virtual user 70
voice telephony 153–4, 157–60, 182
VOIP (voice using Internet protocols)
    154

warranties
    information systems outsourcing
      148
    pensions 320–1, 330–3
    public sector outsourcing 248–9
website hosting 189–207
    acceptable use policies 198–9
    audit 196
    benchmarking 195–6

capacity 202
charges 195
data protection 196–7
force majeure and disaster recovery
  198
hardware 200–1
network 202–3
selection of suppliers 189–94
service credits 203–4
service levels 200–3
software 201

statement of work 199–200
term (period) of contract 195
termination and termination
  assistance 197–8
terms and conditions of agreement
  195–9
**withholding taxes on cross border
  payments** 355
work backlogs 29
working conditions
  transfer of undertakings 295–6

Drafting Confidentiality Agreements

Mark Anderson

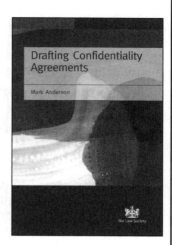

Confidentiality agreements are an important feature of a wide variety of business negotiations. This book gives practical assistance to lawyers and commercial managers who need to draft or negotiate a confidentiality agreement. It includes a summary of the law of confidence as it affects commercial relationships.

The book is divided into three parts:

- a practical explanation of how English law protects confidential information in a business context
- a discussion of commercial practice in relation to confidentiality agreements, including commentary on the terms of such agreements
- a selection of precedents for confidentiality agreements.

The practical nature of the book is enhanced by arguments for and against particular provisions, points to watch out for in confidentiality agreements and model wording for a range of different situations.

The book is accompanied by a free CD-ROM containing easily customised precedents for a variety of situations.

1 85328 871 3   May 2003   128 pages   £39.95

Available from Marston Book Services:
Tel. 01235 465 656.

The Law Society

Enterprise Act 2002

The New Law of Mergers, Monopolies and Cartels

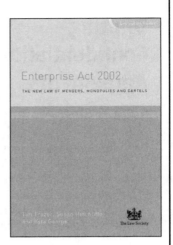

Tim Frazer, Susan Hinchliffe and Kyla George

The Enterprise Act 2002 has radically changed the UK's competition law regime. This book provides you with a clear, comprehensive and immediate guide to the new merger control and market investigation procedures and the sanctions against cartel activities.

Key features include:

- detailed guidance on the practical impact of these sweeping changes and the new powers of the competition authorities
- explanation of how the new rules interact with the existing competition rules under the Competition Act 1998
- relevant sections and schedules of the Enterprise Act 2002 are reproduced in full.

This time-saving book brings together all of the UK competition rules in one single, concise reference work. It is ideal for senior managers and commercial lawyers who need to be thoroughly briefed on the new systems and penalties from a very early stage.

1 85328 896 9   February 2003   528 pages   £49.95

Available from Marston Book Services:
Tel. 01235 465 656.

The Law Society

Design Law

Protecting and Exploiting Rights

Margaret Briffa and *Lee Gage*

This practical new book guides
practitioners through the fast
changing and increasingly complex
area of design law. It clearly outlines
each of the different types of design
protection, demonstrating how best
to exploit designs to their full commercial potential and guard
rights against infringement.

The book highlights the factors that need to be considered when
selecting an appropriate method of design protection and offers
practical advice on how to set about obtaining and enforcing
rights.

More current than any other work on the subject, the authors provide authoritative notes on the latest law and cases.

The practical nature of the book is enhanced by case studies,
examples of good and bad practice, workflow diagrams, checklists,
and relevant statutory materials and precedents.

1 85328 817 9   December 2003   320 pages   £59.95

Available from Marston Book Services:
Tel. 01235 465 656.

The Law Society